Pioneers in Development

A WORLD BANK PUBLICATION

Pioneers

Lord Bauer
Colin Clark
Albert O. Hirschman
Sir Arthur Lewis
Gunnar Myrdal
Raúl Prebisch
Paul N. Rosenstein-Rodan
Walt Whitman Rostow
H. W. Singer
Jan Tinbergen

in Development

edited by Gerald M. Meier and Dudley Seers

PUBLISHED FOR THE WORLD BANK □ OXFORD UNIVERSITY PRESS

Oxford University Press

NEW YORK OXFORD LONDON GLASGOW
TORONTO MELBOURNE WELLINGTON HONG KONG
TOKYO KUALA LUMPUR SINGAPORE JAKARTA
DELHI BOMBAY CALCUTTA MADRAS KARACHI
NAIROBI DAR ES SALAAM CAPE TOWN

First printing June 1984

EDITOR   Jane H. Carroll
BOOK DESIGN   Brian J. Svikhart
FIGURES   Catherine Kocak

Library of Congress Cataloging in Publication Data

Main entry under title:

Pioneers in development.

Includes index.
 1. Economic development—Addresses, essays, lectures.
I. Bauer, P. T. (Péter Tamás)   II. Meier, Gerald M.
III. Seers, Dudley.
HD74.P56 1984   338.9   84-5775
ISBN 0-19-520452-2

Foreword

PIONEERS—in any field—are creative and courageous people. Were they not, they would not have risked reaching out to break new ground and to seek new solutions. They are rarely content to stay put with the conventional, or to stand pat on the obvious. They are fired by an insistent curiosity that drives them to burrow deeper and ferret out the unexpected.

That is why it is worthwhile to get to know them.

In the complex arena of international development economics, this new volume is an invitation to do just that. Here are ten pioneers of that difficult discipline, who have helped define the debate over development issues during the past forty years. They have been not only dedicated teachers and scholars, but active, responsible practitioners as well.

You can read in these pages their candid reflections on their own pioneering work, as well as the perceptive critiques of a select group of their younger colleagues. All in all, it is a stimulating and controversial intellectual bill of fare—and a nutritious one.

We in the World Bank are delighted to have hosted these lectures, and we look forward to further series of similar events. Without question, the international development effort is one of the central historical movements of our era. Its outcome in the decades immediately ahead will largely shape the character of international life throughout the next century.

As development proceeds and conditions change, the world is going to need an ongoing supply of innovators in development strategy. Let us hope that it will be as fortunate with its future pioneers as it has been with those whom this volume commemorates.

A. W. Clausen
President, The World Bank

April 1984

v

Contents

Foreword   *A. W. Clausen   v*

Preface   *Gerald M. Meier   ix*

Introduction

The Formative Period   *Gerald M. Meier   3*

Pioneers

LORD BAUER   *25*

Remembrance of Studies Past: Retracing First Steps   *27*
Comment   *Michael Lipton   44*
Comment   *T. N. Srinivasan   51*

COLIN CLARK   *57*

Development Economics: The Early Years   *59*
Comment   *Graham Pyatt   78*

ALBERT O. HIRSCHMAN   *85*

A Dissenter's Confession: "The Strategy of Economic
Development" Revisited   *87*
Comment   *Carlos F. Diaz Alejandro   112*
Comment   *Paul P. Streeten   115*

SIR ARTHUR LEWIS   *119*

Development Economics in the 1950s   *121*
Comment   *Arnold C. Harberger   138*

GUNNAR MYRDAL   *149*

International Inequality and Foreign Aid in Retrospect   *151*
Comment   *Hla Myint   166*

RAÚL PREBISCH   *173*

Five Stages in My Thinking on Development   *175*
Comment   *Albert Fishlow*   *192*
Comment   *Jagdish N. Bhagwati*   *197*

PAUL N. ROSENSTEIN-RODAN   *205*

Natura Facit Saltum: Analysis of the Disequilibrium
Growth Process   *207*
Comment   *Dragoslav Avramovic*   *222*

WALT WHITMAN ROSTOW   *227*

Development: The Political Economy of the Marshallian
Long Period   *229*
Comment   *Gerald Helleiner*   *262*
Comment   *Azizali F. Mohammed*   *268*

H. W. SINGER   *273*

The Terms of Trade Controversy and the Evolution of
Soft Financing: Early Years in the U.N.   *275*
Comment   *Bela Balassa*   *304*

JAN TINBERGEN   *313*

Development Cooperation as a Learning Process   *315*
Comment   *Michael Bruno*   *332*

Postscript

Development Dichotomies   *Paul P. Streeten*   *337*

Index   *363*

Preface

IT IS A RARE OCCASION when the pioneers of a subject can be called back to reflect on why they said what they did some thirty or forty years ago—and to assess their earlier thoughts in light of the subsequent evolution of the subject they helped to establish. Such is the occasion of this book.

In the late 1940s and 1950s, several seminal works in development economics appeared as the countries of Asia, Africa, and Latin America attempted to emerge from their pervasive and persistent poverty. The impulse behind this book is the desire to recapture the spirit and the economic thought of that pioneering period.

To do this, ten pioneers were invited by the World Bank to prepare the essays that appear in this book—Lord Bauer, Colin Clark, Albert O. Hirschman, Nobel laureate Sir Arthur Lewis, Nobel laureate Gunnar Myrdal, Raúl Prebisch, Paul N. Rosenstein-Rodan, Walt W. Rostow, Hans W. Singer, and Nobel laureate Jan Tinbergen.

When the Second World War ended, economists were challenged by the urgent problems of development. During the next decade a few central articles, official reports, and books came to dominate the thinking about development. The authors of these studies were the pioneers who initially shaped the subject by introducing concepts, deducing principles, and modeling the process of development. Some of the pioneers were stimulated to analyze development problems by their previous academic interests, some by their experience in related policymaking activities, some out of idealism, and others by a basic intellectual curiosity.

In this book, the pioneers have been asked to reassess the main themes of their early work and to reconsider their assumptions, concepts, and policy prescriptions in relation to the way the course of development has proceeded since their pioneering days.

In their individual papers, they now recapture the intellectual excitement, expectations, and activism of that unique pioneering period. Not only do their papers display autobiographical charm but, taken as a set, they also offer an unusual opportunity for a retrospective view of what has happened to development economics. And the retrospective view naturally has implications for future directions of the subject.

The pioneers initially prepared their papers for lectures presented at the World Bank. Following each public lecture, a small seminar was arranged with commentators offering a critique. A number of contemporary development economists served as commentators: Dragoslav Avramovic, Bela Balassa, Jagdish Bhagwati, Michael Bruno, Carlos Diaz-Alejandro, Albert Fishlow, Arnold Harberger, Gerald Helleiner, Michael Lipton, Azizali F. Mohammed, Hla Myint, Graham Pyatt, T. N. Srinivasan, and Paul Streeten.

This book presents the papers of the pioneers, together with the comments. An introductory historical chapter sets the stage, outlining some of the intellectual trends and institutional features that shaped the political and economic environment of the formative period for the pioneers. The final survey chapter synthesizes various issues in development thought and points toward the resolution of unsettled questions in the subject.

The selection of the pioneers was necessarily limited in number. Some pioneers declined the invitation, others were believed to be better placed on a list for a successor volume covering the 1960s. And some pioneers are deceased: references to their works are made in both the introductory and closing chapters.

G. M. Meier and Dudley Seers participated in organizing the lecture series and were responsible for editing the essays and comments. Chapter 1 was to be under their joint authorship, but the death of Dudley Seers in March 1983 required that the volume be completed with only one editor. Dudley Seers's final writings were directed to this project, and his intellectual zeal and ceaseless striving to find a solution to the problems of development have been of lasting value in fashioning this volume, which will stand as a tribute to his achievements.

A general expression of thanks must be offered to the many members of the World Bank who contributed their advice and services in the arrangement of the lecture series and the preparation of this book. Especially helpful have been Sidney C. Chernick and F. Leslie C. H. Helmers. The support of Hollis B. Chenery, Mahbub ul Haq, and Ajit Mozoomdar was much appreciated during the initial planning period. For their help in processing the typescript, I am grateful to the editorial staff of the World Bank, Richard Carroll of the Economic Development Institute, Barbara Taylor of the Institute of Development Studies at the University of Sussex, and Pat Sharp of Stanford University; their assistance has been exceptional both in quantity and quality.

G. M. M.

Stanford, California
January 1984

Introduction

The Formative Period

Gerald M. Meier

THE SUBJECT MATTER OF DEVELOPMENT ECONOMICS is at once among the oldest and newest branches of economics. Beginning with Adam Smith's *Inquiry into the Nature and Causes of the Wealth of Nations*, classical economists sought to discover the sources of economic progress and to analyze the long-run process of economic change. As Nobel laureate Arthur Lewis reminds us, what Smith called "the natural progress of opulence" is what we today call "development economics." During a long interim, however, the marginalist analysis of neoclassical economists introduced a static frame of thinking and shifted interests to the narrower problems of resource allocation and the theory of exchange. And the depressed conditions of the interwar period gave rise to the Keynesian analysis of short-period business cycles and the possible threat of secular stagnation in mature capitalist nations. A return to growth and development as the grand theme of economics did not come until after the Second World War. The late 1940s and 1950s then became in many respects the pioneering period for the "new" development economics that focused on the development problems of Asian, African, and Latin American countries.[1]

The Colonial Background

Introducing his *Theory of Economic Growth* in 1955, Lewis stated "A book of this kind seemed to be necessary because the theory of economic

Gerald M. Meier is Professor of International Economics at Stanford University.

1. This chapter is not intended to be a survey of the development contributions of all those who wrote during this formative period. Instead, it concentrates on the intellectual and institutional environment in which the pioneers wrote. In addition to the pioneers represented in this book, this chapter refers only to some pioneers who are deceased and to some economists who analyzed some of the same issues as did the pioneers.

For a survey of the very limited discussions of economic development prior to 1945, see H. W. Arndt, "Development Economics before 1945," in Jagdish Bhagwati and

growth once more engages world-wide interests and because no comprehensive treatise on the subject has been published for about a century. The last great book covering this wide range was John Stuart Mill's *Problems of Political Economy* published in 1848."[2]

Economic thought is commonly induced by the need to solve policy problems. This was certainly true for the early period of thinking about development. Development economics did not arise as a formal theoretical discipline, but was fashioned as a practical subject in response to the needs of policymakers to advise governments on what could and should be done to allow their countries to emerge from chronic poverty. As their essays and biographies reveal, many of the pioneers in development were active in policymaking positions during the 1940s and 1950s.

The attention to postwar international reconstruction gave rise to three early works on development: Eugene Staley's *World Economic Development*,[3] Kurt Mandelbaum's *Industrialization of Backward Areas*,[4] and Paul N. Rosenstein-Rodan's article on "Problems of Industrialization of Eastern and South-Eastern Europe."[5]

Staley recognized that "there will be an insistent demand in many parts of the world for rapid progress in economic development after the war." His study explored the likely economic effects on the advanced industrial countries of development elsewhere—especially the effects of international investment for development purposes and of shifts in production, consumption, and trade.

Mandelbaum attempted to present a quantitative model of industrialization for the overpopulated and backward areas of Eastern and Southeastern Europe. The "depressed areas" of this region were believed to suffer from a lack of industrial development, which was driving the growing population into rural and urban occupations of very low productivity. As the foreword stated, "The vicious circle of population pressure, poverty, and lack of industries is by no means confined to this corner of Europe; it is present in other European countries and is most clearly seen in the Far East. That south-eastern Europe was selected as an example is partly accidental, and partly due to the fact that material about conditions in south-eastern Europe is slightly more plentiful than that dealing with other over-populated areas." Mandelbaum argued that the economic case for the industrialization of "densely populated backward countries" rests

Richard S. Eckaus, eds., *Development and Planning: Essays in Honor of Paul N. Rosenstein-Rodan* (London: Allen and Unwin, 1972), pp. 13–29. For the classical period, see Lord Robbins, *The Theory of Economic Development in the History of Economic Thought* (London: Macmillan, 1968).

2. W. Arthur Lewis, *The Theory of Economic Growth* (London: Allen and Unwin, 1955), p. 5.

3. Montreal: International Labor Office, 1944; the quotation below is from p. 12.

4. Oxford: Basil Blackwell, 1947.

5. *Economic Journal*, vol. 53 (June-September 1943).

upon the "mass phenomenon of disguised rural unemployment." The principal barriers to higher employment were lack of demand and scarcity of capital. To overcome these, state intervention in a backward area was believed necessary so that redistributive measures might raise "necessary consumption" and thus counteract the potential deficiency of demand and directly relieve poverty; such measures might also institute a regime of state-enforced savings in support of a higher rate of capital formation. The increase in the rate of output and some needed adjustments of technology were derived from the aim of attaining full employment within about one generation.[6]

Rosenstein-Rodan recalls the essentials of his development theory in his chapter, "Natura Facit Saltum," below.

The problems of development were thrust upon economists by the breakup of colonial empires in Asia and Africa during the Second World War and shortly thereafter. Nationalist demands of the interwar period were fulfilled in the postwar period, and imperialism and colonialism were in full retreat. The charter of the United Nations pointed to the goal of colonial emancipation. In the short span of five years after the war, India, Pakistan, Ceylon, Burma, the Philippines, Indonesia, Jordan, Syria, Lebanon, and Israel all became independent. Colonialism was on the way out far more speedily than had first seemed possible at the end of the war, and many more colonies soon emerged as nations.[7]

Centuries of history were reversed. Unlike the League of Nations, the United Nations became immediately enmeshed in the colonial problem, and the Asian-African bloc symbolized a fundamental change in the balance of world forces. The self-assertion of Asian and African peoples through nationalism and political self-reliance led to a drive for development. The leaders of the new nations insisted that international attention be given to their development problems. Areas that had been considered in

---

6. *Industrialization of Backward Areas*, pp. iii, 2, 20ff. For a recent review of Mandelbaum's early study, see Hans Singer, "A Generation Later," *Development and Change*, vol. 10 (1979).

Two other early studies along some lines similar to Mandelbaum's were A. Bonné, *The Economic Development of the Middle East: An Outline of Planned Reconstruction* (London: Kegan Paul, 1945); and Sir P. Thakurdas and others, *A Plan of Economic Development for India* (London: Penguin, 1944).

7. In 1954 Cambodia, Laos, and a divided Viet Nam became self-governing, and in 1957 Malaya received its independence from Britain. In Africa, Libya was made independent, Eritrea was joined with Ethiopia, and Somaliland was promised independence in 1960. Sudan, Morocco, Tunisia, and Egypt were removed from imperial control. The Gold Coast was transformed into independent Ghana. Togoland, the Cameroons, and Guinea soon followed to independence. In the Caribbean, Puerto Rico and the Netherlands Antilles achieved new styles of self-government, and the Federation of the British West Indies approached independence within the Commonwealth. See Rupert Emerson, *From Empire to Nation* (Boston: Beacon Press, 1960); and Henri Grimal, *Decolonization* (London: Routledge and Kegan Paul, 1978).

the eighteenth century as "rude and barbarous," in the nineteenth century as "backward," and in the prewar period as "underdeveloped" now become the "less developed countries" or the "poor countries"—and also the "emergent countries" and "developing economies."

But how was development to be achieved? Although political independence could be legislated, economic independence could not. Nationalism could intensify the demand for accelerated transformation of the economy, but the process could not be simply willed. An understanding of the forces of development was necessary, and the design of appropriate policies to support these forces was essential. To accomplish this, the creative participation of economists was needed.

The earlier study of colonial economics would no longer suffice. Previous courses in colonial economics had catered mainly to those working in, or hoping to enter, the colonial services. In retrospect, the world assumed in these courses seems essentially static. Trade fluctuation had been a basic problem of the interwar years, and the main objective, implicitly at least, had been stabilization. This reflected both the needs of the colonial powers (especially those with interests in Africa where commodity exports were important) and the Keynesian fashion then current. Insofar as social and political change was considered, it was depicted as gradual progress requiring economic stability. The economic role of the state was very limited. The war not only disrupted the colonial systems; it upset this narrow way of perceiving problems. The newly independent governments were consequently under pressure to produce development, not stability.

The term "economic development" was rarely used before the 1940s.[8] During the pioneering period most economists came to interpret economic development as denoting growth in per capita real income in underdeveloped countries. Some, however, emphasized that development meant growth plus change, especially change in values and institutions.[9] For the underdeveloped countries, Hla Myint also distinguished between the

8. H. W. Arndt, "Economic Development: A Semantic History," *Economic Development and Cultural Change* (April 1981).

9. Substantial studies in this area were made by Bert F. Hoselitz. See his *The Progress of Underdeveloped Areas* (Chicago: University of Chicago Press, 1952); "Non-Economic Barriers to Economic Development," *Economic Development and Cultural Change* (March 1952); "Social Structure and Economic Growth," *Economia Internazionale* (August 1953); "Non-Economic Factors in Economic Development," *American Economic Review* (May 1957); and *Sociological Aspects of Economic Growth* (Glencoe, Ill.: Free Press, 1960).

Also see E. E. Hagen, "The Process of Economic Development," *Economic Development and Cultural Change* (April 1957).

Of earlier interest was the discussion of social dualism by J. H. Boeke, *Economics and Economic Policy of Dual Societies* (New York: Institute of Pacific Relations, 1953); and B. H. Higgins, "The 'Dualistic Theory' of Underdeveloped Areas," *Economic Development and Cultural Change* (January 1956).

"underdevelopment" of their natural resources and the economic "backwardness" of their people. Myint stated that there is "a greater need in the study of backward countries than in that of the advanced countries to go behind the 'veil' of conventional social accounting into the real processes of adaptation between wants, activities, and environment . . . In practice there is a real danger of the macro-models of economic development 'running on their own steam' without any reference to the fundamental human problems of backwardness on the subjective side."[10]

The meaning of development also began to be expressed in quantitative terms. Simon Kuznets painstakingly assembled considerable empirical evidence.[11] While emphasizing a cumulatively large rise in a country's per capita product, Kuznets was also concerned to note the implications of this rate—structural changes that necessarily accompany it and the large modifications in social and institutional conditions under which the increased product per capita is attained.

Early on, however, Jacob Viner levied strong criticism of the current criteria of development. He argued that even though per capita wealth, income, and production were all increasing, the population might still have increased substantially, and "the numbers of those living at the margin of subsistence or below, illiterate, diseased, undernourished, may have grown steadily consistently with a rise in the average income of the population as a whole."[12]

If the new nations were to face their development problems, they would now have to look beyond colonial economics. As Nobel laureate Gunnar Myrdal observed, the "colonial theory" was only too often apologetic writing that attempted to absolve the colonial regimes from responsibility for the conditions of underdevelopment.[13] The failure to develop was frequently attributed to conditions of tropical climate, population pres-

10. Hla Myint, "An Interpretation of Economic Backwardness," *Oxford Economic Papers* (June 1954), p. 149.

11. Simon Kuznets, "Quantitative Aspects of the Economic Growth of Nations: I. Levels and Variability of Rates of Growth," *Economic Development and Cultural Change* (October 1956); "Quantitative Aspects of the Economic Growth of Nations: II. Industrial Distribution of National Product and Labor Force," *Economic Development and Cultural Change* (July 1957); "Toward a Theory of Economic Growth," in Robert Lekachman, ed., *National Policy for Economic Welfare at Home and Abroad* (New York: Columbia University Press, 1955); "Economic Growth and Income Inequality," *American Economic Review* (March 1955); and *Six Lectures on Economic Growth* (Glencoe, Ill.: Free Press, 1959).

12. Jacob Viner, *International Trade and Economic Development* (Oxford: Clarendon Press, 1953), pp. 99–100. S. Herbert Frankel also emphasized this quotation in his *Some Conceptual Aspects of International Economic Development of Underdeveloped Territories*, Princeton Essays in International Finance no. 14 (Princeton University, May 1952), p. 3.

13. Gunnar Myrdal, "Need for Reforms in Underdeveloped Countries," in S. Grassman and E. Lundberg, eds., *The World Economic Order: Past and Prospects* (London: Macmillan, 1981), pp. 502–06.

sure, lack of resources, or too rigid and irrational institutions and values that made the people unresponsive to opportunities for improving their incomes and living standards. The postwar wave of decolonization created an entirely new situation.

Moreover, from the viewpoint of the governments of the major capitalist countries, there was grave danger that former colonies might, if there was little social progress, fall under communist domination: investment opportunities and access to markets and sources of raw materials would then be diminished. In addition, egalitarian and humanitarian tendencies had been reinforced by wartime propaganda. A political basis thus emerged in the early 1950s for large-scale financial and technical aid from the richer countries. Many economists in Europe and North America began to fashion tools for analyzing the problems of "underdevelopment." So the pedigree of Development Economics reads "by Colonial Economics out of Political Expediency."[14]

Postwar International Organization

During the war President Roosevelt had proclaimed the "four freedoms," including "freedom from want . . . everywhere in the world," as

14. Dudley Seers, "The Birth, Life and Death of Development Economics," *Development and Change*, vol. 10 (1979), p. 708.

At Oxford, S. Herbert Frankel was appointed the University's Professor of Colonial Economic Affairs in 1946; Hla Myint introduced a seminar on Economics of Underdeveloped Countries in 1949–50; and other lectures in development were presented in the early 1950s at Oxford by Peter Ady and Ursula Hicks. W. Arthur Lewis was appointed Reader in Colonial Economics in the University of London (London School of Economics) in 1947, and in 1948 went to Manchester where he began lecturing systematically on development economics from about 1950. At Yale, Henry Wallich introduced a development course in 1952–53, and the following year Henry Bruton also taught a graduate development course. In 1953–54, John Kenneth Galbraith began a seminar at Harvard on economic and political development. Others who started teaching in the development field during the 1950s at Harvard were Alexander Eckstein, A. J. Meyer, Robert Baldwin, David Bell, E. S. Mason, and Gustav Papanek. A seminar on theories of economic development, with a special effort to integrate economic and psychological theories, was offered by G. M. Meier and David McClelland at Wesleyan University in 1955. McClelland was to draw upon this seminar for his *The Achieving Society* (Princeton, N.J.: Van Nostrand, 1961). Meier was at the same time writing with R. E. Baldwin, *Economic Development: Theory, History, Policy* (New York: Wiley, 1957).

Throughout the 1950s there was also an expansion in the number of journals devoted to economic development. The *Ceylon Economist* began publication in 1950; *Economic Development and Cultural Change*, in 1952; *Pakistan Economic and Social Review*, 1952; *Indian Economic Review*, 1952; *Indian Economic Journal*, 1953; *Social and Economic Studies* (University of West Indies), 1953; *East African Economic Review*, 1954; *Middle East Economic Papers*, 1954; *Malayan Economic Review*, 1956; *Nigerian Journal of Economic and Social Studies*, 1959. The number of articles in development theory and development policy as reported in the *Index of Economic Articles* tripled in the decade between 1950–54 and 1960–64.

postwar objectives of the Western allies. The United Nations charter also included among its objectives the promotion of "higher standards of living, full employment, and conditions of economic and social progress and development." The Bretton Woods conference, however, remained largely immune from these aspirations—even though the International Monetary Fund (IMF) and the International Bank for Reconstruction and Development (IBRD, or the World Bank) were later to assume ever increasing importance in the international development effort.

It seems clear from the membership that the Bretton Woods conference was called primarily to establish the IMF, and that the World Bank was a distinctly secondary issue. Most of the developing countries were still colonies, and only a relatively few, mainly independent nations of Latin America, were invited. The political power lay with the United States and Britain, and from the outset it was apparent that issues of development were not to be on the Bretton Woods agenda.

Of the countries invited to Bretton Woods, Lord Keynes could write in a dispatch to the British Treasury: "Twenty-one countries have been invited which clearly have nothing to contribute and will merely encumber the ground, namely, Colombia, Costa Rica, Dominica, Ecuador, Salvador, Guatemala, Haiti, Honduras, Liberia, Nicaragua, Panama, Paraguay, Philippines, Venezuela, Peru, Uruguay, Ethiopia, Iceland, Iran, Iraq, Luxemburg. The most monstrous monkey-house assembled for years. To these might perhaps be added: Egypt, Chile and (in present circumstances) Yugo-Slavia."[15]

At Bretton Woods, the developing countries tended to view themselves more as new, raw-material-producing nations and less as countries with general development problems. Comprehensive strategies of development and policies to accelerate national development were yet to be identified. The Brazilian delegation introduced a draft proposal for an international conference to promote stability in the prices of primary international commodities, claiming that "fluctuations in the prices of primary products during the interwar period were as much of a curse as recurring large scale unemployment." For the successful attainment of the objectives pursued by the IMF and the World Bank, it was thought necessary to promote stability in prices of raw materials and agricultural prices. Cuba endorsed a conference to promote the "orderly marketing of staple commodities." The delegation from Colombia urged that future agreements on commercial policy should consider the "need for enlarging the consuming markets for foodstuffs and raw materials, the prices of which before the war were notoriously far out of proportion to the prices of manufactured articles" that primary producing countries "were obliged to buy from the great industrial nations." Bolivia was concerned about "cooperation in the organization and implementation of international commodity agreements

15. Donald Moggridge, ed., *The Collected Writings of John Maynard Keynes* (London: Macmillan and Cambridge University Press, 1980), vol. 26, p. 42.

designed to maintain fair and stable prices, and provision for the orderly distribution of raw materials throughout the world." But these proposals came to naught, as did a consolidated resolution for "orderly marketing of staple commodities at prices fair to the producer and consumer alike" proposed by Peru, Brazil, Chile, Bolivia, and Cuba.[16]

In 1947, representatives of fifty-three nations also met in Havana to discuss the formation of an International Trade Organization (ITO) to complement the IMF and the World Bank. As proposed in the Havana charter, the ITO was not only to govern trade barriers, but was also to deal with private foreign investment, infant industries, international commodity agreements, state trading, cartels, and restrictive business practices. The General Agreement on Tariffs and Trade (GATT) was originally designed to serve merely as a temporary expedient until ratification of the Havana charter. But the ITO met opposition in the U.S. Congress,[17] and only GATT survived as the narrower substitute, becoming permanent in 1955.

In its initial provisions, GATT did relieve less developed countries of some obligations. The Agreement referred specifically to the type of country "the economy of which can only support low standards of living and is in the early stages of development." Such a country was offered the privileges of withdrawing a tariff concession, increasing tariff rates to permit protection of an infant industry, and invoking quota restrictions on imports "in order to safeguard its external financial position and to insure a level of reserves adequate for the implementation of its program of economic development."[18] Under the latter provision, the developing countries were able to follow import substitution programs and to protect their domestic industries through quotas imposed under the guise of balance of payments support.

GATT did not allow, however, as much special treatment for developing countries as they had sought through the Havana charter. The controversial issue of allowing different trade rules for countries according to their different stages of development has persisted. The request for special and differential treatment for less developed countries remains prominent in the call for a New International Economic Order.

---

16. U.S. State Department, *Proceedings and Documents of the United Nations Monetary and Financial Conference* (Washington, D.C.: U.S. Government Printing Office, 1948), vol. 1, pp. 332–36, 429–30, 482–85.

17. See William Diebold, Jr., *The End of the ITO*, Princeton Essays in International Finance no. 16 (Princeton University, October 1952).

18. See GATT, Articles XII, XIV, XVII. GATT Working Party reports and other studies addressed the problems of development during the 1950s. Especially notable was the report by a panel of experts, with Gottfried Haberler as chairman, which examined the importance and prospects of maintaining and expanding the export earnings of the developing countries; GATT (Haberler Report), *Trends in International Trade* (Geneva, 1958).

Early U.N. Reports

Together, the IMF, the World Bank, and GATT formed the outlines of an international public sector. Purposive action was to be taken to attain the multiple objectives of full employment, freer and expanding world trade, and stable exchange rates. But of what direct benefit were these postwar institutions to be for the newly developing countries? Had the institutions been created simply to deal with the previous economic crisis—the Great Depression of the 1930s? The economics of every period and place reflects not only contemporary political demands but crucial professional inter-pretations of the actual developments of the recent past. British and American economists continued to dominate the economics profession, and their main topic of professional discussion in 1945–50 was not the war of 1939–45, which did not lend itself easily to analysis with tools of the profession or fit squarely into ideological debates. The overriding preoccupation remained with the Great Depression of the 1930s, a period about which the profession retained some feeling of guilt. Economists had been slow to realize the magnitude of the depression and to analyze its causes, or to point the way to economic recovery. By the late 1940s, however, the Keynesian revolution was sweeping all before it, and the "new economics" was established to prevent a recurrence of the 1930s. Domestic full-employment programs were to be instituted, and interna-tionally, the Bretton Woods order was to provide additional institutional underpinning.

Regional commissions of the United Nations also assumed an active role in examining development problems. Most prominent was the Economic Commission for Latin America (ECLA), organized in 1948 and based in Santiago, Chile. In 1950, Raúl Prebisch was appointed executive secretary of ECLA. In the previous year, Prebisch had written *The Economic De-velopment of Latin America and Its Principal Problems*.[19] On the basis of this study and subsequent studies, ECLA became the recognized spokesman for Latin America's economic development. During its first five years, ECLA was elaborating the development doctrines reviewed by Prebisch in the volume just cited. ECLA then turned to intensive studies of Latin American economies with the aim of "programming their future development."[20] Since about 1958, ECLA has concentrated on Latin American economic integration and cooperation.

19. New York: United Nations, 1950.
20. See ECLA, *An Introduction to the Technique of Programming*, first presented at an ECLA session in 1953 and printed in 1955. Also, Fernando Henrique Cardoso, "The Originality of the Copy: The Economic Commission for Latin America and the Idea of Development," in a Rothko Chapel Colloquium, *Toward a New Strategy for Development* (New York: Pergamon, 1979).

The promotion of programming was particularly significant for its attempt to provide quantitative guidance in the establishment of aggregate and sectoral projections on the basis of empirical knowledge. Techniques were examined to allow the projection of domestic demand in accordance with consumer budget studies, the projection of the capacity to import on the basis of foreign exchange earnings, estimates of savings ratios and capital-output ratios, and the application of various investment criteria and input-output analysis. Given the target of an increase in per capita income, these techniques were then to allow the programming of the path of development to achieve the target.

Another notable part of ECLA's work was the promulgation of "structuralism."[21] In brief, this was an argument that the causes of Latin American inflation were to be found not in excess demand but in particular structural bottlenecks that emerged during the process of development—especially in the supply shortfalls of the agricultural and export sectors.[22] The inflation was believed to be inevitable, and orthodox monetarist measures could suppress it only by stopping the very process of economic development. But it was thought that the structural inflation could be cured by well-devised economic development programs. To overcome agricultural bottlenecks and foreign exchange shortages, Latin American countries were advised to change their structure of production and of imports and exports. Industrialization via import substitution became the advocated strategy. Implementing this analysis, ECLA's policies emphasized the need for "programmed" industrialization via import substitution based on protectionist policies.

During the period 1949–51, three important reports were issued by groups of experts under United Nations auspices. The first—*National and International Measures for Full Employment* (1949)—stemmed mainly from the desire to prevent a recurrence of the 1930s. Nonetheless, it was also a force for economic development since it advocated international investment for development purposes and urged an extension of activities of the IMF and the World Bank.

The second report—*Measures for the Economic Development of Under-Developed Countries* (1951)—addressed squarely the special problems of the developing world and considered what obstacles had to be

21. Structuralism later evolved into "dependency" theory. See the discussion in Paul Streeten's essay, "Development Dichotomies," below.

22. Structuralist explanations of inflation in Latin America were opposed to monetarist explanations such as were advanced by the IMF. See Roberto de Oliviera Campos, "Two Views on Inflation in Latin America," in A. O. Hirschman, ed., *Latin American Issues* (New York: Twentieth Century Fund, 1961); Dudley Seers, "A Theory of Inflation and Growth in Underdeveloped Economies Based on the Experiences of Latin America," *Oxford Economic Papers* (June 1963); David Felix, "Structural Imbalances, Social Conflict, and Inflation," *Economic Development and Cultural Change* (January 1960); and Leopoldo Solís, "Mexican Economic Policy in the Post-War Period: The Views of Mexican Economists," *American Economic Review*, Supplement (June 1971), pp. 34–43.

overcome and what "missing components" had to be supplied in order to promote development.[23] The report emphasized the accumulation of physical capital, stating:

> It is a commonplace that economic progress is a function, among other things, of the rate of new capital formation. In most countries where rapid economic progress is occurring, net capital formation at home is at least 10% of the national income, and in some it is substantially higher. By contrast, in most underdeveloped countries, net capital formation is not as high as 5% of the national income, even when foreign investment is included. In many of these countries, the savings have been sufficient only to keep up with population growth, so that only a negligible amount of new capital, if any, has actually become available for increasing the average standard of living. How to increase the rate of capital formation is therefore a question of great urgency.[24]

Considering various domestic measures for mobilizing resources for capital formation, the report recognized the existence of surplus labor. "In many underdeveloped areas, the population on the land is so great that large numbers could be withdrawn from agriculture without any fall in agricultural output and with very little change of capital techniques. If this labor were employed on public works, capital would be created without any fall in other output, or in total consumption."[25]

The third report—*Measures for International Economic Stability* (1951)—called attention to "the special difficulties of the poorer underdeveloped countries" (p. 13). It advocated international action to reduce the vulnerability of underdeveloped economies to fluctuations in the volume of trade, to promote a larger flow of international capital, to maintain steady development programs, and to reduce fluctuations in the prices of primary products.[26]

Formative Influences

As countries became independent and as the new international institutions were formed, there arose a need for policy advice on development

23. The first group of experts was composed of John Maurice Clark, Nicholas Kaldor, Arthur Smithies, Pierre Uri, and E. Ronald Walker. The group who wrote the second report included Alberto Baltra Cortez (Chile), D. R. Gadgil (India), George Hakim (Lebanon), W. Arthur Lewis (England), and T. W. Schultz (United States).

24. United Nations Department of Economic Affairs, *Measures for the Economic Development of Under-Developed Countries* (New York, 1951), p. 35.

25. Ibid., p. 41. Criticisms of this report were expressed by S. Herbert Frankel, "United Nations Primer for Development," *Quarterly Journal of Economics* (August 1952); and P. T. Bauer, "The United Nations Report on the Economic Development of Under-Developed Countries," *Economic Journal* (March 1953).

26. This third group of experts was composed of James W. Angell, G. D. A. McDougall, Hla Myint, Trevor W. Swan, and Javier Marquez.

problems. Economists were called upon for such advice. But from whence were they to derive their policy proposals? In seeking to formulate their analyses of the process of development and to draw policy inferences, the pioneers were subject to a number of background influences: experience with Soviet planning, national economic management during the Great Depression, wartime mobilization of resources, and the postwar Marshall Plan for the recovery of Western Europe. These experiences carried some implications for development policy. But there was no distinct discipline of development economics that could be readily applied to the problems confronting the less developed countries.[27]

The possibilities of central planning had been demonstrated by the experience of the U.S.S.R. Prior to the war the U.S.S.R. had adopted a strategy of deliberate industrialization, formulated in a series of five-year plans.

The period of depression in the 1930s had also aroused particular attention to the plight of the primary producing countries that suffered deterioration in their commodity terms of trade and a loss of foreign exchange. Pessimistic views with respect to primary product exports followed from the depression experience. The decline in export prices, the low price elasticities and income elasticities of demand for primary products, and unstable foreign exchange receipts—all these adverse characteristics led to export pessimism. Instead of relying on primary product exports, many countries—especially in Latin America—had turned to import substitution during the depression, and the import substitution strategy had been pursued even more vigorously during the war.

The Great Depression also gave rise to Keynesian analysis. Although the type of unemployment that pervaded the poorer countries was believed to differ from the Keynesian type of mass unemployment that results from a deficiency of aggregate demand during depressions in advanced industrial countries, Keynesian analysis nonetheless exerted a strong influence on development economics.[28] By contradicting orthodox economics, Keynes had prepared the way for an alternative approach to economic problems. By assigning a larger role to the public sector, he had also prepared a case for discretionary national economic management. And public policy formation became a much more active force in national economies. Full

27. Lauchlin Currie directed the first World Bank country study mission to Colombia in 1949. He recalls that "there were no precedents for a mission of this sort and indeed nothing called development economics. I just assumed that it was a case of applying various branches of economics to the problems of a specific country, and accordingly I recruited a group of specialists in public finance, foreign exchange, transport, agriculture and so on." Lauchlin Currie, *Obstacles to Development* (East Lansing: Michigan State University Press, 1967), pp. 30–31.

28. For a provocative interpretation of the influence of Keynes and his followers on development thought, see Elizabeth S. Johnson and Harry G. Johnson, *The Shadow of Keynes* (Oxford: Blackwell, 1978), chap. 17.

employment, social security, the political and social responsibility of government—all these attributes of the welfare state carried over to newly independent governments.

A spirit of policy-optimism characterized the early views of these development economists. The optimism derived from the wartime demonstration of what could be achieved by the mobilization of resources once a nation was given an overriding national objective and a sense of priorities. In addition, the successful effort at postwar reconstruction in Western Europe through the help of foreign aid and some economic planning and cooperation generated optimism for the task of economic development in Latin America, Asia, and Africa.

Experience with wartime planning influenced the war on poverty. Planning was viewed as a mechanism to overcome deficiencies of the market price system and as a means of enlisting public support to achieve national objectives. In Britain, the White Paper on Employment Policy (1944), the Beveridge report on *Full Employment in a Free Society* (1945), and the Oxford Institute of Statistics' *Economics of Full Employment* (1945) emphasized the need for national employment policies to achieve full employment in peacetime as had been done in wartime. For some economists, such as Hans Singer, who had been concerned with the depressed areas within Britain, there were now similar problems in the less developed areas. Paul Rosenstein-Rodan referred to "the common characteristics of underdevelopment" in the "five vast international depressed areas," the Far East, colonial Africa, the Caribbean, the Middle East, and Eastern and Southeastern Europe.[29] For some, the domestic welfare state was to be elevated into the welfare world.

Furthermore, during the war, colonial governments in British Africa and the British Caribbean had to do some planning to qualify for British aid. After the war, the British Colonial Development and Welfare Act (1945) also required planning. Planning had also been undertaken by the French, Portuguese, and Belgians for their colonies.

The postwar debate on the role of planning thus became significant for strategies of industrialization, import substitution, and the mobilization of resources in the interest of national development. Although not directly related to the less developed countries, there were implications for development planning in the influential works by Oliver Franks, *Central Planning and Control in War and Peace* (1947), James E. Meade, *Planning and the Price Mechanism* (1948), and W. Arthur Lewis, *Principles of Economic Planning* (1949).

Although the Keynesian type of unemployment was denied, other major themes of the 1950s—the emphasis on capital accumulation, industrialization, and planning—might be traced to a Keynesian background.

---

29. Paul N. Rosenstein-Rodan, "The International Development of Economically Backward Areas," *International Affairs* (April 1944).

The extension of Keynesian short-run employment theory into long-run growth theory in the form of the Harrod-Domar equation ($g = s/k$, where g is the growth rate, s the savings ratio, and k the capital-output ratio) implied that the growth rate could be maximized by maximizing the marginal saving from output growth and by minimizing the incremental capital-output ratio (ICOR).[30]

Some of the authors in this volume recall the emphasis on capital accumulation. So, too, did Ragnar Nurkse look to "balanced growth"— the synchronized application of capital to a wide range of industries—to break the

> vicious circle of poverty . . . Economic progress is not a spontaneous or automatic affair. On the contrary, it is evident that there are automatic forces within the system trying to keep it moored to a given level . . . An increase in production over a wide range of consumables, so proportioned as to correspond with the pattern of consumers' preferences does create its own demand . . . A frontal attack—a wave of capital investments in a number of different industries—can economically succeed while any substantial application of capital by an individual entrepreneur in any particular industry may be blocked or discouraged by the limitations of the preexisting market . . . [T]hrough the application of capital over a wide range of activities, the general level of economic activity is raised and the size of the market enlarged . . . [Balanced growth] is a means of getting out of the rut, a means of stepping up the rate of growth when the external forces of advance through trade expansion and foreign capital are sluggish or inoperative.[31]

Maurice Dobb also concluded that "The largest single factor governing productivity in a country is its richness or poorness in capital instruments of production. And I think that we shall not go far wrong if we treat capital accumulation, in the sense of a growth in the stock of capital instruments—a growth that is simultaneously qualitative and quantitative—as the crux of the process of economic development."[32] Both Nurkse and

30. R. F. Harrod, "An Essay in Dynamic Theory," *Economic Journal* (March 1939); Harrod, *Toward a Dynamic Economics* (London: Macmillan, 1948); Evsey Domar, "Capital Expansion, Rate of Growth and Employment," *Econometrica* (1946).

31. *Problems of Capital Formation in Underdeveloped Countries* (Oxford: Blackwell, 1953), pp. 10, 13–15; and "The Conflict between 'Balanced Growth' and International Specialization," *Lectures on Economic Development* (Istanbul: Faculty of Economics, Istanbul University, and Faculty of Political Sciences, Ankara University, 1958), pp. 171–72.

32. *Some Aspects of Economic Development* (Delhi: Delhi School of Economics, 1951), p. 7; see also Dobb, *An Essay on Economic Growth and Planning* (New York: Monthly Review Press, 1960).

But compare the statement by Alec Cairncross at an International Economic Association's Round Table on Economic Progress in 1953 that "there is greater danger that the importance of capital in relation to economic progress will be exaggerated than that it

Dobb argued that surplus labor could be used to create capital.[33]

Some pioneers also recall the emphasis on industrialization. During the 1950s India was of special concern, and the "Mahalanobis model" that underlay the Indian second five-year plan gained considerable attention. This model considered the choice between investing in machines to make consumption goods and in machines to make machines to make consumption goods. It concluded that a shift toward the latter composition of heavy industry as against light industry would, after a time, result in a higher level and faster growth rate of consumption than would an investment program placing more emphasis on the production of consumption goods.[34]

At the same time as pessimistic conclusions were being reached about the capacity to export primary products and to pursue export-led development, optimistic views were being expressed on the capacity to accelerate development through the extension of the public sector and the institution of wide-ranging governmental policies within a development plan. The combination of external pessimism and internal optimism is reflected in the writings of some of the pioneers. Although some advocated a lighter type of planning through the market system,[35] there was initially greater

---

will be underrated . . . [T]he most powerful influence governing development . . . is not the rate of interest or the abundance of capital; and the most powerful influence governing capital accumulation, even now, is not technical progress." "The Place of Capital in Economic Progress," in Leon H. Dupriez, ed., *Economic Progress* (Louvain: Institut de Recherches Economiques et Sociales, 1955), p. 248.

33. Also of interest was the "critical minimum effort" thesis presented by Harvey Leibenstein, *Economic Backwardness and Economic Growth* (New York: Wiley, 1957), chap. 8; and Leibenstein, "Theory of Underemployment in Backward Economies," *Journal of Political Economy* (April 1957).

34. For an elaboration, see "Development Dichotomies" below. Also, Jagdish N. Bhagwati and Sukhamoy Chakravarty, "Contributions to Indian Economic Analysis: A Survey," *American Economic Review* (September 1969), pp. 5–8; M. Bronfenbrenner, "A Simplified Mahalanobis Development Model," *Economic Development and Cultural Change* (October 1960). For other contemporary discussions of planned economic development in India, see B. Datta, *The Economics of Industrialization* (Calcutta: World Press Private, 1952); B. R. Shenoy, *Problems of Indian Economic Development* (London: Asia Publishing House, 1958); and Shenoy, *Indian Planning and Economic Development* (London: Asia Publishing House, 1963).

The strategy of industrialization was also discussed by T. Balogh, "Note on the Deliberate Industrialisation for Higher Incomes," *Economic Journal* (June 1947); H. Belshaw, "Observations on Industrialisation for Higher Incomes," *Economic Journal* (September 1947); W. S. Buchanan, "Deliberate Industrialisation for Higher Incomes," *Economic Journal* (December 1946); and H. Frankel, "Industrialisation of Agricultural Countries and the Possibilities of a New International Division of Labour," *Economic Journal* (June–September 1943).

35. A strong case for the market mechanism as against detailed planning, as the preferable instrument of economic development, was made by Harry G. Johnson, "Planning and the Market in Economic Development," *Pakistan Economic Journal* (June 1958).

enthusiasm for centralized planning that relied on comprehensive controls.

The United Nations group of experts recommended as early as 1951 that the "government of an underdeveloped country should establish a central economic unit with the functions of surveying the economy, making development programs, advising on the measures necessary for carrying out such programs, and reporting on them periodically. The development programs should contain a capital budget showing the requirements of capital and how much of this is expected from domestic and from foreign sources."[36]

Development programs, national planning boards, and industrial development corporations soon proliferated. Moreover, the economist's tool kit began to provide some modern techniques that could support the formulation of a development plan—especially input-output analysis, dynamic programming, and simulation of growth models. These techniques provided tests for the consistency, balance, and feasibility of plans. Visiting missions and foreign advisers began to cooperate with local planning agencies in producing analyses and policy recommendations underlying development plans. A development plan commonly aimed at a forced take-off and high-speed development, with a large amount of public investment and deliberate industrialization at its core, and supplanted the market mechanism with physical planning that involved the government in numerous decisions of a direct, specific character.[37] At a lower level of planning, increasing attention was given to the allocation of investment techniques, and different views of investment criteria were promulgated.[38]

From the emphasis on capital accumulation, industrialization, and planning, there emerged a case for foreign aid. The resource gap between

36. United Nations Department of Economic Affairs, *Measures for the Economic Development of Underdeveloped Countries.*

37. The "Soviet way of industrialization" had some influence in stimulating planning. See the writing by Maurice Dobb, *Some Aspects of Economic Development*; Paul Baran, "On The Political Economy of Backwardness," *Manchester School of Economic and Social Studies* (January 1952); and Baran, *The Political Economy of Backwardness* (New York: Monthly Review Press, 1957).

38. W. Galenson and H. Leibenstein, "Investment Criteria, Productivity, and Economic Development," *Quarterly Journal of Economics* (August 1955); A. K. Sen, "Some Notes on the Choice of Capital Intensity in Development Planning," *Quarterly Journal of Economics* (November 1957); Sen, *Choice of Techniques* (Oxford: Blackwell, 1960); H. B. Chenery, "The Application of Investment Criteria," *Quarterly Journal of Economics* (February 1953); Alfred E. Kahn, "Investment Criteria in Development Programs," *Quarterly Journal of Economics* (February 1951); O. Eckstein, "Investment Criteria for Economic Development and the Theory of Intertemporal Welfare Economics," *Quarterly Journal of Economics* (February 1957); H. B. Chenery and Kenneth S. Kretschmer, "Resource Allocation for Economic Development," *Econometrica* (October 1956); and H. Leibenstein, "Why Do We Disagree on Investment Policies for Development?" *Indian Economic Journal* (April 1958).

the domestic investment required to fulfill the development plan's target growth rate and the possible amount of domestic savings would be filled by foreign aid.

In the U.N. report by the group of experts in 1951, estimates were made of the total capital required by all developing countries to support an annual rate of growth in per capita national incomes of 2 percent over the 1950–60 period. Of the total annual requirements of $19 billion, it was estimated that only $5 billion could be met by domestic savings, leaving about $14 billion a year to be covered by foreign capital. It was argued that much of this foreign capital must come from foreign governments and multinational agencies in the form of grants and other concessional aid.

In his inaugural address in 1949, President Truman had also announced his Point Four Program for technical assistance. Economists believed that, along with foreign capital, it was desirable to borrow new technology and acquire know-how from abroad in order to absorb the additional capital more rapidly. To utilize the inflow of capital productively, the developing country had to acquire the missing components of technology, skills, and management, but it was thought that these could be imported.

Leading Issues

To determine the sources of growth and delineate strategies of development, the pioneers had to conceptualize, deduce principles, build models, and establish empirical relationships. In this undertaking, the field of economic history was to be revitalized from the perspective of development.[39] The theory of development policy, however, posed more of a challenge and required fresh thinking. Rather oddly, in retrospect, most of those who began theorizing about underdeveloped countries were citizens of the developed countries. But though the Anglo-American tradition of economics dominated, many of the early development economists began to question the relevance of neoclassical doctrines and of Keynesian analysis for the new problems of development.

Gunnar Myrdal, for instance, called upon the underdeveloped countries to produce a new generation of economists who might create a body of thought more realistic and relevant for the problems of their countries:

39. Besides Walt Rostow's *The Stages of Economic Growth* (as discussed in his chapter, "Development: The Political Economy of the Marshallian Long Period," below), the development lessons of economic history are emphasized by H. J. Habakkuk and Alexander Gerschenkron. See Habakkuk, "The Historical Experience on the Basic Conditions of Economic Progress," in Leon H. Dupriez, ed., *Economic Progress* (Louvain: Institut de Recherches Economiques et Sociales, 1955), pp. 149–70; Gerschenkron, "Social Attitudes, Entrepreneurship, and Economic Development," *Explorations in Entrepreneurial History* (October 1953), pp. 1–19; and Gerschenkron, *Economic Backwardness in Historical Perspective* (Cambridge, Mass.: Harvard University Press, 1962).

In this epoch of the Great Awakening, it would be pathetic if the young economists in the underdeveloped countries got caught in the predilections of the economic thinking in the advanced countries, which are hampering the scholars there in their efforts to be rational but would be almost deadening to the intellectual strivings of those in the underdeveloped countries.

I would, instead, wish them to have the courage to throw away large structures of meaningless, irrelevant, and sometimes blatantly inadequate doctrines and theoretical approaches and to start their thinking afresh from a study of their own needs and problems.[40]

Unlike the neoclassical economists who assumed a smoothly working market price system, some of the early development economists adopted a more structuralist approach to development problems. Structuralist analysis attempted to identify specific rigidities, lags, shortages and surpluses, low elasticities of supply and demand, and other characteristics of the structure of developing countries that affect economic adjustments and the choice of development policy.[41] Some of the authors in this volume— Lewis, Myrdal, Prebisch, Singer, and Rosenstein-Rodan—departed from the flexibility and substitutability of neoclassical economics and introduced elements of structural analysis.

Also prominent was Ragnar Nurkse's argument that the developing countries could no longer rely on economic growth being induced from the outside through an expansion of world demand for their export of primary commodities, and that the less developed countries must pursue balanced growth conforming to the income elasticities of internal demand.[42]

Although many others did not take as extreme a position as did Myrdal or the structuralists, there was still wide questioning of how traditional analysis might be amended and extended to be more applicable to development problems. The market price system could not be simply assumed, but first had to be instituted in the emergent nations. The invisible hand was difficult to see.

At the same time, however, as many of the early development economists rejected the teachings of neoclassical economics, there were some who warned that the analysis of development problems should not be "price-less," that the functions of prices should not be ignored, that the economic responses to individual incentives should not be overlooked,

40. Gunnar Myrdal, *Rich Lands and Poor* (New York: Harper, 1957), pp. 103–04.

41. H. B. Chenery, "The Structuralist Approach to Economic Development," *American Economic Review* (May 1965).

42. Ragnar Nurkse, *Problems of Capital Formation in Underdeveloped Countries*, chap. 1; *Patterns of Trade and Development*, Wicksell Lectures (Stockholm: Almqvist and Wiksell, 1959); and "The Conflict Between 'Balanced Growth' and International Specialization."

and that the government should not intervene in the market price system. Such a view dominated the work by P. T. Bauer and B. S. Yamey, *The Economics of Under-developed Countries.*[43]

On issues of trade policy, there were notable critics of import substitution and protectionist policies. Jacob Viner rejected the Prebisch-Singer doctrine of secular deterioration of the terms of trade of developing countries and argued against import-substituting industrialization.[44] Viner also pointed out that

> while it is true that the ratio of nonagricultural to total population tends to be highly correlated positively with per capita income, the degree of industrialization may be and often is a consequence rather than a cause of the level of prosperity, and that where agriculture is prosperous, not only do tertiary or service industries tend spontaneously to grow but there is a widespread tendency to use disposable surplus income derived from agricultural prosperity to subsidize uneconomic urban industry, with the consequence that the overall level of per capita income, while still comparatively high, is lower than it would be if urban industry were not artificially stimulated.[45]

After surveying the dynamic benefits of international trade, Gottfried Haberler also concluded that trade "has made a tremendous contribution to the development of less developed countries in the 19th and 20th centuries and can be expected to make an equally big contribution in the future, if it is allowed to proceed freely." Haberler argued that

> Development policy should be such as to work through and with the help of the powerful forces of the price mechanism instead of opposing and counteracting the market forces. This holds for measures in the area of international trade as well as in the domestic field. I should like to repeat my conviction that the latter—action in the field of education, health, public overhead investment—are more important than the negative policy of import restriction. The latter is, of course, much easier than the former. For that reason, it is likely to be overdone, while the former is apt to be neglected.[46]

43. Chicago: University of Chicago Press, 1957.

44. Jacob Viner, *International Trade and Economic Development* (Oxford: Clarendon Press, 1953). Charles Kindelberger also questioned the empirical basis of the alleged deterioration in the terms of trade: *The Terms of Trade: A European Case Study* (New York: MIT Press and Wiley, 1958); and "Terms of Trade and Economic Development," *Review of Economics and Statistics*, Supplement 40 (February 1958). See also T. Morgan, "The Long-Run Terms of Trade between Agriculture and Manufacturing," *Economic Development and Cultural Change* (October 1959).

45. *International Trade and Economic Development*, p. 97. See also Viner, "Stability and Progress: The Poorer Countries' Problem," in Douglas Hague, ed., *Stability and Progress in the World Economy* (London: Macmillan, 1958), pp. 41–101.

46. *International Trade and Economic Development* (Cairo: National Bank of Egypt, 1959), p. 6.

J. R. Hicks also emphasized the dynamic benefits of trade, related increasing returns and the productivity of investment to the volume of trade, warned against a heavily protected home market for consumption goods, and foresaw the possibility that underdeveloped countries could become exporters of manufactured goods. Also significant were articles on international trade by Hla Myint.[47]

Some may choose to summarize the mainstream development economics of the 1950s as being structural, shaped by trade pessimism, emphasizing planned investment in new physical capital, utilizing reserves of surplus labor, adopting import substitution industrialization policies, embracing central planning of change, and relying on foreign aid.[48] But there were crosscurrents, and the period was characterized by vigorous debate over some leading issues.[49] Especially notable were controversies over balanced growth versus unbalanced growth, industrialization versus agriculture, import substitution versus export promotion, planning versus reliance on the market price system. The debates on some of these issues are still unresolved.

In the following pages, the pioneers again speak for themselves. They are invited to recapitulate the main themes of their early work, to indicate what theoretical position and policies they were trying to rebut or support, and to consider how their position may have changed in light of the development experience of the past quarter century.

In considering their papers, the reader may now ask: Did the pioneers establish economic development as a special branch of economics? Of their contributions, which remain insightful and valid? What questions remain unsettled? And where does the subject of economic development go from here?

---

47. J. R. Hicks, *Essays in World Economics* (Oxford: Clarendon Press, 1959), pp. 161–95. Hla Myint, "Gains from International Trade and Backward Countries," *Review of Economic Studies*, vol. 22, no. 58 (1954–55); and "The 'Classical Theory' of International Trade and the Underdeveloped Countries," *Economic Journal* (June 1958).

48. Ian M. D. Little believes these "were the main features of the dominant school, and they are only slightly caricatured." *Economic Development* (New York: Basic Books, 1982), p. 119.

49. An editorial in *Economic Development and Cultural Change* (March 1952), p. 3, stated: "Even a casual glance at the existing literature reveals not only the absence of a satisfactory theory but also the absence of agreement as to which of the many problems apparent to the observer are important for study. The research worker seeking pathways to adequate theory finds no blazed trails, but instead a veritable jungle of vicious circles, obstacles to change, and necessary (but never sufficient) preconditions for economic growth."

Pioneers

Lord Bauer

P. T. BAUER was born in Budapest in 1915. He is a Fellow of the British
Academy, Fellow of Gonville and Caius College, Cambridge, and was
Smuts Reader in Commonwealth Studies, Cambridge University, 1956–
60, and Professor of Economics (with special reference to economic development in underdeveloped countries) at the London School of Economics, 1960–83. He was raised to the peerage in 1983.

His early publications stem from field work in Malaya and West Africa.
His books include *The Rubber Industry* (Cambridge, Mass.: Harvard
University Press, 1948); *West African Trade* (Cambridge, Eng.: Cambridge University Press, 1954; London: Routledge and Kegan Paul, 1963);
with B. S. Yamey, *The Economics of Under-developed Countries* (Chicago: University of Chicago Press, 1957); *Economic Analysis and Policy
in Underdeveloped Countries* (Durham, N.C.: Duke University Press,
1957; Cambridge, Eng.: Cambridge University Press, 1958); *Indian Economic Policy and Development* (London: Allen and Unwin, 1961; Bombay: Popular Prakashan, 1965); with B. S. Yamey, *Markets, Market
Control and Marketing Reform* (London: Weidenfeld and Nicolson,
1968); *Dissent on Development* (London: Weidenfeld and Nicolson,
1971; Cambridge, Mass.: Harvard University Press, 1972); *Reality and
Rhetoric: Studies in the Economics of Development* (Cambridge, Mass.:
Harvard University Press, 1984).

Among his articles are "The Working of Rubber Regulation," *Economic Journal*, September 1946; with B. S. Yamey, "Economic Progress
and Occupational Distribution," *Economic Journal*, December 1951;
with F. W. Paish, "Reduction in the Fluctuations of Incomes of Primary
Producers," *Economic Journal*, December 1952; with B. S. Yamey, "East-
West/North-South," *Commentary*, September 1980.

Lord Bauer has published extensively on major issues in the general field
of economic development, including the role of trading activity and the
significance of the informal sector in developing countries; the role of cash
crops in development; the relation between economic progress and occupational distribution; conceptual and practical problems of price and
income stabilization; and the operation of commodity agreements. His

25

contributions also offer an effective critique of received opinion on such issues as the vicious circle of poverty, the widening gap of income differences within and among countries, the operation of foreign aid, and the theory and practice of development planning. He has also written on questions of methodology in economics, notably on the tendency in modern economics to ignore the interaction of variables and parameters.

Remembrance of Studies Past:
Retracing First Steps

THE FOLLOWING is a reasonable summary of the principal components to the burgeoning development literature of the early postwar years.[1]

External trade is at best ineffective for the economic advance of less developed countries (LDCs), and more often it is damaging. Instead, the advance of LDCs depends on ample supplies of capital to provide for infrastructure, for the rapid growth of manufacturing industry, and for the modernization of their economies and societies. The capital required cannot be generated in the LDCs themselves because of the inflexible and inexorable constraint of low incomes (the vicious circle of poverty and stagnation), reinforced by the international demonstration effect, and by the lack of privately profitable investment opportunities in poor countries with their inherently limited local markets. General backwardness, economic unresponsiveness, and lack of enterprise are well-nigh universal within the less developed world. Therefore, if significant economic advance is to be achieved, governments have an indispensable as well as a comprehensive role in carrying through the critical and large-scale changes necessary to break down the formidable obstacles to growth and to initiate and sustain the growth process.

These ideas became the core of mainstream academic development literature, which in turn has served as the basis for national and international policies ever since. Even when some elements of the core have disappeared from more academic writings, they have continued to dominate political and public discourse, an instance of the lingering effects of discarded ideas.

My earliest investigations of economic issues in LDCs were not inspired by these topics; in fact, they were altogether unconnected with them.[2] I

1. Detailed references to the early development literature are given in my *Dissent on Development* (London: Weidenfeld and Nicolson, 1971; and Cambridge, Mass.: Harvard University Press, 1972), passim, especially chaps. 1 and 2.

2. The results of my studies are to be found in the following publications: P. T. Bauer, *The Rubber Industry* (Cambridge, Mass.: Harvard University Press, 1948); *Report on a Visit to the Rubber-Growing Smallholdings of Malaya, July–September 1946* (London: Colonial Office, 1948); *West African Trade* (Cambridge, Eng.: Cam-

came to this general area through two studies, one of the rubber industry of Southeast Asia, and the other of the organization of trade in the former British West Africa. I spent more than ten years on these studies during the 1940s and 1950s when I was for substantial periods in each of the two regions. What I saw was starkly at variance with the components of the emerging consensus of mainstream development economics listed above. My enquiries into and observation of economic, social, and political life in these two major regions provoked a lasting interest in general development economics. Although my ideas have developed much since the completion of these studies, they have not moved closer either to the tenets of the development orthodoxy of the 1950s or to their subsequent modification.

[1]

Even before setting foot in Southeast Asia and West Africa I knew that many of their economies had advanced rapidly (even though they were colonies!). After all, it required no instruction in development economics to know that before 1885 there was not a single rubber tree in Malaya nor a single cocoa tree in British West Africa. By the 1930s there were millions of acres under these and other export crops, the bulk of them owned and operated by non-Europeans. But while I knew this and a good deal else about local conditions, I was nevertheless surprised by much of what I saw, including the extensive economic transformation occurring in large areas and the vigor of economic life of much of the local populations. In Malaya (now Malaysia), for example, the economic activity of the many towns and large villages, the excellent communications, and the evident prosperity of large sections of the non-European population reflected a world totally different from the largely empty and economically backward Malaya of the nineteenth century. The results of somewhat similar, though less extensive, changes were evident also in West Africa, most notably in southern Nigeria and the Gold Coast (now Ghana). How was all this possible if there was any real substance in the central ideas of the contemporary development economics?

bridge University Press, 1954; London: Routledge and Kegan Paul, 1963); *Economic Analysis and Policy in Underdeveloped Countries* (Durham, N.C.: Duke University Press, 1957; and Cambridge, Eng.: Cambridge University Press, 1958); and, with B. S. Yamey, *The Economics of Under-developed Countries* (Chicago: University of Chicago Press, 1957), and some of the essays in *Markets, Market Control and Marketing Reform* (London: Weidenfeld and Nicolson, 1968). I want to make it clear that since 1951 I have worked so closely with Basil Yamey that the ideas in this paper are his as much as mine. It is for convenience of exposition alone that I do not make the distinction in the text between our joint work and my own.

In the earliest stages local supplies of capital were minimal. In Southeast Asia, however, the export market for rubber (and to a lesser extent other products such as tin) attracted investment by European enterprises, particularly for such purposes as the development of rubber estates in hitherto empty jungle. Where local labor supplies were inadequate, as in Malaya and Sumatra, the Western enterprises organized and financed large-scale recruitment and migration of unlettered workers, mainly from China and India. The activities of the Western enterprises induced unintended and unexpected sequences. For instance, Chinese traders were drawn into the rubber trade. Some started their own plantations, while others brought seeds and consumer goods to the indigenous people of Malaya and the Netherlands Indies (now Indonesia). They thereby encouraged the local population to plant rubber trees and to produce for the market. By the late 1930s, over half of the rubber acreage of Southeast Asia was owned by Asians. This acreage represented the results of direct investment despite initially low incomes.[3]

The history was somewhat different in West Africa. In this region there were (and are) no European-owned plantations. The large area under cocoa, groundnuts, cotton, and kola nuts has been entirely occupied by farms established, owned, and operated by Africans. The extensive capital involved was made available partly by European trading firms which financed local traders, and partly by direct investment by Africans, the latter in important instances carried out by migrant farmers in regions far from their homes.

In all this the role of traders was crucial: Sir Keith Hancock has rightly called West Africa "the traders' frontier." The traders made available consumer goods and production inputs, and provided the outlets for the cash crops. Their activities stimulated investment and production. The part played by what used to be called inducement goods—a term once a household expression but now rarely encountered in modern development literature—was notable. The sequence showed the inappropriateness of the notion of the international demonstration effect, the idea that access to cheap consumer goods, especially imported goods, retards development in the LDCs by raising the propensity to consume of the local populations.

The rapid economic progress generally in these areas, of which the large-scale capital formation in agriculture by the local people was a major

---

3. The plantation rubber industry comprises smallholdings, that is, properties of less than a hundred acres each, and estate properties of more than a hundred acres each. Smallholdings, which account for well over half the total area, are entirely in Asian ownership. By now well over half of the estates are also in Asian, largely Chinese, ownership. In a private communication in January 1983, W. G. G. Kellett, who was for many years chief statistician of the International Rubber Regulation Committee and subsequently of the International Rubber Study Group, put the present Asian ownership at well over 90 percent.

component, cannot be squared with the idea of the vicious circle of poverty and stagnation. It would have been a freak of chance if I had happened on the only two regions in the less developed world where people had managed to escape the imperatives of a law of economics. In fact, of course, the notion of the vicious circle of poverty, that poverty is self-perpetuating, is belied by evidence throughout the developed and less developed world, and indeed by the very existence of developed countries.

The notion is not rescued by the suggestion, much canvassed since the 1950s, that the production of commodities for export resulted merely in enclaves operated by Westerners without benefit to the local people. As I have said, a large part of production, and sometimes the entire output, was (and remains) in the hands of the local population. The same applies to the associated activities of trade and transport. Had this been otherwise, the development of export crops could not have transformed the lives of the local people as it has done. In these regions, as in many others, the pervasive economic advance has made it possible for much larger populations to live longer and at much higher standards.

A developed infrastructure was not a precondition for the emergence of the major cash crops of Southeast Asia and West Africa. As has often also been the case elsewhere, the facilities known as infrastructure were developed in the course of the expansion of the economy. It is unhistorical to envisage an elaborate and expensive infrastructure as a necessary groundwork for economic advance. Countless people in trading and transport often performed the services usually associated with capital-intensive infrastructure. For instance, human and animal transport, the contacts between numerous traders, and long chains of intermediaries were partial but effective substitutes for expensive roads and communication systems.

[2]

The historical experience I have noted (and which had its counterpart in many LDCs) was not the result of conscription of people or the forced mobilization of their resources. Nor was it the result of forcible modernization of attitudes and behavior, nor of large-scale state-sponsored industrialization, nor of any other form of big push. And it was not brought about by the achievement of political independence, or by the inculcation in the minds of the local people of the notion of national identity, or by the stirring-up of mass enthusiasm for the abstract notion of economic development, or by any other form of political or cultural revolution. It was not the result of conscious efforts at nation building (as if people were lifeless bricks, to be moved about by some master builder) or of the adoption by governments of economic development as a formal policy goal or commitment. What happened was in very large measure the result of the individual voluntary responses of millions of people to emerging or expanding opportunities created largely by external contacts and brought to their notice in a variety of ways, primarily through the operation of the market. These developments were made possible by firm but limited government, without large expenditures of public funds and without the receipt of large external subventions.

The nature of these responses in turn exposed for me the hollowness of various standard stereotypes. It was evident that the ordinary people of the LDCs were not necessarily torpid, rigidly constrained by custom and habit, economically timid, inherently myopic, and generally deficient in enterprise. In a decade or two, the illiterate peasantry of Southeast Asia and West Africa planted millions of acres under hitherto unknown cash crops, rubber and cocoa, which take five years to become productive. The large volumes of direct investment to achieve this were made possible by voluntary changes in the conduct, attitudes, and motivations of numerous individuals, in many cases involving the sacrifice of leisure and the modification of personal relationships. Yet Malays, Indonesians, and Africans were precisely among those who were depicted (as they still sometimes are) as incapable of taking a long view or of creating capital, and as being hobbled by custom and habit.

The establishment and operation of properties producing cash crops are entrepreneurial activities. So also are the ubiquitous trading and transport activities of local people. The contention is thus invalid that entrepreneurial skills and attitudes are lacking in LDCs. Indeed, they are often present but take forms which accord with people's attributes and inclinations and with local conditions and opportunities. In many parts of the less developed world there is evidence of much enterprise and risk-taking, often on a small scale individually, but by no means confined to agriculture and trading.

The contribution to economic development of the numerous small and large-scale entrepreneurs (farmers, traders, industrialists, and so on) highlights the generally melancholy record of the entrepreneurial efforts of LDC governments—all too often financed at large cost from revenues derived by taxing the producers of cash crops. It is often claimed in the development literature, in support of the alleged need for extensive state control and direction in the economies of many LDCs, that their populations lack entrepreneurs. Should the people of a particular country in fact be without entrepreneurial talents or inclinations, it is difficult to see how the politicians and civil servants from this population could make up for the deficiency.

In the less developed world, willingness to bestir oneself and to take risks in the process is not confined to entrepreneurs in the accepted sense of the term. Hundreds of thousands of extremely poor landless rural people have migrated thousands of miles to improve their lot. The large-scale migration from southeastern China and southern India to Fiji, Malaya, and the Netherlands Indies is well known. In my work I was able to show that very poor illiterate people were well informed about economic conditions in distant and alien countries, and that they responded intelligently to the opportunities they perceived.[4]

[3]

When I began my work, the emerging ideas on economic development assigned decisive importance to the ratio between number of people on the one hand, and available resources—land and other natural resources, as well as capital—on the other. Given the size of population, physical resources were all that mattered. Apart from age and sex differences, people were envisaged as homogeneous from an economic point of view. All this can be seen in the construction of the growth models of contemporary economic literature and in the discussion these inspired. The only partial qualification was provided in the growing emphasis on human differences resulting from capital embodied in people.

My existing skepticism about this approach was soon and amply reinforced by what I saw in Southeast Asia. The differences in economic performance and hence in achievement among groups were immediately evident, indeed startling. Perhaps the clearest demonstration that people, even with the same level of education, cannot be treated as being uniform in the economic context was to be found in that region.

Many rubber estates kept records of the daily output of each tapper, and distinguished between the output of Chinese and Indian workers. The output of the Chinese was usually more than double that of the Indians, with all of them using the same simple equipment of tapping knife, latex cup, and bucket. There were similar or even wider differences between Chinese, Indian, and Malay smallholders when I visited several hundred smallholdings in Malaya in 1946. The pronounced differences between Chinese and Indians could not be attributed to the special characteristics often possessed by migrants, as both groups were recent immigrants. The great majority of both Indians and Chinese were uneducated coolies, so that the differences in their performance could not be explained in terms of differences in human capital formation. The Chinese performance in Malay was especially notable. Not only had practically all the Chinese been very poor immigrants, but also they were subject to extensive adverse discrimination imposed by the British administration and by the local Malaya rulers.

Of course, differences among groups were not limited to expertise in rubber tapping or in other aspects of rubber production. They were pervasive throughout the local economies in the establishment and run-

4. See *The Rubber Industry*, chap. 15 and app. D; and *Economic Analysis and Economic Policy*, chap. 1.

ning of plantations and mines and of industrial and commercial undertak-
ings. These differences in no way resulted from differences in the initial
capital endowments of the groups. In fact, of course, these differences
meant that the various groups made vastly different contributions to
capital formation; these contributions in turn were conditioned not only
by differences in productivity but also by differences in personal preferences and motivations and social arrangements. I was to encounter similar
phenomena in West Africa, in the Levant, in India, and elsewhere.

I should not have been so greatly surprised by what I found. After all, I
was aware of the pronounced differences in economic performance among
different cultural groups as a feature of much of economic history, and of
the fact that groups discriminated against were often especially productive
and successful. My temporary oversight was probably due to my having
succumbed to the then prevailing view that the less developed world newly
discovered by Western economists was somehow different. I had also
fallen victim to the notion of the primary and overwhelming importance of
physical resources (including capital) as determinants of real incomes—a
short period of aberration in which I ignored what I knew of economic
history. And I, like others, may have been bemused by figures of average
incomes calculated for entire populations without regard to ethnic (and
for that matter age) composition.

I might note here that many millions of very poor people in the Third
World today, as in the past, have ready access to cultivable land, and also
that conventional labor-to-land ratios are meaningless. Such groups as
aborigines, pygmies, and various African tribes are extreme cases of
poverty amid abundant land. Even in India, much land is officially classified as uncultivated but usable.

The small size and low productivity of many farms in the Third World
reflect primarily want of ambition, energy, and skill, not want of land and
capital. In any case, it was borne in on me that the notion of uncultivable
land is misleading, since cultivability depends heavily upon the economic
qualities of the people as well as on official policies affecting the use of
land. Examples of the last point include the price policies of governments,
control of immigration and inflow of capital, and the terms on which state
lands are made available.[5]

Although the discussion of them has been largely taboo in the postwar
development literature, the reality and importance of group differences in
economic performance cannot be disputed. The subject is virtually proscribed in the profession, even when these differences serve as major
planks in official policy, as they do in Malaysia and elsewhere.

---

5. The distinction between cultivable and uncultivable land is arbitrary. Adam
Smith noted that grapes could be grown in Scotland. The arbitrary nature of the
distinction is highlighted by the experience of areas such as Holland, Venice, Israel, and
other Middle Eastern countries.

Discussion of the reasons for group differences in performance and of their likely persistence would be speculative, and economic reasoning is not informative on these questions. But this provides no excuse for the systematic neglect of group differences by economists. Such differences are plainly relevant for assessment of the economic situation and prospects in Third World countries (and elsewhere too), and for the concept and implications of population pressure. It follows also that the relation between economic development and population growth cannot be examined sensibly on the basis simply of numbers and resources.

[4]

Considerations such as those set out so far have reinforced my reluctance to attempt to formulate a theory of economic development, and also my rejection of theories based either on sequential stages of history or on the conventional type of growth model. The inadequacy of these theories is in any case revealed by their inability to account for the well-attested phenomenon of economic decline (whether absolute or relative). Moreover, economic development is but one facet of the history of a society, and attempts to formulate general theories of history have so far been conspicuously unsuccessful, even though many distinguished minds have addressed the question. Not surprisingly, some of these attempts have yielded informative insights, but none of sufficient generality to serve as a basis for a theory of development.

In the more narrowly economic context, I found the approach embodied in the conventional growth models to be unhelpful and even misleading. The approach focuses on independent variables which I came to know were unimportant. Again, it ignores the interplay between the chosen variables and parameters. Thus, the models take as given such decisive factors as the political situation, people's attitudes, and the state of knowledge.[6] Attempts to increase the stock of capital—for instance, by special taxation or restriction of imports—greatly affect these and other factors treated as parameters, and have repercussions typically far outweighing the effects on development of any increase in capital which might ensue. These shortcomings are apart from basic problems of the concept

---

6. As I have observed in other places, these growth models have been inspired by Keynes: "We take as given the existing skill and quantity of available labour, the existing quality and quantity of available equipment, the existing technique, the degree of competition, the tastes and habits of the consumer, the disutility of different intensities of labour and of the activities of supervision and organisation, as well as the social structure..." (J. M. Keynes, *The General Theory of Employment, Interest and Money* [London: Macmillan, 1936] p. 245). This drastic simplification is doubtfully appropriate even for the analysis of short-term growth in an advanced economy. It is altogether inappropriate to discussion of long-term progress of LDCs.

and measurement of capital, and of the distinction between investment and consumption. This distinction is especially nebulous in the conditions of LDCs, where the use of inducement goods often results in improved economic performance, and consumption is thus complementary to, rather than competitive with, saving and investment.

Since the Second World War an aggregative and quantitative approach has predominated in development economics. Such an approach may have been inspired by the growth models which confine themselves to aggregates such as capital, labor, and consumption. Acceptance of this general approach has had the comforting corollary that the economy of an LDC could be studied on the basis of readily accessible statistics, and also that it was legitimate to dispense with both direct observation and nonquantitative information generally. This neglect in turn has led to an uncritical acceptance of the available statistics. The very large biases in international income statistics, as well as changes in their incidence over time, have been ignored in much of development economics. Again, in the statistics used in development economics, direct capital formation in agriculture has been undervalued or, more often, neglected altogether. Yet this form of capital formation is quantitatively and qualitatively significant in the advance from the largely subsistence activities characteristic of many LDCs. Perhaps more serious in its repercussions has been the failure to recognize this form of capital formation in analyses of economic growth and hence in proposals for promoting growth. Thus fiscal policies for accelerating capital formation have often been advanced without recognition of their necessary effects on direct capital formation in agriculture. In practice, the untoward results of this oversight have been compounded by the habit, itself encouraged by the aggregative approach, of the neglect of prices as determinants of the choice of economic activities.[7]

The use of occupational statistics presents some instructive examples of inappropriate reliance on accessible data and of the neglect, even atrophy, of direct observation. Occupational statistics suggested that in LDCs almost the entire population was engaged in agriculture. For instance, this was a theme of the official reports on West Africa and the literature based on them which I consulted before my first visit. Trade and transport barely figured in the official census or in Lord Hailey's *An African Survey* (London, 1938). I was therefore much surprised by the volume of trading activity and the large number of traders that I was soon able to observe. It became clear that the official statistics were misleading because they did not and could not reflect the prevailing incomplete occupational specialization. In households classified as agricultural it was usual for some of the members to trade regularly or intermittently, regardless of sex and also largely regardless of age.[8]

7. See *Economic Analysis and Economic Policy*, chap. 2; and *The Economics of Under-developed Countries*, chap. 10.
8. See *West African Trade*, chap. 2.

West African experience, which was clearly not unique, except perhaps in the extent of participation in trading, led me to examine and overturn the prevailing Clark-Fisher hypothesis that economic advancement entails a movement of labor progressively from primary to secondary and then to tertiary economic activity.[9] I showed that the theory rested on misleading statistics; that tertiary activities were a miscellany of activities united only by their output being nonmaterial; that they did not have the common feature of high income elasticities of demand, and that many tertiary activities were indeed necessary for emergence from subsistence production in poor countries; that in small-scale trade and transport in LDCs labor can easily be substituted for capital; and that the belief was unfounded that technical progress was necessarily more pronounced in the production of goods than in that of services. Furthermore, the common aggregation of economic activities into three distinctive groups was shown to be of no value for analysis or for sensible policy prescriptions. Yet the notion is still alive that the tripartite classification of economic activities not only is valid and firm but can serve as a basis for policy.

In the general context of development economics, the various preceding examples of misleading aggregation are overshadowed by a practice which I have not yet discussed here. This is the treatment of the world as being two distinct aggregates, the rich and progressing countries and the poor and stagnating countries. The second and much larger aggregate consists of practically the whole of Asia and Africa and the whole of Latin America. This collectivity is envisaged as broadly uniform, caught in a vicious circle of poverty, separated from the rich countries by a wide and widening gap in incomes, and afflicted moreover by generally deteriorating terms of trade in its exchanges with the other aggregate.

In fact, this picture does not bear any resemblance to reality. It does not do justice to the rich variety of humanity and experience in the less developed world, and to the rapid growth of many formerly poor countries and the prosperity of large groups there. The inappropriate lumping together of all so-called LDCs has made it more difficult for economists and others to reject the prevailing notions to which I have drawn attention at the beginning of this chapter, and therefore to recognize the inappropriateness of the policy prescriptions derived from them. I now see far more clearly than I did when my studies began how inappropriate was the division of the world into the two supposedly distinct aggregates.

[5]

In the early postwar development literature trading activity was very largely ignored. It was ignored in the statistics, in the discussion of de-

9. References to the relevant writings of Colin Clark and A. G. B. Fisher are in *Markets, Market Control and Market Reform*, chaps. 1 and 2, which are revised versions of two articles (with B. S. Yamey) in the *Economic Journal* (December 1951 and March 1954).

velopment prospects, and in the planning literature, as well as in the plans themselves. When considered at all, the discussion of trade was couched typically in perjorative terms. For instance, it was viewed as a hotbed of imperfections and as a source or manifestation of waste. Hence there followed policy proposals for the replacement of private trading arrangements by the establishment of state trading and state-sponsored cooperative societies.

In contrast, the indispensable role of traders, especially in the development of cash crops, was evident in my inquiries both in Southeast Asia and West Africa and in other LDCs I came to know.

I noted what had often been observed by economic historians, administrators, and other observers, that traders provided and extended markets and thereby widened the opportunities open to people as producers and consumers.[10] Traders brought new and cheaper goods to the notice and within the reach of people, a process which induced better economic performance. Sometimes small-scale traders penetrated areas before explorers and administrators had reached them. Without trading activities there could be no agricultural surplus. Traders linked producers and consumers, created new wants and encouraged or even made possible the production necessary for their satisfaction. More generally, they acquainted people with the workings of an exchange economy and the attitudes appropriate to it. By extending people's economic horizons and by establishing new contacts, the activities of traders encouraged people to question existing habits and mores, and promoted the uncoerced erosion of attitudes and customs incompatible with material progress. Moreover, trading widely proved to be a seedbed of entrepreneurial activities extending beyond trading itself. Thus enterprising and successful traders at times initiated or expanded their farming interests (many in any case were part-time farmers). Trading brought to the fore entrepreneurs who perceived economic opportunities and were ready to pursue them. It was not surprising that successful transport and manufacturing enterprises were often established by traders, both local and expatriate.

These dynamic effects of the activities of traders were largely ignored in the postwar development literature. The role of traders in bringing about a more effective interregional and intertemporal allocation of output may have been more widely recognized. But even where this was recognized, the activities of traders and the organization of the trading system were subjected to much misconceived analysis and criticism. For example, the multiplicity of traders and the vertical subdivision of trading activity into many successive stages were often criticized. I showed that these features could be explained by the relative scarcity of capital and administrative skills, the possibilities in trade of substituting labor for capital, and the

10. Since I refer to my observations in the early postwar period, I use the past tense. However, the role of traders still applies generally wherever they are allowed to operate. See *West African Trade*, chap. 2; and *Markets, Market Control and Marketing Reform*, chaps. 1 to 3.

availability of large numbers of people for part-time or full-time trading activity. My observations and analysis of trading activities and arrangements gave rise to much subsequent work by economists and anthropologists. Professor Walter Elkan has gone as far as to suggest that this early work pioneered recognition of the presence and significance of what has come to be termed the informal sector in LDCs, and initiated the study of its economics.[11]

Further, my work enabled me to expose the underlying flaws in familiar proposals and policies for restructuring the trading sector in LDCs. These measures ranged from restriction of the number of traders, and the enforced elimination of particular stages in the chain of distribution, to large-scale state support for cooperative trading and to the suppression of private traders and their replacement by state trading organizations. The adoption of such measures in various LDCs has had the unsurprising consequences of restricting the opportunities for producers and consumers, of entrenching inefficiency in the trading sector,[12] and of obstructing economic progress and the widening of horizons. Most of these so-called reforms have caused widespread hardship and have locked many people into subsistence production.[13]

[6]

Since at least the 1930s both popular and academic literature have decried the fluctuations in the prices of primary products, especially those produced in LDCs. Commodity stabilization schemes have now been major items on the agenda for several decades.

Commodity schemes have usually been proposed as instruments for the reduction of price fluctuations. In practice, however, the objective has usually been the monopolistic raising of prices. This is transparent today when commodity schemes are envisaged as a form of resource transfer from the West to the Third World. But the monopolistic intention was already clear in the interwar regulation schemes, such as International

11. Walter Elkan and others, "The Economics of Shoe-Shining in Nairobi," *African Affairs*, vol. 81, no. 23 (April 1982).

12. It is difficult to explain in retrospect why it was almost universally accepted as axiomatic in the early development economics that cooperative enterprises had such particular economic virtues that they should enjoy extensive state support and protection. A cooperative society is simply a form of economic organization. As such, it does not inherently have access to efficiency superior to that of other types of organization, private or public. If cooperative societies had such attributes, they would not have needed official favors. I discussed these issues fully in *The Economics of Underdeveloped Countries*, chap. 14.

13. See "The Economics of Marketing Reform," in Bauer and Yamey, *Markets, Market Control and Marketing Reform*.

Rubber Regulation. I was to study this in detail and was able to document that, while rubber regulation did not stabilize prices,[14] it did widen fluctuations in output and probably also in producer incomes. Among other untoward effects, it imposed hardship on potential producers who were generally much poorer than were the beneficiaries.

Subsequently, I examined in depth the operations of the official West African marketing boards.[15] These state organizations were given the sole right to buy for export and to export the controlled products. The proclaimed purpose of these arrangements was to stabilize the prices received by producers, and even to improve them. In fact, they promptly developed into a system of paying producers far less than the market value of their produce—they were, in effect, an instrument of heavy, persistent, and discriminatory taxation. Over extended periods they destabilized producer prices and incomes. I drew attention to major effects of this heavy taxation, notably that it reduced the development of cash crops and private savings, obstructed the emergence of a prosperous African peasantry and middle class, and served as a dominant source of money and patronage for those with political power. Thus, paradoxically, although stabilization is typically invoked as cover for the monopolistic raising of producer prices, in this instance it was invoked as cover for persistent underpayment of producers made possible by the monopsony powers of the boards.[16]

My work on rubber regulation and on the marketing boards together had various spin-offs. First, it showed that the smoothing of fluctuations needs to be clearly distinguished from other objectives of official schemes, such as monopolistic raising of prices or taxation of producers by underpaying them. Second, it also showed that even if the reduction of fluctuations was the genuine objective of a scheme, its implementation would run up against formidable conceptual and practical problems. These included the problems of determining on an up-to-date basis the long-term trend of prices; of choosing between the setting of producer prices at the discretion of the authorities or in accordance with an announced formula; of choos-

14. See *The Rubber Industry*, passim, especially pt. 3 and statistical app. 2.

15. See *West African Trade*, pt. 5; and *Markets, Market Control and Marketing Reform*, chaps. 8 and 9.

16. When I first published my findings, they were received with indignation by official spokesmen and by fellow economists. As late as the mid-1950s the supporters of the marketing boards argued that the boards were engaged only in price stabilization. By the 1960s it was widely accepted that they were, and had been all along, instruments of taxation. It is also now generally agreed that the proceeds of this taxation were in large measure wasted.

The marketing boards were to a considerable extent descended from largely unsuccessful private produce-buying cartels; state monopsonies were introduced at the instigation of members of these cartels. See my *Dissent on Development*, essay 12; the original version appeared in *Journal of the Royal Statistical Society* (1954), pt. 1.

ing between stabilization of prices and stabilization of producer incomes; and of choosing the frequency and amplitude of the adjustments in producer prices. Third, my work and the response it elicited from Professor Milton Friedman[17] led me to question whether the exercise of government power was desirable or necessary for producers to achieve price or income stabilization if they felt the need for it. If stabilization of disposable incomes is desired, producers on their own account can set aside reserves on which to draw in times of adversity. If necessary, they can form voluntary associations to help them achieve this purpose.

[7]

The truth of the French saying, "rien ne vit que par le détail," impressed itself upon me in the course of my work in Southeast Asia and West Africa. Much of this work uncovered phenomena and relationships which had not been acknowledged adequately either in previous studies of these regions or in the more general economic texts. I list briefly a number of these matters not already discussed in this essay; fuller treatments are to be found elsewhere in my publications. However, several of the issues raised or illustrated are of some general significance and interest.

The supply of smallholders' rubber had commonly been instanced as a classic case of a backward-sloping supply function. In fact, it was possible to establish not only that the supply curve was forward-rising but also that this was fully recognized in the implementation of official policy (for instance, in the imposition of special export taxes to curtail smallholders' exports under rubber regulation). The much higher density of planting on rubber smallholdings than on the estates used to be attributed to the crude methods used by smallholders. In fact, it could be shown to reflect differences in the availability of factors of production to the two broad groups of producers. Further, even the short-period supply price of rubber could not be estimated simply by reference to current outlays, but had also to include the expected reduction of future revenues through the current consumption of the latex-containing bark. Again, cost of production was found to vary greatly with the current product price (much more so than with the scale of operations). Thus cost of production, and therefore the supply price, depended significantly on expected future prices as well as on current prices.[18] When it is recognized that current and prospective product prices affect costs, it is then not legitimate to treat supply as independent of demand (as is the standard practice in microeconomic theory).

I found that the standard expositions of monopoly and of its measure-

17. Milton Friedman, "The Reduction of Fluctuations in the Incomes of Primary Producers: A Critical Comment," *Economic Journal* (December 1954).
18. On the supply of rubber, see *The Rubber Industry*, chap. 4 and app. E.

ment were incomplete, even misleading. Rubber regulation covered many thousands of producers, none of whom controlled even 2 percent of total supplies of a highly standardized product or had any influence on prices. The controlling authority, on the other hand, faced a much less than perfectly elastic demand. This combination was very different from the situation typically analyzed in monopoly theory. In the study of West African trade, statistics accessible to me showed that the degree of concentration was systematically higher for standardized products than for differentiated products. This was contrary to what I expected to find from contemporary discussions of product differentiation. In both Southeast Asia and West Africa the number of trading points diminished steadily from the urban centers to the outlying rural areas. Yet I found this to have no systematic relation to the intensity of competition: the effective degree of monopoly could not be predicted at all reliably from the number of traders present. The small trader in a remote village was exposed to competition from many sources, including itinerant peddlers and farmers acting as part-time traders. The number of traders, however, became important in determining the strength of competition whenever entry was officially restricted. Even then, diversity among the traders (such as ethnic diversity or differences in length of establishment) could modify the effect of numbers on competition.

That detailed statistics can be revealing was shown by statistics of the prices of official rights to export rubber from Malaya. These could be made to reveal both the de facto extent of restriction and the very low supply price of large quantities of smallholders' rubber. Closer examination of the statistics of total estate production and those of locally registered companies disclosed that rubber regulations treated U.K.-registered companies more favorably than locally registered companies, and estates more favorably than smallholdings. The statistics could be used also to measure the effect of the 100 percent excess profits tax on the level of production.

Direct observation in conjunction with certain statistical series, especially transport statistics, helped to uncover the large volume and importance of kola nut production and trade in Nigeria, activities entirely in the hands of Africans and virtually unremarked in official and other publications. Again, detailed examination of the working of import and price controls in wartime and postwar West Africa made clear that quite momentous political and social consequences could follow from apparently innocuous official measures.

[8]

During the latter part of the 1950s I first wrote on two major issues in development economics: comprehensive planning and foreign aid. I was subsequently to develop my analysis and conclusions when these two subjects came to loom more largely both in the academic development literature and even more in public discussion. I noted then that comprehensive central planning was certainly not necessary for economic advance; it was much more likely to retard it. It did not augment resources, but only diverted them from other public and private uses. It reinforced the authoritarian tradition prevailing in many LDCs. And it also divorced output from consumer demand and restricted people's range of choice.

On foreign aid I wrote little, beyond saying that it was not indispensable for the progress of poor countries and that it often served to underwrite and prolong extremely damaging policies commonly pursued in the name of comprehensive planning.[19]

I see no reason to retract the findings and assessments set out in this summarized version of my earlier writings. But I must acknowledge a serious misjudgment. I failed then to appreciate the pervasive significance of the politicization of economic life in LDCs. Except in my treatment of the West African marketing boards, I was apt to analyze the more specifically economic implications and effects of individual policy measures without appreciating adequately how they contributed to the general politicization of life in many LDCs. By the late 1950s the principal measures included state monopoly of major branches of industry and trade, including agricultural exports; official restrictive licensing of industrial and other activities; controls over imports, exports, and foreign exchange; and the establishment of many state-owned and state-operated enterprises including state-supported and state-operated so-called cooperatives. Several of these individual measures gave governments close control over the livelihood of their subjects. When applied simultaneously, these measures conferred even greater power on the rulers.

In these conditions the acquisition and exercise of political power became all important. The stakes, both gains and losses, in the struggle for political power increased. These developments enhanced uncertainty, anxiety, and political tension, especially in the many LDCs which comprised distinct ethnic, religious, or linguistic groups. They thereby diverted people's energies and resources from economic activity to the political arena.

These developments and their repercussions have become much more pronounced and widespread since the 1950s. Not only the economic but even the physical survival of large numbers of people have come to depend

19. My subsequent writings on planning and foreign aid can be found in *Dissent on Development* and in *Equality, the Third World, and Economic Delusion* (London: Weidenfeld and Nicolson; and Cambridge, Mass.: Harvard University Press, 1981). I have returned to these two subjects in my book, *Reality and Rhetoric: Studies in the Economics of Development* (London: Weidenfeld and Nicolson; and Cambridge, Mass.: Harvard University Press, 1984).

on political and administrative decisions. Productive ethnic minorities have been conspicuous among the victims. What I saw only dimly in the 1950s has therefore become a major theme in some of my more recent writings.

Comment

Michael Lipton

In 1946 a young economist, hired by the British Colonial Office, visited Malayan rubber smallholdings. His *Report* truly lived in its details. Unlike many others before and since, he did not overrepresent roadside farms and thus avoided biasing his enquiries; he did cross-check reports of income and outlay within each interview; and, above all, he acquired a deep technical understanding of the crop under study. This allowed him to explain why rules that prohibited new rubber planting, but allowed replanting, unfairly and inefficiently helped big estates at the expense of smallholders.[1] He shows how rubber smallholdings contained both highly efficient growth potential and the best chance of self-improvement for the working poor, yet were held back to protect powerful and relatively inefficient European-owned estates.[2] The tools of bias included policy and research skewed against smallholders; local trading monopoly; and government failure to engage in competing trade, to provide inputs and research for smallholder needs, to ensure the representation of smallholders on crucial decisionmaking bodies, and even to protect smallholder land against waterlogging.[3] To remedy these deficiencies the author proposes, among other things, specific, promising, and imaginative government involvements.[4] Is this, too, Peter Bauer?

In his work (as in Bartok's) one has to reconcile three periods: the involved, creative fieldwork of youth; the increasingly confident, general

Michael Lipton is a Fellow at the Institute of Development Studies, University of Sussex.

1. P. T. Bauer, *Report on a Visit to the Rubber-Growing Smallholdings of Malaya, July-September 1946* (London: Colonial Office, 1948), pp. 10, 11, 25.

2. Ibid., pp. 23, 64, 44. Bauer's passionate and specific concern for the fate and prospects of the poor in this document (see especially p. 27, para. 144) contrasts strikingly with some of his more recent general writing about, for example, "relief of poverty or some other purpose unrelated to development" (P. T. Bauer, "Foreign Aid and Its Hydra-headed Rationalizations," in *Equality, the Third World, and Economic Delusion* [London: Weidenfeld and Nicolson, 1981], p. 101).

3. *Report on a Visit to the Rubber-Growing Smallholdings of Malaya*, pp. 40–57, 60–63.

4. Ibid. and pp. 64–65, 87–90.

and provocative, but also strident and (as it were) supra-empirical middle period; and, in maturity, mellowness. In the present paper, aid and planning are once more neither indispensable nor sufficient for development—not, as in the middle period, its implacable enemies.[5] However, this new paper contains enough "middle Bauer" for us to contrast it, usefully, with the earlier practical experience and theory building.

Lord Bauer is a *classical* economist. Enterprise, trade, enlargement of markets: these are the engines of development. Bauer makes no neoclassical claim that all businessmen act like profit-maximizers, or would maximize welfare if they did. For Bauer, it is the move from subsistence to ever larger markets that counts. His early Malayan work combined this classical emphasis on the role of trade with awareness of "sporadic buyers' rings," of "unduly high dealers' margins," and hence of the need for a larger number of competing "Government buying stations."[6] Perhaps because of his growing fear of politicization, Bauer has recently muted this classical stress on the need for the state to protect the poor from trusts—on Adam Smith's perception that "People of the same trade seldom meet together, even for merriment and diversion, but the conversation ends in a conspiracy against the public, or in some contrivance to raise prices."[7] Bauer's work shows, nowadays, little Ricardian fear that rising shares in GNP of differential rent or monopoly quasi-rent—whether to OPEC, landlords, or formal industry—may erode rewards to, or finance for, enterprise.

Nevertheless, Bauer's generally classical approach is exemplified by his opposition to barriers against trade, investment, and migration and by his tributes to "individual voluntary responses of millions of people to . . . opportunities created largely by external contacts and brought to their notice . . . primarily through the operation of the market." This theory of development is backed by Bauer's Malayan and West African evidence of extremely widespread entrepreneurial, especially small-farmer, response; Bauer was one of the first to show, and to insist against the researchers in the capital cities, that small farmers are shrewd profit-seekers and effective innovators, often outperforming large estates. Before Hirschman, he stressed that such people's investments might precede, not follow, infrastructure.[8] (One might add that the wrong sort of infrastructure—for instance, a premature access road, effectively subsidizing mass-produced competition—frequently nips such local enterprise in the bud.)

However, there is an odd thing about Baverian classicism. It is the

5. P. T. Bauer, *Dissent on Development* (London: Weidenfeld and Nicolson, 1971), pp. 69–94.

6. *Report on a Visit to the Rubber-Growing Smallholdings of Malaya*, p. 61.

7. Adam Smith, *The Wealth of Nations*, 1st ed. 1776 (New York: Modern Library, 1937), p. 128.

8. See A. O. Hirschman, *Strategy of Economic Development* (New Haven, Conn.: Yale University Press, 1958).

attempt *both* to believe in this market theory of development, *and* to reject "general theories of history" in common with the Hayek–Popper–London School of Economics school. The gap between classical theory and anti-theory is to be bridged in two ways. Neither is satisfactory.

First, Bauer—while advancing a particular, data-based account of quasi-classical development in specific countries—rejects both general, formal macro models of development and their data base.[9] That rejection depends on his views that the variables in these models are relatively unimportant, a matter to which I revert later; and that the data are no good. The latter objection, for most of Asia and Latin America, is out-of-date. We now know a good deal about important quantities that used to be left unmeasured. Self-consumed farm output has been included (by means of crop-cutting samples) since the early 1950s. Rural nonfarm employment, long measured in India, has now been assessed in many micro environments elsewhere—even for people who are mainly farmers.[10] "Biases in international income statistics," a recurrent concern of Bauer's, have been corrected by moves toward a purchasing-power comparison at least since the late 1950s; such corrected data (due to Kravis's work under World Bank auspices) are now available for many developing countries.[11] In any case, if the data were no good, we should have no reason to accept or reject any of Bauer's three approaches: his early account of quasi-classical growth (albeit with some state intervention) in specific cases; his later claims that such growth, without aid or planning, was in most cases the best chance for development; or his denial that *any* development path can be generally valid. Models and data, explicit or implicit, are the only way to test theories against each other.

Second, Bauer rejects metatheories, which might imply endogenous, socioeconomic explanations of why quasi-classical development paths sometimes work and sometimes fail. He does so because the *chance* that particular countries happen to be inhabited with particular cultural or ethnic groups is to him crucial. He argues, for instance, that Chinese rubber tappers work harder than Indian ones, and that some groups just

---

9. See both the present paper and *Equality, the Third World, and Economic Delusion*, pp. 262–66.

10. Enyinna Chuta and Carl E. Liedholm, *Rural Non-Farm Employment: The State of the Art*, MSU Rural Development Paper no. 4 (East Lansing: Michigan State University, Department of Agricultural Economics, 1979); and recent rounds of the Indian *National Sample Survey*.

11. This process started in the 1950s with the Milton Gilbert and Irving B. Kravis studies for the Organisation for European Economic Co-operation (now the OECD). The World Bank's International Comparison Project, under Dr. Kravis's guidance, already covers about twenty-five developing countries. The latest publication, containing references to the earlier work, is Irving B. Kravis, Alan Heston, and Robert Summers, *World Product and Income: International Comparisons of Real Gross Product* (Baltimore, Md.: Johns Hopkins University Press, 1982).

are "especially productive and successful."[12] Although such claims—they are hardly explanations—should indeed be researched and not "proscribed,"[13] careful enquiry almost always reveals endogenous and temporary, not exogenous and hereditary, determinants of "group differences in economic performance" (for example, in the Punjab[14]). Moreover (especially in a world of intermarriage, migration, Galtonian "regression toward the mean" of genetic characteristics, and integrated gene pools), such explanations as "Group X works harder" are very unsatisfactory. They are residual—confessions of ignorance. People believed God caused lightning directly, until the explanation was discovered scientifically.

Bauer is forced to oscillate between classical theory and anti-theory for a most interesting reason. His early work was on some developing, export-crop-based economies of Southeast Asia and West Africa. There, the presumptions for the classical model were largely fulfilled. The export crops attracted "investment by European enterprises" in estate development in Southeast Asia and "extensive capital [from] European trading firms" in West Africa. Attractive prices for those crops, "largely empty" cultivable land, and (initially at least) high income- and price-elasticities of demand then permitted widespread entrepreneurial response by indigenous smallholders. In Malaya, Bauer courageously sought to get the colonial state, largely representative as it was of European big capital, off the smallholders' backs, so they would not be prevented from planting more rubber or from obtaining relevant research and inputs.[15] In West Africa, as Bauer showed[16] (but increasingly since his warnings), expansion prospects have been set back by marketing boards and other devices, purportedly for stabilization, but in reality to transfer resources from dynamic, poor farmers to the burgeoning, inefficient apparatus of the urban state.[17] *Few, if any, parts of today's developing world, however, are*

12. Some particularly regrettable reflections on the alleged incapacity of certain U.S. American Indians to develop appear, without evidence, in *Dissent on Development*, p. 97.

13. It is no more—and no less—disgraceful to shout down the arguments for inherited (and even perhaps racially specific) indicators of intellectual capacity, than it is to accept these propositions without testing them properly, or to assume that *even if true* (and the evidence appears to show that they are false) they could justify discrimination against a group of human beings on the grounds of low IQ, hereditary or environmental, average or median or top-percentile.

14. M. S. Randhawa, *Green Revolution* (New York: Wiley, 1974).

15. *Report on a Visit to the Rubber-Growing Smallholdings of Malaya*, passim, especially pp. 87–90.

16. P. T. Bauer, *West African Trade* (London: Routledge and Kegan Paul, 1963); "Operations and Consequences of Statutory Export Monopolies of West Africa," *Journal of the Royal Statistical Society*, vol. 1 (1954).

17. Michael Lipton, *Why Poor People Stay Poor* (Cambridge, Mass.: Harvard University Press, 1977), pp. 294–96.

like the export-crop economies of, say, Malaya or the Gold Coast in the late 1940s in the relevant respects.

Hence Lord Bauer is, in my view, constantly compelled to throw rather flimsy intellectual bridges from his early work—in countries where resource endowments and market opportunities attracted private foreign capital to initiate indigenous growth, in a way reminiscent of the classical thesis—to other developing countries. Bauer recognizes that, despite many different policies, few such countries have spread development to vast numbers of exporting smallholders, as did Malaya and Ghana.[18] Hence classical paths cannot be a *general* predictive base for development theory. Remembering Malaya and West Africa in the 1940s, Bauer both insists on the validity of the classical pattern, and develops reasons—ethnic, cultural, or metatheoretic—why *no* pattern can be expected to apply everywhere.

The problems that result are nicely, and jointly, pinpointed by Bauer's treatment of overseas capital, aid, commodity agreements, Harrod-Domar models, and vicious circles of poverty. Export-crop production and trade in Dutch and British colonies in some areas received significant inflows of private foreign capital from 1900 to 1940. The local farmers and traders in a few such areas—having much spare land and enjoying population growth well below present rates in poor countries—built significant growth, quite widely shared, upon these inflows. Because rubber (and tin) and, in the early stages, cocoa and robusta coffee faced promising markets, international commodity cartels—or even agreements—were nuisances, not necessities. But were these realities too specific and temporary to allow us to transfer the lessons to other situations? If so, does Bauer's attachment to the classical market model force him to reject generalization, aggregation, even theory itself, in order to reconcile the early successes he knew in detail with the biased, unsatisfactory, partly planned, partly aided, but undoubtedly growing and developing realities of the past three decades?

We can usefully start with Bauer's remark that "conventional growth models" focus on "variables which I came to know were unimportant." These explanatory variables are, typically, domestic and foreign savings and investment. These are linked in conventional models to growth via the propensity to save and the marginal productivity of capital. (All this can be, and often is, disaggregated ad lib.) In Bauer's youthful studies, private foreign capital—for planting or trading—came in to develop and exploit major new export-crop opportunities on empty land. The variables of the conventional growth models—savings, investment, productivity of capital—indeed seemed "unimportant" because their values were overwhelmingly favorable.

18. Polly Hill, *Migrant Cocoa Farmers of Southern Ghana* (New York: Cambridge University Press, 1963).

"Rapid economic progress" involving "large-scale capital formation in agriculture by the local people," says Bauer, "cannot be squared with the idea of the vicious circle of poverty and stagnation." On the contrary: shared progress if there are initial capital inflows and subsequent widely spread opportunities, and vicious circles of stagnation if there are not, are two different ways of stating the same point. The Indian Punjab, despite the massive early investments of the government in irrigation and extension and research, since 1960 tells a similar story of progress. With favorable natural resources (especially favorable ratios of good land and improved techniques to people), initial nonlocal capital inflows, and promising markets, both the marginal productivity of capital and the propensity to save will be high enough to attract major domestic savings, embodied in productive investments.

These variables, when very favorable, seem "unimportant"—but they interact to help LDCs break out of the vicious circles. When circles remain vicious, the "unimportant" variables are unfavorable: in Madhya Pradesh or the Sahel or Bangladesh, private domestic savings ratios *are* kept down by low incomes, which *are* perpetuated by underinvestment because of low savings, so that planned public or aid-based funds become vital to supplement the savings and to raise the productivity of capital through research and training. (Incidentally, both savings and investment can easily be redefined to include outlays on health and education.) In these places, again in a vicious circle, hunger depresses productivity, which in turn keeps down food production and maintains hunger. *Opportunity*, as in Bauer's experiences of West Africa and Southeast Asia, is needed to attract the initial inflow of private capital, and the local response to it, in order to reverse the vicious circle of stagnation—to turn it into a virtuous circle of higher savings rates, more investment, higher incomes, then more savings again; or higher labor productivity, more food, less hunger, and higher productivity again.

Consider the opposite extreme to the lands of Bauer's youth, to those ideal places and times to serve as test cases for classical development. Consider Bangladesh today. Big private capital inflows are very unlikely. This is because Bangladesh's main export crops, jute and tea, face highly price-inelastic and income-inelastic market demand.[19] Instability superimposed on such gloom is unattractive to investors, at least until there is a reliable international commodity agreement. Moreover, Bangladesh's ratio of people to good land is so high (and so dynamic) that spare land for

---

19. Although demand for Bangladesh's two main exports, jute and tea, is highly price-inelastic (in each case about minus 0.33), Bangladesh looms so large in the world jute supply that its *own* revenue falls if it increases output and exports of jute. In the case of tea, Bangladesh's share in world exports is very small, but revenue gained from extra production is offset by a loss, about twice as large (because price-elasticity of demand is minus 0.33), in revenue for other tea exporters, all developing countries.

any crop is almost nil.[20] In addition, the people in Bangladesh (unlike those in Malaya and Ghana in 1945) are almost all too poor to save much. With population growth approaching 3 percent, average income barely above the poverty line and hence little domestic savings capacity, and marginal capital-output ratios of at least 3, circles do hiss viciously whatever one's suspicions of such aggregates, especially since many people are so hungry that their productivity as food growers suffers. All the components of the classical growth pattern—initial foreign capital inflows, promising and elastic export-crop markets, spare land, and people able to finance savings to transform it—happily typified the countries that formed Lord Bauer's mental set. All are missing in Bangladesh: circles *are* vicious; capital and saving, and the parameters linking them to output and income respectively, *are* crucially important; large concessional inflows of capital *are* necessary (though not sufficient) to turn the vicious circles into virtuous ones; and inelastic commodity demands, by imposing unfavorable price trends upon unpredictable instability, *do* render the control of such instability through international commodity agreements important and desirable, though probably not essential to development.

Lord Bauer has contributed great insights into the real possibilities, in lucky places, of classical development paths. Other lucky places such as the Republic of Korea and Taiwan, because forced by the occupying power to redistribute land rights to efficient small farmers (and because supplied by that power with massive aid and fairly open access to markets), have subsequently made a success of something like a neoclassical path, albeit modified by initially heavy trade protection, persistently pervasive planning of credit and investment, and some political repression. At the other end of the spectrum, a Cuba or a China can also credibly claim to have abolished most of its absolute poverty—but in ways that combine inefficiency, often negative growth, and, once again, political repression. Much the most interesting cases, in my view, are places such as Sri Lanka, Costa Rica, and some states of India, where public sector action has successfully and substantially reduced poverty, yet where—despite great, persisting inefficiencies and inequities—both real growth and political freedom persist. All get some foreign aid and some private capital. None fits neatly into anyone's model of development. But the search for general theories must go on.

---

20. In most of Indonesia, Egypt, India, and Bangladesh, the statement that "small size and low productivity of many farms in the Third World reflect primarily want of ambition, energy, and skill, not want of land and capital" is wholly inapplicable—not least because, as with Bauer's Malayan smallholders, smaller farms almost always produce more net value added per acre than large ones (R. A. Berry and W. R. Cline, *Agrarian Structure and Productivity in Developing Countries* [Baltimore, Md.: Johns Hopkins University Press, 1979]).

Comment

T. N. Srinivasan

LORD BAUER HAS ONCE AGAIN succeeded in being provocative in this remembrance as in most of his earlier writings. While he has not changed his views of the development process over a period of three decades, except for admitting a single serious misjudgment in not appreciating the pervasive significance of the politicization of economic life in the less developed countries, he has presented an expurgated version of them here. For an unvarnished, no punches pulled version, one has to read a collection of some of his writings published in 1981.[1]

It is difficult to quarrel with his summary of the early development literature. However, it is worth recalling that many of the pioneers, particularly those from the relatively advanced developing countries, viewed the problem as one of achieving in one or two generations a level of development that it took several generations to achieve in the developed countries. Further, the only experience of such rapid transformation that was then available was that of Soviet planning. With hindsight, of course, one may fault some of the early writers for their naiveté in believing that a Soviet-style central economic planning is possible in a less developed country without a Soviet-style political structure.

Bauer has conveniently summarized his own views of the process of development in section 2 of his paper. However, his review of Ali Mazrui's book, *The African Condition*, is far more revealing. While many thinkers in the developing world viewed economic and social development as a process of modernization in the sense of applying scientific methods and technology without giving up traditional values, Bauer views it differently: "The concept of material progress, of steadily increasing control of man over his environment, is Western, as are the modes of conduct which derive from it. . . . But the ideal of modernization without Westernization is self-contradictory."[2]

T. N. Srinivasan is Samuel C. Park, Jr., Professor of Economics at Yale University.

1. Peter Bauer, *Equality, the Third World, and Economic Delusion* (London: Weidenfeld and Nicolson, 1981).

2. Ibid., p. 205.

Pioneers such as Theodore Schultz have emphasized that human capital formation—the development of education and skills as well as of institutions that provide incentives and allow individuals to respond to them—are crucial in modernization. Bauer states:

> African backwardness amidst ample natural resources is only one conspicuous example of the fact that material progress depends on personal qualities, social institutions and mores, and political arrangements which make for endeavour and achievement and not simply physical resources. The relative lack of able and effective people is crucial.[3]

But for Bauer the economic argument is not enough. He proceeds to link inadequate human capital formation to what one may euphemistically call "national characteristics and attitudes." For instance, he cannot resist pointing out that

> In historical times the achievement of Black Africa [that is, most of the continent of Africa] has been negligible compared with that of Asia and Europe. This in no way justifies enslavement or humiliation. . . . Before the closing decades of the nineteenth century [Africa] was without the rudiments of civilized or modern life. For instance, before the arrival of Europeans in sub-Saharan Africa all transport was by muscle, almost entirely human muscle unaided by the wheel. . . What Shiva Naipaul says about Zambia in his recent book, *North of South: An African Journey*, applies widely in Black Africa: "Expatriates staff the mines, the medical services, the factories, the technical colleges, the universities. Without them, the country would fall apart. Zambia makes nothing; Zambia creates nothing. The expatriate lecturer in English waved apologetically at the handful of books, perhaps half a dozen on the library shelf. 'There,' he said, 'that's it. That's all the Zambian literature there is.' For him, the paucity is a source of genuine embarrassment. 'I would dearly love to teach something Zambian to my students. But what can I do if there's nothing.' "[4]

This penchant for tarring a whole continent of nations with a single brush leads Bauer to assert

> Some of the attitudes in India which are most adverse to material change are indeed unique to the country are especially pronounced there, such as the operation of caste system, the veneration of the cow, the reluctance to take animal life, and contemplative, non-experimental outlook.
>
> Although Indians have many valuable economic qualities, especially when they are not hampered by a very restrictive social environment, they are nevertheless generally less ingenious, energetic, resourceful and

3. Ibid., pp. 193–94.
4. Ibid., pp. 194–95.

industrious than the Chinese, as is suggested by the relative performance above of Chinese and Indian emigrants.[5]

It is an elementary fact that in an appropriate environment, the non-development-oriented attitudes somehow tend to disappear, if they were indeed constraints. After all, until recently in the span of history, many Western observers held Bauer-like views of the Japanese! Jagdish Bhagwati quotes the following from a report written in 1915 of an Australian expert invited by the Japanese government:

My impression as to your cheap labour was soon disillusioned when I saw your people at work. No doubt they are lowly paid, but the return is equally so; to see your men at work made me feel that you are a very satisfied *easy-going race* who reckon time is no object. When I spoke to some managers they informed me that it was impossible to change the *habits of national heritage*.[6] [Emphasis added.]

Bauer's policy recommendations are predictable: a severely limited role for government, almost exclusive reliance on the market, including reliance on world capital markets rather than foreign aid for external capital needs, and so on. Although he believes that the West can contribute to the Third World development by reducing its barriers against Third World exports, he is more cautious on the free movement of people. If trade liberalization makes substantial headway, he is willing to consider "conditions under which freer immigration policy might be practical in certain countries."[7]

He believes that foreign aid should be left to voluntary charitable agencies. It should be in the form of cash grants for projects. His views on funding for the International Development Association and on World Bank research are worth quoting:

In June 1976, a referendum was held on a Swiss government proposal to provide substantial funds to the official International Development Association for handouts to Third World governments. The proposal was heavily defeated and at the same time, the Swiss voluntarily contributed large sums to a fund for the victims of an earthquake in Italy as well as to many Third World charities. Thus the public can distinguish official aid from voluntary charity. . . .

Over the imprint of the Bank, senior staff members have been able to publish reports and studies which are riddled with simple violation of common sense, fact and logic. The paucity of critical comment, indeed

5. Peter Bauer, *United States Aid and Indian Economic Development* (Washington, D.C.: American Enterprise Institute, 1959), pp. 23, 112.

6. Jagdish Bhagwati, "Development Economics: What Have We Learnt?" Distinguished Speakers Lecture, Manila, Asian Development Bank, October 1983.

7. Bauer, *Equality, the Third World, and Economic Delusion*, p. 131.

often the commendation of altogether incompetent World Bank publications, reflects in part the prestige and strength of the Bank, and in part the approval of its ideology by the academics and the media. The Bank has given aid used to support inhuman and coercive policies in the Third World—all without endangering the position or prestige of the Bank and mostly without eliciting critical comment.[8]

While I agree with Lord Bauer that a much greater reliance on markets is called for in many developing countries, I find in his writings more polemics and debating points than depth. A far deeper analysis of the role of markets and development can be found in the few pages of Kenneth Arrow's presidential address to the American Economic Association. A fascinating historical analysis of why Europe developed while India and China did not is available in a book by an Australian economic historian, E. L. Jones.[9] I confine myself to Professor Arrow's discussion.

He pointed out that while "the now demonstrated fact that flexible exchange rates are a feasible way of conducting international finance is a triumph of theoretical insights over practical men's convictions," one of the two major failures of neoclassical economics as an explanatory mechanism has been "the incompatibility of recurrent periods of unemployment in the history of capitalism with a neoclassical model of general market equilibrium." The other failure identified by Professor Arrow is of greater interest for my present purposes. He argued that

> inequality in economic development among countries, and among groups and regions within a country, provides a second and somewhat complicated difficulty for neoclassical theory. A purely neoclassical answer would explain differences in per capita income by differences in physical and human assets per capita. This, of course, raises the further question, how this came to be, which would require a fully dynamic model to answer. But the more compelling problem is that the differences in income seem too vast to be explained by factor differences. Indeed, in the presence of international trade, and especially international capital movements, wage differences should be strongly reduced compared to what would occur in autarkic states . . .[10]

Professor Arrow suggested that differences in the production-possibility sets of different countries could be a possible answer, only to dismiss this as a partial answer in that it raised further questions, for the differences in production-possibility sets among contemporaries can be due only to constraints on the transmission of knowledge, in a broad sense, across national boundaries. This led him to put his finger on the failure of

8. Ibid., pp. 129, 131.

9. *The European Miracle* (New York: Cambridge University Press, 1981).

10. Kenneth J. Arrow, "Limited Knowledge and Economic Analysis," *American Economic Review* (March 1974), pp. 1–10.

markets for future goods, in part because of large enforcement costs with respect to future contracts as compared with contemporaneous contracts, and in part because of the many uncertainties about the future. In particular, the markets of credit and capital goods, he suggested, are most likely to be subject to imperfections or even nonexistence. And nonexistence or imperfection of even a single market has spillover effects on other markets and can destroy the optimality of competitive equilibrium.

Once nonexistence or imperfect functioning of markets is admitted, the normative characterization of a global competitive equilibrium as reflecting an efficient and Pareto optimal allocation of resources among countries and individuals no longer holds. If markets fail, Professor Arrow argued, other social devices are likely to be invented, such as government intervention, codes of conduct for economic agents, or economic organizations with some power between the neoclassical competitive firm and an all-encompassing government.

One of the more exciting areas of current research involves investigations into the role of alternative institutional and contractual arrangements that exist in the absence of a complete set of insurance and future markets. In fact, the various types of land tenancy, labor hiring, credit, and selling arrangements observed in developing countries are institutional responses to the absence of markets. A fuller understanding of their systemic role in concrete sociopolitical-economic contexts is essential in devising developmental policies. In the absence of such understanding, a discussion of the place of markets or, for that matter, central planning cannot go very much beyond assigning totemic value to either. Further, since governments, just as markets, can be and often are imperfect, and are subject to lobbying, interventions to correct market imperfections that are optimal in theory may turn out to be worse than no interventions at all. Rather than fulminations against government intervention, such as Bauer has given us, we sorely need an analysis of development which treats the government as *one* of the many forces that influence its course and which draws on the rich comparative country experience and data that the World Bank must surely have.

Colin Clark

COLIN CLARK was born in 1905 in London. He was educated at Winchester and Oxford, receiving his B.A. in 1928, M.A. in 1931, and a D. Litt. (Oxon) in 1971. After receiving his first degree, he took part in a social survey of Merseyside and was on the staff of the British Economic Advisory Council from 1930 to 1931. He was a lecturer at Cambridge University between 1931 and 1937. From 1938 to 1952 he served in various high-level Australian government positions, including Under-Secretary of State for Labour and Industry, Financial Advisor to the Treasury, and Director for the Queensland Bureau of Industry. In 1953 he returned to the University of Oxford as Director of the Institute for Research in Agricultural Economics, remaining in this post until 1969. He is presently Department of Economics Research Consultant at the University of Queensland, Australia.

Among his publications are *The National Income, 1924–31* (London: Macmillan, 1932); *National Income and Outlay* (London: Macmillan, 1937); *A Critique of Russian Statistics* (London: Macmillan, 1939); *Conditions of Economic Progress* (London: Macmillan, 1940, 1957); *The Economics of 1960* (London: Macmillan, 1942); *Growthmanship* (London: Institute of Economic Affairs, 1961); with M. R. Haswell, *Economics of Subsistence Agriculture* (London: Macmillan, 1964); *Starvation or Plenty?* (New York: Taplinger, 1970); *Population Growth and Land Use* (London: Macmillan, 1967, 1977); *Poverty before Politics* (London: Institute of Economic Affairs, 1977); with Jan Carruthers, *The Economics of Irrigation* (Liverpool: Liverpool University Press, 1981); and *Regional and Urban Location* (St. Lucia: University of Queensland Press, 1982).

His numerous books and articles have been directed toward quantitative international studies of national products, a questioning of capital investment as a determining factor in growth, a study of limitations of taxation and proposals for its reduction, analysis of agriculture's role in developing countries, and a recognition of the beneficial effects of population growth.

Development Economics:
The Early Years

DURING MY YEARS AT CAMBRIDGE from 1931 to 1937 I was first occupied with studies on British national product or, as it was generally then called, national income. The last available study, by Bowley and Stamp, published in 1927 related only to 1924, and nothing had been done to bring the information up to date.

It has only recently become known that an official British government study of national income had been prepared, also relating only to 1924, but with some interesting figures of factor distribution, not yet available elsewhere.[1] Publication was suppressed, however, on the extraordinary grounds that industrial employers had complained that these figures would be used against them in wage negotiations.

My first publication on British national product, covering the years 1924–31, appeared in 1932; a more thorough study, which appeared in 1937, also made provisional attempts at long-period historical comparisons and at quarterly information for recent periods.[2] This publication, however, caused a break in the international studies which I had already commenced and which were to conclude in the publication of *The Conditions of Economic Progress* in 1940.[3]

At that time, and for many years afterwards, it was believed that the key factor in economic growth was the accumulation of capital. As early as 1937 I began profoundly to question this doctrine, in the concluding paragraphs of the book *National Income and Outlay*. We know now that such an accumulation is a *necessary* but not a *sufficient* condition for economic progress, an important logical distinction. On this more below.

[1]

Work on *The Conditions of Economic Progress* and the outlining of all of its chapters were undertaken one bright spring day in 1935. I was

1. *Inland Revenue Report on National Income 1929*, University of Cambridge, Department of Applied Economists, 1977.
2. *The National Income, 1924–31* (London: Macmillan, 1932); *National Income and Outlay* (London: Macmillan, 1937).
3. London: Macmillan, 1940, 1951, 1957.

engaged to be married, and my future wife had pointed out to me, gaily but firmly, that I was leading an unduly leisured life.

Those who knew Keynes personally are now considerably diminished in number—it was Keynes who recommended me for the University Lectureship in Economic Statistics at Cambridge in 1931. I was present at the seminar where Keynes first released his biography of Jevons, and was much encouraged by the phrase that Jevons was the first to bring to economics "the prying eyes and fertile controlled imagination of the natural scientist"—natural science having been my own background. (It was also in this paper that Keynes made the aggressive comparison that "Jevons chiselled in stone, where Marshall knits in wool.") It has always been my profound conviction that economics should be based on the empirical observation and classification of what has actually been happening, with theory occupying only a secondary position. It was on this principle that I wrote *The Conditions of Economic Progress*, which, I was told, had some influence on economic thought (a clandestine translation even circulated in wartime Japan).

From my earlier work in the British government's Economic Advisory Council, I had come to appreciate that laws of economics are to be deduced from comparative observation, rather than from a priori postulates. The Economic Advisory Council was a large unwieldy body with a few economists among scientists, businessmen, and bankers, and its early discussions were confused and purposeless. In time, however, Keynes came to dominate its proceedings. I prepared a number of statistical reports for the council, in which Keynes took a considerable interest.

Soon the Economic Advisory Council's principal concern was with attempts, entirely unsuccessful, to counter the rapidly spreading effects of the great world economic depression of the 1930s. In my position on the Economic Advisory Council staff, one of the first observations I was able to demonstrate was that, at that time (in 1930), the rise in unemployment in Britain could be fully accounted for by the loss of exports. This in turn could be fairly fully accounted for by the heavy loss in purchasing power of the primary-producing countries, due to the extreme fall in the prices of their goods on the world market. Britain's two principal export markets then were India and Australia.

Keynes at that time had just completed his lengthy book, *A Treatise on Money*, now almost totally overshadowed by his subsequent *General Theory*. He was soon drastically to modify many of the ideas in the earlier book. It was indeed fascinating to watch, in Whitehall and in Cambridge, the progressive development of his ideas which later reached the world in the *General Theory*.

Most British economists at that time—but not Keynes—were in a mood of extreme pessimism, probably the still prevailing aftermath of the suffering of the First World War, in which so many of their friends had died. Their pessimism was not only about the impossibility of countering any of the effects of the world recession, but about Britain's economic situation even before it started. On the crude information then available, I was able to show that productivity per man-hour in British industry had shown a moderate advance in the 1920s. Leading economists of that time just refused to believe this simple fact.

It was not long, however, before the principal economists—led by Keynes—not to mention the politicians, reached what seemed to them the obvious conclusion that the best thing to do about the world depression was to unload some of its consequences onto other countries by abandoning the long-established British tradition of free trade, and by restricting imports by tariffs or other means. That a secondary consequence of such action might be a further fall in British exports did not occur to them. There is a clear and sinister resemblance to the present situation.

Keynes's principal opponent on the free trade issue was Lionel Robbins, recently appointed professor in the London School of Economics. But while Keynes was feeling his way toward a policy of increased public investment and temporary toleration of budget deficits, Robbins took the opposite position, based on a most improbable theory developed by Austrian economists, that the right solution in such a time of extreme depression was further to restrict consumption.

Lord Robbins has recently expressed regret for the position he then took, and Professor Hayek, while maintaining his general theory, agrees that in Britain's peculiar circumstances in 1925–31 of an overvalued exchange rate, a general expansion of demand would have been the right policy.

It is now all too clear what should have been done then: we should have accepted Keynes's policies for expanding demand and also preserved free trade to enable other countries to share the benefits. Such a policy would have necessitated a devaluation of the exchange rate. This came about in any case in September 1931, but neither Keynes nor Robbins had advocated it. The only public figure advocating exchange devaluation at that time was the trade union leader Ernest Bevin, who later became well known in the Churchill and Attlee governments. Britain then (unlike its present position) still figured prominently in world trade, and such a policy might have had a chance of inaugurating world economic revival.

What was going on then in Britain was similar to what was happening in all the other advanced economies. They were so fully occupied with their own problems that they had not the smallest thought to spare for the troubles of the poor and developing countries.

There is considerable truth in the saying that it is important to have information, but more important to have information in time. Strange though it may seem, *The Conditions of Economic Progress* was almost the only source of information at the time about the comparative real products of different countries. At the beginning of 1941, in making an assessment of the comparative economic resources of the belligerents at that time (including the German-occupied territories), the *London Times* had to quote from a Queensland Bureau of Industry publication. It appears that this dearth of information may have continued for some years after the war.

[2]

My first concern with the economics of the developing countries began with a casual but profound conversation with Austin (now Sir Austin) Robinson. The right opening for a lecture course in economics, he said, was to tell your class that per head real income in India was only about a quarter, or at any rate some low fraction (we had very little idea in those days) of per head income in Britain. What were the causes of this situation?

Austin and Joan Robinson had spent some time in India, where he had held the position of tutor to the crown prince of Gwalior in the 1920s. At that time about a quarter of India was ruled by hereditary princes, with only indirect supervision by the British authorities. Both of the Robinsons developed an active interest in India's economic problems. They were commissioned to prepare a report on the highly complex issue of the financial position of the princely states in a proposed reorganization of the Indian government.

During the years since that time, India and other developing countries have occupied most of Austin Robinson's attention. Joan Robinson, on returning to Cambridge in 1928, was first occupied with her extensive study *The Economics of Imperfect Competition*, much of which she later wanted to disavow, but then turned her attention to macroeconomics, with considerable though not exclusive attention to the developing countries, and finally to China.

It was not long after this initial conversation with Austin Robinson that I was appointed supervisor to V. K. R. V. Rao, then a keen but unknown student, subsequently to have a highly varied and prominent career, including the vice chancellorship of Delhi University, and a position in the Indian central government as minister of transport. Rao was then undertaking a thesis which eventually appeared as *The National Income of British India, 1931–32* (excluding the princely states, about which little information was available).[4] We saw nothing incongruous about embarking on such a study in Cambridge, where much of the reference material was found to be available, supplemented by a few postal questionnaires on some technical points.

This, however, was not the first study of Indian national income. The first was an approximate order of magnitude obtained, as long ago as 1869, by Dadabhai Naoroji, a most unusual scholar who contested an

4. London: Macmillan, 1940.

election as a radical and won a seat in the British Parliament, which he was constitutionally entitled to do. A number of subsequent studies before Rao's showed that per head real income in India, while probably advancing, was doing so at an extremely slow pace.

I was asked by the Indian Planning Commission for a report on the prospects for economic development, which I prepared in November 1947, a few months after India had attained independence. I had two most interesting interviews, one with Lord Mountbatten, the governor general who had skillfully administered the transfer of powers, and one with Mahatma Gandhi, who was to be assassinated a few weeks later. Gandhi (nobody will believe this) proved to be a convinced free-market economist, strongly critical of the price controls, rationing, and compulsory purchase of farm crops which the Nehru government was then introducing. The right solution, he said, was to raise the price of food, then everyone would have to work harder. The source of India's troubles was that the people were thoroughly idle.

Examination of the extremely scanty information available in 1947 suggested that the long-term rate of growth of real product per head in the past had been of the order of magnitude of 0.5 percent a year. Most Indian economists at that time were expecting no better for the future—indeed, even less if there were to be no substantial capital inflow from abroad. In fact, in spite of all the mistakes which have been made, the per head growth rate subsequently attained has been about three times the rate then expected. Population growth may after all have been a beneficial factor.

Among other research workers in Cambridge whom I supervised at that time were Alexander (now Sir Alexander) Cairncross, who was working on nineteenth-century British investment history, and Richard (now Sir Richard) Stone, who had spent a number of years in India in his younger days, where his father was a judge. At this time, however, he expressed profound skepticism about Rao's attempt to obtain a measure of Indian national product.

Since those days India has been the developing country with which I have had the closest connection. I have visited India more than a dozen times, sometimes on official business, sometimes unofficially. I have also been asked to prepare official economic reports on Sri Lanka in 1947 and on Pakistan (then including Bangladesh) in 1952. I have paid only very short visits to any African or Latin American countries.

[3]

As in the case of India, we can hardly start on the economics of a developing country without some information, however approximate, about national product. Information about imports and exports is generally available, but this does not get us very far. The other main source of information is the census. But even the advanced countries are now discovering, to their dismay, that at this date there is still significant underenumeration in the census. This is probably very much worse in the developing countries—after all, the average uninformed man still thinks that the census has something to do with military service or taxation—so we cannot obtain accurate estimates even of rates of population growth.

It is true that the quality of census taking varies considerably from one country to another. The worst example of all was Nigeria, where the census results were deliberately falsified for the sake of gaining additional seats in the Federal Assembly.

The economist hopes to obtain census information about the distribution of employment. But the Indian census has been one of the worst in the world not only because of the obscurity of its definitions, but also because of the frequency with which they have been drastically changed. On the face of it, however, the Indian census seems to show that the proportion of the labor force engaged in agriculture has changed little, if at all, since the first census in 1881—a sure sign of the extreme slowness of economic growth.

It is now universally recognized (though I do not think that this was the case when I was writing *The Conditions of Economic Progress*) that economic advance leads to a declining proportion of the labor force being engaged in agriculture. However, some of those engaged in formulating policy in some developing countries have treated this relationship as if it were reversible—that is, as if the creation of industrial employment would automatically enrich the country. What a disastrous error. India, under the guidance of a leading scientist, followed a most peculiar line of reasoning. Population, he pointed out, was increasing, therefore we need more food. To produce more food we need fertilizer. So far, correct. Then we must produce the fertilizer—the possibility of importing was apparently not considered. And to construct fertilizer plants we need steel. Therefore as much as possible of our available resources should go into building large steel works. Perhaps because of the extraordinary conditions under which it is produced, steel attracts emotional attributes which prevent rational discussion. Once when I was asked in India whether further investment in steel works should be undertaken, I replied that this was a problem in comparative religion.

India is far from being the only developing country which has made such errors. There is some truth in the lampoon that the real needs of a developing country are a steel works, an airline, a six-lane highway, and an invitation for the president to address the Washington Press Club. One consequence of such follies is that the world is now hopelessly overcapacitated with both steel works and airlines, and it will take a long time to absorb the surplus.

The worst of all cases of such misjudgment was in Mao's China. Somebody had told Mao, and he wrote in his book, *Socialist Upsurge*, that about one-third of China's agricultural labor force was redundant and should be transferred to other employment. This was in fact attempted in the Year of the Great Leap Forward, 1958, when Mao apparently believed (at any rate for a time) what had been told him about the harvest having been doubled in a single year. The result was what now has been admitted to have been a disastrous famine.

We do not know why Mao obtained his misinformation—at one time he appeared to have some Indian advisers!

A simple reference to the already abundant information collected by J. L. Buck in the 1930s (*Chinese Farm Economy*, University of Nanking Press) would have shown that the Chinese farm economy was usually one of labor shortage rather than underoccupation, apart from the two cold months of December and January. After all, to put it simply, if you are going to cultivate a country the size of China with hand hoes—very few draft animals and still fewer tractors were available—you are going to need the labor of something like 600 million people.

[4]

There has been a great deal of misunderstanding about the supposed surplus of agricultural labor force in developing countries. This arises from the practice of looking at the data on an annual basis. Once we analyze monthly labor requirements, we find that the cultivator in the developing countries—after long months of enforced idleness in which the climate is too dry or too cold, as the case may be, for agricultural operations—is often faced with periods of serious labor shortage, particularly in the rice planting and harvesting seasons. This is true of China, where in most regions unoccupied labor is found only in the two coldest months of the year. In the more advanced rural economies, however, as in Japan, these seasonal fluctuations in labor requirements can be reduced to a very low level by careful diversification of crop and livestock production.

In 1935 I began studying the agricultural outputs of the developing countries and presented a preliminary paper to that year's meeting of the British Association for the Advancement of Science. This led to the preliminary international comparison of agricultural outputs per worker in *The Conditions of Economic Progress*, and a more thorough and up-to-date study, begun in some time I spent at the Food and Agriculture Organization in 1951, eventually published in *Journal of the Royal Statistical Society* in 1954.[5]

There are enormous international differences in agricultural productivity, whether measured per man or per hectare. My work was taken as a

5. "World Supply and Requirements of Farm Products," *Journal of the Royal Statistical Society*, vol. 117, no. 3 (1954).

basis by Hayami, who proceeded to make international comparisons for the years around 1960 on three different price-weighting systems. It is now clear, from the work of Yujiro Hayami and Vernon W. Ruttan,[6] that we must distinguish the situation in countries where the limiting factor in agricultural production is land, and fertilizers, insecticides, and the like may be regarded as "land supplements," from the situation where the limiting factor is labor, which can be successfully supplemented by machinery. One of Professor John Kenneth Galbraith's activities as U.S. Ambassador in India was to persuade people to regard fertilizer as a "land substitute."

[5]

We come now to our central subject, namely the international comparison of real incomes. International comparisons of money wages had been available for some time. The problem was to obtain comparable information on prices.

After a highly tentative effort by the British Board of Trade (the government department then responsible for statistics) to make some international comparison of real wages in 1904, the first systematic study appears to have been that of the International Labour Office (ILO) in the 1920s, based on wage data, related to preliminary international comparisons of prices. These price comparisons did not go much beyond staple foodstuffs, fuel, and rent. The International Labour Office was encouraged in its efforts by the Ford Motor Company, which was establishing branches all over the world. Its executives thought it their duty to attempt to pay comparable real wages everywhere, taking relative prices into account.

In the statistical office in Paris in 1935 I was surprised to observe on the staircase a cupboard full of what appeared to be discarded clothing. "Now you can see our difficulties," a French statistician explained to me. Ford Motor Company, wishing to bring clothing into its comparisons, actually delivered specimens of the garments to be included in the index. Conspicuous among these was a crudely colored, thick, checked shirt. In Detroit it was specified as the working costume of a manual worker doing heavy work. In Paris at the same time, however, it was regarded as an ultra-fashionable garment, purchased only by rich young men at specialty shops.

The Ford-ILO enquiry ran into worse troubles when publication of the results became a political issue. Not surprisingly, Italy appeared at the lower end of the table. The bombastic Mussolini, who had recently seized absolute power, said that he could not tolerate Italy being internationally

---

6. *Agricultural Development: An International Perspective* (Baltimore, Md.: Johns Hopkins University Press, 1971).

insulted in this manner. Other countries also showed themselves sensitive about their relative positions in the table, so the work was abandoned. In any case, the work covered only price comparisons among the advanced countries, with no information on the developing countries.

However, I had to take this work as a basis. The ILO prepared some further information on rents, and I was able to obtain some information on international comparisons of prices of what were then called "luxury goods" (though they certainly would not be so called now). These improved price comparisons, with index numbers on alternate and "ideal" bases, were published in *Weltwirtschaftliches Archiv* in 1938.[7]

For reliable information on this subject we have had to wait right up to the present day. In 1954, under the auspices of the Organisation for European Economic Co-operation (now the OECD), Milton Gilbert and Irving Kravis prepared comprehensive comparisons (covering capital goods and public expenditure as well as private consumption) on the comparative purchasing power of money in a number of the leading industrial countries.[8] Even on this evidence alone it was clear that to assume that the purchasing power of currencies could be equated to their exchange rates would lead to misleading results. With few exceptions, the purchasing power of the currency of a country of low real per head income must be *higher* than indicated by its exchange rate. This case was first clearly set out by Roy Harrod in *International Economics* in 1933.

Let us simplify the issue. The output of the two countries being compared consists in each case of some agricultural and industrial products which are traded fairly freely on world markets, and services and other products which can only be sold locally. We then have the proposition, which appears to be true in every case, that productivity in these service and related industries is not advancing, in time or between countries, so rapidly as in the first group of industries. When goods are freely traded internationally, wages and other factor incomes in the first group of industries will be, on the whole, adjusted to the relative exchange rates of the two countries' currencies. But the service and related industries in the more advanced country, while not so much above the poor country in relative productivity as are the industries trading in international markets, nevertheless will have to pay wages and other factor incomes comparable with the internationally trading industries. The relative prices of services of a given quality may therefore be expected to be higher in the higher-income country. This is found to be true, with some qualifications— productivity in service industries can sometimes advance quite rapidly, and factor incomes in the service industries are not always precisely

7. "International Comparison of National Income," *Weltwirtschaftliches Archiv*, vol. 47, no. 1 (1938).

8. *An International Comparison of National Products and the Purchasing Power of Currencies* (Paris: Organisation for European Economic Co-operation, 1954).

adjusted to those in manufacturing. But on the whole, depending on the relative importance of the different factors in the situation, the overall purchasing power of money in a low-income country must be higher than indicated by its exchange rate, and the difference in per head income therefore *less* than suggested by a crude comparison of national products converted on exchange rates.

It is only recently that the Gilbert-Kravis study has been supplemented by more complete work by Kravis and others, covering now a number of developing countries.[9] Some of their results are surprising. In some cases, such as a comparison of per head incomes between India and the United States, crude comparisons of income per head based on the rupee exchange rate have to be adjusted by a factor of more than three.

The preparation of *The Conditions of Economic Progress*, from 1935 to 1939, was first interrupted, as stated above, in 1937 by the publication of a more detailed study of British national income; and a year later by a short study, *A Critique of Russian Statistics*, published in 1939.[10] It sought to bring the U.S.S.R. into the comparison by valuing its agricultural and industrial output at prices prevailing in Western Europe, a method first suggested by Polanyi. The results came out low. At first I was inclined to give not a political but a Malthusian explanation (as indeed Keynes had done regarding the appalling Russian famine of 1921). Critics, however, soon pointed out that Russian population growth was slowing down. Indeed, Stalin suppressed the results of a census taken in 1937 (with the expected remarks about the census officials being fascists, Trotskyites, or whatever) because the result came out too low. The census was in fact not taken until 1939 and came out with a population only just in excess of that which Stalin had claimed several years earlier. The loss of life during the "collectivization" of agriculture and the subsequent famine, between 1929 and 1933, was estimated at an order of magnitude of at least 6 million.

Regarding the service industries, it became apparent to me at an early stage that, while we had a reasonable amount of information about agriculture, mining, and manufacturing and some about construction, we had virtually no information about output or about prices in the service industries, a large and increasing sector in the economy of every country.

---

9. Irving B. Kravis, Zoltan Kenessey, Alan Heston, and Robert Summers, *A System of International Comparisons of Gross Product and Purchasing Power* (Baltimore, Md.: Johns Hopkins University Press, 1975); Irving B. Kravis, Alan Heston, and Robert Summers, *International Comparisons of Real Product and Purchasing Power* (Baltimore, Md.: Johns Hopkins University Press, 1978); Irving B. Kravis, Alan Heston, and Robert Summers, *World Product and Income: International Comparisons of Real Gross Product* (Baltimore, Md.: Johns Hopkins University Press, 1982); and Kravis and others, "Real GDP per Capita for More than One Hundred Countries," *Economic Journal* (June 1978).

10. London: Macmillan, 1939.

The rising employment in the service industries was apparent from census results, however, and in more recent times, in some countries, from social insurance statistics.

In 1932 I organized a study group in the Royal Statistical Society in England on the service industries. We were able to do little more than draw attention to the extraordinary gaps in our knowledge. Even now there are still many service industries on which we have virtually no information about productivity or prices. In national accounts as well as in international comparisons, such services (for example, teaching, government service, domestic work) can be included only on the basis of the number employed in them; that is, on the assumption that their productivity never changes, which clearly is untrue. Yet when we proceed from national to regional statistics, we find that services, if defined in the broad sense to include transport and distribution, amount to some 80 percent of the whole product of some of the most economically advanced regions.

The communist countries omit them altogether. Marxism, in view of the curious philosophical materialism on which it is based, denies that services can be regarded as a form of production—though an exception is made for services "incorporated" in material goods, such as transport, distribution, and restaurant services. But the services of housing, health, education, government, and the like must, according to this philosophy, be treated only as forms of consumption and not regarded as part of the national product.

Adam Smith had a curious definition, based on the durability of the product. A repair service, for instance was real because it produced something which lasted. But musicians could not be regarded as yielding a product because their performance was only enjoyed at the time.

But there have been many others besides Marxians who could not understand services as part of the national product. A favorite line of reasoning, if it can be so called, using the values of Edwardian England, took a rich property owner with an income of £5,000 a year, who employed a secretary at £500 a year, who in his turn employed a gardener at £50 per year. National income statisticians would regard their combined income at £5,550. But the true figure, it was said, should be only £5,000—because the other incomes were dependent on the first income. This reasoning is a sort of updated physiocracy. The physiocrats held that it was only agricultural output which mattered—a doctrine that lasted until well into the present century. In its revised form, this doctrine held that it was only material production which mattered.

I came across these ideas as late as 1938, in a fierce controversy in the New Zealand press. By the standards of that time, New Zealand was once one of the world's most advanced economies and had a relatively large service sector. New Zealand national product estimates at that time in circulation, prepared by methods of almost incredible crudity, and omitting almost entirely the service sector, were coming out far too low. When I was able to make an independent investigation and to assure New Zealanders that their national product was much higher than they supposed, they were offended rather than pleased.

[6]

That agriculture should show a decline in its relative importance in employment and in national product, with manufacturing showing first a rise and then a decline in favor of services, was a generalization first made as long ago as the seventeenth century by Sir William Petty. This was a principal subject of observation, with extensive studies of the available material, current and historical, in *The Conditions of Economic Progress*. I was unable to give full analytical explanations, which indeed even now partly escape us. We have to deal with the interactions of both income and price elasticities of demand for the products of the three sectors, and the labor required per unit of output of each. The productivity of labor in agriculture, we used to suppose, advanced fairly slowly and steadily. It accelerated greatly after 1945 in many countries, however, apparently because of an accumulation of technical improvements whose application had for various reasons been delayed. This acceleration in productivity had most unexpected effects on the proportion of the labor force required in agriculture and also on the world terms of trade for agricultural products, of which more below.

In all countries observed (except for the case of India mentioned above) the agricultural proportion of the labor force has been showing a long-period decline, but at varying rates. In many developing countries with high rates of total population growth, this *relative* decline may still mean a continued absolute increase in the number employed in agriculture. Economic development policies should therefore be prepared which take this factor into account—often they do not.

Conversely, the advanced countries faced substantial absolute declines in agricultural employment. This was true even in agricultural exporting countries such as the United States, where the absolute number employed in agriculture was at its maximum about 1920.

When working for the British government's Economic Advisory Council I had to prepare some information for a committee on emigration. At that time, the extraordinary idea prevailed that the right solution for the British unemployed was to send them to Australia and New Zealand to start farming. I still remember the committee's consternation when I found that even in New Zealand the absolute number employed in agriculture was declining.

Now that we have Kravis's latest results on international comparisons of purchasing power we can examine the international relativity of the prices of services, where such prices have been directly measured, though not of course where they have been valued by the crude method of equating output to input of labor. Insofar as productivity in services rises less rapidly than in agriculture and manufacturing, we would to that extent expect services to be relatively low-priced in the low-income countries. We should expect the same, perhaps to a lesser extent, for the output of construction, which is a composite of goods and services. In the low-income countries covered by Kravis the results are somewhat mixed. Services and construction are found to be comparatively cheap in India, but not in Kenya, with uncertain results for the other developing countries. But at any rate examination of these results does not support the hypothesis that *no* improvement in service productivity is possible.

We can also get some idea of the relative productivity of the service industries if we have long-period data on comparative prices of commodities and of services within one country. Such data are available for Japan and France. Unfortunately, they point in different directions. The Japanese data going back to 1926 indicate service prices were keeping almost in line with commodity prices; that is, service productivity was advancing almost as rapidly as commodity productivity. For France, for the earlier years (the data go back to 1900) service prices were relatively low, indicating apparently service productivity rising less rapidly than commodity productivity, although there may be the qualification that factor incomes were not equalized between the commodities sector and the service sector.

It may be asked whether the Japanese figures should be called in question. But Japan has a high reputation for statistical precision. And the conclusion to which they point—that productivity has risen in commodity production—is on the whole supported by the international comparisons. We are left in the dark, however, when we attempt to gauge whether the quality of services has improved or deteriorated.

Combining national historical (including U.S.) and international comparisons, we reach the tentative conclusion that service productivity can (though it does not always) rise at a rate comparable to commodity productivity at lower-income levels, but in due course some sort of barrier is reached, with service productivity advancing less rapidly—that is, with the relative prices of services steadily rising.

The evidence points to a fairly high income elasticity of demand for services. However, there is a substantial price elasticity of demand too. Domestic service and restaurant service are two examples of services with high labor content, whose relative price must therefore rise as wages rise. It must be price elasticity of demand, in the advanced countries, which has almost terminated the demand for domestic service and checked the otherwise expected growth of the demand for restaurant service.

[7]

In 1938 I was appointed to a position in the state government of Queensland, Australia, which combined acting as economic and financial adviser to the state Treasury, supervising certain large public works, acting as state statistician, and various other duties. I also had discussions with the government of New Zealand at the same time. Both for Australia and for New Zealand it was clear to me that the cardinal issue in economic policy was what was to be expected in the future for the world terms of trade for agricultural exports, and I began a concentrated attack on this problem. The result was *The Economics of 1960*, written in 1940, published in 1942.[11] I expected then a very large postwar improvement in the world terms of trade for agricultural products. What happened in fact was a brief period of such improvement, peaking at a high level in 1951, followed by a steady decline.

It is worth tracing how little went right and how much went wrong in *The Economics of 1960*, as a warning to those engaged in long-period economic projections—though these are absolutely necessary for rational policy formation.

In the concluding section of this book I speculated on what is sometimes called the long or Kondratieff cycle. Kondratieff's original proposition related to price movement only, but subsequent thinking has related it also to movements of investment, international trade, and terms of trade for primary products. I think that there is something in the idea. I saw it then, and I see it now, as predominantly a cycle of investment. World investment, both internally within countries and across international borders, accelerates for various reasons until the world reaches a condition of "capital satiation," and in consequence for a long period investment is slowed down.

The expansion period is one of comparatively good terms of trade for primary products and conversely. A period of fifty years can be roughly fitted to the whole cycle, approximately half of "capital satiation" and half of "capital hunger," though the cycle is interrupted by wars and by demographic changes. The satiation phase I estimated then (and still do) as having started some years before 1929. But worldwide wartime capital destruction quickly brought this stage to an end and ensured a longer than usual period of capital hunger, beginning in 1945. I did not venture then to predict, though I might well have, that the next downward phase of the long cycle would begin in the mid-1970s.

One surprising prediction in *The Economics of 1960* was that Russia would become the world's largest importer of agricultural products, which is now nearly coming true—though much later than 1960. Another was that the declining trend of world fertility would be reversed and population growth again accelerated. This certainly took place in the 1950s—though this prediction was based on intuition rather than on formal analysis.

The main faults in the predictions were as follows:

11. London: Macmillan, 1942.

1. The income elasticity of demand for food in the advanced countries was overestimated. My figures were taken from observed income elasticities in household expenditure surveys. But these represent prices containing very large elements of costs of transport, distribution, and the like. Income elasticities of demand for food at farm gate are much lower. We should also consider the whole question of whether static cross-section studies give a valid indication of expected dynamic change.
2. Productivity per man-year of agricultural labor was estimated, on experience up to that time, with advances of the order of magnitude of only 1.5 percent a year. As mentioned above, this suddenly changed after 1945 in most of the advanced countries.
3. The possible rate of industrialization, or, to be more precise, the rate of growth of nonfarm employment, in the developing countries was very much exaggerated.

Soon I saw this third point as the most important issue. It was central to the economic report which I prepared for Pakistan in 1952. (This was a confidential diplomatic document not intended for publication; I have been told, however, that it was later published in full in the *Proceedings* of the Pakistan Legislative Assembly.) It appeared that, however favorable the circumstances, there was an upper limit to the absolute (not relative) rate at which nonfarm employment could increase. The comparative information which I had before me at that time related to Japan for the whole period since the beginning of industrialization in the 1870s, to Canada in the first decade of the present century, a period of unprecedented growth, and to the U.S.S.R. under Stalin. The conclusion I drew, principally on the Japanese evidence, was that there was an upper limit of 4 percent a year to the rate at which any country could advance its nonfarm employment, whether its rate of population growth was high or low. The U.S.S.R. was the exception which tests the rule. Stalin's attempt to force the pace after 1928 led not only to agricultural disorder and famine, but also to transport and industrial breakdown. "I will not drive and whip the country any further," Stalin is reported to have said in 1933. Rate of growth of nonfarm employment is, for developing countries, much more readily measurable than growth of nonfarm output. As far as we can predict a relation between the two, we may expect it to be nonlinear. Initially, economies of scale may be reached where difficulties of management, congestion of infrastructure, and other factors may have the opposite effect.

Subsequent evidence, however, has shown the 4 percent limit to be much too cautious. A number of countries have shown much higher figures than this in recent years, headed by the Republic of Korea with a steady 8 percent until recently, although this country now appears to be in a state of disorganization. Perhaps, however, such general improvement throughout the world in the rate at which industrialization could proceed should have been expected. Education, transport, means of communication have all shown great advances in comparison with the experience of nineteenth-century Japan, taken as a base measurement.

[8]

As we became aware of the poverty of the developing countries and their need for rapid development, there was a tendency to think that this was mostly due to lack of capital and could quickly be put right by adequate transfers of capital. The famous Harrod-Domar formulation purported to show how a country could grow on its own capital accumulation—capital transfers from elsewhere were not considered. Output was seen as a simple Cobb-Douglas function of labor and capital inputs, each with its own exponent, but with the exponents adding up to one or approximately so, slight differences being allowed to account for economies of scale. All this reasoning was based on the fallacious assumption described above. Although capital investment was undoubtedly a *necessary* condition of economic growth, it must not also be regarded as a *sufficient* condition. The limits imposed by difficulties of organization, shortages of managerial skill, inadequate infrastructure, or other causes in fact imposed a maximum rate of growth of nonfarm employment somewhere between 4 and 8 percent a year, whatever the capital inputs.

It was in the 1950s, from Robert Solow in the United States and Odd Aukrust and Olavi E. Niitamo in Scandinavia, that we began to get long-period production functions based on some knowledge of the historical levels of capital input. The Cobb-Douglas function worked only with very large residual terms for a combination of effects which we still find difficult to classify—technical improvement, economies of scale, better organization, education, or whatever it may be.

Another question which exercised us then, and exercises us now, is whether capital transfers, such as they are, are best in the private or in the public sector. Examples of extravagance and waste in capital spending by the public sector in some countries have aroused suspicion.

The cardinal question here is political. Sir Dennis Brogan, professor of politics at Cambridge, coined the remarkable phrase that "Asian politicians like having their arms twisted." What he meant was that politicians in developing countries come under such overwhelming pressure from their families, friends, or tribal associates for a share in what they regard as the loot that it is very difficult for them to refrain from diverting some of the funds under their charge—unless, as Brogan indicated, they were under even stronger pressure from international authority. The World Bank's reputation stands high (I hope that this is merited) for the strictness with which it discounts local politics and sends its own accountants and engineers to check every detail of the expenditure of the funds advanced by it.

For countries in the earliest stages of economic development, the most valuable investments are in infrastructure, particularly for transport, without which only a localized subsistence agriculture is possible, and for water supply, without which infectious diseases cannot be kept in check. Both roads and water supply must be public investments. We have the interesting paradox, pointed out by transport economists, that the poorer the country, the better the roads that it needs. For bad roads lead to a quicker deterioration of vehicles, which soon adds up to a capital loss much greater than the cost difference between the good and the bad road.

In those days also we tended to overstate capital requirements. I put the figure too high in a paper on capital requirements given at the Plenary Session of the United Nations Conference on Development at Lake Success in 1949. A normal capital-output ratio of four was widely believed in at that time. In fact, it is very rarely as high as this, even if housing and public investment are included. The experience of Japan, for which we have fairly good information over the whole cycle of development, shows the capital-output ratio rising to a maximum in the 1920s, followed by a fall. Many technical and organizational improvements can be capital-saving—a fact not recognized by the classical economists.

At a later date, an interesting conversation with the Polish director of planning led me to inquire into the capital requirements of agriculture. The Polish planning authorities at that time (in the 1960s) thought that capital requirements in agriculture were high relative to those in industry, and that the best policy for Poland's economic future might be to develop as an industrial and mining exporter and agricultural importer. (How wrong these plans seem to have gone!) I found that capital requirements per unit of output in agriculture, as it was generally then practiced, were indeed high in comparison with those of industry. But this was principally the consequence of the fragmentation of holdings into suboptimal units, with consequent unduly high requirements per unit of output for buildings, equipment, and livestock. In the case of agriculture, technical improvements and decline in employment may themselves be expected to bring about a substantial fall in the capital-output ratio.

[9]

Nearly everyone then, as indeed most people now, tended to regard population growth as an adverse factor, using up limited supplies of capital to bring a growing population to a given level of capital stock per head, and leaving very little for "deepening" per head capital. A fundamental assault on this position was first made by Everett Hagen at the

1953 conference of the Association for Research on Income and Wealth—his paper in fact was not published until very much later. International comparisons indicated that geographical density of population on the one hand, and its rate of growth on the other, both tended substantially to reduce per head capital requirements. In other words, marginal capital requirements for the expansion of output seem to be very much less than average per head requirements.

Hagen made a further important point. Rapidly growing population has the effect, to use his curious phrase, of "absolving" the country from the consequences of errors in investment. Both public authorities and private investors are capable of making serious errors in their investment decisions, as we know all too well. But with growing population a mistaken piece of physical investment is much more likely to find an alternative use than in a state of stationary population.

Keynes reasoned in a similar manner, when he published *The End of Laissez-Faire* in 1926. Europe, he thought, was then approaching a state of stationary population, and he stated the proposition in the converse manner: the mistaken judgments of private investors had in the past done comparatively little economic harm, but they would become much more harmful with a stationary population and therefore more in need of government regulation—at that time it was believed that government regulation was always done with wisdom. By 1937, however, Keynes had ingeniously inverted his own argument. Free private investment, he considered, was inherently desirable, and this is much more readily obtainable under conditions of increasing population.

It was not until the 1960s that I began to develop the line of thought, published in *The Economics of Subsistence Agriculture* (with M. R. Haswell)[12] that improvements in agricultural productivity must be regarded as another *necessary* condition for industrial development. Both international comparisons and time series indicated that a rising proportion of the labor force in nonfarm occupations was only possible if agricultural productivity not only rose, but rose at an increasing pace (the nonfarm proportion of the labor force rising as a linear function of the *logarithm* of farm productivity). The only exceptions were when a developing country could produce what we labeled "food substitutes"—mineral or forest products, or occasionally manufactures, which could be exported to world markets—and would bring in food imports which could partially substitute for the productivity of the country's own agriculture. This proposition of course is based on the simplest common sense. You cannot employ an industrial population if you cannot feed them. In addition, economic development necessitates an increasing volume of imports (though many planners seem to have neglected this issue). These have to be paid for, and

12. London: Macmillan, 1964.

in most developing countries (apart from the exceptions mentioned above) the only possible exports are agricultural products.

The central illustration of this principle was the early development of Japan, where rising agricultural productivity, supplemented from the 1890s onward by some manufactured exports, formed the basis for a rate of rise of nonfarm employment considerably greater than elsewhere.

The Japanese-American economist Nakayama objected to this whole concept. Although he was able to show some misstatement of agricultural output in the earlier years, his general case was thoroughly demolished by Yujiro Hayami and Saburu Yamada.[13] This is much more than a simple problem in Japanese economic history, because it refers to the prime exemplification of the most important of all development principles, namely that (except for countries richly endowed with minerals) improvement in agricultural productivity is a prior condition for successful development.

13. In *Agriculture and Economic Growth: The Japanese Experience*, K. Ohkhawa, ed. (Princeton, N.J.: Princeton University Press, 1969).

Comment

Graham Pyatt

OVER THE YEARS Colin Clark has written on a good many subjects, but these remarks on his contribution as a pioneer of development economics focus essentially on three areas in which his contribution is most often recognized. These are:

- The evolution of sector balance between agriculture, industry, and services as real incomes rise
- The international comparison of real incomes in terms of what has come to be known as purchasing power parity
- The determinants of agricultural productivity and the economic consequences of population growth.

For Colin Clark, these three subjects are not independent, and if his contributions to them are not integrated in a neat theoretical whole, then at least we can recognize that they were all present "one bright spring day in 1935," as he tells us, when the initial outline of his seminal work, *The Conditions of Economic Progress*, was drafted in response to a gay chiding for indolence from his wife-to-be. And if I am less than critical here in commenting on these contributions, it is in part because I fear that Colin Clark has received less recognition than he deserves; and for the rest, perhaps because his contributions need to be appreciated in a perspective which cannot necessarily be taken for granted among today's economists.

Something akin to this last point may have been in his mind when he wrote "the first edition [of *The Conditions of Economic Progress*] was written during the period 1935–39 and the preface to that edition, written in early 1939, deplored, perhaps in unnecessarily violent language, the continued preference of the English university economists for economics as a study based upon speculation and theoretical reasonings, rather than as a science based on the collection and examination of the actual facts of the economic world."[1]

Graham Pyatt is Senior Adviser, Development Research Department, at the World Bank.

1. *The Conditions of Economic Progress*, 2d ed., 1951.

Those who have worked with Hollis Chenery over the years will be familiar with the calligraphy displayed prominently on his office wall: "If the facts do not fit the theory, then the facts are wrong." The issue identified by Clark remains, then, and it was not the last time that Colin Clark was to be proved wrong when he followed the quotation I have cited with the observation that "what was said [in the preface of the first edition] is now, fortunately, quite obsolete." I have never as yet had the opportunity to ask Chenery in what spirit one was meant to react to his wall hanging. But that there is continuity of a major intellectual tradition from Clark to Chenery in the investigation of patterns of development is not to be disputed. Any gap is in the data base, not in the approach.

Clark's insistence on empiricism as the proper basis for economics permeates his work, which demonstrates an enormous energy and diligence in the sifting and collation of data. As a champion of the empirical, who has more than once been able to debunk modish theories by confronting them with facts, Colin Clark may well be excused for not having maintained a more balanced view on the importance of a priori reasoning to the development of economic science. As it is, he would today most likely be categorized as an economic statistician, rather than as an economist. For his own part, I suspect, he would take more kindly to the label of "politikal arithmetician." Not only are the great seventeenth-century pioneers of this "arithmetik," Sir William Petty and Gregory King, obviously among Clark's heros, but also his approach to economics reflects a view of the subject which places it lexicographically as subservient to political science, which in turn is dominated by history and ultimately by moral philosophy. This is the context, then, for the remark in his paper that whether India should build more steel mills "was a problem in comparative religion." It also prompts the thought that intellectually Colin Clark is a historian among economists, and this is not the only sense in which a direct comparison with Simon Kuznets is appropriate.

Agriculture versus Industry versus Services

> As time goes on and communities become more economically advanced, the numbers engaged in agriculture tend to decline relative to the numbers in manufacture, which in turn decline relative to the numbers engaged in services.
>
> —THE CONDITIONS OF ECONOMIC PROGRESS, 3D ED.

This generalization by Clark is traced back by him to Sir William Petty (circa 1691) and might well be referred to as the Petty-Clark law (especially if phrased with more emphasis on tendencies, in much the same spirit as the caveats in Engel's original articulation of the law named after him). It is presented by Clark as "a wide, simple and far-reaching generalisation" supported by massive empirical evidence and elements of a conceptual framework, drawing on income and price elasticities of final demand, the importance of intermediate goods, and stylized facts as to movements in labor productivity.

This contribution is so well known that two comments on it may suffice here. The first is that, as far as I know, the law still lacks a closed, formal, analytical exposition of its essentials, although it is of course implicit in many of the disaggregated macro models and a root of the rich vein of literature on patterns, as noted earlier. Second, in his paper Colin Clark is obviously concerned that the logic of the law has been perverted by some in drawing the incorrect inference that creation of industrial jobs will necessarily raise real incomes. I wonder whether Clark is quite fair here in failing to reference other, more acceptable, logic to support the conclusion that an early start on manufactures is in a country's longer-term development interest. The cases of India and China, which he cites in his paper, strike me as being more persuasive in relation to autarky than to industrialization.

The International Comparison of Real Income and Real Product

Colin Clark is undoubtedly a pioneer not only of development but also of national accounts, as evidenced by his considerable achievement in *National Income and Outlay* (1937). The two strands come together—I doubt if they were ever separate in Colin Clark's thinking—in *The Conditions of Economic Progress*, where the comparison of real products over time and across nations is the initial focal point of the analysis, especially in the second (1951) and in the much expanded third (1957) editions. It is unfortunate that Kravis and others (1975)[2] do not address the intellectual history of work in this area, and hence the place of Colin Clark in it. However, I understand that Sir Richard Stone is taking up the matter, while Clark himself gives detailed earlier references in both the second and third editions of *The Conditions*. Be this as it may, the result of Clark's monumental personal effort is a detailed set of estimates of national product in international (U.S.) and oriental (Indian) units for no less than twenty-nine countries. One cannot but be impressed by Clark's magnanimity, then, to read on page 71 of the third edition: "After all the above text had been set up in type, a new and greatly improved comparison for five leading countries was published by Messrs. Milton Gilbert and Irving Kravis . . . while previous studies have referred to the prices of consumable

2. Irving B. Kravis, Zoltan Kenessey, Alan Heston, and Robert Summers, *A System of International Comparisons of Gross Product and Purchasing Power* (Baltimore, Md.: Johns Hopkins University Press, 1975).

goods and services only, this study also covers the prices of investment goods and of government services." The breakthrough was made possible by the availability, thanks to the U.S. Department of Commerce, of national accounts at constant 1939 prices for 1950 and intervening years, and of the implicit price deflators. Colin Clark turns these new data to good effect (drawing also on Kuznets's *National Product since 1869*) to produce long time series for many countries in his much larger sample.

Colin Clark had already pointed the way in his earlier editions,[3] although the proper treatment of services remains a vexed question, even with the resources made available for primary data collection in recent years.[4] Moreover, the need for shortcut or reduced information methods remains. It may yet prove appropriate to resurrect the techniques that Clark deployed in the early years to meet this need. It is undeniably correct to acknowledge Colin Clark as a pioneer not only in devising methods of computing purchasing power parity, but also in applying them to the understanding of development.

Agricultural Productivity and Population Growth

As I have noted previously, the three topics selected for discussion here are far from independent in Colin Clark's thinking. After his statement, quoted above, on the relative size of agricultural, industrial, and service employment, Clark moves on to an appreciation of Petty's understanding of these phenomena and their association with the significantly higher standard of living of the Dutch relative to the British and French in the late seventeenth century. "He [Petty] found good government to be a significant factor in their prosperity, but he specially goes out of his way to commend the economies arising from a dense population. After a century and a half of Malthusian propaganda we come to regard dense populations, including our own, with some suspicion; and have lost sight of the obvious fact that, until a certain degree of population density has been attained, no civilisation at all is possible" (*The Conditions of Economic Progress*, 3d ed., pp. 492–93). Economies in capital required through population growth are similarly referred to when Colin Clark cites Everett Hagen on the matter, presumably to strengthen a general argument—for which other pieces are assembled in Clark's 1954 paper to the Royal Statistical Society[5]—that "Malthusian propaganda" is just that.

3. Indeed, his "international unit" for making international comparisons of national income first appeared in 1937 in an article in *Weltwirtschaftliches Archiv*.

4. World Bank participation in the International Comparison Project dates back to 1968.

5. "World Supply and Requirements of Farm Products," *Journal of the Royal Statistical Society*, ser A., vol. 117.

These other pieces refer, on the one hand, to a detailed analysis of consumption and Engel's law and, on the other, to a similar investigation of levels and trends of labor productivity in agriculture. Both, of course, are in international units—and oriental units also, when possible. (It makes some difference.)

Colin Clark's basic point, here as elsewhere, is that international comparisons reveal enormous potential for growth in labor productivity within agriculture. In subsequent discussion of the paper before the society, Dudley Stamp and Sir Arthur Lewis, among others, queried the relevance of this as compared with the productivity of land, since it is land that is potentially in short supply. As Lewis put it, "If the world became short of food it would find all the labour or machinery needed for increasing supplies, but could it find the land?" Colin Clark's answer was to cite the contemporary Dutch case where "the area required for the support of one person was a little under one acre." Taken together with Professor Stamp's earlier comment in the discussion—"If we look for an increase in world food production the easiest way is to consider one of the still most underdeveloped of all the great agricultural countries, the United States"—the Malthusian specter of a world food shortage starts to evaporate.

And so it has proved historically, a fact in which Colin Clark may take some satisfaction, notwithstanding his failure to foresee the development of the United States as a major food exporter. Indeed, his prediction in 1954 was the exact opposite.

A further weakness in Colin Clark's analysis was the cursory treatment of low-income countries, which may well have been inevitable to a degree because of the relatively limited data available, but hardly commensurate with the numerical importance of their populations. In any event, we now know that productivity per acre is high by international standards in much of the Third World, and the evidence suggests that this may well have been true for many years. Yet subsistence has also been a problem. It is hard to concur, therefore, with the statement in the paper that, in postwar India, "population growth may, after all, have been a beneficial factor." Demand pressure may have raised total output, but hardly output per head.

In conclusion, I wish to make three general points.

First, Colin Clark has contributed enormously to our understanding of the facts of development. His personal productivity (without a computer!) has been staggering, and the generalizations he has extracted from these facts are proven foundations of development economics.

Second, there is implicit in much of his work a reluctance to develop theoretical constructs. Colin Clark would apparently much rather gather more facts, which is so admirable a trait in his historical work but, at some point, leads to a lack of final articulation in the numbers, as in his *National Income and Outlay* or his paper on "World Supply and Requirements of Farm Products."

Third, I return to Colin Clark's own hierarchy of disciplines, where political science lies above economics and below history. He has occasionally expressed himself most forcefully on the potential of politics to interfere with the smooth regulation of economic affairs, especially at the international level. But in his main works, at least, there is little on the political economy of development and the distribution of power or assets within a population. Colin Clark observes, as a historian, that potential exists—in agriculture, for example—but tells us little or nothing about how it might be realized. His contribution has indeed been to provide the facts, soundly based in economic concepts and in both a broad historical and international perspective. If we look elsewhere for what to do about these facts, we should not underestimate the contribution of a man who has played such an enormous role in providing a vantage point. Beyond that, Colin Clark's greatest contribution may be that his message for development is ultimately an optimistic one: not that it will happen, but that it could.

Albert O. Hirschman

ALBERT O. HIRSCHMAN was born in 1915 in Berlin. He left Germany in 1933 and studied economics in Paris, London, and at the University of Trieste where he received his doctorate in 1938. He served in the French army in 1939–40 and emigrated to the United States in 1941. After two years at the University of California (Berkeley) and three years in the U.S. army, he joined, in 1946, the Federal Reserve Board where he worked on the financial problems of postwar reconstruction of Western Europe. From 1952 to 1956 he lived in Bogotá, Colombia, first as Financial Adviser to the National Planning Board and then as private consultant. In 1956 Hirschman went to Yale University, and then taught at Columbia (1958–64) and Harvard (1964–74). Since 1974 he has been Professor of Social Science at the Institute for Advanced Study in Princeton, New Jersey.

His early books remain influential: *National Power and the Structure of Foreign Trade* (Berkeley: University of California Press, 1945; expanded edition, 1980); *The Strategy of Economic Development* (New Haven: Yale University Press, 1958); and *Journeys toward Progress* (New York: Twentieth Century Fund, 1963).

Among his numerous other books and articles, the following titles convey some notion of his innovative and wide-ranging contributions: *Development Projects Observed* (Washington, D.C.: Brookings Institution, 1967); *Exit, Voice and Loyalty: Responses to Decline in Firms, Organizations and States* (Cambridge, Mass.: Harvard University Press, 1970); *A Bias for Hope: Essays on Development and Latin America* (New Haven: Yale University Press, 1971); *The Passions and the Interests: Political Arguments for Capitalism before Its Triumph* (Princeton, N.J.: Princeton University Press, 1977); *Essays in Trespassing: Economics to Politics and Beyond* (New York: Cambridge University Press, 1981); *Shifting Involvements: Private Interest and Public Action* (Princeton, N.J.: Princeton University Press, 1982); and "Rival Interpretations of Market Society: Civilizing, Destructive, or Feeble?" *Journal of Economic Literature* (December 1982).

A Dissenter's Confession:
"The Strategy of Economic Development" Revisited

> Ah, what happened to you, you my written and painted thoughts! Not long ago you were so colorful, young and malicious, so full of thorns and secret spices that you made me sneeze and laugh—and now? Already you have doffed your novelty, and some of you, I fear, are about to become truths: so immortal do they already look, so distressingly honorable, so boring!
>
> —NIETZSCHE

WHEN I RECEIVED THE INVITATION to participate in the symposium as one of the "pioneers" alongside Raúl Prebisch, Gunnar Myrdal, Arthur Lewis, and other such luminaries of development economics, my first reaction was one of surprise. Not that I doubted my status as a luminary; but, in my own mind, I still saw myself as a rebel against authority, as a second-generation dissenter from the propositions that, while being themselves novel and heterodox, were rapidly shaping up in the 1950s as a new orthodoxy on the problems of development. Had my once daring and insurgent ideas then become classic, respectable, that is, "distressingly honorable" and "boring" in the manner of Nietzsche's plaint? Perhaps. In any event, I must somewhat revise the picture I had of myself. Viewed in perspective, my dissent, however strong, was in the nature of a demurrer *within* a general movement of ideas attempting to establish development economics as a new field of studies and knowledge.[1] My propositions were at least as distant from the old orthodoxy (later called neoclassical economics) as from the new. In retrospect, therefore, it is only natural that my work should be lumped with the very writings I had chosen as my primary targets.

---

1. There were other such demurrers. A striking case of convergence with my thinking is Paul Streeten's article "Unbalanced Growth," *Oxford Economic Papers*, N.S., vol. 2 (June 1959), pp. 167–90. His article and my book, *The Strategy of Economic Development* (whose working title was for a long time "The Economics of Unbalanced Growth"), were written quite independently. Paul Streeten tells me that the printing of his article was delayed for several months by a printers' strike, otherwise his defense of unbalanced growth might have come out before mine.

In an earlier essay,[2] I have written in the most objective way I could muster about the development of our discipline. To repeat myself as little as possible I shall do the opposite in this paper, which will therefore be totally subjective and self-centered. First, I shall attempt to present the personal background and principal motives for the positions I took in *The Strategy of Economic Development*. Next, I shall look at the main propositions put forward in that book in the light of subsequent developments and present-day relevance.

Developing a Point of View

There is nothing quite like a good story to lend authority to a half-truth. For a long time, when people asked me how I came to hold the views I proposed in *The Strategy of Economic Development*, my stock answer was: I went to Colombia early in 1952 without any prior knowledge of, or reading about, economic development. This turned out to be a real advantage; I looked at "reality" without theoretical preconceptions of any kind. Then, when I returned to the United States after four and a half years' intensive experience as an official adviser and private consultant, I began to read up on the literature and discovered I had acquired a point of view of my own that was considerably at odds with current doctrines.

It is a nice line, and not *notably* untrue; but now I want to tell a more complex story.

The Marshall Plan Experience and Other Personal Background

I did go to Colombia without being well read in what development literature existed at the time.[3] But I had just been working, with intensity and occasional enthusiasm, on postwar problems of economic reconstruc-

---

2. "The Rise and Decline of Development Economics" in *Essays in Trespassing: Economics to Politics and Beyond* (Cambridge, Eng., and New York: Cambridge University Press, 1981), chap. 1. There will be several references here to this book as well as to *The Strategy of Economic Development* (New Haven: Yale University Press, 1958; and New York: Norton, 1978) and to *A Bias for Hope: Essays on Development and Latin America* (New Haven: Yale University Press, 1971). Their titles will here be shortened to, respectively, *Trespassing, Strategy,* and *Bias.*

3. I had participated in one conference on development, held at the University of Chicago in 1951, which was notable primarily for the active participation of some eminent anthropologists and for the fact that this was the occasion for Alexander Gerschenkron to unveil his masterpiece, "Economic Backwardness in Historical Perspective." The proceedings of the conference were published as *The Progress of Underdeveloped Areas,* Bert Hoselitz, ed. (Chicago: Chicago University Press, 1952), to which I contributed a paper, "Effect of Industrialization on the Markets of Industrial Countries," a topic far removed from development economics as such. The conference stimulated my interest in the problems of development.

tion and cooperation in Western Europe, as an economist with the Federal Reserve Board, from 1946 to 1952.

In particular, I was dealing with economic reconstruction in France and Italy, and with various schemes for European economic integration, such as the European Payments Union, that were central to the Marshall Plan concept. I came out of this experience with the following impressions or convictions: (1) Orthodox policy prescriptions for the disrupted postwar economies of Western Europe—stop the inflation and get the exchange rate right—were often politically naive, socially explosive, and economically counterproductive from any longer-run point of view. The advocates of orthodoxy seemed to have "forgotten nothing and learned nothing" since the days of the Great Depression. (2) The innovators who, to their lasting credit, proposed the creative remedies embodied in the Marshall Plan and, in justification, propounded novel doctrines, such as the "structural dollar shortage," soon became unduly doctrinaire in turn.

These innovators exhibited a perhaps inevitable tendency to take themselves and their ideas too seriously. This was particularly and understandably true for their balance of payments projections, for aid was given in proportion to prospective balance of payments deficits so that the projection exercises assumed crucial economic and political importance. To be effective advocates within the Executive Branch and in relations with Congress we had to exhibit far greater confidence in those statistical estimates than was warranted by the meager extent of our knowledge and foreknowledge, a "dissonant" situation leading to the development of a character trait known as charlatanism in some, and to active dislike of the whole procedure and withdrawal therefrom in others. Moreover, in order to be disavowed as little as possible by emerging reality, Marshall Plan administrators attempted to *make* their estimates come true by taking a considerable interest in the domestic plans and policies that shaped the external accounts of the aid-receiving countries.

During my six years in Washington I sided in general with the innovators, but not without some reservations. From the French and Italian experiences I had lived through in the 1930s, I had come away with a healthy respect (based on watching the misadventures of the French economy) for the efficiency of the price system, particularly with respect to the effect of exchange rate changes on the balance of payments,[4] and with a correlative distrust (based on watching Fascist economic policy in the second half of the 1930s) of peacetime controls, allocations, and grandiloquent plans. Having studied the expansion of Nazi Germany's influence in Eastern and Southeastern Europe, the background to my first book,

---

4. See my paper "Devaluation and the Trade Balance: A Note," *Review of Economics and Statistics*, vol. 21, no. 1 (February 1949), pp. 50–53, which was a late fruit of that experience.

National Power and the Structure of Foreign Trade,[5] I had developed a special sensitivity to the propensity of large and powerful countries to dominate weaker states through economic transactions. I therefore felt a natural concern and aversion when Marshall Plan administrators were aggressively pressing their views about appropriate domestic programs and policies upon countries such as Italy that were large-scale beneficiaries of aid. They did so for the best of motives—they sincerely sought for Italy not only the "right" balance of payments deficits, but a more prosperous economy and a more equitable society. But it was perhaps because they felt thus unsullied by imperialist concerns that the aid administrators thought they were justified in pursuing their objectives in an imperious manner. Fortunately this phase lasted only a short time since Marshall Plan aid to Europe was terminated, in surprising accord with the original time table, after only five years—thereby putting an end also to much of U.S. leverage.

Revolting against a Colombian Assignment

So I went to Colombia with some preconceptions after all. During my first two years there I held the position of economic and financial adviser to the newly established National Planning Council. The World Bank had recommended me for this post, but I worked out a contract directly with the Colombian government. The result was administrative ambiguity which gave me a certain freedom of action. I was in the employ of the Colombian government, but obviously also had some sort of special relationship with the World Bank, which had taken an active part in having the Planning Council set up in the first place and then in recruiting me for it.

My natural inclination, upon taking up my job, was to get myself involved in various concrete problems of economic policy with the intention of learning as much as possible about the Colombian economy and in the hope of contributing marginally to the improvement of policymaking. But word soon came from World Bank headquarters that I was principally expected to take, as soon as possible, the initiative in formulating some ambitious economic development plan that would spell out investment, domestic savings, growth, and foreign aid targets for the Colombian economy over the next few years. All of this was alleged to be quite simple for experts mastering the new programming technique: apparently there now existed adequate knowledge, even without close study of local surroundings, of the likely ranges of savings and capital-output ratios, and those estimates, joined to the country's latest national income and balance of payments accounts, would yield all the key figures needed. I resisted being relegated to this sort of programming activity. Having already plunged into some of the country's real problems, I felt that one of the

5. Berkeley, Calif.: University of California Press, 1945.

things Colombia needed least was a synthetic development plan compiled on the basis of "heroic" estimates. This was a repetition, under much less favorable circumstances (the quality of the numbers was much poorer), of what I had most disliked about work on the Marshall Plan.

One aspect of this affair made me particularly uneasy. The task was supposedly crucial for Colombia's development, yet no Colombian was to be found who had any inkling of how to go about it. That knowledge was held only by a few foreign experts who had had the new growth economics revealed to them. It all seemed to be an affront to the Colombians who were, after all, struggling or tinkering with their problems in many fields through a great variety of private decisions and public policies. My instinct was to try to understand better *their* patterns of action, rather than assume from the outset that they could only be "developed" by importing a set of techniques they knew nothing about. True, this paternalistic mode of operation was given much encouragement by the Colombians themselves who were, initially at least, treating the foreign advisers as a new brand of magicians, and who loved to pour scorn on themselves by exclaiming at every opportunity "Aquí en el trópico hacemos todo al revés" (Here in the tropics we do everything the wrong way around). But the foreign advisers and experts took such statements far too literally. Many Colombians did not really feel all that inept. For at least some of them the phrase implied that, in the particular environment in which they operated, they might well have worked out by trial and error some cunning principles of action, of which they were themselves hardly conscious, that might seem perverse to outsiders, but have actually proven quite effective.

Searching for Hidden Rationalities

This was exactly what I thought worth exploring. I began to look for elements and processes of the Colombian reality that *did* work, perhaps in roundabout and unappreciated fashion. Far more fundamentally than the idea of unbalanced growth, this search for possible *hidden rationalities* was to give an underlying unity to my work. It also gave it vulnerability.

To uncover the hidden rationality of seemingly odd, irrational, or reprehensible social behavior has been an important and quite respectable pastime of social scientists ever since Mandeville and Adam Smith.[6] If successful, the search results in those "typically counterintuitive, shocking" discoveries on which social science thrives.[7]

My principal findings of this kind were the possible rationality ("uses") of (1) shortages, bottlenecks, and other unbalanced growth sequences in the course of development (*Strategy*, chaps. 3–7); (2) capital-intensive

6. In the humanities, the tradition goes much further back, at least to Erasmus's *Praise of Folly*.

7. See "Morality and the Social Sciences: A Durable Tension," in *Trespassing*, chap. 14, p. 298.

industrial processes (chap. 8); and (3) the pressures on decisionmakers caused by inflation and balance of payments deficits (chap. 9). I shall discuss later these key themes of my book. But I must say something right away about the vulnerability that comes with such discoveries.

Once the discoveries were made and proudly exhibited, there arose, inevitably and embarrassingly, the question: Would you actually *advocate* unbalanced growth, capital-intensive investment, inflation, and so on? The honest, if a bit unsatisfactory, answer must be: yes, but of course within some fairly strict limits. There is no doubt that the unbalanced growth strategy can be overdone, with dire consequences. But I stand by the concluding paragraph of an article I wrote jointly with C. E. Lindblom to bring out the similarity of our approaches in different fields:

> There are limits to "imbalance" in economic development, to "lack of integration" in research and development, to "fragmentation" in policy making which would be dangerous to pass. And it is clearly impossible to specify in advance the optimal doses of these various policies under different circumstances. The art of promoting economic development, research and development, and constructive policy making in general consists, then, in acquiring a feeling for these doses. This art . . . will be mastered far better once the false ideals of "balance," "coordination," and "comprehensive overview" have lost our total and unquestioning intellectual allegiance.[8]

Another problem arises in connection with that embarrassing question about advocacy. Social scientists who discover the hidden rationality of a social practice should be aware that they frequently act as something of a spoilsport: once the uses of unbalanced growth or of inflation are discovered and explained, the attempt consciously to apply these notions and to replicate the earlier successes is likely to stumble for various reasons. For one, policymakers who up to then had merely backed into such devices will now tend to overdo and otherwise abuse the newly discovered knowledge.[9] Moreover, various affected parties will neutralize much of the policy by acting in anticipation of it once it is expected, in line with reasoning made familiar by the rational-expectations argument.

Thus the discovery of hidden rationalities clearly yields "dangerous knowledge." But, as is well known, knowledge is intrinsically dangerous. And this simple observation gives me a chance to turn the tables on my critics. As long as the findings I had come up with were dangerous there was at least some chance that they truly constituted new knowledge. This

---

8. "Economic Development, Research and Development, Policy-Making: Some Converging Views" (1962), reprinted in *Bias*, pp. 83–84.

9. I noted this previously for the combination of inflation and overvaluation which permitted the financing of import-substituting industrialization in many countries in the 1950s. See *Trespassing*, p. 110.

is more than can be said for quite a few of the bland and banal pieties that have been paraded under the banner of either "principles of development planning" or "efficient allocation of resources!"

Uncovering hidden rationalities permitted me to fight against what I perceived as two very different, yet interrelated evils. On the one hand, as already noted, I reacted against the visiting-economist syndrome; that is, against the habit of issuing peremptory advice and prescription by calling on universally valid economic principles and remedies—be they old or brand new—after a strictly minimal acquaintance with the "patient." But, with time, another objective was assuming even more importance in my mind: it was to counter the tendency of many Colombians and Latin Americans to work hand-in-glove with the visiting economist by their own self-deprecatory attitudes. As I put it in another article written shortly after *Strategy* was published: "Some of my main contentions could serve to reconcile the Latin Americans with their reality, to assure them that certain ubiquitous phenomena such as bottlenecks and imbalances in which they see the constantly renewed proof of their ineptness and inferiority are on the contrary inevitable concomitants and sometimes even useful stimulants of development."[10]

Because Latin Americans were wont to issue blanket condemnations of their reality they became incapable of learning from their own experiences, so it seemed to me. Later, in detailed studies of economic policymaking, I even coined a term for this trait: the "failure complex," or *fracasomania* in Spanish and Portuguese.[11]

At this point, however, my bias for hidden rationalities might seem to harbor yet another danger. Was it not going to make me blind to the imperative need for change in societies where economic growth was frustrated at every turn by antiquated institutions and attitudes as well as by exorbitant privilege? Was my enterprise then going to end up as a giant exercise in apology for the existing order (or disorder)? This danger actually never bothered me much, for the simple reason that the hidden rationalities I was after were precisely and principally *processes of growth and change already under way* in the societies I studied, processes that were often unnoticed by the actors immediately involved, as well as by foreign experts and advisers. I was not looking for reasons to justify what was, but for reasons to think that the old order was already changing. In this way I tried to identify progressive economic and political forces that

10. "Ideologies of Economic Development in Latin America," first published in 1961 and reprinted in *Bias*, pp. 310–11.

11. See my *Journeys toward Progress: Studies of Economic Policy Making in Latin America* (New York: Twentieth Century Fund, 1963; Norton, 1973); and "Policymaking and Policy Analysis in Latin America—A Return Journey" (1974), reprinted in *Trespassing* as chap. 6. In both works, but particularly in the latter, I pointed out that *fracasomania* (the failure complex) could lead to real *fracasos* (failures).

deserved recognition and help. This position did put me at odds with those who judged that the present society was "rotten through and through" and that nothing would ever change unless everything was changed at once. But this utopian dream of the "visiting revolutionary" seemed to me of a piece with the balanced growth and integrated development schemes of the visiting economist.[12]

A Paradigm of My Own?

My basic concern with the discovery of hidden rationality shows up in my first general paper on development, written in 1954 after two years in Colombia, for a conference on Investment Criteria and Economic Growth at the Massachusetts Institute of Technology.[13] Here I presented, besides a critique of what I called "The Myth of Integrated Investment Planning," two empirical observations which could qualify as investment critieria. One was about the superior performance of airplanes in comparison with highways in Colombia (the need for adequate maintenance and efficient performance in general being far more compelling in the case of airplanes), a point which later led me to a general hypothesis about the comparative advantage less developed countries have in certain types of activities. The other observation dealt with what I then described as "the impact of secondary on primary production" and later named "backward linkage." Both observations served to justify investments (in case of airlines) or investment sequences (in the case of backward linkage) that seemed questionable or *al revés* (the wrong way around) from the commonsense point of view.

In 1954 these were isolated observations. But they remained key elements of the conceptual structure that I erected three years or so later in *Strategy*. I now searched for a general economic principle that would tie them (and several related propositions) together. To this end, I suggested that underdeveloped countries need special "pressure mechanisms" or "pacing devices" to bring forth their potential. In my most general formulation I wrote: "development depends not so much on finding optimal combinations for given resources and factors of production as on calling forth and enlisting for development purposes resources and abilities that are hidden, scattered, or badly utilized" (*Strategy*, p. 5).

I presented this point as a special characteristic of the underdeveloped countries and implicitly granted that the advanced countries continued to be ruled by the traditional principles of maximization and optimization, on the basis of given and known resources and factors of production. Actually, these principles were to be impugned in short order, or were

12. For some elaboration, see *Journeys*, pp. 251–56.
13. Reprinted in *Bias*, chap. 1.

already being impugned, precisely for the advanced countries, by various important contributions of other economists. For the business firm, Richard Cyert and James March documented the importance of what they called "organizational slack," on the basis of Herbert Simon's pioneering work on "satisficing" as opposed to "maximizing." Adopting the concept of "inducement mechanism," Nathan Rosenberg showed how the pattern of inventions and innovations in the advanced countries simply does not follow the gradual expansion of opportunities as markets and knowledge grow, but has been strongly influenced by special "inducing" or "focusing" events such as strikes and wars. Finally, Harvey Leibenstein built his X-efficiency theory on the notion that slack is ubiquitous and effort sporadic and unreliable, again in the absence of special pressure situations.[14]

It appears, therefore, that the very characteristics on which I had sought to build an economics specially attuned to the underdeveloped countries have a far wider, perhaps even a universal, range and that they define, not a special strategy of development for a well-defined group of countries, but a much more generally valid approach to the understanding of change and growth. In other words, I set out to learn about others, and in the end learned about ourselves.

As many anthropologists have discovered and taught us, this is by no means an unusual meandering of social thought and knowledge. Nor does it come to me as a disappointment that I must give up the pretense of having discovered *the* distinguishing characteristic of underdeveloped societies. There always was some irony, not to say inconsistency, in the intellectual path I had followed. First I rejected the old and new paradigms of others and stressed the importance of steeping oneself in the Colombian reality—from which I eventually emerged with a triumphant paradigm of my own! So I am quite happy at this point to renounce that claim,[15] especially as long as some of my more specific findings and suggestions (frequently generated only by means of my overall conceptual scheme) continue to lead an active life of their own. I shall now show that this is indeed the case.

14. H. A. Simon, "A Behavioral Model of Rational Choice," *Quarterly Journal of Economics*, vol. 69, no. 1 (February 1955), pp. 99–118; Richard M. Cyert and James G. March, *Behavioral Theory of the Firm* (Englewood Cliffs, N.J.: Prentice-Hall, 1963); Nathan Rosenberg, "The Direction of Technological Change: Inducement Mechanisms and Focusing Devices," *Economic Development and Cultural Change*, vol. 18, no. 1 (October 1969), p. 18; and Harvey Leibenstein, "Allocative Efficiency versus X-Efficiency," *American Economic Review*, vol. 56, no. 3 (June 1966), pp. 392–415, and *Beyond Economic Man* (Cambridge, Mass.: Harvard University Press, 1976).

15. In order not to be misunderstood I must emphasize that I do not renounce my basic idea (about the need for pacing devices and so on), but only the claim that with it I had hit upon the *distinguishing* characteristic of a certain group of (economically less developed) countries.

The Life of Some Specific Propositions

Linkages

If a popularity contest were held for the various propositions I advanced in *Strategy*, the idea of favoring industries with strong backward and forward linkages would surely receive first prize. The linkage concept has achieved the ultimate success: it is by now so much part of the language of development economics that its procreator is most commonly no longer mentioned when it is being invoked.

A major battle I fought in *Strategy* was against the then widely alleged need for a "balanced" or "big push" industrialization effort; that is, against the idea that industrialization could be successful only if it were undertaken as a large-scale effort, carefully planned on many fronts simultaneously. To contradict this idea I pointed to the processes of industrialization that could in fact be observed in Colombia and other developing countries. Their entrepreneurs, domestic and foreign, had apparently hit upon a good number of *sequential* rather than *simultaneous* solutions to the problem of industrialization, but the more typical sequences were often unusual by the standards of experience in the more advanced countries. Precisely for this reason, these sequences were either not easily perceived or, once noted, were judged to be characteristic of an inferior, inefficient, or (according to a term that became fashionable in the 1960s) "dependent" industrialization.

My approach was exactly the opposite. Following Gerschenkron, I saw originality and creativity in deviating from the path followed by the older industrial countries, in skipping stages, and in inventing sequences that had a "wrong way around" look. It was surely this attitude that permitted me to ferret out the backward and forward linkage dynamic and to acclaim as a dialectical-paradoxical feat what was later called, with disparaging intent,[16] import-substituting industrialization: in its course, a country would acquire a comparative advantage in the goods it imports; for the "fatter" the imports of a given consumer good grew, the greater was the likelihood that, in Hansel and Gretel fashion, they would be "devoured" or "swallowed" by a newly established domestic industry (*Strategy*, chap. 7). My intent throughout was to underline the originality of these various dynamics, as well as the feasibility, then in doubt, of a sequential approach. As with unbalanced growth, there was of course danger that the dynamics I celebrated could be overdone, to the point of setting up a highly inefficient industrial structure. But is it not unreasonable to ask the inventor of the internal combustion engine to come up immediately with a design for pollution control and airbags?

16. *Trespassing*, p. 127, n. 39.

Be that as it may, as an analytic tool the linkages have led an active life over the past twenty-five years. They have been particularly useful in orienting various historical studies of developing economies.[17] It has been much more difficult to turn the linkage criterion (priority to investment in industries with strong linkage effects) into an operational device for industrial planning, with the help of input-output statistics. A great deal of discussion about appropriate measurement has taken place.[18] The most extensive and successful study of this sort to date has been undertaken by the Regional Employment Program for Latin America and the Caribbean (PREALC) of the International Labour Office.[19] It uses the linkage concept for the purpose of measuring employment creation, rather than industrial expansion in terms of value added. The idea is of course to help in devising an industrialization strategy that would maximize employment. One empirical finding of the study deserves special notice: once the indirect employment effects (via backward and forward linkages) are taken into account, investment in large-scale (capital-intensive) industry turns out to be just as employment-creating as investment in small-scale (labor-intensive) industry for the industrially advanced countries of Latin America.

The linkage concept was devised for a better understanding of the industrialization process, and initially most applications were in this area. Fairly soon, however, the concept caught on even more in the analysis of the growth patterns of developing countries during the phase when their principal engine of growth was (or is) the export of primary products.[20] Very different growth paths were traced out by countries exporting copper rather than coffee, and these differences were difficult to explain by the traditional macroeconomic variables. The linkages permitted a more detailed look, yet stopped short of the wholly descriptive account that had been practiced by Harold Innis and other practitioners of the so-called staple thesis.

17. Albert Fishlow, *American Railroads and the Transformation of the Ante-Bellum Economy* (Cambridge, Mass.: Harvard University Press, 1965); Judith Tendler, *Electric Power in Brazil: Entrepreneurship in the Public Sector* (Cambridge, Mass.: Harvard University Press, 1968); Michael Roemer, *Fishing for Growth: Export-led Development in Peru, 1959–1967* (Cambridge, Mass.: Harvard University Press, 1970); Scott R. Pearson, *Petroleum and the Nigerian Economy* (Stanford, Calif.: Stanford University Press, 1970); and Richard Weisskoff and Edward Wolff, "Linkages and Leakages: Industrial Tracking in an Enclave Economy," *Economic Development and Cultural Change*, vol. 25 (July 1977), pp. 607–28.

18. See the symposium on linkage effect measurement in *Quarterly Journal of Economics*, vol. 90, no. 2 (May 1976), pp. 308–43.

19. Norberto E. García and Manuel Marfán, "Estructuras industriales y eslabona-mientos de empleo" [Industrial structures and employment linkages], Monografía sobre empleo 126 (Santiago, Chile: PREALC, December 1982), processed (to be published in Spanish and English, with a preface by the present author, by the International Labour Office).

20. For a more extensive treatment of this topic, see *Trespassing*, chap. 4, "A Generalized Linkage Approach to Development, with Special Reference to Staples."

At this point the linkage concept proliferated. In analogy to backward and forward linkage, consumption linkage was defined as the process by which the new incomes of the primary producers lead first to imports of consumer goods and then—in line with the "swallowing" dynamic—to their replacement by domestic (industrial or agricultural) production. Similarly, fiscal linkage is said to occur when the state taxes the newly accruing incomes for the purpose of financing investments elsewhere in the economy. Such fiscal linkages are either direct, as when the state is able to siphon off a portion of exporters' profits through export duties or royalties, or indirect—in this case the various incomes earned through exports are not tapped directly, but are allowed to generate a flow of imports which are then made to yield fiscal revenue through tariffs.

Once the various ways through which exports of primary products can give rise to further economic activities had come into view, it became clear that some of the linkages are usually to be had only at the cost of doing without some of the others. In this manner, typical *constellations* of linkages could be identified for different kinds of primary commodities; as a result, it became possible to differentiate what had long been designated "export-led growth" and treated as a unified and transparent process. More important still, this approach almost compels one to consider the interaction between the social structure and the state, on the one hand, and the more narrowly economic factors, on the other.

Latitude in Performance Standards

While the linkages, in their increasingly numerous varieties, help us understand how one thing leads to another in economic development, an even more basic inquiry is how one firm or productive operation can be made to *endure* as an efficiently performing unit of the economic system. The answer to this question yielded what was, in my opinion—and, once again, in that of any market test—the other major find I made in Colombia. It had its origin in the already noted observation about the comparative efficiency (and maintenance) of airplanes and highways and was developed in *Strategy* (chap. 8) into the much more general point— sometimes called the Hirschman hypothesis—contrasting machine-paced with operator-paced machinery, and process-centered with product-centered industrial activities.[21] An implication was that a certain type of

---

21. The hypothesis lent itself to testing by empirical data; if it were true, the productivity differentials between advanced and less developed countries would be larger in certain types of industries than in others. A large number of attempts at testing have been made and are reviewed in Simon Teitel, "Productivity, Mechanization, and Skills: A Test of the Hirschman Hypothesis for Latin American Industry," *World Development*, vol. 9, no. 4 (1981), pp. 355–71. See also M. Shahid Alam, "Hirschman's Taxonomy of Industries: Some Hypotheses and Evidence," *Economic Development and Cultural Change*, vol. 32 (January 1984), pp. 367–72.

capital-intensive, advanced technology could be more appropriate, in a country with little industrial tradition, than the labor-intensive technology and "idiot-proof" machinery—contrary to some of the most frequent, automatic, and insistent advice proffered by visiting experts.

I became fascinated with this point for several reasons. First, it permitted me to indicate another hidden rationality: the widely noted preference of developing countries for advanced technology and capital-intensive industry with a flow process was perhaps not in all cases a damaging bias, based exclusively on misguided prestige-seeking.

Second, I had come upon a concept or criterion that was helpful in understanding a number of social and economic processes: the greater or smaller extent of latitude in standards of performance (or tolerance for poor performance) as a characteristic inherent in all production tasks. When this latitude is narrow the corresponding task has to be performed *just right*; otherwise, it cannot be performed at all or is exposed to an unacceptable level of risk (for example, high probability of crash in the case of poorly maintained or poorly operated airplanes). Lack of latitude therefore brings powerful pressures for efficiency, quality performance, good maintenance habits, and so on. It thus substitutes for inadequately formed motivations and attitudes, which will be *induced* and generated by the narrow-latitude task instead of presiding over it.

Here, then, was another promising "wrong way around" sequence. Ever since Max Weber, many social scientists looked at the "right" cultural attitudes and beliefs as necessary conditions ("prerequisites") for economic progress, just as earlier theories had emphasized race, climate, or the presence of natural resources. In the 1950s, newly fashioned cultural theories of development competed strongly with the economic ones (which stressed capital formation), with Weber's Protestant Ethic being modernized into David McClelland's "achievement motivation" as a precondition of progress and into Edward C. Banfield's "amoral familism" as an obstacle. According to my way of thinking, the very attitudes alleged to be preconditions of industrialization could be generated on the job and "on the way," by certain characteristics of the industrialization process.[22]

The emphasis on latitude in performance standards as a variable influencing efficiency also had a bearing on approaches that regard certain economic institutions as necessary conditions for development. For many economists, competition is the all-powerful social institution bringing pressures for efficiency. Strangely and somewhat inconsistently, some of these economists seem intent on granting competition a monopoly in this endeavor. But with competition being so often quite feeble and with the battle against inefficiency and decay being so generally uphill, why not search and be grateful for additional mechanisms that, to paraphrase

22. Alex Inkeles and David H. Smith, *Becoming Modern* (Cambridge, Mass.: Harvard University Press, 1974).

Rousseau, force man to be efficient? In *Strategy*, lack of latitude seemed to me to hold considerable promise in this regard. Twelve years later I stressed another such mechanism: protests, complaints, and criticism by consumers and, more generally, by members of organizations when the quality of the organization's output deteriorates. This I called "voice," and the interaction of voice with competition, called "exit" for greater generality, involved me in the writing of another book.[23]

One matter I notice only now, with much surprise over the underlying unity of my thought: there appears to be a real affinity between these two mechanisms, which I developed quite independently one from the other. Narrow-latitude tasks will, if performed poorly and (ex hypothesi) disastrously, give rise to strong public concern and outcry—to voice. This is obvious in the case of airplane crashes and was specifically noted in *Strategy* for another concrete example of a narrow-latitude task, road construction using a certain technology. I cited the opinion of a highway engineer who favored low-type bituminous surfaces on relatively low-traveled routes, rather than gravel and stone surfaces, for the reason that "local pressure would be applied to the Ministry of Public Works to repair the deep holes which will develop in cheap bituminous surfaces if maintenance and retreatment is delayed, and that such pressure would be greater than if a gravel and stone road is allowed to deteriorate."[24] Maintenance of cheap bituminous surfaces is therefore a narrow-latitude task that, if neglected, is likely to give rapid rise to strong voice (the results of poor performance being intolerable).

It could be argued that, in this case and in that of airplanes, voice is the only available mechanism since these are instances of natural or institutional monopoly (in the case of air transportation being reserved to one national airline). This is not so, however; even when competition is lively for narrow-latitude products or services—for example, pharmaceuticals—public regulation is generally present, testifying to the presence of public concern and to the feeling that, because of the possibly disastrous consequences, the assurance of the "right" level of quality cannot be left to market forces. I had earlier pointed out that voice is likely to come to the fore when there is a strong public interest—for example, because of concerns for health and safety.[25] The narrow-latitude criterion leads to the same conclusion.

If there is a strong affinity between narrow-latitude and voice, one would expect a corresponding association between exit (that is, competition) and wide-latitude goods and services. These are items that can be and are produced and marketed to very different quality standards, without lower quality having disastrous effects. It is indeed correct that, with

---

23. *Exit, Voice, and Loyalty* (Cambridge, Mass.: Harvard University Press, 1970).

24. *Strategy*, p. 143. This passage is part of a letter to me from a highway engineer who was then working in Colombia as a consultant to the World Bank.

25. *Trespassing*, p. 217.

regard to such goods and services, comparison shopping and competition in general come peculiarly into their own. The attractiveness of Milton Friedman's proposal for introducing competition into primary and secondary education may precisely derive from the wide-latitude characteristic of education. It is a fact that the quality of education varies widely and that this variability is both inevitable (because of varying teacher quality, for one) and tolerated by the public, however disastrous the individual and social effects of poor education may in fact be. On this score, then, I must grant that education seems to be a task whose performance might be improved by competition. For reasons I have discussed elsewhere,[26] however, the maintenance and improvement of quality in education still seem to me to require, on balance, a strong admixture of voice.

Even before I came to write on exit and voice, the concept of lack of tolerance for poor performance continued to yield dividends. In *Development Projects Observed*[27] a major chapter, entitled "Latitudes and Disciplines," deals with a large variety of pressures for performance stemming from various characteristics of the project: spatial or locational latitude, temporal discipline in construction, tolerance for corruption, latitude in substituting quantity for quality, and so on. These categories proved quite useful in understanding the specific difficulties and accomplishments of different projects.

Yet later I found that I was by no means the inventor of these concepts of latitude or discipline and of their uses, but that I had some illustrious predecessors, such as Montesquieu and Sir James Steuart! These thinkers were evidently not concerned with the functioning of development projects or the efficiency of industry; they had more portentous matters on their mind—their overriding concern was the more or less tolerable performance of the state. But here their reasoning was very close to mine; they were looking for ways of constraining the latitude of the state, of repressing the "passions" of the sovereign, and they thought they found a solution in the expansion of the "interests" and the market. I shall not retell this tale here, but merely meant to indicate the straightforward connection between my interest in the comparative performance of airlines and highways in Colombia and the principal theme of *The Passions and the Interests*.[28] Here also, I came up against the limits of latitude concept, but that is another story.

Views on Inflation and Balance of Payments Problems

One of the pleasant experiences in writing a book rather than an article is that the ideas one starts out with are given enough breathing space so they can fully unfold and expand in all kinds of originally unanticipated

26. *Trespassing*, pp. 219–22.
27. Washington, D.C.: Brookings Institution, 1967.
28. Princeton, N.J.: Princeton University Press, 1977.

directions. This is what happened with *Strategy*. The book's basic theses on unbalanced growth and sequential problem-solving eventually yielded positions of my own on the problems of inflation, balance of payments disequilibrium, and population pressures (chap. 9), as well as on regional development (chap. 10). In the following I shall limit myself to just two of these topics.[29]

INFLATION. With its shortages and bottlenecks, the unbalanced development path I had described as most typical, "conveys an almost physical sensation of inflationary shocks being administered to an economy" (p. 158). Relative price rises, so I argued, play an important role, via more or less elastic supply responses, in overcoming the imbalances. In the process, however, "with any given level of skill and determination of [the] monetary and fiscal managers" (p. 158), the general price level will be subject to upward pressure, especially if supply responses are weak or slow in some key sectors such as food and foreign exchange (pp. 162–63). In this manner, I put forward a view on inflation that was just then being elaborated within the U.N. Economic Commission for Latin America as the "structuralist," as opposed to the "monetarist," approach. That very view came to the fore in the North, without any reference to its Southern antecedents of course, under the name of "supply-shock inflation" during the oil crises of the 1970s and their monetary repercussions.[30]

In presenting inflation as the unfortunate, but to be expected side effect of a certain type of growth process, I had in mind the comparatively moderate inflations—in the 20 to 30 percent range—that Colombia and Brazil were then (in the 1950s) experiencing. I advocated implicitly a greater comprehension on the part of the advanced countries and the international financial institutions (the International Monetary Fund and the World Bank), which at that time considered any two-digit inflation as evidence of profligate fiscal and monetary policies that had to be corrected before further development finance was made available. Particularly in the Brazil of the Kubitschek years this policy seemed to me highly ill-advised,

29. At the time my book appeared, my most "scandalous" position was the one I expressed on population pressures. I maintained that, in certain circumstances, such pressures could be considered as stimulants rather than as depressants of development. I do not wish to return to the argument here, except to point out that my position was later given considerable support through the influential writings of Ester Boserup, who stressed the effects of population growth on the introduction of new agricultural techniques. See her books, *The Conditions of Agricultural Growth* (New York: Aldine, 1965), and, more recently, *Population and Technological Change* (Chicago: University of Chicago Press, 1981).

30. An extended retrospective treatment of these matters is in my survey article, "The Social and Political Matrix of Inflation: Elaborations on the Latin American Experience," in *Trespassing*, chap. 8.

and I still believe that it bears some responsibility for the tragic "derailment" of Brazilian politics from 1958 to the military takeover in 1964.[31]

BALANCE OF PAYMENTS PROBLEMS. This brings me to the balance of payments problems of developing countries. Once again I analyzed pressures on a country's international accounts as "part and parcel of the process of unbalanced growth" (*Strategy*, p. 167) rather than as primarily the reflection of macroeconomic disequilibrium between domestic savings and investments. In this perspective, the needs of developing countries for international financial assistance do not arise so much from the fact that they are too poor to save the amounts needed to achieve some growth target—this was the then current rationale for foreign aid—as from some disproportionalities that arise in the growth process. At some stage the need of the expanding economy for imported inputs outpaces its ability to increase exports, unless the country is lucky enough to produce some items that are in rapidly expanding demand on the world market. In other words, the need for financial assistance from abroad would by no means be greatest when the country is poorest, but would be liable to bulge—perhaps several times—in the course of development as certain initially import-intensive economic activities are being put into place. The point was once again to get away from the excessive simplicities of certain growth models and to argue that balance of payments pressures, like inflation, are not necessarily reflections of profligate fiscal and monetary policies.

So much for the effect of growth on the balance of payments. How about the equally important inverse relation—the effect of foreign exchange abundance or stringency on growth? Here I put forward an idea that I have since used in a number of increasingly broad contexts.[32] It was based on a simple observation: after a period of comparative foreign exchange *affluence* that causes certain consumption habits, based on imports, to take root, the experience of foreign exchange *shortage* has often set in motion industrial investments designed to produce the previously imported goods that are now sorely missed. It therefore looked as though some alternation of good and hard times (with regard to foreign exchange availability) could be particularly effective in fostering industrial development. Still in *Strategy*, I made a similar point with regard to

31. For a critical evaluation of World Bank policy in Brazil during the 1950s, see Edward S. Mason and Robert E. Asher, *The World Bank since Bretton Woods* (Washington, D.C.: Brookings Institution, 1973), pp. 660–62.

32. The idea was originally expressed in a discussion paper written for a conference of the International Economic Association held at Rio in 1957. See Howard S. Ellis, ed., *Economic Development for Latin America* (New York: St. Martin's Press, 1961), p. 460; and *Strategy*, pp. 173–76.

regional development (chap. 10). I saw certain advantages in an underdeveloped region (such as northeastern Brazil) being closely integrated with
the country's more advanced provinces, whereas other kinds of development stimuli would arise from withdrawal and insulation. Later on, I
wrote about the virtues of *some* oscillation between contact and insulation
in connection with both foreign trade and investment.[33]

This thesis was not going to make me popular either with the advocates
of delinking or with their neoclassical opponents.[34] Once again, moreover,
it was sure to disappoint those looking for operational policy advice: first,
the optimal width of the oscillation between foreign exchange affluence
and penury is impossible to define; second, such ups and downs are
generally not subject to a single country's control. If it is correct, my point
has nevertheless important implications: it makes policymakers aware
that each situation brings with it its own set of opportunities (and of
possible calamities).

The principle of oscillation is obviously a close relative of the strategy of
unbalanced growth which, in spite of the commanding position it occupies
in my book, has not yet been discussed here as such. Since I have some new
thoughts on this topic, I left it for the concluding section.

The Politics of Unbalanced Growth

To write in praise of lack of balance is evidently a provocation for which
a price must be paid. The worst penalty is not inflicted by the critics, but by
those who proclaim themselves devoted disciples and commit all kinds of
horrors in one's name. Here is a striking example of this sort of occur-
rence.

On a visit to Argentina around 1968, shortly after the military coup that
toppled the civilian regime of Illia and brought to power General Onganía,
I was told by a high-ranking official, "All we are doing is applying your
ideas of unbalanced growth. In Argentina we cannot achieve all our
political, social, and economic objectives at once; therefore we have
decided to proceed by stages, as though in an unbalanced growth sequence. First we must straighten out the economic problems, that is,
restore economic stability and stimulate growth; thereafter, we will look
out for greater social equity; and only then will the country be ready for a
restoration of civil liberties and for other political advances." I was of
course appalled by this "application" of my ideas. It seemed quite prepos-
terous to me on various counts. After all, the imbalances I had written

33. See *Bias*, pp. 25 and 229–30.
34. An excellent survey of the pros and cons of delinking is in Carlos F. Diaz
Alejandro, "Delinking North and South: Unshackled or Unhinged?" in Albert Fishlow
and others, *Rich and Poor Nations in the World Economy* (New York: McGraw-Hill,
1978), pp. 87–162.

about were far less grand than those referred to by my Argentine interlocutor. They had been confined to the economic sphere and were concerned with disproportionalities between sectors, such as industry and agriculture, and even more with interactions between much more finely subdivided subsectors. Because of the interdependence of the economy in the input-output sense, the expansion of one sector or subsector ahead of the other could be relied on to set forces in motion (relative price changes and public policies in response to complaints about shortages) that would tend to eliminate the initial imbalance. As I put it in a letter to André Gunder Frank, who had written one of the more perceptive reviews of my book[35] (this was before his "development-of-underdevelopment" phase):

> If one wants to move [straight] from one equilibrium position to the next, then, because of the discontinuities and invisibilities *that I take for granted*, the "big push" or "minimum critical effort" is indispensable. But if we assume that intermediate positions of development-stimulating disequilibrium are sustainable at least for limited time periods, then we can manage to break down the big push into a series of smaller steps. In other words, I am in favor of utilizing the energy which holds together economic nuclei of given minimum size in the *building up* of these nuclei. (Letter of August 18, 1959; emphasis in the original.)

In addition to making clear my position as dissent from a dissent (without a return to the original orthodoxy), this passage well illustrates my conception of the unbalanced growth process as something fueled and justified by the "energy which holds together" the various sectors and branches of the economy and which would ensure that the various imbalances would be approximately self-correcting.

Even for intersectoral imbalances, my principal concern was not so much to praise imbalance in general as to draw a distinction between "compulsive" and merely "permissive" sequences. On the basis of this distinction, I was critical of the then prevailing emphasis on investments in infrastructure (*Strategy*, chap. 5). Further, I noted that in regional development the process of unbalanced growth is fundamentally different from unbalanced growth in the sectoral sense because of the weakness of the forces making for restoration of interregional balance (chap. 10). Hence, it is illegitimate to invoke the unbalanced growth idea when there are no compelling reasons why an advance in one direction and the ensuing imbalance should set countervailing forces in motion. In the Argentine case I have cited, it was impossible to detect any such forces unless one trusted the self-proclaimed intentions of the new regime (that came duly to naught) or the dubious correlations between economic growth and

---

35. "Built-in Destabilization: A. O. Hirschman's Strategy of Economic Development," *Economic Development and Cultural Change*, vol. 8, no. 4 (July 1960), pp. 433–40.

the growth of democracy adduced by the more sanguine political-development theorists of the time.

But there is another, perhaps more interesting, way in which the Argentine sequence differed from the one I had talked about. My Argentine interlocutor conveniently failed to mention that the military had just ordered severe curtailments of political freedoms. Whatever economic advance the new regime would bring was being achieved at the cost of previously political and civil rights of the citizens. Later on these rights were to be restored—perhaps, in turn, at the cost of some of the previous economic advances? This sort of (implicit) sequence is again very different from the one I had had in mind: in my scheme one sector, say, manufacturing industry, was to move ahead without any simultaneous expansion in power or transportation or agriculture, but certainly not at the expense of these sectors. Nevertheless, there is here some scope for reflection and, at long last, for self-criticism. Is it really true that the process of unbalanced growth, as sketched in *Strategy*, never implies actual retrogression for any economic agents? Probably not. When industry advances and uses the *existing* power and transportation facilities, then, in the absence of excess capacity, there are fewer such facilities available for the traditional users who will therefore be worse off. The same is likely to hold, with rather more serious consequences, for an isolated advance of industry while agricultural output remains stationary.[36]

It appears therefore that, for some of these purposes, I have to redraw the diagram by which I have attempted to portray the unbalanced-growth process.[37] The comparatively innocuous pattern of figure 1 is transformed by the preceding considerations into the more problematic pattern of figure 2, where at each stage in the sequential growth process the income-receivers of one of the two sectors are gaining at the expense of those of the other sector. As drawn, to reflect the eventual all-around increases in output, the incomes received in both sectors are growing in the course of the process as a whole, but at any one point Sector A is gaining at the expense of Sector B or vice versa, making for what might be called an *antagonistic* growth process. Note that antagonistic is very different from zero-sum since all-around growth is in effect being achieved.

36. This matter could obviously be elaborated at considerable length. The effect of unbalanced growth on sectoral incomes in a two- or three-sector economy depends on the intersectoral terms of trade, and it is conceivable that the incomes generated in the expanding sector would decline rather than expand. Harry G. Johnson's classic article, "Economic Expansion and International Trade," is still a good starting point for the analysis of the various possibilities. See *Manchester School of Economic and Social Studies*, vol. 23, no. 2 (May 1955), pp. 96–101.

37. The most straightforward such presentation is in the already cited article, co-authored with C. E. Lindblom, "Economic Development, Research and Development, and Policy Making: Some Converging Views," p. 65; in *Strategy*, a similar, but more complex diagram is on p. 87.

Figure 1. *Balanced and Unbalanced Growth*

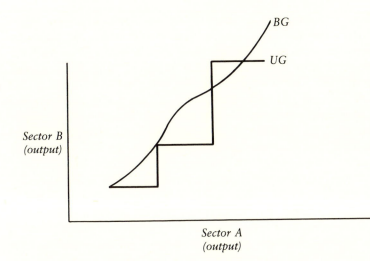

Sector B
(output)

Sector A
(output)

Figure 2. *Antagonistic Growth*

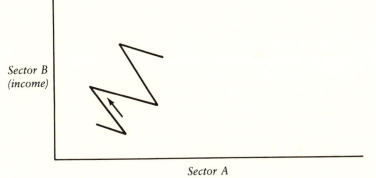

Sector B
(income)

Sector A
(income)

I had not noticed that my unbalanced growth path had these antagonistic implications. Had I done so I might have inquired into the political
consequences and prerequisites of the process. For it to unfold, a certain
level of tolerance for increasing inequality in the course of growth appears
to be required. This matter was later investigated in my article, "The
Tolerance for Income Inequality in the Course of Economic Development,"[38] but only after the antagonistic potential of the development

38. First published in 1973 and reprinted in *Trespassing*, chap. 3.

process had led to civil wars and various other disasters. Along with my fellow pioneers, I thus stand convicted of not having paid enough attention to the political implications of the economic development theories we propounded.[39]

But perhaps it was not altogether unfortunate that we were myopic and parochial. Had we been more far-sighted and interdisciplinary, we might have recoiled from advocating any action whatever, for fear of all the lurking dangers and threatening disasters.

Take my own case. In the hopeful 1950s I found it quite daring and paradoxical enough to advocate a growth pattern corresponding to figure 1. I just *had* to repress the thought that the process depicted there implies to some extent the antagonistic process shown in figure 2. Twenty-five years later we have learned so much, alas, about the enormous difficulties and tensions that come with any social change that the antagonistic growth process portrayed in figure 2 no longer looks as gratuitously harrowing as would have been the case earlier. In fact, I now want to argue that the process of antagonistic unbalanced growth—it could be called "sailing against the wind"—is far more common than one might think.

In figure 2 we are free to make the two coordinates represent not the incomes of two important social groups, such as workers and capitalists, but more generally two important social objectives such as economic stability (internal and external) and growth, or growth and equity (a less unequal distribution of income and wealth), or, for that matter, equity and stability. As soon as we do so we realize that sailing against the wind is actually how Western societies have frequently been traveling when they were moving forward at all.

I have two reasons to suggest. First, each of these objectives is so difficult to achieve that progress with just one of them requires the utmost concentration of intellectual energies and political resources. The result is neglect of other crucial objectives, a neglect which subsequently comes to public attention; the resulting criticism then leads to a change in course, to a new concentration—and a new neglect.

Second, I want to argue that the sailing-against-the-wind pattern is congenial to the democratic form of government, and particularly to the two-party system of democratic governance. If, in such a system, each of the two parties retains a characteristic physiognomy or ideological consistency of its own, then each party will give very distinct priorities to such social objectives as growth, equity, and stability; with the parties alternating in power, society is likely to move, in the best of circumstances, as though it were sailing against the wind.[40]

39. For an early critique of this sort, see Warren F. Ilchman and R. C. Bargave, "Balanced Thought and Economic Growth," *Economic Development and Cultural Change*, vol. 14, no. 4 (July 1966), pp. 385–99.
40. An empirical study and verification for twelve Western European and North American nations during the postwar period is in Douglas A. Hibbs, Jr., "Political

It does seem, at first blush, an odd and even perverse way of moving forward—a course in which some important social group is constantly aggrieved and attacked and some primary social objective constantly disregarded and even set back. Yet this may be the characteristic, even the only available pattern, of progress in a society which lives by the canons of competitive politics. Such a society is necessarily divided into "ins" and "outs," with the interests and aspirations of the latter being neglected until it is their turn to take over and to turn the tables on their opponents.

In sum, the art of moving society forward in a democracy is to do so in spite of substantial and justified discontent on the part of some important groups, followed by similar discontent on the part of others. At any one point in time, there is always not only strife and clash and conflict, but also loss of some valuable terrain previously gained. Yet it is possible that all-around progress is being achieved behind the back, so to speak, of the parties and groups in conflict. Democracy is consolidated when, after a few alternations of the parties in power, the various groups come to realize that, strangely enough, they have all gained.

There can of course be no certainty that the antagonistic moves here described will actually have this happy outcome. They can just as well do the opposite—in figure 2 the movement would simply have to be visualized as taking place in the direction opposite to that of the optimistic arrow there shown. In such circumstances democracy will be proclaimed to be in crisis and to be involved in playing zero- or negative-sum games. "Fundamental" solutions will now be sought, such as an end to the "destructive" party struggle and a national accord on basic objectives, so that society can move forward along a "balanced" path with simultaneous progress being made toward each and every one of the agreed-upon objectives. Such is the ever present corporatist and authoritarian temptation that arises when a pluralist regime puts in a poor performance. Our antagonistic, sailing-against-the-wind growth pattern makes it clear that another solution might also be available, one that has the considerable merit of not jettisoning the pattern of competitive politics.

By now my self-criticism of unbalanced growth has obviously taken a strange turn. I started by faulting myself for not having recognized, in the course of my advocacy of unbalanced growth, that such growth could imply for a while an actual decline in the incomes of the initially nonexpanding sector. But then I established a connection between this antagonistic growth model and the awkward way in which a democracy typically moves forward. Thus my self-blame soon ran out of steam, and I ended up presenting this growth model as a remarkable social invention by means of which pluralist politics and the achievement of multiple social objectives can be reconciled.

Parties and Macro Economic Policy," *American Political Science Review*, vol. 71, no. 4 (December 1977), pp. 1467–87.

What I have done, once again, is to show that the unbalanced growth model of *Strategy*, originally intended exclusively for the better comprehension of processes in developing countries, has its uses, after a slight transformation, in dealing with problems of political economy in the advanced countries. And this demonstration gives me considerable satisfaction: in the end, the advanced countries too are forced into awkward solutions to their problems, they too do things seemingly *al revés*, the wrong way around!

Conclusion

Our instructions from the organizers of these lectures said—in effect, though not in these exact terms—that we should both celebrate and criticize (in the light of intervening events and experiences) our ideas of yesteryear. Like my distinguished fellow pioneers, I have found it difficult to be evenhanded in this dual task. Moreover, what started out here and there as a confession of sins tended to end up, curiously enough, as a confession of faith.

It is probably a futile exercise to go back to a work, some twenty-five years later, and to pronounce some ideas as still good, others as disproven; some as having had a wholesome influence, others as having been harmful—and then to strike a balance with a bottom line. It makes more sense to attempt what Benedetto Croce pointed to with one of his titles that read *What Is Alive and What Is Dead in Hegel's Philosophy*, that is, to evaluate what is alive and what is dead of our work.[41] There too, of course, the authors themselves are poor judges, and all they can do is to try to convince the reader that there is quite some life left in those old "written and painted thoughts" and that they continue to evolve in interesting ways.

One last remark, on the impact of new ideas. Since my thoughts on development were largely dissents, critical of both old and new orthodoxies, they have led to lively debates, thus helping, together with the contributions of others, to make the new field of development economics attractive and exciting, back in the 1950s and 1960s. I rather think that this was the major positive contribution of my work as well as its principal impact.

Perhaps there is a general point here. The effect of new theories and ideas is much less direct than we often think: to a considerable extent, it comes by way of the general impetus that is given to a certain field of studies. As a result of a few contributions, that field suddenly comes alive with discussion and controversy and attracts some of the more intelligent, energetic, and dedicated members of a generation. This is the indirect, or

---

41. *Ciò che è vivo e ciò che è morto nella filosofia di Hegel* (Bari: Laterza, 1907).

recruitment, effect of new ideas, as opposed to their direct, or *persuasion*, effect which is usually the only one to be considered. It happens frequently that the recruitment effect is far more significant and durable than the persuasion effect. The importance of the recruitment effect explains, among other things, why the influence of new ideas is so unpredictable and why it is so difficult—and often ludicrous—to assign intellectual responsibility for actual policy decisions, let alone for policy outcomes.

The field of development studies is a remarkable case in point. After the success of the Marshall Plan, the underdevelopment of Asia, Africa, and Latin America loomed as the major unresolved economic problem on any "Agenda for a Better World." At the same time, various contending views came forward on how best to tackle that problem. The recruitment effect of this combination of circumstances was notable. As the problem turned out to be tougher and more hydra-headed than any of us had anticipated, this was most fortunate. In this manner, we, the so-called pioneers, can take pride, not in having solved the problems of development, but in having contributed to attracting into our field a large number of people who will carry on.

Comment

Carlos F. Diaz Alejandro

WHAT HAS HIRSCHMAN REBELLED AGAINST? His paper gives us generous clues: the France of the 1930s taught him to suspect both gold standard practical orthodoxy and populist simplicities, as one hopes young Chileans have learned from the excesses witnessed in their country during the 1970s. Hitler and Mussolini warned Hirschman about planning. Even during the slack 1930s he could observe the power of the price system and the dangers of thoughtless interventionism; he became, if not an elasticity-optimist, at least a devaluation-optimist, in the sense of discovering that the worse the current account situation was, the more likely was its improvement following devaluation. Marshall Plan experiences reinforced his doubts about planning exercises in which "if you give me the intercept, I will give you the slope."

From these origins, Hirschman went on to search for "hidden rationalities." This crucial methodological decision puts him in the middle, or rather in the vanguard, of mainstream economics. Young 1980s economists, schooled in choice-theoretic models with uncertainty, imperfect information, and missing markets are likely to find Hirschman not so much a heterodox rebel but rather a forerunner and a rich source of ideas and testable hypotheses. Hirschman himself notes how recent industrial organization literature emphasizes a number of notions found in his early writings. One is even tempted to point out similarities between Hirschman and conservative economists associated with the old Chicago School: suspicion of planning, faith in the rationality (hidden or otherwise) of the peasant and other private agents, skepticism about foreign aid and bureaucratic "experts" administering it, a delight in shocking, counterintuitive results, and an optimism and bias for hope many critics of mainstream economics find so offensive. But there are important differences. Searching for inducement mechanisms, Hirschman explores beyond the market; hence government is not viewed as intrinsically stupid and inefficient. Early exposure to Hegel, Marx, and other Continental thinkers

Carlos F. Diaz Alejandro is Visiting Professor of Economics at Columbia University, on leave from Yale University.

gave Hirschman not only a taste for standing things on their heads, but also an admirable willingness to trespass outside the market and to pretend that there are no boundaries among the social sciences. Furthermore, aware of the substance of what today would be called moral hazard, asymmetric information, and costly supervision of effort (as in the classic example of airplane maintenance as opposed to road maintenance), Hirschman displayed, in contrast with "old Chicago," a greater skepticism regarding the efficiency of the invisible hand.

So Hirschman has been a rebel and a dissenter not so much against the major traditions of mainstream, academic economics, but against the simplifications, banalities, and limitations of practical orthodoxy *and* heterodoxy, and against the charlatanism of practitioners impatient with subtleties and the "pale cast of thought." The Hirschman rebellion has been at its finest when fighting vulgar recipes imposed on the weak or the vanquished.

Let me now turn to criticisms of the Hirschman style. He notes in his paper an early objection: what is the operational content of his work; what exactly is his policy advice; did he really mean that imbalances should be deliberately engineered? Hirschman's kingdom is no longer of *that* world; he replies, basically, that this is not his business. In a profession characterized by excess supply of aspirants to positions in councils of economic advisers and an unseemly eagerness to peddle nostrums in the mass media, I find his answer quite satisfactory and refreshing. The ex-practitioner has become a shining example of scholarly defiance, responsible only for generating mind-expanding ideas and maintaining academic pulchritude.

What about the "idiot disciple" syndrome? Are not the Hirschman paradoxes a joy when spun by the master, but dangerous in the hands of mediocre followers, hence to be labeled poison? Traditional academic immunity would also be enough to dismiss this charge, but perhaps this and the previous criticism deserve a more Hirschmanian exploration.

Hirschman's results typically involve the conclusion that a little bit of something is a good thing, but too much of it is bad. Timing and intensity matter a good deal, but his analysis remains qualitative. Formalization and quantification, without which optima cannot be pinned down, are absent. This is a pity, not so much because the policymaker is left without a recipe for action, but because the scientific validity of his propositions are left not quite ready for testing. Furthermore, his style of analysis, like labor-intensive techniques in the tropics, may be said to have too many permissive sequences and too wide a tolerance for sloppy imitation, in contrast with the narrow tolerance and somewhat mechanical pacing generated by analytical styles relying more on capital-intensive quantification and formal model-building.

Could we devise curricula and inducement mechanisms so as to produce two, three, more Hirschmans? It is both a tribute to his style and a criticism of it that it leaves behind no obvious foundation on which to build a school. But rather than lament that Mozart did not leave behind formulas on how to produce at least a few Mozarts in each generation, we should rejoice on having been graced by a one-of-a-kind visitation.

Flirting with ungrateful perversity, one last criticism may be considered. In his search for "hidden rationalities" in the tropics, has not Hirschman sometimes overshot, and justified policies which were really *al revés?* In his sympathetic attempt to understand, has he not forgiven too much, indulging in a new kind of paternalism? Old debates come to mind on the extent of import-substituting industrialization and on mechanisms for promoting it. Without reviewing those controversies, I would conclude that there is a little, but not much, to this criticism.

Let me close by remarking on some omissions in the Hirschman paper and by reflecting on development economics. The Rojas Pinilla interlude in Colombian history appears to have had little impact on Hirschman's thinking about the interaction of politics and economics in the breakdown of democratic government, a subject of compelling fascinations to Hirschman and other social scientists interested in Latin America during the 1970s. Perhaps the other omission was motivated by a modest reluctance to say "I told you so": the Alliance for Progress is mercifully ignored.

Hirschman notes in his paper that apparently deviant phenomena first observed and analyzed in the lush tropics have been, later on, also perceived in the cool regions of the world. Development economics, as created by pioneers like Hirschman, may be said to have been at its best as a School for Scandal, a frontier where the profession lowered its cognitive dissonance defenses and allowed itself to be surprised. Inevitably, many "discoveries" dissolved under closer scrutiny, while the robust ones were incorporated into mainstream economics. As long as the tropical periphery remains with us, there will be room for venturesome explorers willing to bear the phoenix-spangled banner of development economics. For having recruited us to serve under this multicolored flag, and for bearing it erect against petty and gross tyrants, we are grateful to rebellious Albert O. Hirschman.

Comment

Paul P. Streeten

The princes of Serendip, who did everything badly with fortunate results, are outnumbered by the disciples of the engineer Murphy, for whom anything that can go wrong will go wrong.

—CHARLES P. KINDLEBERGER,
"GOVERNMENT AND INTERNATIONAL TRADE,"
PRINCETON ESSAYS IN INTERNATIONAL FINANCE.

After reading Albert Hirschman's paper I was dazzled by its brilliance and by the unity of so many different ideas. "Only connect" and connect with connections! The world made sense and everything fell into place.

But when the blinding glare of the dazzle fades, there are certain questions one would like to ask. First, there is a systematic asymmetry underlying Hirschman's analysis which he himself expresses in the title of one of his books: *A Bias for Hope*. Things turn out better than we have a right to expect according to a more unbiased analysis. It is, of course, true that unbalanced growth creates incentives for decisions, highlights signals, and mobilizes motivations. If the task is to create pressures for action, unbalanced growth is the way to do it. But surely it also creates opposition, resistances, and counterpressures. Import-substituting industrialization, as we now know, has created very powerful vested interests that resist the change to more outward-looking policies. What is needed is a policy that creates an excess of positive stimuli over negative ones, and this is one argument for balanced growth. Unbalanced growth can be understood as a process or as an objective. It makes better sense as the former, if that excess exists.

In his diagram of antagonistic growth, Hirschman envisages the possibility that we lose something on one axis but gain more on the other, so that the direction is upward. He invited us to put objectives of policy on the two axes. Let these be full employment and price stability. Alas, the path has been downward to the southwest; we now have considerably higher rates of inflation and more unemployment, partly as a result of the

Paul P. Streeten is Professor of Economics and Director of the World Development Institute, Boston University.

expectations and pressures that have built up through stop-go policies, a form of unbalanced growth. Since many countries have succeeded in combining high rates of inflation, high levels of unemployment, and large balance of payments deficits, one would expect, in a symmetrical universe, the reversal of all government policies, like turning a stocking inside out, to produce a combination of all blesssings. But the universe does not seem to be symmetrical.

Take another example. According to the Principle of the Hiding Hand people tend to underestimate the difficulties of the task they set themselves, but unexpected fortunate events that serve as challenges to human creativity can turn disasters or failures into successes. But can there not be also unexpected unfavorable events? The Principle of the Hiding Hand says that the underestimate of the difficulties is offset by the underestimate of our creative responses to these difficulties. But creative responses presuppose that there are opportunities on which to exercise the creativity. (Adam Smith thought that "the over-weening conceit which the greater part of men have of their own abilities, is an ancient evil remarked by the philosophers and moralists of all ages."[1] The San Lorenzo irrigation project in Peru suffered delays, but these were compensated by its learning effects. Because the Aswan High Dam in Egypt prevented the rich sediment of the Nile from being deposited, however, manufactured fertilizer had to replace it, and much of the electricity that was intended to improve the lives of Egyptian peasants was needed to make up for the damage. Could we not design the Principle of the Hiding Fist, which is related to Murphy's law, according to which "if anything can go wrong, it will." When insurance companies thought that paying patients to get a second opinion would reduce unnecessary surgery, the result was more surgery. People who had resisted the knife on one doctor's word were persuaded by two. Reduced latitude may increase incentives to good performance, as in the maintenance of Colombian airplanes, but increased latitude may reduce it. When cars were made more crash resistant, accidents rose because drivers took more chances. When, some years ago, Congress wanted to ensure that the big oil companies did not monopolize crude oil supplies, it set aside crude, at low prices, for small refineries. That produced a boom in tiny, inefficient refineries and a shortage of refinery capacity for unleaded gasoline required by the new cars. In *Shifting Involvements*,[2] Hirschman argues that people require a taste for public activity for its own sake, but he ignores the fact that we may also come to dislike it for its own sake when the intrinsic pleasures disappoint us. And so on.

Hirschman's bias would be justified if it were simply to counterbalance

1. *The Wealth of Nations*, Edwin Cannan, ed. (London: Methuen, 1950), vol. 1, p. 109.
2. *Shifting Involvements: Private Interest and Public Action* (Princeton, N.J.: Princeton University Press, 1982).

biases that normally go the other way. But as a full analysis of what happens, it does seem to me somewhat unbalanced, which of course would recommend it in Hirschman's scheme. Another defense would be that he points only to possibilities, not to necessities or even probabilities. But how illuminating is this? If my aunt had wheels, she would be an omnibus. Is this a useful maxim for a minister of transportation?

Hirschman says that there has been a proliferation of linkages. Indeed, there have been production, consumption, and employment linkages; horizontal and vertical linkages; forward, backward, and lateral linkages; fiscal, foreign trade, and investment/savings linkages; and informational, technical, financial, procurement, locational, managerial, pricing, and other linkages.

But the linkage concept does presuppose a ceilingless economy. Not resources but decisionmaking is the bottleneck. The dispute over whether it is resources or decisions that impede progress underlies much of the controversy about development—indeed, about economic policy. Imagine two missions going to a country to make recommendations about taxation. The first mission believes resources are scarce and decisions will automatically follow the availability of resources. They recommend higher taxation in order to set free the resources for the priority objectives. The other mission believes decisions are the scarce factor and resources will flow as soon as entrepreneurial talent is activated. They recommend reduced taxation, because this would convey the signals and the incentives to the decisionmakers. Which is the right policy depends, of course, partly on the economy in question, but a basic dilemma between resources and incentives, between means and motives, between the will and the way remains. And a Bias for Despair could argue that whenever the will is there, there is no way, and whenever the way is there, there is no will, as in the case of the leaky roof that never gets repaired.

As a more constructive suggestion, I should like to invite Albert Hirschman to apply his notion of unbalanced growth to the interaction between ideas and interests in the history of thought and action. Keynes thought that it was the power of ideas that is, for good and ill, more important than vested interests. Marx thought that it was class interests that determine the superstructure of ideas. It would be consistent with Hirschman's approach to say that there is a continuing interplay between interests and ideas. It might be worth pursuing this interaction in specific areas, such as the controversy over industry versus agriculture, the population problem, or the issue of migration and brain drain. Together with the Bias for Hope this approach would be a counterweight both to those who emphasize ignorance and stupidity as the principal obstacles to progress (like Count Oxenstierna) and to those who stress wickedness, selfishness, or cupidity as the barriers. We might see that progress has been made and that the new problems in the sphere of ideas and of interests are often the result of the successful solution of the first generation of problems.

There is something irresistibly attractive in counterintuitive results. Social scientists thrive on them. But we should not despise truisms simply because they are true. Certainly, the flush of discovery of a new truth often has the appearance of the paradoxical. But in listening to Albert Hirschman, we are sometimes tempted to reflect: "It is paradoxical but nevertheless false."

Sir Arthur Lewis

NOBEL LAUREATE ARTHUR LEWIS was born in Saint Lucia, British West Indies, in 1915. He left school at the age of fourteen, having completed the curriculum, and went to work as a clerk in the civil service. In 1932, when he was old enough to do so, he took the examination for a St. Lucia government scholarship and elected to go to the London School of Economics. He received the Bachelor of Commerce degree in 1937 and a Ph.D. in industrial economics in 1940. Between 1938 and 1948 he served as a lecturer at the London School of Economics before becoming a full professor at the University of Manchester in 1948. At Manchester, he began his systematic research in development economics, and also pursued research in the history of the world economy since 1870.

Since 1957 he has spent nearly as many years in administration as in academic scholarship. During the six years from 1957 to 1963, he was in turn U.N. Economic Adviser to the Prime Minister of Ghana, Deputy Managing Director of the U.N. Special Fund, and Vice-Chancellor of the University of the West Indies. From 1970 to 1974 he was President of the Caribbean Development Bank.

Since 1963, he has been at Princeton University where he occupies the James Madison Chair of Political Economy. In 1978, Sir Arthur was decorated by the Queen of England, and in 1979 he received the Nobel Memorial Prize in Economic Science for his classic work in development economics.

Among his earliest development studies are "An Economic Plan for Jamaica," *Agenda*, vol. 3, no. 4 (November 1944); "Industrialisation of Puerto Rico," *Caribbean Economic Review*, December 1949; *Industrial Development in the Caribbean* (Port-of-Spain, Trinidad: Caribbean Commission, 1949); with others, *Measures for the Economic Development of Under-Developed Countries* (New York: United Nations, 1951); and *Aspects of Industrialisation* (Cairo: National Bank of Egypt, 1953).

His most celebrated works in development economics were written in the mid-1950s: "Economic Development with Unlimited Supplies of Labor," *Manchester School of Economic and Social Studies*, vol. 22, no. 2 (May 1954); and *The Theory of Economic Growth* (London: Allen and Unwin, 1955).

Among his many other books are *Economic Survey, 1919–39* (London: Allen and Unwin, 1949); *The Principles of Economic Planning* (London: Allen and Unwin, 1949); *Politics in West Africa* (London: Allen and Unwin, 1965); *Development Planning: The Essentials of Economic Policy* (London: Allen and Unwin, 1966); *Some Aspects of Economic Development* (Accra: Ghana Publishing Co., 1969); *Aspects of Tropical Trade, 1883–1965* (Stockholm: Almqvist and Wiksell, 1969); *Growth and Fluctuations, 1870–1913* (London: Allen and Unwin, 1978); and *The Evolution of the International Economic Order* (Princeton, N.J.: Princeton University Press, 1978).

From some fifty articles, the following may be specially cited: "World Production, Prices and Trade, 1870–1960," *Manchester School*, vol. 20, no. 2 (1952); "International Competition in Manufactures," *American Economic Review*, vol. 47, no. 2 (1957); "Unlimited Labour: Further Notes," *Manchester School*, vol. 26, no. 1 (1958); "Employment Policy in an Underdeveloped Area," *Social and Economic Studies*, vol. 7, no. 3 (1958); "On Assessing a Development Plan," *Economic Bulletin of Ghana*, vol. 3, nos. 6–7 (1959); "A Review of Economic Development," *American Economic Review*, vol. 55, no. 2 (1965); "The Dual Economy Revisited," *Manchester School*, vol. 47, no. 3 (1979); and "The Slowing Down of the Engine of Growth" (Nobel Lecture), *American Economic Review*, vol. 70, no. 4 (1980).

Development Economics in the 1950s

THE MANDATE GIVEN TO ME is to advertise myself; to recall what I was thinking about in the 1950s and how things have turned out. This has its attractions since some of my earlier books are still in print and could do with such a boost, but I have resisted this temptation. I have chosen instead to write a brief sketch of the problems with which development economists were then wrestling, with only occasional references to my own part. I have also narrowed the agenda to the two major obsessions of the day: what is the appropriate size of the industrial sector, and how is modernization to be financed.[1]

Industrialization

What limits the size of the manufacturing sector? The preliminary answer—the productivity of the farmers whose marketable surplus will exchange for manufactures—has been in our literature a long time, since it was provided by Sir James Steuart.[2] In Adam Smith this proposition became the key to understanding what he called "The Natural Progress of Opulence"—what we would call today "development economics." Adam Smith added an escape clause. If the farmers' surplus was small, the expansion of industry might still be supported by exporting manufactures.[3]

These propositions were not known, or if known not usually understood, in 1950, so the question was debated interminably by the supporters of industry and the supporters of agriculture. I supported both. As I put it in 1949, writing on industrialization of the British West Indies, "A poor people spends a very high proportion of its income on food and shelter,

1. The most important topics excluded are models of historical change, like those of W. W. Rostow, and the quantitative study of sectoral changes associated with development led by Colin Clark, Simon Kuznets, and Hollis Chenery.

2. Sir James Steuart, *An Enquiry into the Principles of Political Economy*, Bk. I, chaps. 8 and 20.

3. Adam Smith, *The Wealth of Nations*, Bk. III, chap. 1.

and only a small proportion on manufactures. At their present low standard of living, the number of persons for whom West Indians can provide
employment in manufacturing by their own purchases is extremely
small."[4] I took it for granted that overpopulated countries like the West
Indies or India could not feed themselves over the next twenty-five years,
and would have to import food and raw materials and export
manufactures.[5] But in writing about the Gold Coast I laid emphasis on the
need for an agricultural policy that would have equal priority with import
substitution.[6]

The agricultural option is really two options: to export or to produce for
the home market.[7] Hence three strategies are available for supporting
industrialization: (1) to export more agricultural commodities (or minerals, which I shall not pursue); (2) to develop a self-sufficient economy,
emphasizing the home market; or (3) to export manufactures. All three
strategies imply vigorous industrial and agricultural policies. They differ
only in their foreign exchange requirements and yields.

In theory, there is no need to choose between these strategies, since each
must be taken to the margin of advantage. Appropriate data for a development plan matrix, if such data existed, would optimize the allocation of
resources between domestic and foreign trade. But in addition to the
unavailability of data and the crucial guesswork as to the future, it
happens that each of these strategies develops in practice its own momentum, institutions, power structure, infrastructure, and outlook, so that one
or another tends to dominate decisionmaking. Even if there were not real
economic forces pushing this way, economic philosophers tend to become
emotionally wedded to one or another of these strategies, and to emphasize all the arguments against the other two.

So it came about that most of what was said in the 1950s about
development strategy defended or attacked one of these three strategies,
and I shall use them as the framework of my comment.

Agricultural Exports

Let me begin with the strategy based on exporting agricultural products.
The high emotional content of this discussion is well known. Myint[8]
originates the argument in Adam Smith's "vent for surplus," and we can

4. "The Industrialisation of the British West Indies," *Caribbean Economic Review*
(May 1950), para. 50.

5. W. A. Lewis, *The Theory of Economic Growth* (London: Allen and Unwin,
1955), pp. 329, 351–52.

6. *Report on Industrialisation and the Gold Coast* (Accra: Government Printing
Department, 1953).

7. The same good may be produced both for export and for domestic consumption;
for example, rice in Burma.

8. H. Myint, "The Classical Theory of International Trade and the Underdeveloped
Countries," *Economic Journal* (June 1958).

finger several cases that fit his model—Burma, Thailand, Gold Coast, Uganda, and others. Whether exports are an engine of growth or a handmaiden is of no significance. If the growth of industrial production for the home market is raising imports, then more exports will be needed. Alternatively, if agricultural exports are rising, any trade multiplier in excess of unity will stimulate industrial production for the home market. The historian wishes to know which came first; the economist is concerned that they henceforth match each other.

In the 1950s two arguments were developed against the agricultural export strategy: the terms of trade argument and the dependency argument. The terms of trade argument was in two parts, one historical and one theoretical. The historical argument was that since the commodity terms of trade have had a long-term bias against agriculture, primary production should be avoided. I never subscribed to this position. In *Economic Survey*, published in 1949, I said

> In the past hundred years primary production has not failed to respond to the growth of manufactures; and if the economies of Asia are fructified by an influx of knowledge and of capital, which will stimulate both their manufactures and their primary production, there is no *a priori* reason to expect these two to grow at incompatible rates.[9]

Throughout most of this argument the data used related to U.K. prices, whether of manufactures or of primary products. My contribution was to construct an index of the prices of tropical products and an index of the prices of manufactures. These indexes showed that the terms of trade were more or less constant between 1870 and 1927, fell off during the Great Depression, and were back at the same level in the 1950s. But this index was not published until 1969.[10]

The theoretical argument is different from the historical. Whatever may have happened in the past, if primary producers develop their exports faster than the industrial countries demand, then the terms of trade must move against them. I spent some time trying to figure out what rate of growth of trade in primary products would leave the terms of trade unchanged in long-run equilibrium. Ultimately I settled for a rate of 85 percent (plus or minus) of the growth of industrial production in countries in the Organisation for Economic Co-operation and Development (OECD).[11] Neisser and Modigliani and Polak were on the same track.[12]

9. W. A. Lewis, *Economic Survey* (London: Allen and Unwin, 1949), p. 197.

10. W. A. Lewis, *Aspects of Tropical Trade, 1883–1965* (Stockholm: Almqvist and Wiksell, 1969).

11. W. A. Lewis, "World Production, Prices and Trade," *Manchester School of Economic and Social Studies* (May 1952).

12. Hans Neisser and Franco Modigliani, *National Incomes and International Trade* (Urbana, Ill.: University of Illinois Press, 1953); J. S. Polak, *An International Economic System* (London: Allen and Unwin, 1954).

That is a short-term answer. In a 1954 article[13] I argue that in the long run in the less developed countries (LDCs) it is the factoral terms of trade that determine the commodity terms, and not the other way around. The factoral terms have moved continually against the LDCs since the beginning of the nineteenth century. The basic way to stop this is continually to raise the productivity of LDC farmers producing for the domestic market, thereby increasing the supply price of export crops.

The dependency argument is not like the usual arguments against imports, which turn on the difference between money costs and real costs, but is primarily about power and its cumulative accretion. Here is a brief summary. A peripheral country that begins to export agricultural commodities becomes paralyzed in ways that preclude an industrial takeoff. Its trade and all that goes with it—shipping, banking, insurance, port facilities—fall into the hands of a few foreigners, with or without association with a few rich local families. The profits of this trade are transferred overseas instead of being invested in the country. The best jobs are reserved to foreigners, so that local talent is untrained and unable either to compete in the old trades or to start new ones. The talented young become frustrated, lose confidence in their abilities, emigrate, or lower their horizons. Domestic industries are destroyed by imports. The foreign companies are interested in foreign trade and, if they can, will block attempts to create new industries that might diminish their trade or render it more costly. Mass advertising teaches the people to prefer imported consumer goods to their own products, thereby raising the propensity to import foreign brands or materials or machinery in place of local resources. This trend imperils the balance of payments, makes it harder to provide jobs, and pushes displaced workers back into the subsistence sector.[14]

This is a reasonable description of what was happening in most tropical colonies in the first half of the twentieth century, though it exaggerates the share accruing overseas, and underplays the superior investment in schools and other services in the colonies with highest exports per head. But it is not clear why independent countries should fall into such a trap. Thus, it is not a good description of Brazil, around 1880, which had already begun to build its own industrial bourgeoisie; or of Argentina, which was bossed by its great landowners rather than by foreign capitalists; or of the countries of Southern and Eastern Europe, whose stagnation through the nineteenth century is as much a puzzle for development analysts as is the history of Mexico.

For these reasons, my book of 1955 admitted the validity of elements of

13. "Economic Development with Unlimited Supplies of Labour," *Manchester School of Economic and Social Studies* (May 1954).

14. This is a composite of many different writers. The leader of the dependency school is André Gunder Frank; see, for example, his *Capitalism and Underdevelopment in Latin America* (New York: Monthly Review Press, 1967).

dependency theory, but limited its value; and my piece for the International Economic Association conference of 1962, though warmer, was equally restrictive.[15] The dependency theory seemed to me to be important for the study of the second half of the nineteenth century, but not the second half of the twentieth century when independent governments were engaged in restructuring the place of foreigners in the country. As a contribution to deciding whether the small farmers should be encouraged to plant more tea or rubber, it seemed to me unhelpful.

Dependency belongs to a class of arguments that rejects the economists' usual objective, the maximization of output at prices equal to marginal costs. In dependency one seeks instead fast independent growth. In this class also belongs a preference for one set of institutions rather than another (for example, family farms as opposed to plantations) which will yield different outputs and prices. A basic needs strategy may also be in this class. Hanging over all is the problem that, since prices reflect the original and intervening distribution of resources, one can get several Pareto optimal price and allocation "solutions," no one of which is superior to all others. This is bad enough where the population is homogeneous in religion, race, language, and tribe; in plural societies ministers choose between one technology and another, one geographical layout and another, or one objective and another in terms of the demographic characteristics of gainers and losers, and may be doing so without malice in order to maintain national unity. Our welfare economics does not yield "scientific" solutions, but is rather a branch of Western political philosophy. Plural societies must develop their own system of evaluation.

Import Substitution

Let me set this aside, as most economists do, and come back to the fold. Apart from doubting the effects of exporting primary products, development economists were happily engaged in their traditional occupation of showing why, if not controlled, imports will be excessive.

One of the traditional arguments turns on money cost, as reflected by the market, not being the same as real cost. Manoilescu had spelled this out in 1931, with his claim that wages are always higher in manufacturing than in agriculture and therefore exaggerate the real cost of manufacturing. Around this we built the case of unemployment created by success. Take an export industry such as bauxite in Jamaica that can afford to pay wages three or more times higher than the rest. Wages in that industry pull up wages in all other industries beyond what they can pay. The success of this industry is therefore paralleled by even greater unemployment else-

15. *The Theory of Economic Growth*, pp. 347–50; and "Economic Development and World Trade," in E. A. G. Robinson, ed., *Problems in Economic Development* (London, Macmillan, 1965).

where, but there is no shortage of foreign exchange and so no pressure to devalue. I articulated this argument for Jamaica in 1964; Dudley Seers at about the same time reached a similar conclusion for Venezuela, using a wages fund approach.[16] But not much notice was taken of us until the Netherlands began to experience the same phenomenon. Nowadays it is known as the Dutch disease, and its Europeanization has raised its academic standing. This line of analysis leads to shadow prices and benefit-cost analysis—a treacherous swamp, but unavoidable if one is to make decisions involving international trade.

In addition to arguments involving shadow pricing, development economists rounded out the arguments involving time (the learning factor), scale, externalities, or complementary (networks). These arguments were already in the theory books, though normally ignored in analytical casework. Two more fundamental objections were also uncovered, one relating to resource mobility and the other to the inelasticity of export earnings.

The framework of international trade theory is that commodities may move across frontiers and therefore have everywhere the same price (excluding transport costs), whereas resources—labor, land, and capital—cannot cross frontiers and have different prices. If one is talking about the sugar industry in the late 1920s, which was dependent on migrant labor and foreign capital, the theory of international trade is hardly relevant. Capital will move to equalize its marginal productivities everywhere, and so will labor; as a result, submarginal countries will have no population. When making policy recommendations for the Ivory Coast, does one include the migrants from Upper Volta in the group whose income is to be maximized or treat them as an input at predetermined prices? The point is specially relevant when one is talking about customs unions, common markets, and optimal currency areas. When British economists were asked whether they favored joining the Common Market, half said yes and talked about the law of comparative cost. The other half said no and trembled at the possibility that British skilled labor, capital, and entrepreneurship would migrate to the continent, leaving the island in stagnation. Whose welfare is to be maximized?

The relevance of migration is enhanced by the phenomenon of the "growth pole," also elaborated by development economists, including Myrdal and Hirschman.[17] This refers to the tendency for people to mass in great urban concentrations, seldom exceeding 1 million before this century, but now up to as many as 13 million, well beyond the margin where the gain from geographical propinquity exceeds the cost of congestion. If

16. *Jamaica's Economic Problems* (Kingston, Jamaica: Gleaner Co., 1964). Dudley Seers, "The Mechanism of an Open Petroleum Economy," *Social and Economic Studies*, vol. 13, no. 2 (June 1964).

17. A. O. Hirschman, *The Strategy of Economic Development* (New Haven: Yale University Press, 1958); and Gunnar Myrdal, *Economic Theory and Underdeveloped Regions* (London: G. Duckworth, 1957).

we wish to assess the effects of forming a customs union we have to ask where the growth poles are, and in what directions populations will flow. Comparative cost is then a minor element in the story. Much of the disillusionment with customs unions over the past thirty years comes from applying the wrong theories: foreign trade theory instead of location theory.

The case of inelastic export earnings was also opened up in the 1950s. International trade theory assumes that a country can always earn more foreign exchange by exporting more commodities or services. It is, however, logically possible for a country to have difficulty in earning more, whether because of barriers to its trade, low elasticities of supply, or low elasticities of demand for its products; or because its wage level is so tightly secured to its cost of living that devaluation raises costs in the same proportion. This opens up a number of possibilities:

- The two-gap model, worked on especially by Chenery,[18] in which extra saving cannot be converted into imports of capital goods and is therefore frustrated.
- Structural inflation, a concept introduced to Anglophones by Dudley Seers,[19] in which the marginal propensity to import exceeds the marginal propensity to export. Originally a Latin American export, this argument was discounted by OECD spokesmen until the British adopted it to explain their own stop-go system; so now it is included in the canon.
- Balanced growth, which we owe to Rosenstein-Rodan.[20] If imports and exports cannot be increased, production must follow a balanced growth path. This would be facilitated by issuing indicative plans and by small countries joining into customs unions within which large-scale industries might be operated more efficiently.

The logic of these three models seemed to me unchallengeable, and I was never involved in the huge critical literature that emerged. Most of this ignored the basic assumption and was unhelpful, except for Hirschman's stimulating treatise on the forces that convert imports into import substitutes.[21] I did become involved with the Rosenstein-Rodan recommendations, especially the making of indicative plans and the creation of customs unions.[22] But neither of these movements has been as successful as

18. For the model in operation, see H. B. Chenery and Peter Eckstein, "Alternative Policies for Latin America," *Journal of Political Economy* (July 1970), pt. 2.

19. Dudley Seers, "A Theory of Inflation and Growth," *Oxford Economic Papers* (June 1962).

20. P. N. Rosenstein-Rodan, "Problems of Industrialization of Eastern and South-Eastern Europe," *Economic Journal*, vol. 53 (June–September 1943).

21. Hirschman, *The Strategy of Economic Development*.

22. After a number of field experiences, I wrote a book on making indicative plans: *Development Planning* (London: Allen and Unwin, 1966). My 1950 piece, "The Industrialisation of the British West Indies," included the case for a customs union.

we had hoped, partly because the difficulty of earning foreign exchange, from which the models were derived, turned out to be not as great as we had feared; and partly because the planners were slow in learning that market prices are more powerful incentives than ministerial speeches.

Self-sufficiency

Self-sufficiency is the part of the import substitution strategy that relates to food production for the domestic market. Once one has grasped the point that agriculture and industry provide markets for each other's output, theoretical dispute ceases. Practical planning is more difficult. We do not know exactly how much to spend to set food production on a 3 percent or a 4 percent growth path. We do know that expansion of the extension system and the rest of the agricultural package takes time and runs into its own administrative bottlenecks. So we choose a program that seems administratively viable as well as reasonably effective for the money.

The principal reason for our limited success on this front has been that, with exceptions, the developing countries did not wake up to the importance of agriculture until rising food deficits began to produce rising foreign exchange bills. Economists on the whole are not to blame for this. Nothing was more popular with us in the 1950s than land reform, on grounds both of equity and of expected effect on output. (I wrote two articles on this subject.[23]) The Third World's failure with agriculture has been mainly at the political level, in systems where the small cultivator carries little political weight.

The agricultural problem is not simple, however. The wet tropics is capable of having its food production grow at 4 percent a year over the next thirty years, but we do not know how to average even 2 percent a year over that period in the dry tropics. At least 500 million people live on the fringes of the great Asian and African deserts, where rainfall is either inadequate or uncertain. This is one of the reasons for the wide spread of LDC growth rates and of LDC per capita incomes. These gaps will widen until the agronomists make a major breakthrough in tropical dry farming.

Exporting Manufactures

The last option is to export manufactures. This is the obvious strategy for countries that are overpopulated, and several of us were saying this from the 1940s onward. But the current expansion did not come from this.

23. "Issues in Land Settlement Policy," *Caribbean Economic Review* (October 1951); and "Thoughts on Land Settlement," *Journal of Agricultural Economics* (June 1954).

It followed upon import substitution. The backlog permitted manufacturing for the home market to grow by as much as 7 to 10 percent a year for a couple of decades, after which it was exhausted, and fast industrialization could then be sustained only by exporting manufactures. This was like the breaking of a spell. For over a century tropical peoples had been told that manufacturing industry was unsuitable for their countries, and that their comparative advantage lay in exporting agricultural commodities. Then suddenly they were selling manufactures in the markets of developed countries, and the leaders of these developed countries were running around in a panic and adopting special discriminatory measures to keep out LDC manufactures. It involved a spiritual revolution as great as that experienced by economists over the age of thirty who were converted to Keynesianism in 1936.

One aspect of the export of manufactures that causes pain is its dependence on foreign entrepreneurship. LDCs manage without multinational corporations in agriculture, public utilities, banking, and wholesaling, in which they were concentrated before 1950, and from which they are now disappearing. In manufacturing, multinationals contribute high technology to industries where technology is changing rapidly, but these are of interest only to the more sophisticated LDCs. For standard items such as shoes or cement the technology is available to all, and factories can be purchased off the rack. More widely significant is that multinational corporations frequently also contribute access to markets. These may be domestic markets that they have been supplying with imports. Where multinationals tend to be indispensable is in initiating exports of manufactures to other markets in which they are already established. Domestic entrepreneurs learn how to sell manufactures overseas, but foreigners usually take the first steps.

I have never felt that LDCs should hold back the diversification of their manufacturing sectors from fear of multinationals, since in independent countries they operate on the country's terms or not at all. The most important control is the use of work permits to force the firms to hire and train local recruits at managerial and professional levels. I have received much criticism for this stand over the past thirty years, but the heat seems to be diminishing as Third World governments gain confidence in their own bargaining skills.

The future of the option to export manufactures cannot be predicted. World trade in manufactures could not grow indefinitely at 10 percent a year when world production of manufactures was growing at only 5 to 6 percent a year. The behavior of the developed countries is also not predictable; their attitude toward free trade in manufactures will be affected by whether they return to fast growth of GDP. Third World exports to each other are just beginning to take off; they will presumably grow fast if the industrial countries are protectionist, and less fast if the industrial countries maintain an open door.

Finance

In the 1950s we were obsessed not only by the appropriate size of the industrial sector but also by how modernization was to be financed. This second obsession was widely but not universally dominant. The approach of many older economists was that the world's capital is scarce and should be invested where it would be most profitable. If that turned out to be the rich countries, then so much the worse for the poor countries. Other economists thought that the amount of capital required would not prove to be a problem because the absorptive capacity would prove to be small—even Myrdal touted the low absorptive capacity. Eugene Black told a U.N. delegation of which I was a member, in 1951, that the maximum amount the Third World could absorb in Bank lending would be $250 million a year. I never took any of this capacity talk seriously because my mother had brought me up to believe that anything they can do we can do. This is not a scientific proposition, but it turned out to be true, since by 1960 the capacity of LDCs to absorb capital fruitfully was being demonstrated by their low capital-output ratios.

Capital Intensity

We were much concerned about the economical use of capital, which sprouted a large literature in the first half of the 1950s. A famous article by Galenson and Leibenstein[24] invited us to choose capital-intensive strategies, as did P. C. Mahalanobis in expounding his plan framework for India. But most economists rejected their reasoning, preferring the analysis and conclusions of neoclassical shadow prices. The Indian government put a lot of resources into modernizing small-scale workshop and handicraft production. My 1955 book has several pages on the subject. We did not espouse the extremist position of Schumacher,[25] but most of us desired new and more appropriate technologies to be devised and utilized.

This discussion involved setting the present against the future. Should we adopt policies which would hold down mass consumption now in favor of a faster rate of growth of output, or should we have more consumption now and not so large an increase a decade later? The appendix to my 1955 book argued the case for moderation. The popular view today that the economists of the 1950s did not care about distribution is wide of the mark. As I mentioned before, we were all in favor of land reform, for reasons of equity as well as output. As for the urban worker, I wrote in 1955:

24. W. Galenson and H. Leibenstein, "Investment Criteria, Productivity and Economic Development," *Quarterly Journal of Economics* (August 1955).
25. E. F. Schumacher, *Small Is Beautiful* (New York: Harper and Row, 1973).

Neither is there any excuse for not developing a proper range of social services—medical services, unemployment pay, pensions and the like—in the absence of which the industrial worker is forced to keep one foot in the village so that he can return to it in case of need. The effect would be a healthier labour force, more settled, and more anxious for improvement on the job. These things cost more, but they also pay off in extra productivity, as well as in human happiness.[26]

My concern in those days was not with the amount of money paid to urban workers, which I assumed would be directly related to the productivity of the small farmers, but rather with the social wage, especially education, health services, water supplies, workmen's compensation, unemployment pay, pensions, and such. This network of social provision seemed to me, as a social democrat, to be one of the best products of the past hundred years. Now as then I single out education, about which I wrote in 1955 in the course of a thirty-five page chapter on "Knowledge," which was probing for priorities: "The difficulty education raises is that it is both a consumer and an investment service. In so far as it is an investment, it contributes directly towards increasing output."[27] I followed this up with three articles and a section in my book, *Development Planning*.[28] But I did not get into the mainstream of the enormous literature initiated by Gary Becker in 1964. This was because whatever value the econometric exercises may have in measuring the private rate of return, they are quite misleading as measurements of the social rate of return, especially in developing countries. The line I was following led instead to manpower budgeting, a less controversial subject, but what the ministry has to use in the end, despite its weaknesses.

Sources of Finance

The government was going to need a lot of money, given the cost of the social programs and its contribution to financing capital formation. In 1956, along with Alison Martin,[29] I started a line of inquiry to establish norms of government revenue and expenditure. This stimulated a string of articles by other writers. In the hands of the staff of the International Monetary Fund, the subject metamorphosed into a test of how much revenue one could reasonably expect governments to raise, given the different structures of their economies; and this looked as if it might even

26. *The Theory of Economic Growth*, pp. 193–94.
27. Ibid., p. 183.
28. The articles were: "Education and Economic Development," *Social and Economic Studies*, vol. 10, no. 2 (1961); "Education for Scientific Professions in the Poor Countries," *Daedalus*, vol. 91, no. 2 (1962); and "Secondary Education and Economic Structure," *Social and Economic Studies*, vol. 13, no. 2 (1964).
29. "Patterns of Public Revenue and Expenditure," *Manchester School of Economic and Social Studies*, vol. 24, no. 3 (1956).

become one of the elements determining how much assistance a country deserved to receive.

Taken as a group, governments of less developed countries (LDCs) have, in fact, passed reasonable tests. There are four times as many children in school as there were in 1950. The infant mortality rate has fallen by three-quarters. The multiplication of hospital beds, village water pipes, all-season village roads, and other mass services is faster than at any period in the history of the countries now developed. Much of the disillusionment with the results of the past three decades originates with people who do not understand the importance of the social wage, who have no idea what the conditions of the masses were like in 1950, or who have forgotten the extent to which LDC peoples live in semi-arid lands for which we have yet to make the technological breakthrough.

In the event, part of the answer to where money for capital formation is to come from is taxation. LDC governments need to have surpluses of current revenue plus public enterprise profits over current expenditures, and do in fact have substantial surpluses. But the bulk of the finance, even with foreign aid, has to come from increases in private domestic saving. The problem was to elucidate how this comes about.

How had it come about in the nineteenth century? For Europe it was from a rising share of profits in the national income. And what caused this rise in the share of profits? Neoclassical economics was no help. Keynes's model provided for the profits share to rise in the cyclical upswing. The evidence showed, however, that profits share and the savings share were more or less constant in the long run after 1870, in both Britain and the United States. What we were getting from the neoclassicists, whether Duesenberry or Friedman or Modigliani, were demonstrations of how to combine long-run savings constancy with short-run savings volatility. This was of no use to us, since what we were trying to understand was a long-term rise in the savings propensity.

As I was walking down a road in Bangkok one morning in August 1952, it suddenly occurred to me that all one needed to do was to drop the assumption—then usually (but not necessarily) made by neoclassical macroeconomists—that the supply of labor was fixed. Assume instead that it was infinitely elastic, add that productivity was increasing in the capitalist sector, and one got a rising profits share. It also occurred to me that this model would solve another problem that had bothered me since undergraduate days: what determined the relative prices of steel and coffee? I had been taught that marginal utility was the answer to this question, but this answer made no sense to me. If, however, one assumed an infinite elasticity of labor in terms of food to the coffee industry, and an infinite elasticity also in terms of food to the steel industry, then the factoral terms of trade between steel and coffee were fixed, and marginal utility was out the window.

So in three minutes I had solved two of my problems with one change of assumptions. Writing this up would take four articles from me, and further exploration by Fei and Ranis and others.[30] The thing became for a time a growth industry, with a stream of articles expounding, attacking, testing, revising, denouncing, or approving. The upshot seems to be that the model is illuminating in some places at some times, but not in other places or other times. This was said when it was first presented.

What was the basis of near infinite elasticity? Critics fastened on disguised unemployment among small farmers in a half-dozen overpopulated countries, but this was only one item in a long catalog covering four pages of the first article. Other items were: technological unemployment, which Marx thought powerful enough by itself to create a growing labor surplus; underemployment in urban areas, in what has now come to be called the informal sector; the movement of women from the household into the labor market; and the increase of population. This last turned out to be the dominant factor. With population growing at 3 percent a year, the supply of labor could not be other than very highly elastic.

Population deserves more than a mention. I think the biggest mistake development economists were making in the 1950s was to underestimate the likely growth of population. We expected it to average 1.5 percent. That the death rate might drop by 10 to 15 points per thousand over the next ten years never entered our heads.

Rapid population growth was a blow to development in LDCs in ways that I enumerate, but do not need to elaborate. It aggravated the food problem, already acute in the semi-arid lands. It put stress on the balance of payments. In countries already overpopulated, it reduced the savings potential. It led to rapid urbanization, which is extremely expensive in terms of infrastructure.

Rapid population growth also made the problem of urban unemployment insoluble. This first struck me in Ghana in 1954. I wrote about it in 1957, saying:

> [Urban unemployment] is also due partly to the growing wage gap itself, which by raising the level of those who have employment in the towns, attracts more and more people to come into these towns. It is very difficult to know how to cope with this increase in urban unemployment. The normal way to cope with unemployment is to provide work, but this is no solution in this case. On the contrary, it merely aggravates the problem, because the more work you provide in the towns, the more people will drift into the towns, and there is no certainty that you can

---

30. Interest was greatly stimulated by an article by Gustav Ranis and John Fei, formalizing various aspects of the model, and by their book, *The Development of the Labor Surplus Economy* (Homewood, Ill.: Richard D. Irwin, 1964).

win the race ... No one ought to say that he knows how to cure unemployment in this situation.[31]

This problem still remains without solution, except insofar as the solution is to make more jobs in the countryside. Todaro's model[32] and the subsequent literature on migration and the labor markets are illuminating, but we need clearer links between growth poles and migration, and we also need to hear more from the sociologists and the historians about why people move, other than for wage differentials.

Now let me come back to my question: where had the money come from to pay for modernization in the past? The short answer was that profits had risen relative to the national income, because productivity had risen faster than wages. I was frequently attacked for recommending this change in income distribution, but I was not making recommendations; I was trying to understand, not to prescribe. This was not specifically a capitalist answer, since the same answer could be reached for the U.S.S.R., with the profits of the state firms and the turnover tax performing the same function as the sources of increasing savings.

Inflation

Ragnar Nurkse opened the door to what looked at first like a painless solution: use surplus labor for capital formation. A great deal of construction can be done with minimal equipment: building roads, bridges, irrigation channels, terraces, anti-erosion barriers, and so on. The meaning of surplus labor gave rise to an unhelpful literature. Nurkse believed that one could mobilize people for capital works at certain times of the year without reducing other output significantly. Both the works and the people would be rural. It was obvious that one could do this in the six months of the agricultural off-season, and obvious that one could not do it during the four weeks of harvesting. Argument centered on whether in some parts of India the labor force in agriculture could be reduced by as much as 5 percent of the farmers of five acres or less, without a significant fall in total output. Why this became the issue is not clear, since those schemes in practice are timed to complement the agricultural season and not to compete with it.

By definition, surplus labor could be used without reducing other output significantly, especially during the long agricultural off-season. It was therefore costless in real terms. We had great hopes in the 1950s for the

31. "Employment Policy in an Underdeveloped Area," *Social and Economic Studies*, vol. 7, no. 3 (1958); and "Unemployment in Developing Countries," *The World Today*, vol. 23, no. 1 (1967).

32. M. P. Todaro, "A Model of Labor Migration and Urban Unemployment in Less Developed Countries," *American Economic Review*, vol. 59 (1969).

community development movement using unpaid labor, and some governments made a go of it, but enthusiasm usually petered out. Labor has to be
paid whether it is in surplus or not.

Since the use of surplus labor results in increased output, one is tempted
to bring this about by increasing the money supply. How much inflation
this would cause must be analyzed at two levels. At the primary level the
amount of inflation would depend on what the surplus labor was used for.
If it was used productively, say, to dig irrigation channels and thereby
increase the output of mass consumer goods, we would be matching extra
money with extra consumer goods, and the inflation would be damped. If,
however, the money was used to pay soldiers or civil servants, without
increasing the output of consumer goods, we would get the full blast of
inflation.

The secondary level is the reaction to the inflation created at the first
level. The money spent there enters into circulation and turns up as extra
incomes for various groups of people. If those who gain invest the proceeds productively, we get a secondary round of additional capital formation. If not, they consume more and others consume less. Whether the
gainers can retain their gains depends also on the simple-mindedness or
powerlessness of the people who lose. If the losers are able to insulate
themselves against inflation—for example, by having their wages and their
lendings indexed—then the propensity to save would not be changed.

Most of the debate on inflation is about what happens at the secondary
level, and it ignores the fact that the primary objective of spending is
attained whatever the secondary consequences may be. Putting the primary and the secondary levels together offers four corner choices. In one
corner is productive primary use plus an increased propensity to save, and
the resultant inflation is damped. In the opposite corner is wasteful primary expenditure and zero addition to saving, so inflation is maximized. I
entered the 1950s standing firmly in the first corner, but quit the 1950s
disillusioned into expecting only the opposite extreme. That is to say, I was
hopeful in 1950 that a country like India could launch a big program of
land improvement and would not be deterred from this merely because it
might raise the price level by 3 percent a year. There was some such
program, especially for irrigation, but it was not big enough. Instead, the
continent where inflation raged was Latin America, where neither the
primary nor the secondary phases contributed significantly to capital
formation, since "rational expectations" by now prevailed. As I put it to
the Rio Conference on Inflation and Growth in Latin America in 1963:

A big inflation cannot go on for long without turning into spiral inflation, because in a big inflation everybody soon gets the point, and learns
to protect himself by demanding higher money income. In this sense, by
having prolonged large spiral inflations, which have achieved nothing,

Latin America has already wasted her inflationary potential, and barred herself from turning now to useful self-liquidating inflations.[33]

The Rio conference was more widely concerned with the connection between monetary equilibrium and balance of payments equilibrium—a topic about which Latin American economists had been fighting with the IMF throughout the 1950s. In the 1960s developed countries began to have the same problems with Bretton Woods as the LDCs, and by the 1970s were using essentially the same language that had originated in Latin America. The subject now has an enormous bibliography.[34]

Foreign Aid

The economists of the 1950s sought answers to three questions. The first was: why did LDCs need foreign aid when the countries now developed had not needed it? Some of our answers have survived less well than others.

We used to talk about the need for a big push, and about the low-level equilibrium trap, but have fallen silent about these.

We used to point out that the industrial countries had all been borrowers at some point—even Britain in the eighteenth century and the United States in the nineteenth. But these were small amounts.

We produced the two-gap model to show why countries may be forced to save less than they would like to, but this was hard to square with the buoyancy of world trade in the 1950s and 1960s.

We noted that LDCs were growing about twice as fast as European countries grew in the nineteenth century—partly because of the population explosion—and therefore needed higher investment ratios.

Finally, we made the point that LDCs are also urbanizing more than twice as fast as was Western Europe around 1900, and this is an expensive process.

The second question that worried us was: who should get foreign aid? The question was not asked of bilateral aid, which was distributed on political lines. But there were already sizable multilateral programs, and the LDCs kept asking the General Assembly to establish a large U.N. concessional fund. What would be the basis for distributing such a fund?

There were many candidates. Rosenstein-Rodan published a list emphasizing absorptive capacity.[35] The Alliance for Progress was to emphasize good performance in social and economic policies. I emphasized good

---

33. "Closing Remarks," in W. Baer and I. Kerstenetzky, eds., *Inflation and Growth in Latin America* (Homewood, Ill.: Richard D. Irwin, 1964), pp. 31–32.

34. My small contribution to this was historical. "The LDCs and Stable Exchange Rates," Per Jacobsson Lecture, in IMF, *The International Monetary System in Operation* (Washington, D.C., 1977).

35. P. N. Rosenstein-Rodan, "International Aid for Underdeveloped Countries," *Review of Economics and Statistics* (May 1961).

performance in raising the share of saving and taxes in national income.[36] Chenery emphasized balance of payments needs, especially where reflected in two-gap disabilities. In the end, the prize went to distribution on the basis of poverty, giving proportionately more to the poorer countries. The U.N. made a list of the twenty-five least developed countries and asked bilateral as well as multilateral donors to give priority to them. This basis of choice runs the highest risk of waste, but may also be the most worthwhile.

The third question we asked ourselves was how to prove to the rich countries that they would benefit economically by giving to the poor. We have the theoretical tools for tackling this subject—economies of scale, external economies, the terms of trade, comparative cost, growth poles—but since the answer yielded by our tools is that the result may go either way, we cannot reach a conclusion without collecting a lot of data, measuring a lot of elasticities, and guessing a number of possibilities. So this question remains in the sphere of problems to which there is no satisfactory solution at the level of economic analysis. For my part, the maxim that the rich should help the poor suffices, but it is not an economic theorem.

Conclusion

Let me wind up on finance. My overwhelming impression is that the LDCs have done much better by their own efforts than we had considered likely. Both domestic saving and government revenue have risen to the point that the median share of private consumption in national income has fallen by about ten percentage points over twenty years. This is an achievement on which a country should be congratulated, as should the economists who have pushed in this direction.

The performance is of course mixed. When one lists the factors that cause countries to be at the bottom of the growth list, political instability is prominent; countries grow fastest whose citizens think it safe to save and invest at home. We underestimated this factor in the 1950s. It will probably cease to be so common as the new sovereignties created since the Second World War acquire experience and legitimacy. We also overestimated the likely efficiency of new governments and their commitment to improving the conditions of the poor (which varies widely).

Meanwhile, all LDCs are menaced since 1973 by the international recession, by rising protectionism in the industrial countries, by the high price of oil, and by the enormous debt this has created. These disasters are beyond their control and call for special measures by the whole international community. But the viability of LDCs in normal times, like the 1950s and the 1960s, is now beyond all doubt.

36. "A Review of Economic Development," Richard T. Ely Lecture, *American Economic Review* (May 1965).

Comment

Arnold C. Harberger

PROFESSOR LEWIS has given us a pleasantly wistful and nostalgic tour of development economics in the 1950s, in which are blended many of those nuggets of insight and wisdom for which he is justly famous. The juxtaposition of these two elements enlivens the task I face in commenting on his work.

The nostalgic parts appear to me as being exactly that—these parts invite, indeed virtually demand, a juxtaposition of the approaches and views that were popular in the 1950s with those that are now more current. The emphasis here would be on the evolution of ideas—how fads that attract a lot of attention in an earlier era tend to evaporate, even almost disappear through the erosion of time; and how small seeds, barely noticeable in the earlier period, sprout massive progeny that end up occupying important places in the intellectual vista of a later time.

The nuggets of wisdom are quite the opposite; they render insights and observations that, while not necessarily timeless in a philosophical sense, at least do not appear to be bound to any narrow time dimension within our span of evidence and observation.

In what follows I shall try to explore the interplay of these two quite distinct elements in each main part of Arthur Lewis's paper.

Industrialization

In introducing this topic, Professor Lewis outlines three strategies for supporting industrialization: more agricultural exports, a self-sufficient economy, and export of manufactures. He follows the presentation of these with two sentences:

> In theory, there is no need to choose between these strategies, since each must be taken to the margin of advantage.

Arnold C. Harberger is Gustavus F. and Ann M. Swift Distinguished Service Professor of Economics at the University of Chicago.

This is solid and "timeless" economics, a thought which could be developed so as to present in detail some of the more essential elements of policy economics that are involved in this area. The second sentence, immediately following, says:

> Appropriate data for a development plan matrix, if such data existed, would optimize the allocation of resources between domestic and foreign trade.

Now this sentence harks back to an era long past—in which countries actually spent important amounts of resources in creating development plan matrices and actually took the resulting numbers seriously. This is no longer the vogue, the fruitlessness of the effort having been learned many times over. I would think the modern counterpart of the second sentence would more properly read:

> The optimum allocation of resources between the production of importables, exportables, and nontraded goods and services would result if we had an appropriate estimate of the social opportunity cost of foreign exchange, and if we implemented policies that led economic agents to perceive this (1) as the effective local-currency cost (to them) of the foreign exchange they spent and (2) as the effective local-currency yield (to them) of the foreign exchange they generated, through either export or import-substituting activities.

Thus, although Professor Lewis comes to the "right" conclusion in the first sentence, its force is palliated in the second by what strikes me as unnecessary lip service to a bygone fad.

Agricultural Exports

In the section on agricultural exports we have first a nugget of wisdom. On the idea of a long-term bias against agriculture, Lewis cites his 1949 pronouncement:

> In the past hundred years primary production has not failed to respond to the growth of manufactures; and . . . there is no *a priori* reason to expect these two to grow at incompatible rates.

I consider this conclusion a sound inference from past data, and also a sound deduction from the applicable theory.

But this is followed by an observation that is hard (for me) to understand.

> The factoral terms [of trade] have moved continually against the LDCs since the beginning of the nineteenth century. The basic way to stop this is continually to raise the productivity of LDC farmers producing for the domestic market, thereby increasing the supply price of export crops.

The underlying idea here is that if, perhaps through technical advances, farmers can earn high incomes in producing, say, truck crops for the domestic market, then market equilibrium will require that those left producing export crops also earn higher incomes. The supply curve of export crops will shift to the left, and the world price will tend to go up. However, there is little reason to expect that technical advance will be limited to crops produced for the domestic market; moreover, technical advance itself shifts the supply curve of the affected crops to the right, producing a downward pressure on their price. (Technical advance in the production of a domestic crop would actually tend to draw resources to its production only if the price elasticity of demand for it were greater than unity—a rather unlikely event in the case of agricultural goods produced just for the local market.)

The above interprets the rise in productivity of LDC farmers as stemming from technical advance. Another way of raising the supply price of export products would be through the increase in the demand for agricultural products in the domestic market. This would lead with more certainty to a reduction in the supply available for export, and may be what Professor Lewis had in mind. But it would normally entail (for given technology) a fall rather than a rise in the physical productivity of farmers in producing the affected crops.

My main observation here is that, in general, rises in the productivity of farmers for the domestic market and rises in the supply price of export crops are not readily subject to policy determination by LDC governments, except through the introduction of taxes, subsidies, or other distortions in the affected market. No case is made by Professor Lewis to suggest that such interventions would act as correctives for preexisting negative externalities or distortions; my presumption, therefore, is that no serious policy solution has been proferred.

Dependency Theory

Professor Lewis's judgments on dependency theory appear to me to go straight to the point:

> The dependency theory seemed to me to be important for the study of the second half of the nineteenth century, but not the second half of the twentieth century when independent governments were engaged in restructuring the place of foreigners in the country. As a contribution to deciding whether the small farmers should be encouraged to plant more tea or rubber, it seemed to me unhelpful.

In the text preceding the above, Lewis describes the dependency syndrome as one in which the dominance of foreigners (or colonialists) on the scene limits opportunity for local talent, and biases against domestic development are consciously introduced or perpetuated. I find this a much more congenial definition of dependency than the simple fact that a small country's prosperity depends largely on the movements of the prices of its principal export goods. That kind of dependency prevails (on wheat prices) in Kansas and Manitoba as well as Argentina and (on copper prices) in Montana and Arizona as well as Chile and Zaire.

Import Substitution and Customs Unions

In Professor Lewis's discussion of import substitution and customs unions, his most profound remarks concern the phenomenon of migration.

> [For] the sugar industry in the late 1920s, which was dependent on migrant labor and foreign capital, the theory of international trade is hardly relevant. . . . When making recommendations for the Ivory Coast, does one include the migrants from Upper Volta in the group whose income is to be maximized or treat them as an input at predetermined prices? . . . [Concerning] joining the Common Market, half [of British economists] said yes and talked about the law of comparative cost. The other half said no and trembled at the possibility that British skilled labor, capital, and entrepreneurship would migrate to the continent, leaving the island in stagnation. Whose welfare is to be maximized?

But side by side with these thought-provoking comments we find lip service again being paid to the two-gap model, structural inflation, and balanced growth (linked to the use of indicative plans and, for small countries, to customs unions). Of these Lewis says, "The logic of these three models seemed to me unchallengeable, and I was never involved in the huge critical literature that emerged." He asserts that most of the critical literature was "unhelpful," ignoring the basic assumption. But he does not address the real issues here—the unwillingness of two-gap model enthusiasts (or anybody else) to take seriously, in all policy dimensions, the exaggerated shadow prices of foreign exchange and of capital that are typically produced by such models; the absence of serious evidence on the existence of structural inflation, except when chronic fiscal deficits financed by the printing of money are considered a structural phenomenon (in which case monetarists and structuralists agree); and the implausibility of at least the premise in the statement "If imports and exports cannot be increased, production must follow a balanced growth path."

Nonetheless, and characteristically, he ends the section with a solid proposition:

> But neither [the making of indicative plans nor the creation of customs unions] has been as successful as we had hoped, partly because the difficulty of earning foreign exchange, from which the models were derived, turned out to be not as great as we had feared; and partly because the planners were slow in learning that market prices are more powerful incentives than ministerial speeches.

Self-sufficiency

Professor Lewis's remarks on self-sufficiency have a puzzling prelude and a sobering postlude. The prelude:

> Self-sufficiency is the part of the import substitution strategy that relates to food production for the domestic market. Once one has grasped the point that agriculture and industry provide markets for each other's output, theoretical dispute ceases.

It always seemed to me that self-sufficiency meant having domestic supply equal to (or perhaps greater than) domestic demand. It can be in food, in lumber, in sugar, in steel, in anything. If one is to have it, one cannot have it in everything without totally isolating the economy (or denuding it through perennial export surpluses). One can, moreover, have a very firm strategy of import substitution (say, by a uniform 30 percent tariff) without producing all one's food or providing all one's agricultural products. So I basically fail to perceive self-sufficiency as relating specifically to food production for the domestic market. But much more important, I see enormous scope for dispute (on both theoretical and policy grounds) concerning what incentives, if any, should be given to domestic production of food or of anything else. As far as I can see, the modern answer would begin with the principle set forth above (page 139), in my update of a statement of Lewis, and from there perhaps proceed to set forth particular reasons why in some cases a country should be willing to incur higher domestic resource costs for producing substitutes for imported food than for producing other import substitutes. This line of reasoning is not pursued at all in the paper.

Professor Lewis's sobering postlude:

> [Although] wet tropics . . . food production [can] grow at 4 percent a year . . . we do not know how to average even 2 percent a year over [the next thirty years] in the dry tropics [where] at least 500 million people live . . . This is one of the reasons for the wide spread of LDC growth rates and of LDC per capita incomes. These gaps will widen until the agronomists make a major breakthrough in tropical dry farming.

Professor Lewis is not really referring to self-sufficiency as such, but is rightly recognizing that the future of the half billion people in the dry tropics is likely to be strongly linked to agriculture for decades to come. Food production for local consumption need not expand to meet demand, but any major shortfall will have to be substantially covered by a growing export surplus in items such as cotton, jute, wool, and tea. This observation, however, does not invite policies to discriminate in favor of producing food and other agricultural products at the expense of manufactures, handicrafts, and so on. Rather, it reflects a highly plausible judgment that these latter items are unlikely to provide the source of a major turnabout in the growth prospects of the half billon inhabitants of the dry tropics.

Exporting Manufactures

On the subject of exporting manufactures we benefit once again from Professor Lewis's experience and judgment:

> One aspect of the export of manufactures that causes pain is its dependence on foreign entrepreneurship. . . . I have never felt that LDCs should hold back the diversification of their manufacturing sectors from fear of multinationals, since in independent countries they operate on the country's terms or not at all. The most important control is [to require] the firms to hire and train local recruits at managerial and professional levels.

That genuine externalities are involved in the upgrading of a country's labor force is rarely disputed; moreover, multinationals and other foreign companies have more often gained than lost by replacing their own (expensive) expatriate employees with local, trainable talent that in the end turns out to be just as good, but significantly less costly. The policy suggested by Lewis is in such cases simply a catalyst which sets in motion a process often beneficial to the local population and the foreign company alike.

On LDC Achievements

Professor Lewis serves the profession well in emphasizing that the story of the past two or three decades is not all that bad:

> Taken as a group, LDC governments have, in fact, passed reasonable tests. There are four times as many children in school as there were in 1950. The infant mortality rate has fallen by three-quarters. The multiplication of hospital beds, village water pipes, all-season village roads, and other mass services is faster than at any period in the history of the countries now developed.

Too much of the discussion of LDC problems has focused on the allegedly widening gap between them and the more developed parts of the world. In fact the gap has narrowed significantly in relative terms, dramatically so if one includes in the measure of welfare such items as increased life expectancy, increased educational levels of those still in school, and reduced infant mortality, none of which are directly reflected in our standard macroeconomic measures of real income and product.

Infinitely Elastic Labor Supply

The vision of an infinitely elastic labor supply formed the basis of some of Professor Lewis's most famous early writings and of much subsequent work. Controversy has raged over the subject for something like three decades, and surely it will not be settled here. But perhaps I can help to clarify some of the issues by pointing out that, in my opinion, much of the dispute has been between one group (Lewis's critics) which on the whole interpreted the notion of an infinitely elastic labor supply in a rather precise, technical way, and another group (including Professor Lewis) which interpreted the concept much more loosely.

Taken literally, an infinitely elastic labor supply means that there exists a wage level at which anyone can hire all the workers he wants, and below which he can get no one. It is incompatible with seasonal variations in the agricultural wage (which are very strong, for example, in India and some other Asian countries). Moreover, it is difficult to rationalize a secularly rising real wage under a strict interpretation of infinitely elastic supply. Must not last year's unhired workers plus this year's new additions to the labor force both be fully absorbed *before* real wages (in the open market) can rise? And at that point, is not the surplus fully absorbed?

Lewis lists in his paper some of the sources of infinite elasticity of labor supply:

> What was the basis of near infinite elasticity? Critics fastened on disguised unemployment among small farmers . . . but this was only one item in a long catalog . . . Other items were: technological unemployment, which Marx thought powerful enough by itself to create a growing labor surplus; underemployment in urban areas, in what has now come to be called the informal sector; the movement of women from the household into the labor market; and the increase of population. This last turned out to be the dominant factor. With population growing at 3 percent a year, the supply of labor could not be other than very highly elastic.

Careful scrutiny reveals that none of the above causes leads labor supply to disappear when demand is reduced. Each and every one of them is fully compatible with wages falling when labor demand decreases, and with wages rising when labor demand expands. Each is a good reason why the secular upward trend in real wages has not been stronger, but is not evidence of (or a basis for) infinite elasticity of labor supply.

The problem is a serious one, since most of the conclusions extracted from the infinite-supply-elasticity model do indeed depend on the strict interpretation (rather than any of the many looser ones) of the term.

Migration-fed Unemployment

I was delighted to find in Lewis's paper an old quotation, documenting his early perception of the concept (later emphasized by Harris and Todaro, myself, and numerous others) of migration-fed unemployment. According to this notion, urban unemployment can be an equilibrium phenomenon. When some force holds the urban wage level above the supply price at which migrants are willing to come in from the country-side, they will continue to come until some other factor (in this case, a sufficiently high urban unemployment rate) dissuades them. In Professor Lewis's own words of 1957:

> [Urban unemployment] is also due partly to the growing wage gap itself, which by raising the level of those who have employment in the towns, attracts more and more people to come into these towns. It is very difficult to know how to cope with this increase in urban unemployment. The normal way to cope with unemployment is to provide work, but this is no solution in this case. On the contrary, it merely aggravates the problem, because the more work you provide in the towns, the more people will drift into the towns, and there is no certainty that you can win the race . . . No one ought to say that he knows how to cure unemployment in this situation.

Inflation

One of the most nostalgic notes struck by Professor Lewis in his paper is surely contained in his discussion of inflation. He begins by citing Ragnar Nurkse's idea of using surplus labor for capital formation, and then continues:

> By definition, surplus labor could be used without reducing other output significantly . . . It was therefore costless in real terms. We had great hopes in the 1950s for the community development movement using unpaid labor, and some governments made a go of it, but enthusiasm usually petered out. Labor has to be paid whether it is in surplus or not.

In these few sentences one can see how much our image of labor markets has changed in three decades. The first two sentences reflect the vision of the time—unless people were drawn away from other employments, their labor was "costless in real terms." Yet the multiple alternative activities of the so-called surplus did have some value, at least to those workers themselves (and perhaps their families), and this alternative value, or opportunity cost, was reflected in a positive supply price of labor. There-fore such labor "has to be paid," as Lewis senses when he recalls the promotion of programs with unpaid labor. These programs did not work. Lewis concludes that "labor has to be paid whether it is in surplus or not." Many economists today would say that when labor has to be paid, it usually ceases to be in surplus (that is, costless) in the Nurkse-Lewis sense.

Professor Lewis's next point concerns the relationship between the printing of money to hire surplus labor on the one hand, and the subsequent inflation on the other.

> If [the surplus labor] was used productively . . . we would be matching extra money with extra consumer goods, and the inflation would be slight. If, however, the money was used to pay soldiers or civil servants, without increasing the output of consumer goods, we would get the full blast of inflation.

This remark savors of the "real bills doctrine," though in a somewhat different guise. The modern approach to the problem involved is numerical. Say that national income is initially 100, the money supply 20, and the price level 1.0. Other things being equal, an autonomous increase of 5 in the money supply will bring the price level to 1.25. If, however, the increase of 5 is spent on investment goods, and they in turn have a (rather high) real marginal productivity of 20 percent a year, then output will go to 101, and the price level will go only to 1.24. There is indeed a difference between a highly productive and a zero-productive use of the extra money, but (with plausible parameters) it is so small that in effect it gets lost in the shuffle.

Yet, when all is said and done, Arthur Lewis comes out with a sound judgment.

> In one corner is productive primary use [of newly printed money] plus an increased propensity to save, and the resultant inflation is damped. In the opposite corner is wasteful primary expenditure and zero addition to saving, so inflation is maximized. I entered the 1950s standing firmly in the first corner, but quit the 1950s disillusioned into expecting only the opposite extreme.

Today we would use different wording, but would still come out with the conclusion that price level movement overwhelms the real effects of any major resort to inflationary finance.

Conclusion

As should by now be evident, there is much in Professor Lewis's paper that evokes feelings of nostalgia, but also many of his ideas dating from the 1950s reflect remarkable prescience. In addition, the judgments that he renders from the vantage point of the 1980s distill a professional lifetime of experience, in which he remained ever ready to be sensitive to evidence and to learn from new experience.

Yet one cannot avoid noting a sort of "generation gap." The emphasis on savings is heavy compared with other topics in the economic development field. The implicit judgment that it is good to reduce the share of private consumption in national income is not sufficiently tempered with warnings about public sector waste.

Finally, there is little reflection of some of the main lessons we have learned in the past twenty years. Nowhere in the paper, for example, is the distinction between tradable and nontradable goods, and within the tradables the distinction between importables and exportables, even mentioned, let alone given the weight it came to have in the trade and development literature of the 1970s. Nor does one find reference to the concept of effective protection or to the voluminous literature (both theoretical and empirical) that has grown up around this concept since the 1960s. So too it is with monetary and exchange rate policies. Developing-country experience with the phenomenon of inflation has multiplied in the past decade, both the number of countries affected and the range and variety of inflationary episodes. The same can be said of trade and exchange rate regimes, new varieties of which seem to have emerged as if from a botanical laboratory.

I cite the absence of discussion of these matters, not in criticism—because, after all, a paper entitled "Development Economics in the 1950s" has every right to concentrate on that decade—but as a way of calling attention to the essential nature of the piece. We have here not a view of the 1950s from the standpoint of where economic science has come in the interim (the current "state of the art"), but rather the view of a patriarch who did much to forge the early outlines of development economics, looking back on those exciting and fruitful years.

Gunnar Myrdal

NOBEL LAUREATE GUNNAR MYRDAL was born in 1898 in the village of Solvarbo in Sweden. He received the degree of Doctor of Law in economics from the University of Stockholm in 1927, having written his dissertation on price formation under economic insecurity. Since then he has been the recipient of more than thirty honorary degrees.

His many offices and honors include Lars Hierta Chair in Political Economy and Public Finance at the University of Stockholm, 1933–39; Senator, Swedish parliament, 1935–38, 1943–47; Chairman, Postwar Planning Commission, Sweden 1943–45; Minister of Commerce, Sweden, 1945–47; Executive Secretary of the United Nations Economic Commission for Europe, 1947–57; Professor of International Economics and Director of the Institute for International Economic Studies, University of Stockholm, 1961–65. In 1974, Myrdal received the Nobel Memorial Prize in Economic Science.

After ten years with the Economic Commission for Europe, he undertook a ten-year study of development problems in Asia that resulted in the publication of his monumental *Asian Drama: An Inquiry into the Poverty of Nations*, 3 vols. (New York: Pantheon, 1968). Earlier books that related to development include *Economic Theory and Underdeveloped Regions* (London: Duckworth, 1957; Methuen, 1963), also issued as *Rich Lands and Poor* (New York: Harper, 1957); and *An International Economy: Problems and Prospects* (New York: Harper, 1956).

Among his other books are *Monetary Equilibrium* (1931; translated, London: William Hodge, 1939); *An American Dilemma: The Negro Problem and Modern Democracy* (New York: Harper, 1944); *The Political Element in the Development of Economic Theory* (London: Routledge and Kegan Paul, 1953; Swedish original, 1930); *Value in Social Theory: A Selection of Essays on Methodology*, Paul Streeten, ed. (London: Routledge and Kegan Paul, 1958); *Beyond the Welfare State* (New Haven: Yale University Press, 1960); *Challenge to Affluence* (New York: Vintage, 1962); *Objectivity in Social Research* (New York: Pantheon, 1969); *The Challenge of World Poverty: A World Anti-poverty Program in Outline* (New York: Pantheon, 1970); and *Against the Stream: Critical Essays on Economics* (New York: Pantheon, 1973).

His contributions have been especially notable in the study of racial problems, in methodological questions related to value premises and the political element in economic theorizing, in his institutional approach to social problems, and in his critique of conventional economic theory applied to developing countries.

International Inequality and Foreign Aid in Retrospect

THIS PAPER is directed toward rendering an account of growing pangs of conscience.[1] At the beginning of my research interest in the development problems of underdeveloped countries, I gave unqualified support to the idea that the developed countries should give financial assistance for their development. In my own country, Sweden, I had been active in urging a relatively generous and untied aid program for this purpose. Development aid gradually reached the level, sometimes internationally declared to be a goal, of 1 percent of the national income, and it was planned to reach even higher in the future. Recent happenings in the underdeveloped countries and in the world at large, however, have caused me to doubt whether I was right. Political problems have regularly a moral kernel, and questions of aid are essentially dependent upon moral judgment.

[1]

I do not belong to the true pioneers who, immediately after the war, when the avalanche of liberation from colonial bonds began, and sometimes even in advance of this revolutionary change in the world's political situation, took up the study of the development problems of underdeveloped countries. After returning to Sweden in 1942 upon completing my work on *An American Dilemma*,[2] I became fully occupied in governmental planning activities and, as minister of trade after the war, in guiding Sweden's role to restore trade and financial relations in Europe. My thoughts about the underdeveloped countries on other continents were hazy and not much in focus.

In early 1947, however, I left Sweden to become executive secretary of the United Nations Economic Commission for Europe (ECE). Development problems then came closer. For one thing, some countries, particu-

---

1. The personal and autobiographical direction of my paper has been chosen in agreement with the editors of this volume and actually on their advice.
2. New York: Harper, 1944.

larly those in eastern and southern Europe, were relatively poorer than others. This had to be accounted for in the secretariat's *Annual Economic Surveys*. But by common agreement their development problems were not considered in such a way that the question of financial assistance was raised.

More important for directing my interests to the development problems in Asia and other non-European underdeveloped countries was the close cooperation with the secretariats of the two other economic commissions which soon came into existence for Asia and Latin America. In connection with this cooperation I had the opportunity to make long journeys, particularly in South Asia. I also traveled widely in the Middle East. When Israel, as a member of the United Nations, used its right to participate in the ECE to assist its efforts in opening up trade to European countries, I was active in attempting to draw also the Arab countries into such participation. Together with colleagues in the ECE's secretariat I also spent some time in and made a special study of the regions in the U.S.S.R. bordering on South Asia. My main interest in that study was how the development of those initially underdeveloped districts had been financed within the general budget of the U.S.S.R., which in fact implied development aid on a large scale given within one state.

When in these years I came to approach the problem of the great poverty in the really underdeveloped countries outside Europe, it was natural for me, with my background in Swedish political life, to look upon their economic underdevelopment as a problem of international distributional inequality. We should strive towards creating more of a "welfare world," just as I had been active in helping Sweden come closer to the ideal of a welfare state.

The four lectures I gave in Cairo in 1955 at the invitation of Egypt's Central Bank, published in edited form under the title *Economic Theory and Underdeveloped Regions*, were focused on the international problems of maldistribution.

In that early work, on the basis of Knut Wicksell's hints of "circular and cumulative causation," I showed how in the absence of counteracting policies inequalities would tend to increase, both internationally and within a country.[3] The welfare state that was coming into existence in the rich countries was the result of such policy interventions. I also discussed the biases against the poorer countries in the inherited theory of international trade, particularly the unrealistic idea, then becoming prevalent among economists, that trade in commodities worked for the equalization of factor prices, more especially of wages.[4]

In this and in other early writings of mine there was no thought that the

---

3. *Economic Theory and Underdeveloped Regions* (London: G. Duckworth, 1957), chaps. 2 and 3.
    4. Ibid., chap. 11.

existing great inequality of resources and power within the underdeveloped countries themselves could be part of the explanation of their underdevelopment. This was the time when development was generally simply defined as "growth," which is still often the case among economists, and when increasing internal inequalities were even assumed by some economists to be an inevitable result of growth, an idea I have never shared. On the contrary, I have always seen greater equality as a condition for more substantial growth.

[2]

This was how far my thinking on development and underdevelopment had reached when in 1957 I resigned from my employment with the United Nations in order to give full time to a study of the development problems of the countries in Asia south and west of China and Russia, with the main emphasis on India. That study came to take a much longer time than I and the Twentieth Century Fund, which provided research support, had reckoned. It resulted in *Asian Drama.*[5]

In this study I was brought back to the institutional approach, which twenty years earlier I had been forced to apply when I had innocently undertaken my study of the Negro problem in the United States. I had then rapidly found out that I faced an analysis of the entire American civilization from the point of view of the working and living conditions for the most disadvantaged large group of the American population.

The glaring contradictions between people's conceptions of the race problem in America, which were reflected in the huge literature, both popular and scientific, made me take more seriously my understanding that things look different depending upon where you stand. I had to work with explicit value premises. In *An American Dilemma* they were specified for different problems and all subordinated to what I called the American Creed of liberty and equality of opportunity in the pursuit of happiness.

The "modernization ideals," proclaimed with varying completeness by the intellectuals and governments in Asian countries, were clarified and specified to be used as value premises for the new study. What had often been declared to be inherited "Asian values" were taken into account and, when needed, integrated into the development goals.

The institutional approach meant enlarging the study to include what in a summary way I referred to as "attitudes and institutions." They were found to be largely responsible for those countries' underdevelopment and would have to be changed in order to speed up development.

Methodologically, *Asian Drama* became in a sense a replica of *An American Dilemma.* I retained my predominant interest in the equality

5. New York: Pantheon, 1968.

issue, though in the new study it was directed toward the internal conditions in the underdeveloped countries.[6]

In the 1920s and 1930s, when my research and policy work had focused on conditions in Sweden, I held the view that an equalization in favor of the lower-income strata was also a productive investment in the quality of people and their productivity. And I found support for this opinion in comparisons of different rich nations' growth statistics. It seemed clear that income equalization would have an even greater effect in this direction for underdeveloped countries, where the masses of people are suffering from very severe consumption deficiencies in regard to nutrition, housing, and everything else. *The productivity of higher consumption levels stands for me as a major motivation for the direction of development policy in underdeveloped countries. Higher consumption levels are a condition for a more rapid and stable growth.*

In underdeveloped countries such a redistribution of income cannot, however, be carried out by taxing the rich and transferring money to the poor via social security schemes and other such measures to raise their levels of living. The poor are so overwhelmingly many, and the wealthy so relatively few—and tax evasion among them so common. What is needed in order to raise the miserable living levels of the poor masses is instead radical institutional reforms. These would serve the double purpose of greater equality and economic growth. The two goals are inextricably joined. This implies a fundamental difference from developed countries, where the two goals can be, and often are, pursued separately.

[3]

And so a major part of *Asian Drama* came to deal with the political issues of changing institutions, which were then, as now, avoided by most ordinary economists in their writings on development. The book had to include chapters on population and population policy, landownership and tenancy, conditions of illness and health, education for different strata and in different localities and its quality, and so on. I became the first economist to write about the "soft state" and to have a chapter on corruption, in which I showed how its prevalence was hampering economic growth. Corruption worked in the interests of the rich and powerful, even if it permeated the whole society. Taking all these other things into consideration made the book very bulky, particularly as I was driven to devote much space to methodological explanations in the text and in a number of appendices.

6. For a very condensed recent summary, see my contribution to *The World Economic Order: Past and Prospects*, Sven Grassman and Erik Lundberg, eds. (New York: St. Martin's Press, 1981), chap. 14, "Need for Reforms in Underdeveloped Countries," pp. 501–25.

The book tended to contain relatively few numbers. This was not because I am averse to quantification of knowledge. But the institutional facts are very complicated and cannot be easily reduced to statistical measurement; they have to be described in a less precise form, particularly in a study of general conditions in a whole country. Moreover, institutional research could not rely on the concepts used in ordinary economic literature and borrowed from studies of developed countries: such concepts as income, savings, supply, demand, and prices, all within markets and all in aggregate or average terms. These concepts were seldom adequate to deal with reality in underdeveloped countries.

The widely used concepts of unemployment and underemployment, for instance, have in the underdeveloped countries no precise meaning, except for narrow sections and even there only with reservations. Without a developed labor market in which the workers are split up according to occupation, have knowledge about a market, and are actively seeking employment, the larger part of the actual "worklessness" of people cannot be categorized in these terms.

[4]

The India I saw immediately after liberation and the cruel collisions of partition was in many ways a country that could look forward with hope and confidence to the future. Great Britain under Prime Minister Attlee had given India its freedom without waging a colonial war, unlike the other metropolitan countries in Europe. The Indians were left free to feel that their independence had been won by a struggle that on their part was bloodless and backed by the people. Like Pakistan, India had not been invaded by the Japanese during the war, as had many other countries in the region. The Indian soldiers who had fought under British command had done so abroad.

India inherited a civil service that included a number of native Indians who were trained, organized, and effective. Toward the end of the British raj the civil service was almost free of corruption. The corruption that still existed was among lower Indian officials, particularly in the countryside. The higher civil service had indeed often protected the common people from injustices.

Representative assemblies had been established in colonial times, even if their powers were limited. For more than half a century royal commissions had been set up to prepare reforms, for instance in the field of education, though their recommendations had not so often been carried out. That was a tradition that free India could continue to follow.

In spite of its own great financial difficulties after the Second World War, Britain even paid back some forced credits it had taken from India during the war. Since liberation had finally been won through agreement, established trade relations with the old mother country could be carried on without interruption.

The population explosion that came with the rapid spread of modern, cheap medical technology was, however, not foreseen. As in other under-developed countries, that difficulty was not part of the expectations until the censuses around 1960. But in India, even before independence, studies and proposals for spreading birth control had been initiated, and the idea of controlling population growth had been accepted by Indian intellectual leaders.

With Jawaharlal Nehru at the helm as prime minister, great and apparently successful initiatives were taken in many fields. They were all in the direction of democracy and equalization. The princely states were integrated. India rapidly furnished itself with a new constitution, founded upon the principle of general suffrage for both men and women.

Preparing for further advances in the egalitarian direction, a set of "directive principles" was added to the constitution. But in the constitution itself caste had already been abolished and forbidden. Local government by panchayats had been established. Family legislation had been modernized, so radically that it could hardly be understood by the villagers.

And India began its five-year plans. The Planning Commission had been instituted in 1950 and was linked to the directive principles. Nehru took the chairmanship himself and wrote at the outset a brief introduction, stressing the egalitarian purposes of Indian policies.

Nehru had set out on his personal educational campaign, sometimes speaking several times a day and often to large groupings of common people. India should become a "classless" society on the basis of cooperation. Land reform had been announced to give "the land to the tillers." Education should be radically reformed with the main goal rapidly to make the whole population literate.

This was the mood when I first saw India rather soon after independence. It was then definitely heading in the direction of egalitarian ideals.

[5]

But when I arrived for my study at the end of 1957, things had changed and continued to change in a less encouraging direction. Nehru, like the aging group of the "Servants of India" who had promised themselves to think not of their own interests but of India's future, had not changed his ideals but saw the overwhelming difficulties of realizing them. Soon Nehru himself even planned to leave his post as prime minister and become an itinerant preacher of his gospel in the spirit of Mohandas Gandhi. He was persuaded to retain his political responsibilities and he continued his educational campaign for a democratic India, but he had fewer and fewer possibilities to pursue his ideals.

From the beginning Indian society was, however, very unequal. In colonial times the metropolitan power had almost automatically allied itself with privileged groups in the colony and often created new such groups. To support its reign, the colonial government had an interest in upholding and even strengthening the inherited inegalitarian social structure.

The upper strata, still holding the real power after independence, were a very diversified crowd, ranging from the big industrialists, higher officials, and teachers in secondary and particularly tertiary schools to the landowners and moneylenders in the villages and local officials in collusion with them. The political parties and particularly the Congress party became increasingly financially dependent upon the few wealthy.

Reforms of the basic economic and social structure were not carried out or they were truncated. I remember how once a radically inclined member of Parliament characterized a new tax law as "a tax-exemption law."

Driving out the British in the Gandhian fight for Indian freedom had been a simple issue that could be easily understood and accepted by almost all, even the poorest and most simpleminded. But the new issues that were raised by the demands for reforming independent India were all very complicated and less easily understood by the broad masses of people. They were better understood by the rich and powerful who felt their interests threatened. The poor, whose interests should be protected, were easily deceived and split.

A land reform was a complicated affair in a country with so much tenancy of various sorts and with such a huge group of landless people, most of them of lower caste. Even independent farmers with only very small plots could be mobilized against land reform, although it was not their land that would be taken to give to the totally landless. A gradual increase in population created difficulties, particularly in heavily populated regions. And many other issues split especially the poor and uneducated classes.

Caste, and caste feelings, remained a reality even though abolished by law. In addition, even after separation from Pakistan, India had a huge Moslem population with different ways of life. Tensions of caste and religion remained and sometimes resulted in violent clashes. Such splits clearly hindered efforts to unite poor people to press for reform in their common interest. The spread of corruption in a cumulative way was another obstacle. The big bribes went to people in the upper strata, who could in turn afford to bribe political parties and their individual representatives.

India is rightly called the world's largest democracy, and its government depends upon a Parliament elected by the people, whose participation is on a higher level than, for instance, in the United States. But the Parliament, as I pointed out, is not looking after the interests of the people. And so India remained unreformed or achieved only severely maldirected reforms. Not carried out were the more fundamental reforms needed to democratize the very unequal society inherited by free India.

The other countries in the region that I had set out to study were very different from India and also differed among themselves in regard to the time they gained their freedom, the way they got it, and the economic levels from which they started. I did not find it possible to use a simple, common model for their development, except that they, like India, generally abstained from carrying out the institutional reforms which should have raised the consumption levels of the poor and thereby also their productivity.

An exception is tiny Singapore, one of the few states in the underdeveloped world which has actively fought corruption and also pursued an effective housing policy. But Singapore has had and still has an average income level perhaps ten times higher than that of India. It may also be significant that the Chinese are a majority in Singapore.[7]

[6]

In my work on *Asian Drama* I held to the end my institutional approach and the modernization value premises, together with my conviction that

---

7. Since the completion of my study, a few small economies north of my region have, together with Singapore, had a rapid economic development, namely Taiwan, the Republic of Korea, and Hong Kong. In the economic literature this has commonly been attributed to their being more export-minded and less inclined to hinder imports.

In my view, expressed in *Asian Drama*, the problem in all the poor countries of the region was not that because of the scarcity of foreign exchange they tried to restrict imports, especially of less necessary commodities. Instead, the problem was that under the pressure of business interests they did not counter the direction of their industrial development, as they should have done, by regulation or special taxes. Their import restrictions came thereby to stimulate their production of the less necessary commodities for domestic use. This of course hampered production for export.

For political reasons, Taiwan and Korea from the beginning received tremendously more aid per head from the United States than did India and other countries in the region. This decreased their need to depend on import restrictions. In addition, the United States forced them to adopt a radical land reform policy—as it had done in the defeated Japan, for which the Japanese can now be grateful. During the first few years after the war America was very radically inclined as far as these economies were concerned. This explains their greater freedom to invest in export industries. To do this they did not need to be especially export-minded.

Moreover, all these small economies had been for long periods under Chinese cultural influence. Unlike India and most countries in the region, they had never suffered much from the divisive systems of caste and religion. If in China a poor boy from a village did succeed in getting into an educational career, which of course seldom happened, at the end he was a mandarin, and nobody ever asked from what sort of people he came.

egalitarian institutional reforms to raise the consumption levels of the poor would be the condition for a more rapid development by increasing the productivity of their people. When I later wrote *The Challenge of World Poverty*,[8] I still adhered to this view, as I do today. That book was indeed an effort to condense my earlier, more intensive research into a shorter volume with a definite stress on the policy issues. It thus contained chapters on the institutional approach, the equality issue, land reform, population, health, education, the "soft state," and corruption.

In this new book, however, I also dealt with the responsibility of the developed countries. I criticized their trade policies, and particularly their aid policies. After having informed myself about conditions and policies affecting Latin America and Africa, I widened my criticism to include those regions and their relations with the developed countries.

During the past ten years I have been working on other problems. Under the influence of that type of conservatism from which social scientists are not exempt, I am afraid that whenever I had to explain my views on the development problems of underdeveloped countries, I came to repeat what I had in greater detail formulated in my earlier works. Fresh thinking that could change my views I have done only in regard to the aid problem; otherwise—and I feel with good reason—I have retained my views from earlier periods.

My new thoughts on aid to underdeveloped countries have been formed under the influence of what has happened in the course of the present world crisis and its influence on both developed and underdeveloped countries. I find it therefore practical first to sketch what has happened to the underdeveloped countries in the present world crisis.

I have always felt skeptical about the reliability of the figures on economic growth in underdeveloped countries that are widely quoted in the literature. My skepticism is founded upon what I have seen of how the primary material for these statistics of average real income per head is collected, then summarized into an average figure for an underdeveloped country, afterwards translated into dollars according to a nominal exchange rate, and published by the United Nations Statistical Office.

These figures certainly cannot be expected to understate what has actually happened. It is therefore significant when the 1982 *UN Report on the World Social Situation* concluded that 1981 was the first year in a quarter of a century for which the figures do not show growth. The development since then has surely not made for a change in a positive direction.

The depression in the industrial developed countries is a trend that has not been broken. It has of course tended to hurt the underdeveloped countries by decreasing the demand for their exports of raw materials and still more of industrial goods. At the same time, the tremendously in-

8. New York: Pantheon, 1970.

creased prices of oil have been burdening the great majority of underdeveloped countries who depend upon imported oil.

They have been compelled to seek credits in the capital market, and their indebtedness has grown rapidly. In this credit market the interest rates have been rising, which has worsened still more their balance of payments. Many underdeveloped countries soon reached the level of indebtedness at which they find it difficult to pay interest and amortization. New credits in addition to what they need for that purpose have become increasingly difficult to obtain, and if granted they would only increase the burden of repayment for the future.

I am referring to the great majority of underdeveloped countries that have little or no oil at home. The small oil-producing countries on the Persian Gulf and a few others in a similar situation are outside this discussion.

But some new oil-exporting underdeveloped countries such as Nigeria and Mexico have handled their oil incomes in a squanderous way that has left their large agricultural regions in continuing or increasing poverty and has permitted commercial centers to explode in all sorts of speculative adventures. As a result, they have brought themselves to financial collapse.

Meanwhile, secular changes that are independently tending to hold back underdeveloped countries are continuing as trends. The population explosion goes on. Despite some progress in the spread of birth control in a few countries, which will be increasingly difficult to sustain when poverty is increasing, population growth will continue for decades on about the same levels because of the youthfulness of the present population. In particular, people who will be of working age until at least the turn of the next century are already born. Another secular trend causing increasing difficulties in many underdeveloped countries is rapid deforestation, which destroys the soil and has undesirable effects even on the climate and population growth.

Development efforts have regularly been directed to building up the modern industrial sector, although everywhere it can employ only a minimal part of the total growing work force. Most of the people in the growing city slums who have not been born there are not needed for further industrialization; they are simply refugees from an overpopulated agricultural sector. In agriculture the productivity of land and man remains mostly low and leaves the landless in particular without work for part or all of the year.

The result is increasing mass poverty. Famine becomes an ever more crushing problem. There are indications that the children of the poor who survive starvation come to suffer from retarded brain development and will become a hopeless subclass of mental cripples. This increases the damage caused by the lack of primary education or by schooling that is insufficient or maldirected.

As I see it, poverty in the underdeveloped countries is now almost everywhere increasing and becoming extreme. Robert McNamara, formerly president of the World Bank, established the habit of talking about "absolute poverty." I anticipate that it will become steadily even worse, especially in the poorest of the poor countries. The poverty-stricken are, I am afraid, now becoming a growing portion of the population in all underdeveloped countries.

In addition, conflicts and even open warfare among nations have been and are becoming more common in large parts of the underdeveloped world. Generally speaking, underdeveloped countries are carrying heavier and heavier costs for weapons, even if they are subsidized by the superpowers. Governments in underdeveloped countries are more and more getting into the hands of the rich and powerful. And large parts of the underdeveloped world are now under military dictatorships.

While all this is happening, financial aid rendered by the developed countries is kept on a very low level and has recently been shrinking. The sometimes proclaimed aim of raising it to 1 percent of the national income or 0.7 percent of the gross national product in the developed countries has been fulfilled only by the small Scandinavian countries and the Netherlands. Even in these countries it is now tending to fall. The principle of keeping aid untied from exports from the aid-giving country is gradually being given up even in Sweden. The big industrial countries hold their official aid on a much lower level. In particular, aid from the United States is not distributed according to needs but according to U.S. interests in the Cold War.

In view of the enormous and growing needs in the underdeveloped countries and the small amount of money coming from the developed countries, my conclusion must be that any aid which is made available should be directed to help the increasing masses of poverty-stricken people in the poorest countries and in other underdeveloped countries. Aid should also be made available to the victims of catastrophes that are so much more common in these countries.

The need for aid is continually growing, and I would certainly not make any recommendation to lower the appropriations for aid but would continue to ask for more. But the only "development aid" I would find room for under present circumstances would be directed to the simplest and least costly measures to increase food production, to provide sanitation facilities and to increase their utilization, generally to supply pure water, and also as far as possible to improve health care, particularly for poor families, and to give their children somewhat more of better schooling. This together with securing the availability of contraceptives could well claim the whole part of any so-called development aid. Whatever additional aid could be available will be needed for provision of food.

I am of the opinion that we should discontinue aid for industrial projects, particularly large-scale ones. (Money for such projects decreases the funds available for assisting the poverty-stricken masses.) In any case, such matters should not be handled by the particular administrations set up for planning aid to the underdeveloped countries, but should be left to the ministries of trade and foreign affairs of the donors.

I do not think that such a change in the direction of aid would go against public opinion in developed countries, if people there were better informed. Not only in Sweden but everywhere in the rich countries, much of the propaganda for their giving aid stresses how the utter poverty among masses of people in underdeveloped countries hurts the children. Photographs of their unhappy faces and swollen stomachs are widely used. It is only when the aid problems move upward to governments and parliaments that they come under the influence of business interests.

[7]

In the underdeveloped countries governments are everywhere in the hands of upper-class elites, even in countries that are not under military dictatorship. It is with the governments in power that all business deals have to be negotiated and concluded. And it is with them that even aid matters have to be settled. It has been pointed out that as a result poor people in developed countries are taxed to "aid" rich people in underdeveloped countries.

In recent years underdeveloped countries have more and more established a common front toward the developed nations, even in regard to aid. They demand that the direction of aid and its utilization should be their business, and that the aid projects should fit into their planning. These requests have largely been accepted by the aid-giving countries, who have begun to speak about their aid as "cooperation."

Given the undesirable qualities of the governments in most underdeveloped countries, I think this concession is wrong. I believe that the voters in aid-giving developed countries, if properly informed, would agree with me in demanding more control over how their aid is used and where the money is going. I am well aware that such control is very difficult to exert.

Unofficial organizations in developed countries, such as the Red Cross and various religious and humanitarian organizations, have often been more successful than government agencies in keeping their activities in underdeveloped countries free from side influences from their governments. In my opinion, they should be utilized to a larger extent for handling even official aid.

To sum up, the aid-giving governments should insist upon effectively controlling the use of aid in an underdeveloped country. They should do so even if it would increase the costs of administering aid. In developed countries such guarantees would increase the willingness among ordinary people to give aid. If that type of aid-giving in the interest of the poverty-stricken ever came to be common practice, it would even be one element encouraging more democratic rule in some underdeveloped countries.

For these reasons, I now criticize myself for not having changed my views on aid to the underdeveloped countries until the shocks experienced in the present world economic crisis.

[8]

I will end by commenting upon two proposals for improving the situation in underdeveloped countries, which to me seem rather futile. Facing the situation of increasing mass poverty in underdeveloped countries, the Brandt Commission in 1980 proposed a massive transference of capital to them from developed countries.[9] It would allow these countries to increase their import of development commodities and thereby make possible higher production and employment. It might also increase the import of consumer goods to still the hunger of the people if the governments wanted to do so. Underdeveloped countries are always pressed to utilize every means they can to increase their imports. At the same time, it would also increase employment in the rich developed countries and the utilization of their production facilities. Such capital transference would thus be mutually advantageous.

This proposal agrees with the advice of most professional economists, at least in Western Europe and probably also in the United States, who urge their governments to cooperate in an expansionist economic policy. This advice has not been followed. We have seen less and less of international economic cooperation, while international interdependence has become greater than ever. We have never had so many international conferences for international cooperation and never so little of it. The explanation is stagflation, which is a new phenomenon. All countries have to fight inflation and unemployment and are then compelled to take policy measures hurting each other.

The only originality in the proposal by the Brandt Commission was that the new cooperation should be between two groups of countries, the developed and the underdeveloped. The report met with much sympathy in the world but did not lead to action on the part of the developed countries. Three years later the commission delivered a new report.[10] It showed that in the years since its first report the situation in underde-

---

9. Report of the Independent Commission on International Development Issues (Brandt Commission), *North-South: A Programme for Survival* (Cambridge, Mass.: MIT Press, 1980).

10. Brandt Commission, *Common Crisis: North-South Cooperation for World Recovery* (Cambridge, Mass.: MIT Press, 1983).

veloped countries had severely worsened. The second report also com-
mented upon the very serious situation in the international currency and
credit system, and pointed out how some underdeveloped countries were
near bankruptcy because of their inability not only to get more credits, but
also to amortize and pay interest on old debts.

On this point the Brandt Commission was in line with rescue actions
that were already on their way. The report insisted upon speeding up these
actions and urged an increase in the funds to be made available to the
International Monetary Fund and also to the World Bank. This proposal
may have greater influence on what actually will happen, as it is in line
with policies already being pursued in the interest of the developed countries and their banks which have given these large credits. By itself,
however, it will hardly make more fresh money available to the underdeveloped countries.

[9]

For a still longer time underdeveloped countries have joined together,
rather independently of what type of government they have, to press for
improvements in their economic relations with developed countries. The
United Nations Conference on Trade and Development was an early
outcome of these strivings. Against much resistance it has reached certain
results in some minor questions.

More recently the underdeveloped countries have raised their protest
and demanded a "new international economic order." One world conference after another has been convened to consider that demand. There has
not been unanimity among the underdeveloped countries on what that
new world order should imply, however, and the concrete content has
been rather unclear. But one of the demands has been more aid.

Some developed countries have expressed sympathy for these strivings
and even used them for announcing small adjustments in their aid policies.
Sweden, for instance, has remitted some credits, which were, however,
already written off its own accounts. As the world economic crisis has
continued, I fear that these conferences will remain fruitless. At the Cancun meeting in 1981, called together on the advice of the Brandt Commission, even the United States was pressed to agree to a new meeting of this
type under the United Nations, but it has still not materialized.

Although the developed countries are not prepared to make any substantial concessions in their economic relations with underdeveloped
countries, they generally show their politeness by never asking whether the
underdeveloped countries do not need a new order at home.

Under these conditions, by directing their interests so exclusively to this
rather inconsequential issue, the underdeveloped countries have, I believe,
turned demands for a new economic world order into a sort of alibi for not

reforming the way in which they are governed. Any concessions they might win at these conferences are very small compared with what they should be able to win both economically and socially by the internal reforms I have emphasized in this paper.

Intellectuals, and particularly the academics, whose duty it should be to press for internal reforms, are drawn into putting the blame entirely on those other-worldly international problems. In so doing they escape from being the useful rebels they should be in countries ruled as they are.

Comment

Hla Myint

PROFESSOR MYRDAL BELIEVES that economic growth in the underdeveloped countries has been much less than is stated in the official statistics; that in fact mass poverty "is now almost everywhere increasing and becoming extreme"; and that this is the result not only of the short-run world depression but also of a number of secular factors, notably the continuing population explosion. He traces the root cause of this to the failure of the elitist governments of the underdeveloped countries to carry out radical institutional reforms to counter the cumulative tendency of the free-market forces to aggravate the existing "great inequality of resources and power within the underdeveloped countries themselves." He now feels that aid to the underdeveloped countries should mainly take the form of what may be called "relief aid" to alleviate mass poverty and catastrophes rather than the conventional type of "development aid" directed toward large-scale industrial projects. He describes his paper as "an account of growing pangs of conscience" for not having changed his views on aid "until the shocks experienced in the present world economic crisis."

My comments will be made under three heads. (1) I shall suggest that Professor Myrdal has taken too pessimistic a view of the progress achieved in the past decades by the underdeveloped countries, before the deepening of the current world depression, and that, although there is no ground for complacency, he may well be taking too gloomy a view of the longer-run secular factors. (2) I agree with him that the poor economic performance of many countries is attributable to a failure to undertake internal economic reforms, and I would not myself be too polite to ask "whether the underdeveloped countries do not need a new order at home." Where I disagree with him is with his exclusive emphasis on internal income equalization while denying the need for more outward-looking policies toward foreign trade and foreign investment. (3) I can wholeheartedly support his views on aid in sections 7 and 8 of his paper. I also agree with him on the need to distinguish relief aid from development aid.

Hla Myint is Professor of Economics at the London School of Economics and Political Science.

[1]

Although I have some sympathy for Professor Myrdal's skeptical attitude toward official national income figures, I believe that the broad
dimensions of economic growth in the underdeveloped countries are
reflected fairly convincingly in the figures provided by the annual *World
Development Reports* or in a compilation such as David Morawetz,
Twenty-five Years of Economic Development, 1950 to 1975.[1] Professor
Myrdal is incorrect in thinking that the per capita income figures of the
underdeveloped countries, translated into dollars at the nominal exchange
rate, "certainly cannot be expected to understate what has actually happened." A well-known study has shown that an underestimation of the
real income is likely to occur because of the undervaluation of the non-
traded output. "When the totality of the developed market economies is
compared with the entire group of developing market economies, average
real per capital GDP of the former is 6.4 times that of the latter rather than
the more than 13-fold ratio produced by exchange conversions."[2] In fact, a
country like India is likely to suffer from a large underestimation of its real
GDP per capita both because of its relatively low level of income and also
because of a low ratio of foreign trade to GDP. The rise in real income
implied by the growth rates is also reflected in the declining infant mortality and rising life expectancy among the low-income countries during the
period 1960–75.

Although the burden of population growth in the poorer sections of the
people should not be underestimated, I believe that Professor Myrdal is
painting too gloomy a picture of the overall demographic situation of
underdeveloped countries. Simon Kuznets, after a more systematic empirical analysis, came to a different conclusion: "Thus, one could hardly
argue that in much of Sub-Sahara Africa, Latin America and even Asia, a
reduction of population growth to, say, a tenth of a per cent from the
current annual rate would significantly alleviate the acute growth
problem."[3]

Most economists would nowadays accept the World Bank's estimate
that during the period 1950–75 the per capita income of the underdeveloped countries grew by almost 3 percent a year, an impressive achievement in the face of a rapid population growth of over 2 percent (*World*

1. Since 1978 the *World Development Report* has been published annually for the
World Bank by Oxford University Press, New York. Morawetz's book was published
by Johns Hopkins University Press, Baltimore, Md., 1977.
2. Irving B. Kravis, Alan Heston, and Robert Summers, "Real GDP per Capita for
More than One Hundred Countries," *Economic Journal* (June 1978), p. 241.
3. Simon Kuznets, *Population, Capital and Growth* (London: Heineman Education
Books, 1974), p. 39.

Development Report 1978, p. 3). But this is rather damaging to the older theory of the "vicious circle," and one cannot help feeling that Myrdal's skepticism of the official growth statistics arises from his implicit faith in the theory of "circular and cumulative causation," which has permeated his work from *American Dilemma*, to *Economic Theory and the Underdeveloped Regions*, and thence to *Asian Drama*. I shall turn to this theory for the next part of my comment.

[2]

Myrdal regards his *Economic Theory and the Underdeveloped Regions*[4] as the application of the principle of cumulative causation of inequalities at the international level and his *Asian Drama*[5] as the extension of the same principle to internal inequalities within the individual underdeveloped countries. In this [*Economic Theory*] and in other early writings of mine there was no thought that the existing great inequality of resources and power within the underdeveloped countries themselves could be part of the explanation of their underdevelopment." In *Economic Theory* (p. 55), he wrote: "Basically, the weak spread effects as between countries are thus for the larger part only a reflection of the weak spread effects within the underdeveloped countries caused by their low level of development attained." I take this to mean that the low level of the domestic economic organization is determined *spontaneously* by the natural factors. It was only in *Asian Drama* that he extended the principle of cumulative causation to the policy-induced internal inequalities generated by a failure to carry out radical institutional reforms.

On re-reading Myrdal's *Economic Theory*, I find that his mechanism for the cumulative inequalities at the international level is very sketchily formulated. There was the hypothesis of the weak spread effects because of the underdeveloped state of the domestic framework: "the 'natural' play of the forces in the markets will be working all the time to increase internal and international inequalities as long as its general level of development is low"; there was a reference to Folke Hilgerdt's argument that the gradual filling of the "empty spaces" of the world by labor and capital from Europe has not reduced population pressure in Asia's overpopulated regions; and there was the criticism of Samuelson's factor price equalization theory (*Economic Theory*, pp. 61 and 147–49). I believe that the easy target offered by Samuelson's highly formalized model led Myrdal to throw away the baby with the bath water. This is rather a pity because I believe that when sensibly reinterpreted, the Heckscher-Ohlin factor pro-

---

4. First edition, 1957; hereafter referred to as *Economic Theory*, with page references to the University Paperbacks edition (London: Methuen, 1965).
5. New York: Pantheon, 1968.

portions theory contains an important kernel of truth for the underdeveloped countries. What repels Myrdal (and also myself) is the highly simplified assumptions of the standard trade model of the domestic economy, which amount to an implicit presupposition of a fully developed institutional framework providing a determinate production possibility frontier with the "given" resources and technology. Myrdal rightly starts from the low level of development of the domestic economic organization, but uses it as the basis of his case against freer trade and an outward-looking policy toward foreign investment because he believes that underdevelopment weakens the spread effects. I, on the other hand, would argue that the very underdeveloped state of the domestic economic organization means that we are somewhere within the production possibility frontiers with a greater potential for gains from a more outward-looking policy toward foreign trade and investment than in a fully developed economy.

Myrdal favors a protectionist policy, combining egalitarian domestic reforms with domestic industrialization policies—the resultant internal domestic disequilibrium being insulated from the world market forces by tight economic planning and controls. Myrdal would say that there is something wrong with an underdeveloped country which is *not* suffering from a balance of payments disequilibrium.[6] The conventional neoclassical free-trade economist would insist on appropriate domestic economic policies: an equilibrium exchange rate policy supported by appropriate fiscal and monetary policies and correct pricing of products and factors of production. The neoclassical economist would not neglect public investment in social overhead capital, but since he implicitly starts from a fully developed organizational framework and is concerned only with the correction of the distortions in the allocation of resources with reference to that framework, he tends to ignore the further problem of developing an appropriate organizational framework.

I would go along with the neoclassical economist in stressing the importance of appropriate domestic economic policies, but I would go further and say that the problem of strengthening the organizational framework to enable a country to take advantage of its potential comparative advantage also requires attention. The organizational requirement is *not* exactly symmetrical or neutral for a labor-abundant underdeveloped country compared with a land- or capital-abundant developed country. Comparative advantage offered by an abundance of land and capital can be pursued on the basis of fairly large-scale units of production, whereas comparative advantage offered by an abundant labor supply can be more effectively pursued on a small-scale basis. But catering to the economic needs of a large number of dispersed small-scale units creates an extra demand on the capacity of the domestic economic system to provide an

6. *An International Economy* (London: Routledge and Kegan Paul, 1956), p. 270.

adequate network of marketing and credit and information. Not every labor-abundant underdeveloped country, even if it were following appropriate domestic economic policies in the conventionl neoclassical sense, would be able to comply with these extra organizational requirements. In this context the outward-looking economies (such as Taiwan), which have succeeded in expanding labor-intensive manufactured exports, offer both a vindication of the factor-proportions theory and examples of how appropriate institutional innovation and adaptation may utilize the potential comparative advantage of labor-abundance. In brief, they deliberately encouraged a dispersed pattern of industrialization, in which a decentralized labor-intensive type of small-scale industry operated in close proximity with a dynamic and labor-intensive agricultural sector. This enabled the rural labor supply to be tapped cheaply and flexibly on a part-time or seasonal basis and on a daily community basis in addition to the normal migration to the towns and cities.[7]

This type of institutional innovation, which enables a labor-abundant underdeveloped country to realize its potential comparative advantage from foreign trade, I consider a more potent method of reducing income inequality within a country than Myrdal's proposal for radical institutional reforms combined with an inward-looking policy toward foreign trade and investment. Indeed, it is difficult to be sure what these radical institutional reforms might be. Myrdal candidly admits it is not feasible for underdeveloped countries to redistribute income through taxation or for a densely populated country like India to redistribute land, since there are so many landless people relative to the available land (*Asian Drama*, p. 1380). In contrast, the institutional innovation of the Taiwan type (leaving aside Taiwan's land reforms), combined with the standard neoclassical domestic economic policies, might have helped India to expand its labor-intensive manufactured exports and to defend its textile export markets against the inroads of the East Asian competitors. If India had been able to follow these export-expansion policies, there would have been a markedly greater expansion of employment opportunities for the poor and higher wages for them. Myrdal is of course quite aware of this as a theoretical possibility, but has always been prone to export pessimism. In *Asian Drama* (p. 1203) he wrote: "In general, however, the obstacles to export promotion in manufactures are so great that import substitution usually offers a more promising prospect."

Looking back at the economic performance of the countries considered in *Asian Drama*, I believe that export expansion policies have turned out to be a more promising path toward raising the income levels of the poor than domestic income equalization policies combined with import-

7. See my paper, "Comparative Analysis of Taiwan's Economic Development with Other Countries," *Academia Economic Papers* (Taiwan: Academia Sinica, March 1982).

substitution policies. India, Sri Lanka, and Burma may be regarded as "inward-looking" among the countries considered by Myrdal, and among these South Asian countries Sri Lanka has perhaps gone furthest with internal income equalization policies. In contrast, the Southeast Asian countries, such as Thailand, Malaysia, and the Philippines, have followed more outward-looking policies toward foreign trade and investment. The South Asian countries and the Southeast Asian countries started from approximately the same level of incomes in the 1950s. But after two or three decades, the differential rates of growth associated with the inward- and the outward-looking policies have resulted in a wide divergence of per capita income levels. The Southeast Asian countries now belong to the middle-income countries with per capita income levels two or three times higher than those of the low-income countries of South Asia. On the basis of available information, it is reasonable to conclude that the poorer people in Southeast Asian countries have improved their income levels relative to the poor of South Asia.[8] This does not take account of the spectacular success of the outward-looking policies of the Gang of Four: Singapore, Hong Kong, Taiwan, and Republic of Korea, which Myrdal assigns to a footnote. I believe that, like some other commentators, he tends to exaggerate the role of U.S. aid and land reforms in Taiwan and Korea while underrating the role of their domestic economic policies.[9]

[3]

I can wholeheartedly support Myrdal's criticisms of the current arguments and practice of aid-giving set out in sections 7 and 8 of his paper. I have long felt the necessity of distinguishing the "need criterion" from the "productivity criterion" in aid-giving, criteria that have been blurred by the popularity of "soft loans" supported by soft arguments. Much confusion has arisen from a failure to distinguish five different concepts of aid. (1) First there is "relief" in the form of consumer goods designed to alleviate acute suffering in the short run. This is what Myrdal is emphasizing now.[10] (2) Then there is the Marshall Plan type of "reconstruction aid"

8. A further analysis of the relation between export expansion and income distribution is given in my paper, "Economic Development Strategies of the Southeast Asian Nations and an Assessment of Their future Prospects," for the conference on "The United States, Japan and Southeast Asia: The Issues of Interdependence" sponsored by the East Asian Institute and the International Economic Research Center of Columbia University.

9. For a more systematic assessment, see Walter Galenson, ed., *Economic Growth and Structural Change in Taiwan* (Ithaca, N.Y.: Cornell University Press, 1979), particularly chap. 7 by I. M. D. Little.

10. Myrdal's present position is similar to the position I took in my paper "An Interpretation of Economic Backwardness," *Oxford Economic Papers* (June 1954). I

to repair war damage; this is the "R" in IBRD (International Bank for Reconstruction and Development) and is still relevant given the continuation of serious warfare in Lebanon and many countries in Africa, Asia, and Latin America. (3) "Stabilization aid" is given to ease the shorter-run balance of payments problems; the rationale is to help a country make appropriate adjustments that, by switching resources, will reduce the trade deficit. This may be distinguished from (4) the longer-run "development aid" proper, in the form of investible resources, designed to ease the shortage of domestic savings and to alleviate chronic, as distinct from acute, poverty. (5) Finally, there are various types of aid given, not for the benefit of the aid-receiving countries, but to further the selfish political and economic goals of the aid-giving countries, including aid as a hidden subsidy for their exports. I share Myrdal's distrust of the "global Keynesianism" of the sort underlying the first Brandt Commission report, designed to relieve depression in the advanced countries suffering from "stagflation."

Myrdal used to be a staunch advocate of multilateral aid; I presume that he has now switched over in favor of bilateral aid in which the aid-giving country could control how the aid is used to ensure, not so much an adequate economic rate of return from the chosen project, but an adequate moral rate of return in the relief of poverty. He suggests that aid should be channeled through the ministries of trade and foreign affairs rather than specialist aid agencies. But I must confess that I am still skeptical as to how far official aid is capable of reaching the poor after it has gone through the double filter of the governments of the aid-giving and the aid-receiving countries, each naturally pursuing its own political and economic goals.

---

suggested there that "rather than waste huge sums of money by investing in projects which cannot be justified on the strict productivity principle, it were better to distribute them as free gifts of consumers' goods and services among the poor of Africa." In that paper I also talked about the "disequalizing factors" arising from the free play of the market forces, but this is not the occasion to elaborate the differences between my concept and Myrdal's concept of "backwash" and "spread" effects.

Raúl Prebisch

RAÚL PREBISCH was born in 1901 in Tucuman, Argentina. He was educated at the University of Buenos Aires and has received honorary degrees from universities in several countries.

His posts have included Under Secretary of Finance, Argentina, 1930–32; Executive Secretary to the U.N. Commission for Latin America, 1948–62; Director-General for the Latin American Institute for Economic and Social Planning, 1962–64; Secretary-General to the U.N. Conference on Trade and Development (UNCTAD), 1964–69; and Advisor to the Secretary-General of the United Nations on development problems. He is currently Director of the *CEPAL Review* of the U.N. Economic Commission for Latin America in Santiago, Chile.

In 1974 he was honored with the Jawaharlal Nehru award for International Understanding; in 1977, with the Dag Hammarskjold honorary medal of the German U.N. Association; and in 1981, with the Third World Prize by the Third World Foundation.

His books include *Introducción a Keynes* (Mexico City: Fondo de Cultura Económica, 1947); *Una Neuva Politica Commercial para el Desarrollo* (Mexico City: Fondo de Cultura Económica, 1964); *Transformación y Desarrollo* (Mexico City: Fondo de Cultura Económica, 1965); *Interpretación del Proceso de Desarrollo Latino-Americano en 1949*, U.N. Serie Commemorativa del XXV Aniversario de la CEPAL (Santiago: United Nations, 1973), which also appeared in *Economic Survey of Latin America, 1949* (New York: United Nations, 1950); and *Capitalismo Periférico: Crisis y Transformación* (Mexico City: Fondo de Cultura Económico, 1981).

Among his articles are "Commercial Policy in the Underdeveloped Countries," *American Economic Review*, Papers and Proceedings (May 1959); and "El Desarrollo Económico della América Latina y Algunos de Sus Principales Problemas," *Boletin Económico América Latina*, vol. 7, no. 1 (February 1962).

His writing and activities have been directed toward an understanding of the development of the countries of the world economic periphery, particularly those of Latin America. His policy proposals have been influential, especially in relation to the creation of a New International Economic Order.

Five Stages in My Thinking
on Development

WHEN I STARTED MY LIFE as a young economist and professor during the 1920s, I was a firm believer in neoclassical theories. However, the first great crisis of capitalism—the world Depression—prompted in me serious doubts regarding these beliefs. It was the beginning of a long period of heresies, as I tried to explore new views on development matters. The second great crisis of capitalism, which we are all suffering now, has strengthened my attitude.

In the long lapse of time between these two great crises, my thinking on development has gone through five successive stages under the influence of a changing reality and the broadening of my own experience.

During those hectic years of the Depression I had some influence on the economic policy of my country, Argentina, first as under secretary of finance and later with the Central Bank. During the 1930s I recommended orthodox anti-inflationary measures to eliminate the fiscal deficit and suppress inflationary tendencies, but at the same time I departed from orthodoxy when I had to face a serious balance of payments disequilibrium and advocated a resolute industrialization policy as well as other measures to this end.

My duties during this period did not permit me to devote time to theoretical activities. But after I left these responsibilities in the early 1940s, I spent some years trying to derive some theoretical views from my experience. This was the first stage, before my association with the Comisión Económica para América Latina (CEPAL, the United Nations Economic Commission for Latin America). The second and third stages evolved thereafter, during my cooperation with CEPAL, and the fourth relates to my work in the United Nations Conference on Trade and Development (UNCTAD). The fifth stage corresponds to a final period when, free from executive responsibilities for the first time in many years, I have been able to revise and advance systematically in my thinking.

The First Stage

The first stage evolved after 1943 when, having been forced to leave my public responsibilities, I was able to devote some years to reflection on the meaning of my previous experience. Important theoretical problems emerged in my mind. Why must I depart suddenly from well-entrenched beliefs? Why was it necessary for the state to play an active role in development? Why was it that policies formulated at the center could not be followed at the periphery?

These and other reflections paved the way for the next stage.

The Second Stage

My entry into CEPAL in 1949 took place when my ideas were already reaching maturity, and I was therefore able to crystallize them in various studies published in the early 1950s. In these studies I tried both to diagnose the problems and to suggest policies which would serve as alternatives to those proposed by orthodox thinking. Thanks to the broader horizon which my new responsibilities permitted me, these studies concerned not only Argentina but Latin America as a whole.

In formulating my point of view I mentioned from the beginning the role of technological progress. In particular, my interest was attracted by the question of the international dissemination of technology and the distribution of its fruits, since the empirical evidence revealed considerable inequality between the producers and exporters of manufactured goods on the one hand and the producers and exporters of primary commodities on the other. I tried to understand the nature, causes, and dynamics of this inequality and studied some of its manifestations, such as disparity in demand elasticity and the tendency toward deterioration of the terms of trade for primary commodity exports, which industrialization as well as other policy measures could counteract.

In trying to find an explanation for these phenomena in those years, I put special emphasis on the fact that the countries of Latin America formed part of a system of international economic relations which I named the "center-periphery" system.[1] In reality, this concept had been turning over in my mind for some time. At first I gave it a cyclical character, considering that it reflected the active role of the industrial centers and the passivity of the periphery, where the consequences of the economic fluctuations of the centers were intensified. There was in effect an "economic constellation," at the center of which were the industrialized countries. Favored by this position and by their early technical progress, the industrialized countries organized the system as a whole to serve their own interests. The countries producing and exporting raw materials were thus linked with the center as a function of their natural resources, thereby

---

1. See, in particular, *The Economic Development of Latin America and Its Principal Problems* (New York: United Nations, 1950); and *Economic Survey of Latin America, 1949* (New York: United Nations, 1950).

forming a vast and heterogeneous periphery incorporated in the system in different ways and to different extents.

For each peripheral country, the type and extent of its linkage with the center depended largely on its resources and its economic and political capacity for mobilizing them. In my view, this fact was of the greatest importance, since it conditioned the economic structure and dynamism of each country—that is the rate at which technical progress could penetrate and the economic activities such progress would engender. Similarly, this system of international economic relations exaggerated the degree to which income in the periphery was siphoned off by the centers. Moreover, the penetration and propagation of technical progress in the countries of the periphery was too slow to absorb the entire labor force in a productive manner. Thus, the concentration of technical progress and its fruits in economic activities oriented toward exports became characteristic of a heterogeneous social structure in which a large part of the population remained on the sidelines of development.

My diagnosis of the situation of the countries of Latin America was constructed on the basis of my criticism of the pattern of outward-oriented development, which I considered to be incapable of permitting the full development of those countries. My proposed development policy was oriented toward the establishment of a new pattern of development which would make it possible to overcome the limitations of the previous pattern. This new form of development would have industrialization as its main objective. In reality, my policy proposal sought to provide theoretical justification for the industrialization policy which was already being followed (especially by the large countries of Latin America), to encourage the others to follow it too, and to provide all of them with an orderly strategy for carrying this out. This task was by no means easy, because the recovery of the international economic order after the Second World War and the expansion of exports caused a resurgence of the champions of outward-oriented development and the criticism of industrialization of the periphery.

I should like to underline some aspects of my policy proposals which seem to me to be of particular importance.

Industrialization

The technology of the centers had penetrated mainly into activities connected with primary exports, which responded to the needs of the industrial countries, but not into other activities of peripheral countries where the productivity of a very large proportion of the labor force was very low. The basic problem of development therefore involved raising the level of productivity of the entire labor force. However, export activities suffered from serious limitations from this point of view, for the possibilities of increasing commodity exports were restricted by the relatively slow growth of demand in the centers because of the generally low demand elasticity for primary products and their protectionist policies. Consequently, industrialization had a very important role to play in the employment of these large masses of manpower of very low productivity as well as the manpower released by further technological progress not only in export activities but also in the production of agricultural goods for domestic consumption.

But could industry be developed when costs of production were much higher than in the centers?

Let me repeat that, as a young economist, I was a neoclassicist and fought against protection. But during the world Depression, throwing overboard a substantial part of my former beliefs, I was converted to protectionism.

Theoretically, the problem was put in the following dynamic terms. What is to be done with productive resources when further expansion of primary exports would bring a fall in prices? Should these resources be used to generate additional exports, or should they be allocated to industrial production for domestic consumption?

The most economically advantageous solution depends on the proper combination between these two compatible options. Additional primary exports would be more advantageous provided the export income lost through the fall in prices was not greater than the income lost because of the higher cost of domestic industrial production in relation to imported industrial goods. Once beyond the point where such income losses were the same, the option in favor of industrialization was quite obvious.

This was essentially my reasoning. I underlined that this cost was necessary to accelerate the rate of productive employment and consequently the rate of development. The net economic result was quite positive insofar as the global product could grow faster than the rate of primary exports. But every effort must be made to intensify these exports without overstepping the limits just referred to.

No emphasis was put at this stage on exports of manufactures to the centers, because suitable industrial infrastructure was lacking and conditions in the centers were unfavorable. To spark the beginning of this process I strongly recommended the stimulation of exports of manufactures—as well as primary goods—among Latin American countries. I envisaged preferential arrangements by regions or subregions that would lead in the course of time to a common market.

Conventional economists both in the centers and in the periphery have always attacked (and continue to attack) protection as a form of intervention violating the laws of the market. Industrialization, they claimed, should be spontaneous. If costs of production were higher than in the centers, wages should be adjusted to become competitive. And exchange devaluation was the best instrument to promote both exports and import-substitution. My position, however, was that once the limit already re-

ferred to was passed, additional primary exports that were already competitive would bring a loss of income through the deterioration of the
terms of trade.[2]

From this analysis emerged the conclusion that import substitution
stimulated by a moderate and selective protection policy was an economically sound way to achieve certain desirable effects. Such a policy would
help correct the tendency toward a foreign constraint on development
resulting from the low income elasticity of demand for imports of primary
product by the centers, compared with the high income elasticity of
demand at the periphery for manufactures from the centers. Import substitution by protection counteracts the tendency toward the deterioration
of the terms of trade, by avoiding the allocation of additional productive
resources to primary export activities and diverting them instead to industrial production. (I also recognized other possibilities of counteracting that
tendency by various ways of limiting competition.) Industrialization, in
addition to assisting the overall penetration of technology and creating
employment, promotes changes in the structure of production in response
to this high demand elasticity for manufactures. Therefore, industrialization and increased productivity in primary production are complementary. The more intense the latter, the greater the need for industrialization.

Relations with the Centers

I strongly criticized the insistence of the centers on the outworn idea of
the international division of labor. First they opposed industrialization,
and later they exalted the dominant role of the transnationals in an
efficient process of import substitution. I recognized the importance of
these corporations for introducing technical progress, but at the same time
I emphasized the need for a selective policy in order to avoid the excessive
pressure of profits on the balance of payments, to check their role in the
diffusion of forms of consumption contrary to the accumulation of reproductive capital, and to orient development toward a sense of national
autonomy. I strongly advocated important changes in the trade policy of
the centers, and stressed the need for an enlightened transfer of financial
and technological resources.

Generally speaking, my attack on protectionism at the centers and my
defense of protectionism at the periphery has been misinterpreted. I envisaged the latter type of protection as necessary during a rather long transition period in which these disparities in demand elasticity should be
corrected. Protection at the centers aggravates these disparities, while at
the periphery it tends to correct them, provided they do not exceed certain

2. See my first works in CEPAL already cited, and also "Commercial Policy in the
Underdeveloped Countries," *American Economic Review* (May 1959).

limits. The wider the disparity, the greater the need for import substitution (as well as the promotion of exports of manufactures), especially if the rate of growth of peripheral countries is higher than in the centers.

An important policy consideration emerged from this assertion. The insistence of the centers on reciprocity in trade concessions was generally detrimental to peripheral growth. An increase in exports to the centers by virtue of concessions from the periphery implicitly brings with it an element of reciprocity. Why is this? Because given the high income elasticity, that increase in peripheral exports to the centers is followed by a corresponding expansion in peripheral imports from them. Quite apart from this, I considered that the rationalization of protectionism in Latin American countries was in any case a requirement for sound development.

Planning and the Market

The structural changes inherent in industrialization require rationality and foresight in government policy and investment in infrastructure to accelerate growth, to obtain the proper relation of industry with agriculture and other activities, and to reduce the external vulnerability of the economy. These were strong reasons for planning.[3] Another important one was the need to intensify the rate of internal capital accumulation through proper incentives and other policy measures.

International financial resources were to complement and enhance a country's capacity to save, while changes in the structure of trade were necessary to use these savings for capital goods imports. Planning should help obtain these resources and accomplish the latter objective.

Planning was compatible with the market and private initiative. It was needed to establish certain basic conditions for the adequate functioning of the market in the context of a dynamic economy. But it did not necessarily require detailed state investment, except in infrastructure and development promotion. However, there were other reasons for this.

The Third Stage

The third stage was mainly one of criticism in the late 1950s and early 1960s. I was critical of policy and of ideas, in response to changes occurring in the process of development and my better understanding of problems.

---

3. I advocated planning in particular in *Theoretical and Practical Problems of Economic Growth* (Mexico City: United Nations, 1950); and "Los Principales Problemas de la Técnica Preliminar de Programación," chap. 1 of *Introducción a la Técnica de Programación* (Mexico City: United Nations, 1955).

The Flaws of Industrialization

On the one hand, it was clear that the process of industrialization (at least in the most advanced peripheral countries) had nearly exhausted the possibilities of further import substitution for the internal market of nondurable consumer goods. It was therefore necessary to enter into more complex and difficult forms of industrialization in intermediary products as well as capital goods and durables requiring larger markets. Consequently I advocated suitable measures conducive to a Latin American Common Market.[4]

On the other hand, the reconstruction of the world economy had been completed with the reorganization of the international system of trade and payments to improve its efficiency. New trade possibilities were visualized for the periphery, and I advocated a policy to stimulate exports of manufactures to the centers and to strengthen trade relations within the periphery. My reasoning was that industrialization had been asymmetrical, since it was based on import substitution through protection without corresponding promotion of exports of manufactures. Protection should be matched with selective export subsidies in order to face cost differentials with the centers. Furthermore, industrial policy had been improvised, principally to counteract the effects of a cyclical fall in exports. It was necessary to introduce rationality and correct exaggerations and abuses by reducing duties. Excessive duties not only distorted industrial production but also had adverse effects on exports of primary products.

Income Disparities

Up to this stage I had not paid sufficient attention to the problem of income disparities, except in the case of the outdated land tenure system. Nor had I paid enough attention in the early CEPAL years to the fact that growth had not benefited large masses of the low-income population, while at the other extreme of the social structure high incomes flourished. Perhaps this attitude of mine was a remnant of my former neoclassicism, which assumed that growth in itself would eventually correct great income disparities through the play of market forces.

At the beginning of the 1960s I changed fundamentally, for some estimates made by CEPAL economists about the dimensions of this problem were appalling indeed. What had caused these great disparities? In the light of the theoretical interpretation that I elaborated years later, I confess

4. The idea of a Latin American Common Market was present in my works from the late 1940s. See especially *El Mercado Común Latinoamericano*, pt. 1 (New York: United Nations, 1959).

that I fell into conventional explanations: the concentration of land, excessive protection, and inflation.[5]

Earlier I had frequently emphasized the need to enhance the rate of capital accumulation both in material goods and in the formation of human resources. At this stage I presented a series of projections to show the possibility of achieving this objective at the expense of privileged consumption of the high income strata in order to employ productively those large masses of the population which had not shared in the fruits of development.

Inflation

I frequently dealt with inflation in my writings. Inflation aggravated social disparities but did not help to increase accumulation, as some would expect. On the contrary, it promoted conspicuous consumption. My treatment of this matter was rather conventional, however, with some occasional incursions into structural factors and external vulnerability. I was far from being sympathetic to the views and prescriptions of the International Monetary Fund, but notwithstanding my previous experience at the Central Bank in noninflationary times, I was not able to recommend policies different from those I criticized.

Be that as it may, it took me some years to understand the real meaning of inflation and the process of income distribution. I was intrigued by these phenomena but I could not undertake further efforts at theoretical elucidation, for I had to leave CEPAL to take charge of the establishment and initial years of UNCTAD. That was the fourth stage.

The Fourth Stage

The fourth stage related to my work at UNCTAD (from 1963 to the end of the 1960s) and was oriented toward matters of international cooperation. This new responsibility was a very heavy one, but extremely challenging. I had no time for theoretical pursuits, and I had to have recourse to my previous CEPAL thinking.

Despite the great differences between the countries of the world periphery, there were many common denominators. This enabled me to present a full body of policy recommendations that constituted the starting point for discussion by member governments—or rather discussion and confrontation, for there was no meeting of minds. This was the beginning of the North-South dialogue, although it was and continues to be more a

---

5. See in particular *El Falso Dilema entre Desarrollo Económico y Estabilidad Monetaria* (Santiago de Chile, 1961); and *Towards a Dynamic Development Policy for Latin America* (New York: United Nations, 1963).

series of parallel monologues, not conducive to concrete action, on the most fundamental problems of international cooperation in trade, finance, and technology.

One of the main arguments prevailing in the developed countries was that the developing countries should take adequate measures to deal with their own internal development problems. Far from dissenting from this view, I underlined the need for a global strategy on the basis of joint responsibilities, common objectives, and convergent measures to achieve them.[6]

However, I did not succeed: clear proof that the North was not willing to act nor was the South inclined to engage in the very serious structural transformations needed to pave the way for development and social equity. The problems continue to be essentially the same, but seriously aggravated by the present crisis of the centers.

Although my endeavors at UNCTAD interrupted my theoretical activities, I had the benefit of broadening my field of knowledge and gaining a better insight into the workings of the system, both at the center and at the periphery, and into the complexities of their relationship. This contributed to the fifth stage of my thinking.

The Fifth Stage

The fifth stage really started when, after many years of rewarding international service, I was able to free myself of executive responsibilities. CEPAL put me in charge of its *Review*, where I resumed my theoretical pursuits in a series of articles that formed the basis for my *Capitalismo Periférico* (Peripheral Capitalism).[7] This was the fifth and probably last stage of my thinking in development matters.

The Search for New Answers

From the start, I asked myself some questions of paramount importance which had previously been left without convincing answers. Why was the

6. *Towards a New Trade Policy for Development: Report by the Secretary-General of UNCTAD* (New York: UNCTAD, 1964); *Towards a New Global Strategy for Development: Report by the Secretary-General of UNCTAD* (New York: UNCTAD, 1968); and *Change and Development: Latin America's Great Task* (Washington D.C.: Inter-American Development Bank, 1970).

7. "A Critique of Peripheral Capitalism," *CEPAL Review*, no. 1 (First half of 1976); "Socioeconomic Structure and Crisis of Peripheral Capitalism," *CEPAL Review*, no. 6 (Second half of 1978); "Towards a Theory of Change," *CEPAL Review*, no. 10 (April 1980); "The Latin American Periphery in the Global System of Capitalism," *CEPAL Review*, no. 13 (April 1981); "Dialogue on Friedman and Hayek from the Standpoint of the Periphery," *CEPAL Review*, no. 15 (December 1981); and *Capitalismo Periférico: Crisis y Transformación* (Mexico City: Fondo de Cultura Económica, 1981).

development process accompanied by growing disparities in income and wealth? Why was inflation so persistent, and why could it not yield to the use of conventional means? What were the reasons for some important contradictions in the development process at the periphery which had not occurred in the historical development of the centers, at least not with comparable intensity? Why had the periphery been left behind?

These and other questions dominated my mind and prompted new efforts to find consistent answers. For this purpose I went over my previous ideas very critically. Although it is true that there were some valid elements in them, they were very far from constituting a theoretical system. I arrived at the conclusion that to start building a system it was necessary to enlarge the scope beyond purely economic theory. Indeed, economic factors could not be isolated from the social structure. This was of paramount importance. It would be hopeless to seek a proper answer to these and other important questions within the narrow framework of a purely economic theory.

The Center-Periphery Concept Once Again

My old concept of center and periphery was still valid, but it had to be enriched by introducing some very important consequences of the hegemony of the centers. Obviously it was not my purpose to deal theoretically with the centers. Some facts had to be clarified, however, in order to understand the other side, the periphery.

Technological progress started at the centers and its fruits remained basically there. For better or worse, they did not spread to the periphery through a general fall in prices in relation to increases in productivity. Historically, the role of the periphery had been mainly restricted to the supply of primary products. This explains why the growth of income stimulated demand and continuous technological innovations at the centers and gave great impetus to industrialization. The periphery was left behind not because of malicious design but because of the dynamics of the system.

It so happened that peripheral industrialization had been greatly delayed and took place during successive crises at the centers. This accentuated the tendency of the periphery to imitate the centers—to grow in their image and likeness. We tried to adopt their technologies and life styles, to follow their ideas and ideologies, to reproduce their institutions.

All this penetrated the social structure of the periphery, which lagged considerably behind the most advanced structure of the centers, and brought significant mutations and contradictions that it is of the utmost importance to clarify. This is in fact the clue to understanding why the system tends to exclude socially those at the bottom, why it becomes more and more conflictive in the course of its evolution, and finally why it eventually tends toward a serious crisis.

The Dynamic Importance of the Economic Surplus

I shall try to explain these phenomena in a rather summary fashion. The essence of my interpretation turns around the concept of the economic surplus, that considerable portion of successive increments of productivity that is appropriated by the owners of the means of production, especially those concentrated in the high social strata.

The surplus is a structural phenomenon. In the heterogeneous social structure of the periphery a great proportion of the labor force is employed in activities of very low productivity. By virtue of the process of capital accumulation, this labor force is gradually absorbed into occupations of greater productivity. However, their remunerations do not increase correspondingly because of the regressive competition of those who have remained in occupations of much lower productivity and income (or are unemployed). Only a relatively small fraction of the labor force qualified to respond to the growing requirements of technological advance is in a position to share spontaneously in the fruits of productivity (thanks mainly to its social power).

I attach to the surplus paramount dynamic importance. Indeed, it is the main source of reproductive capital that multiplies employment and productivity. At the same time, however, it is also the means of enhancing privileged consumption by the high social strata which imitate more and more the consumption patterns of the centers.

The privileged consumer society is detrimental to reproductive capital accumulation. It promotes a premature diversification of demand with adverse social effects. To this should be added the disproportionate siphoning-off of income by the centers, specially through transnational corporations, which are closely geared to the privileged consumer society. Here lies the main explanation of the tendency of the system to exclude a sizable proportion of the labor force.

Let us understand clearly the nature of the surplus. It is based fundamentally on sheer economic, political, and social inequality. *And to fulfill its dynamic role it has to grow* in the course of time. There is a dynamic sequence in this process. Increase in reproductive capital accumulation, increase in employment and productivity, further increase in capital accumulation, and so on.

Thus, the continuous growth of the surplus, the rate at which it grows, and the use made of it depend on the successive increments of productivity added to it. In the course of development, however, other forces emerge that try to share in these increases in productivity, and in the long run they tend to weaken the rate of growth of the surplus for a given rate of increase in productivity.

These forces result from changes in the social structure in the course of development when, mainly through industrialization, technology penetrates a broader area. There are then changes in occupation and income, accompanied by changes in the power structure as an integral part of the social structure. This opens the way for the advance of the labor union and the political power of the labor force. This emerging power tends to counteract the power of appropriation of the surplus by the upper strata.

Changes in the Power Structure

The intensity of these changes in power relations depends largely upon the evolution of the process of democratization. When this process is hampered or manipulated by the top strata, the redistributive power of the labor force is limited. When the democratic process advances genuinely, however, that redistributive power augments the effectiveness of democratization.

But that is not all. To this redistributive power of the labor force is added the growing power of the state to share in the fruits of productivity. Part of the growth of the state is due to the spurious absorption of manpower that does not find employment because of the insufficient accumulation of reproductive capital—a situation that thus aggravates this problem of growing state power.

Let me clarify another point. I have been speaking about the behavior of the labor force. This behavior is due to the efforts of workers not only to improve their real earnings, but also to recuperate their losses from taxes that fall directly or indirectly upon them. From this point of view, the labor force is an intermediary in the pressure of the state on the surplus. No wonder, therefore, that when the labor force has that power, taxes falling on them become inflationary.

There are also taxes which are not inflationary, since they fall in one way or another upon the surplus. Even so, by weakening the growth of the surplus, they aggravate the effects of the pressure of the labor force and the state.

What are the results of this dual redistributive pressure? Obviously it tends to increase consumption: private and social consumption by the labor force, and consumption by the state, including military consumption. However, these different forms of consumption do not evolve at the expense of consumption by the high-income groups which enjoy the surplus; instead, each form is superimposed on the others.

Here we are arriving at the gist of our problem. These various forms of consumption cannot continue to increase indefinitely, for they encroach upon the rate of reproductive capital accumulation and thereby impair the dynamic sequence of accumulation, employment, productivity, and accumulation. How long can business enterprises resist the dual pressure of the labor force and the state without transferring this pressure to prices?

The Role of Money

Monetary policy has a great influence on this. Let us look in a very simplified way at its role in the appropriation of the surplus.

The different stages in the productive process, from primary production to the sale of the final product in the market, take a certain amount of time. To increase the production of these final goods it is necessary to begin at the primary stage with an increase in employment.

This is where the role of the monetary authority comes in: to supply the larger amount of money needed to pay the growing wage and salary bill. This increase in money should be just enough to match the growth of final production owing to the growth of employment. If it is less, the increase in productivity will be accompanied by a fall in prices.

This monetary expansion constitutes an integral part of the productive process, a mechanism whereby the surplus is appropriated by the owners of the means of production. The surplus tends to grow continually, whether it is allocated to consumption or to capital accumulation.

What happens, then, when business enterprises demand more money to pay higher remunerations? If the monetary authority follows a restrictive policy to avoid inflation, it can press enterprises to absorb these higher remunerations at the expense of the rate of growth of the surplus. But there is a limit to this policy. Enterprises under pressure of labor power can indeed be constrained to use the increments of productivity and even a part of the surplus that has been growing. This, however, has obvious detrimental effects, not only because it reduces the earning capacity of business, but also because it restricts the dynamic role of the surplus in relation to the rate of capital accumulation and the rate of increase in employment.

The Tendency toward the Inflationary Crisis of the Economic Process

It is understandable that these tensions in the system cannot continue for long, and the monetary authority finally has to yield to the growing pressure of enterprises, labor, and government. Additional money is created to match higher remunerations, and prices go up. It is the beginning of a new type of structural inflation. As the labor force reacts with a new increase in remunerations, the inflationary spiral gathers momentum. Enterprises increase prices expecting to restore the surplus. But this does not last long, because the labor force reacts by pushing up remunerations correspondingly, when they have sufficient power to do so. Therefore capital accumulation suffers to the detriment of development, and the whole process is utterly distorted when the inflationary spiral gathers momentum.

What is to be done, then? In the Latin American experience there are two ways out. One is through monetary policy, that is to say, credit restriction. But this type of inflation cannot be attacked in this conventional fashion, because it turns out to be counterproductive. Enterprises need *more* credit to face the increase in wages and salaries, and if they do not get more, they are obliged to use available credit at the expense of the increase of production in process, that is to say, of working capital. Recession or contraction follows.

The other way to stop the spiral is to control wages and salaries by government intervention and let prices attain their "proper" level. In other terms, this involves restoring the surplus to the detriment of the labor force. The workers must then not only retreat from what they have gained previously but also bear the weight of taxes that they can no longer transfer by readjusting their remunerations.

The state is then required to use force to overcome the political strength of the labor unions and the masses. Consider the paradox: the use of force by the state is justified by invoking the principle that the state should not intervene in the economy! Economic liberalism is strongly proclaimed at the tremendous social and political cost of destroying political liberalism, if we interpret these concepts in their original philosophic unity.

I cannot deny that the restoration of the surplus through implacable control of wages and salaries could raise the rate of accumulation. But at the same time it would give further impetus to the privileged consumer society, and the latter prevails over the former.

I cannot deny, either, that control could reduce, if not eliminate, inflation of internal origin. If this phenomenon nevertheless continues, it is due to external or fiscal inflation or to the abusive expansion of private credit. But in fact this does not worry the dominant groups, provided the growth of the surplus is fully restored and respected.

The Limits of Redistributive Power

The surplus and its dynamic role are based on inequity—technical, economic, and political. Democratic processes have been very effective in improving real earnings and in the evolution of the state. In the present system, however, there is a limit that must not be overstepped by redistributive power, a limit reached when the dynamics of the system is jeopardized. At this limit the surplus and the privileged consumer society have reached their maximum levels, and the redistributive process to improve income distribution cannot proceed further.

I am not implying that the whole surplus could be redistributed and at the same time a larger share given to the state, which generally grows at an exaggerated pace. Indeed, one of the main flaws of the process is to yield to disproportionate consumption of what should be allocated for capital accumulation.

However, there is nothing in the play of the laws of the market or in monetary policy to correct this flaw. Nor is there any safeguard against the use of the democratic process to improve income distribution beyond the aforesaid limit. On the contrary, if this is done the redistributive pressure leads to the crisis of the system. The democratic process tends to devour itself. In the light of what I have said, I must regretfully conclude that in the advanced course of peripheral development the process of democratization tends to become incompatible with the regular functioning of the system. This is not due so much to the failure of that process on account of the political immaturity that prevails in the periphery, but rather to the serious socioeconomic bias of the mechanism for income distribution and capital accumulation in favor of the high social strata.

Let me emphasize, in order to avoid frequent confusion, that the market is far from being the supreme regulator of the economy. Nonetheless, it has considerable economic and political importance. What really matters is the structure behind the market and the arbitrary play of power relations. Let us change the structures, preserve the market, and respect income disparities emerging from different individual contributions to the productive process.

The Market at the International Level

A similar reflection could be made in relation to international market forces. I fully recognize the value of competition, notwithstanding the well-known fact that it is far from being prevalent. For the correct functioning of the international market, however, it is necessary to deal with the consequences of the great structural disparities between the centers and the periphery. I noted earlier that the fruits of productivity are retained mainly in the centers. This increases demand and promotes technological innovations and capital accumulation in the centers, with only appendicular effects on the periphery in the historical development of capitalism.

This pattern of development has left the periphery on the margin of industrialization. When industrialization has started there (typically with a great lag), it has been necessary to resort to protection and subsidies to compensate for the economic and technological superiority of the centers, as I have explained when dealing with the second and third stages. This applies to those industrial activities in which the periphery could compete with the centers. However, the centers are reluctant to admit this competition even when there are no export subsidies.

How can this be explained in the light of the two successful trade rounds (Kennedy and Tokyo)? They have achieved an impressive reduction of duties and restrictions. But these have been mainly for technologically advanced goods resulting from incessant innovations, where the transnationals have made great progress. It is quite understandable that for the time being the periphery has no access to these innovations, nor can it participate (except marginally) in the extraordinary flow of international trade in these goods. This liberal trade policy in the centers is applied to those goods in which the periphery lags behind technologically. In goods where it can compete, the centers are very far from following a liberal policy.

The centers, principally the United States, have emphasized the role of the transnational corporations in the periphery. These corporations are supposed to internationalize production. Primarily, however, they have internationalized consumption by giving impetus to the privileged consumption society.

There is an aspect of paramount importance to which governments of developing countries have not paid sufficient attention. We have not yet been able to break the pattern of isolation these countries inherited from the old framework of the international division of trade. Indeed, most of world trade has been between the centers themselves. Trade of the developing countries has converged on the centers, and the enormous potential for reciprocal trade has been overlooked. From the earliest days of CEPAL I have strongly preached the need for this structural trade reform.[8]

The Historical Hegemony of the Centers

The pattern of trade has been, and continues to be, a factor in the survival of the historical hegemony of the centers over the periphery. This hegemony is changing, but is very strongly buttressed by the fragmentation of the developing world and the economic and technological superiority of the centers. Colleagues of mine, both within and outside of CEPAL, have dealt much better than I with the political and strategic significance of this hegemony. The concept of "dependence" emerged from them. As generally happens, however, the pendulum of controversy went to the other extreme, so that some writers have tried to explain all the flaws of peripheral development as being due to "dependence." No wonder that in their zeal some of them recommend a radical "delinking" from the centers. In my latest book I have tried to present a balanced view of these phenomena of hegemony.[9]

One of the manifestations of hegemony is the resistance of the centers to change in the status quo. I am referring not only to the center-periphery relationship but also to important structural changes within the periphery and within the centers. Immediate interests prevail and when the periphery, rightly or not, hurts these economic or political interests, the centers—especially the principal dynamic center—frequently react with punitive measures; in extreme cases even with military intervention.

8. See, for example, the works already cited in notes 1 and 2.
9. *Capitalismo Periférico*, pt. 4.

The Need to Transform the System

The transformation of the system seems to me inevitable if we are to combine development with social equity and political advance. However, the most widely disseminated doctrinal options do not appear to be of much use for guiding this transformation.

The neoclassical option advocates the restoration of the dynamic growth of the surplus in line with the principles of peripheral capitalism, even though in order to do this it is necessary to stifle the process of democratization by imposing authoritarian regimes. Quite apart from its proven ineffectiveness, this neoclassical option should be rejected because of its renunciation of democratic and liberal political values. The various options which have been supported by democratic movements (such as the Social Democrats or Christian Democrats) usually drift toward mere redistribution and the crises associated with this, without having any idea how to get out of these problems. Orthodox socialism, for its part, puts its faith in state ownership of the means of production and also stifles the democratization process. I therefore believe the time has come to search for a synthesis of both socialism and genuine economic liberalism, and thereby restore that essential philosophic unity of economic liberalism with political liberalism. The discussion of this delicate subject constitutes the last part of my recent book.

Socialism is necessary to ensure the "social use" of the surplus. The rate of capital accumulation and the correction of great social disparities should be the subject of collective decisions, and a new political and economic institutional regime should be established for that purpose. Moreover, economic liberalism is necessary insofar as individual decisions to produce and consume should be left to the market.

We need a policy inspired with a long-term vision on both sides. But the long term starts now with regard to enlightened policy action involving a series of agreed convergent measures. The centers and the periphery are losing a great opportunity. Nothing important is being done to meet a tremendous historical responsibility with far-reaching economic, social, and political consequences for the whole world!

Comment

Albert Fishlow

RAÚL PREBISCH identifies five stages in the evolution of his approach to economic development during a long and distinguished career. Despite, or perhaps because of, a significant commitment to public service, he excludes his policy role in Argentina in the 1930s and passes over rapidly his period as secretary-general of UNCTAD in the 1960s. It is a measure of the importance he has always attached to the value and influence of ideas.

I follow him here in focusing on his seminal contributions to the problems of Latin American industrialization from the late 1940s to the early 1960s, and to his most recent thinking on peripheral capitalism.

Like many of his fellow pioneers, Raúl Prebisch interpreted lagging economic development and income disparities in the developing world as the result of market failure: private calculations and market incentives did not succeed in directing resources where these long-term social returns would be greatest. Unlike others, such as W. A. Lewis or Paul Rosenstein-Rodan, for example, he formulated his views explicitly within an international economic framework and derived important and immediate policy implications. At the heart of the matter is Prebisch's argument that the gains of technological progress, concentrated at the center, will not be appropriately distributed by the prices of center and periphery tradables.

The issue is actually dealt with at two levels. In asserting the unfair operation of the international economy, Prebisch relied upon market imperfections that caused the terms of trade inadequately to favor the periphery: monopoly in the center and/or segmented capital markets in the periphery. These led to excessively high prices of manufactures and excessive production of low-priced primary exports. This strand of the argument, later to be reinforced by criticism of multinationals and their excessive returns, emphasizes the deviation from perfectly competitive comparative advantage. The consequence is a smaller gain from trade for the periphery. This disparity, however, is not necessarily reflected in the movement of the barter terms of trade, but is related to the double factoral terms of trade—corrected for the technical change in each trading partner.

Albert Fishlow is Professor of Economics at the University of California, Berkeley.

Under Prebisch's assumption that productivity increases more rapidly, if not exclusively, in the center, the barter terms could provide the necessary evidence of progressive loss. This line of attack resurfaces later in the guise of unequal exchange. It powerfully condemns the inherent structure of center-peripheral relations and so directly leads on to prescriptions of North-South delinking and radical change rather than to more modest policy intervention.

For all its political sway, the predominant Prebisch emphasis is another: the more mundane behavioral implications of disparate income (and price) elasticities of demand for manufactures and primary products in the center and periphery. These differences predictably guide dynamic comparative advantage and imply a market-signaled, overly large investment in primary production for export in the periphery relative to investment in manufactures. Such a consistent trend in the terms of trade makes present prices an inappropriate signal for accumulation decisions, and justifies public intervention both to limit imports and to promote industrialization. If not, development is eventually checked. Strongly influenced by the experience of the 1930s—both the magnitude of the decline in import capacity and the success of many of the larger Latin American countries in their production of import substitutes—Prebisch also placed great emphasis upon cyclical fluctuations. Balance of payments fluctuations that checked economic growth when export prices fell because of limited domestic flexibility could mean smaller income levels than a less specialized economy might attain. Prebisch, as had other proponents of industrialization before him, had found reason to doubt the wisdom of a division of labor that implied concentration on primary exports.

The timing of his theoretical justification for the import substitution activities of many countries in the region was critical. The postwar period saw actual improvement in the terms of trade for many countries and favorable prospects for exports. Thus it was necessary to invoke long-term and inevitable trends, and normative arguments, to counteract the immediate force of market signals. As Prebisch revealingly comments, "This task was by no means easy, because the recovery of the international economic order after the Second World War and the expansion of exports caused a resurgence of the champions of outward-oriented development . . ." He might have added that the favorable international climate also facilitated the taxing of agricultural exports through overvalued exchange rates without provoking an early balance of payments crisis.

The practical importance of Prebisch's formulation is clear in the sway it held over development policies in the 1950s and 1960s and even subsequently. Despite academic criticism addressed to the persuasiveness of the theoretical case he formulated for protectionism, industrialization, and planning—for those were the critical conclusions—and mounting statistical evidence that the terms of trade had not shown trend deterioration, import substitution dominated. It did so not merely because of the persuasiveness of Prebisch's ideas, but also because of the conditions then prevailing. In the 1950s the terms of trade eroded for many countries from cyclical Korean War highs and discouraged investment in the primary sector because industrialization in many Latin American countries had already reached levels at which national producers represented a significant political voice; increased direct foreign investment made transmission of technology more effective than it had been earlier, and also compensated for increasing deficits on trade account; and national autonomy and increasing state participation were popular political values.

As we all have come to appreciate, and Prebisch among the first, import substitution was not an unmixed blessing. It was a second-best policy imposed to tax agriculture and reallocate resources toward industry that was eventually brought down by the very circumstance it was to avert: a shortage of foreign exchange. Import substitution's bias against exports and its own voracious appetite for imports of intermediate and capital goods created a fundamental disequilibrium. So, too, expanded state activity without concomitant revenues tended to provoke larger deficits and inflationary pressures; when real resource transfer from agriculture to industry became progressively more difficult because of a weaker balance of payments, subsidies to industry were financed by central banks. Finally, the hopes for massive absorption of labor in industry and for a more equitable income distribution were dealt a blow by evidence of widening disparities and privileged, organized urban workers.

Before passing on to Prebisch's responses to such mounting evidence in the late 1950s in his third stage, it is necessary to underline Prebisch's intellectual accomplishment. He had set the terms, not merely for the rich literature in Latin America that followed and would build upon the center-periphery distinction, but also for the subsequent formalization of the foreign exchange constraint in the North American literature. Trade and development themes were subsequently inextricably related, rather than separate compartments.

In his third phase, Prebisch sought to understand what had gone wrong with the import substitution prescription. For one remedy, he encouraged exports of manufactures from the newly emplaced industrial sector as a source of new foreign exchange; subsidies would compensate for overvalued exchange rates. For another, recognizing that scale was a potentially more important constraint as production moved from consumer to intermediate and capital goods, he advocated a Latin American Common Market. That would make a continuing low import coefficient from the outside world compatible with efficiency. For a third, he called attention to the adverse consequences of continuing high levels of protection long after domestic production had begun.

These proposals were within an import substitution framework: they sought to avert the exhaustion of the process, a theme that increasingly figured in the concerns of the Economic Commission for Latin America in the early 1960s. As growth rates decelerated and balance of payments disequilibria proliferated, and as the institutional and structural reforms Prebisch advocated failed to compensate, there was help from an unanticipated source. The Alliance for Progress, embodying many of Prebisch's evaluations of the limits to Latin American development, brought new inputs of official bilateral assistance. Such finance alleviated the constraints many of the countries were facing—but on the whole, only temporarily. Nor was it possible to sustain assistance at the early rate.

In this context of the early 1960s, many of Prebisch's followers advocated more radical solutions. To avert the seeming strangulation of an ever more burdensome foreign exchange constraint, populist options gained in attractiveness. The internal market was posed against the external, the state emphasized at the expense of the private sector, and equity elevated in concern to compete with efficiency. On the other side, the mounting crisis reinforced the desirability of giving more attention to market signals, international and domestic, and of controlling a mounting state sector.

Although Prebisch's inclinations were clearly of the former persuasion, he never went quite so far. Indeed, he candidly tells of his disappointment at the continuing concentration of income, and his dissatisfaction with his treatment of it and the problem of inflation. At this stage he remained an advocate of structural reform. His commitment to the international economy and to reformism is evident in his UNCTAD labors in behalf of generalized preferences and commodity agreements.

More searching revisionism was to await his fifth, and current, phase. Prebisch has now tried to provide more systemic and far-ranging answers to the puzzle of economic development. They have taken the form of a broad assault upon peripheral capitalism as a viable economic form.

The concept of economic surplus is at the core of Prebisch's reformation. The incapacity of peripheral capitalism to sustain the accumulation of this surplus causes the inviability of the form. Accumulation is impossible because it is checked by redistributive claims upon the surplus by the labor force, on the one hand, and the state, on the other. Such a contest over real shares underlies the inflationary process, the conduct—but not the character—of which is influenced by monetary accommodation. Orthodox policy can only provoke decline, an unacceptable and only temporary solution. The eventual inflationary crisis leads to state intervention and repression to destroy the claims of labor. Peripheral capitalism is unable to mediate the conflict between equity and accumulation (and privileged consumption) in a tolerable way.

In this fifth phase, Prebisch brings to center stage the distribution and inflation issues that had earlier been at the margin. He likewise rehearses the center-periphery theme, casting blame on dependency for an imitative consumerism by the upper strata in the periphery, for "the disproportionate siphoning-off of income by the centers," and for a protectionism that inhibits peripheral growth. Above all, the import substitution crisis he had earlier believed avertable now returns as the inevitable collapse of a democratic, capitalist form. It is not difficult to detect the practical source of Prebisch's concern. The frustrations of the last decade in Chile and Argentina are evident.

The alternative Prebisch holds out is a humane, market-oriented social-ism. Whereas earlier the genius of his abstraction of import substitution was its ready conversion to practical implementation, his option now is more utopian. From a previous second-best solution, he has now fixed on the *optimum optimorum*.

It may not be readily attainable or fully necessary. One can accept the reality and the force of tensions he describes without concluding that a self-destructive crisis is the only possible outcome. The gloomy authoritar-ianism of the Southern Cone is not generalizable. There are too many other cases, in Latin America and elsewhere in the periphery, to suggest that public policy is uniformly inadequate to the task of making equity and efficiency compatible. Nor can one speak of authoritarian processes as if they were completely irreversible.

There is, as always, much to ponder and to learn from this fifth, and one hopes not final, phase of Raúl Prebisch's thinking—not least, his own self-critical capacity. I hope he will pardon others of us our less compre-hensive and more policy-oriented visions in the pursuit of the better world to which he has dedicated his own life and work.

Comment

Jagdish N. Bhagwati

To PLACE RAÚL PREBISCH among a *large* field of "pioneers" or "fathers" of development economics is to lose perspective. For those of us who grew up through the 1950s, it is immediately apparent that Prebisch (along with Paul Rosenstein-Rodan, Ragnar Nurkse, and W. A. Lewis, to mention several of the important figures that influenced my generation) belongs to a most distinguished *small* group of pioneers—if "pioneers" refers to Columbus rather than the Mayflower immigrants, Vasco de Gama rather than Robert Clive, or Adam Smith rather than Milton Friedman. Indeed, the innovative entrepreneurs of this volume should have started with a "grandfathers" volume, to be followed by "fathers," "sons," and "grandsons" where I and my distinguished fellow commentator might aspire to be included (despite the reminder from *Buddenbrooks* of the perils that await the third and fourth generations)!

I should also add that, for my generation of economists in the developing countries, preeminence of Raúl Prebisch in a field of obvious importance was a major source of inspiration. To see that one's own can be innovative, ingenious, and important is always, and was then especially, a matter of considerable psychological significance. For, among the colonial attitudes which afflicted our societies in those days was the belief that fundamental thinking required that one belong to the center, not the periphery, in Raúl Prebisch's splendid terminology. Prebisch and Lewis, among a few key figures, helped to shatter that myth decisively. I note this, especially for the "great-grandsons" from the periphery in development economics today who are otherwise likely to pass it by. For, within development economics, the situation has now turned decidedly on its head. The intellectual strength of the periphery, with its economists located both in the center and in the periphery, has now grown to a point of dramatic change: in the 1950s development economists traveled in numbers to the periphery to "advise the natives"; now the same flow is substantially to collaborate with them in dispensing the research funds of the center on the problems of the periphery!

Jagdish N. Bhagwati is Arthur Lehman Professor of Economics at Columbia University.

Turning to Raul Prebisch's paper, I am struck by two things. First, it is remarkable how he has interacted with his economic and political environment and has therefore grown as an economist. Second, if one is interested in the origins of development economics at the end of the Second World War, the similarities and contrasts among Prebisch and some of the other major figures cry out for comment. Let me begin with the latter, rather more general question and then turn to the evolution of Prebisch's own thoughts.

[1]

The second stage that Prebisch describes in his paper is, of course, the one that is best known to economists outside Latin America. It relates to the period when he developed the thesis that the prospect of declining terms of trade for Latin American primary products implied the desirability of import substituting (IS) industrialization. Interestingly, he argues that "as a young economist, I was a neoclassicist and fought against protection. But during the world Depression, throwing overboard a substantial part of my former beliefs, I was converted to protectionism. Theoretically, the problem was put in the following dynamic terms. What is to be done with productive resources when further expansion of primary exports would bring a fall in prices?"

From this and subsequent argumentation in Prebisch's present paper, it is clear that Prebisch was converted to elasticity pessimism by the experience of the Depression and the growth of beggar-my-neighbor exchange restrictions and other inward-looking policies that came in its aftermath. A distinction has to be made, however, between falling terms of trade when the country facing this phenomenon is small in Paul Samuelson's sense, and a similar-sounding but altogether different phenomenon where the country is large and the fall in the terms of trade arises from expanding exports. In the latter case protection could be rational; in the former it could not. Prebisch today writes as if he had made the correct latter assumption (elasticity pessimism) in his writings, whereas many have interpreted his writings to imply the former. Indeed, the secular decline in the terms of trade hypothesis is compatible with either interpretation, since it may come about from growth in the periphery in relation to a stagnant or quota-protectionist center. I am therefore happy to assume now that Prebisch indeed had such elasticity pessimism argumentation in mind and that IS-inducing protection followed appropriately from this understanding of the reality.

Taking this interpretation, I am then struck by the similarity of views in regard to elasticity pessimism that many of the major developmental economists shared at the end of the Second World War. I like to distinguish three different types of elasticity pessimists among these early writers.

First, I must recall Ragnar Nurkse whose celebrated Wicksell Lectures, delivered just before his untimely death, developed a theme of balanced growth that was predicated on a carefully stated belief in elasticity pessimism.[1] Nurkse, who must have been clearly influenced like Prebisch by the post-Depression experience on which he wrote so elegantly, felt that the developing countries were faced by the prospect that trade could no longer serve as an "engine of growth" in Dennis Robertson's graphic phrase. He therefore proposed an inward-looking, balanced growth which meant IS industrialization, since without the benefit of constant terms of trade, growth would have to reflect internal demands. This prescription was not spelled out carefully to argue that the IS industrialization would have to go beyond what a decentralized, functioning market economy would generate, since the elasticity pessimism would *additionally* call for an optimal level and structure of protection (which could well be a set of optimal export tariffs reflecting the foreign elasticities of demand for one's primary exports). But this protectionist implication, spelled out today by Prebisch, was definitely there.

Second, the elasticity pessimism was implicit in the classic 1943 *Economic Journal* paper of Paul Rosenstein-Rodan.[2] Like Nurkse, he argued for balanced growth, but felt the need to have investments coordinated and interlocked in a balanced-growth pattern. The underdeveloped economy was trapped in a low-level equilibrium with no effective inducement to invest: for example, the entrepreneur investing in shoes was not sure about selling shoes unless others invested simultaneously in textiles. This dilemma would, of course, disappear if the country faced constant terms of trade at which these entrepreneurs could atomistically sell what they wished. A necessary condition for Rosenstein-Rodan's analysis and prescription is, therefore, elasticity pessimism. And, in Rosenstein-Rodan's version, the balanced, coordinated growth *explicitly* requires a planning framework, whereas Nurkse's does not.

Third, this planning approach also comes naturally—and from quite another perspective than the inducement-to-invest problem of Rosenstein-Rodan—from the "structuralist" models of Fel'dman in the U.S.S.R. and Mahalanobis in India.[3] These planners also implicitly assumed an extreme

1. *Patterns of Trade and Development* (Stockholm: Almqvist and Wiksell, 1959).

2. "Problems of the Industrialization of Eastern and South-Eastern Europe," reprinted in Amar N. Agarwala and S. P. Singh, eds., *The Economics of Underdevelopment* (New York: Oxford University Press, 1963).

3. G. A. Fel'dman, "A Soviet Model of Growth," in Evsey Domar, *Essays in the Theory of Economic Growth* (New York: Oxford University Press, 1957), pp. 223–61; and Prasanta C. Mahalanobis, "Some Observations on the Process of Growth of National Income," *Sankya*, vol. 12 (September 1953), pp. 307–12.

form of elasticity pessimism since they worked with closed-economy models so that, at the margin, transformation of what was produced into what was needed was shut off. In the two-sector version of their models, these planners developed the case for heavy-sector IS industrialization.[4]

The preceding three forms of elasticity-pessimism-based arguments for IS strategies nonetheless implied alternative versions of policymaking to implement the IS program: (1) In the planning-oriented IS strategy, reading Nurkse somewhat liberally and Rosenstein-Rodan, Feldman, Mahalanobis, and others more literally, the planners proceeded to build up consistent, and then "optimal,"[5] plans, with targets of investments and outputs in different activities, often buttressed by licensing mechanisms. (2) In the more market-oriented IS strategy, the protection implied by elasticity pessimism was conceived to be exactly that and no more. The second approach was, in fact, utilized in the writings of international economists such as Gottfried Haberler, who argued that if one must have protection, one should do it by across-the-board tariffs or promotional measures, eschewing the impulse to plan the IS activities in detail, and by planned and regulated investments.[6]

---

4. In this tradition of "structural" models, I should also include the two-gap models associated with the work of Hollis Chenery, in particular. These were *computable* planning models and were also built on the assumption of elasticity pessimism; the two gaps referred to the ex ante savings and the foreign exchange bottlenecks to increasing the value of the specified objective function. See in particular Jagdish N. Bhagwati, "The Nature of Balance of Payments Difficulties in Developing Countries," in *Measures for Trade Expansion of Developing Countries*, Japan Economic Research Center Paper no. 5 (Tokyo, October 1966), to be reprinted in Jagdish N. Bhagwati, *Wealth and Poverty: Essays in Development Economics*, Gene Grossman, ed. (Cambridge, Mass.: MIT Press, forthcoming); Ronald Findlay, "The Foreign Exchange Gap and Growth in Developing Economies," in Jagdish N. Bhagwati and others, eds., *Trade, Balance of Payments and Growth* (Amsterdam: North-Holland, 1971); Ronald McKinnon, "Foreign Exchange Constraints in Economic Development and Efficient Aid Allocation," *Economic Journal*, vol. 74 (1964), pp. 388–409; and Padma Desai and Jagdish N. Bhagwati, "Three Alternative Concepts of Foreign Exchange Difficulties in Centrally Planned Economies," *Oxford Economic Papers* (November 1979). The best example of the Chenery literature is Hollis Chenery and Michael Bruno, "Development Alternatives for an Open Economy: The Case of Israel," *Economic Journal*, vol. 72 (1962).

5. Nurkse had mentioned that the balanced-growth strategy would require tailoring domestic investments to the income elasticity of demand for different goods. Of course, the logical next step would be to include the entire "final demands" vector and also, in accordance with material-balances and the more sophisticated Leontief input-output procedures, the indirect demands. But all this implies only *consistency*, whereas economists eventually will always maximize. So the consistency models soon gave way to optimizing models, with intertemporal objective functions specified. This latter development in planning models was reinforced by the independent theoretical advances coming in from the work—such as on the turnpike theorem—which stemmed from the capital-theoretic work on heterogeneous-capital models by Samuelson and Solow, among others.

6. *International Trade and Economic Development*, National Bank of Egypt Lectures (Cairo, 1959).

These two IS strategies, one planning oriented and the other market reliant, must be contrasted with yet a third: the approach of Albert Hirschman, who also advocated IS as a strategy for development.[7] In his case, the problem for development was again one of inducing investment, as in Rosenstein-Rodan's classic formulation of many years earlier. Hirschman's solution was very simple: cut off imports and get a ready-made market, so domestic entrepreneurs will jump in.[8] Drawing on the agricultural strategy of "slash and burn," I like to call this the "slash (imports) and grow" IS strategy. It runs against the grain of an economist, for it denies the economic essence of the issue by consigning the notion of costs and benefits to the side! Since many developing countries did wind up in the postwar period with an IS strategy simply as a result of overvalued exchange rates (now understood to imply an inward-looking IS bias), and since we now know that these exchange control regimes were often administered without attention to costs and benefits at any level,[9] many of these developing countries were on a de facto Hirschman strategy of "anarchic" IS industrialization!

The enormous waste that attended the IS strategy has been documented in several empirical studies by the Organisation for Economic Co-operation and Development (OECD) and the National Bureau of Economic Research (NBER). In retrospect, one wonders whether this waste was really essential and not simply a result of the IS strategy pursued in what I have called here the planning-oriented approach, on the one hand, or the anarchic Hirschmanesque approach implied by overvalued exchange rates, on the other hand. Indeed, my own judgment is that many of the costs associated with the IS strategy were the unforeseen results of these two special versions of the strategy.[10] If only the third version—what I

7. *The Strategy of Economic Development* (New Haven, Conn.: Yale University Press, 1958).

8. I am taking the essence of the Hirschman strategy here. He does also advocate attention to "linkages" so as to maximize the investment-inducing effects of any import slashing. This is a nonoperational concept, however, since linkages cannot be defined independently of the decision on which imports to slash and not merely with the aid of information such as income elasticities of demand, and input-output coefficients.

9. For the results of a National Bureau of Economic Research project directed by Anne Krueger and myself on this issue, see Jagdish N. Bhagwati, *The Anatomy and Consequences of Exchange Control Regimes* (Cambridge, Mass.: Ballinger, 1978).

10. I myself have long researched and documented these costs: with Padma Desai in *India: Planning for Industrialization*, for the OECD Development Center (London: Oxford University Press, 1970); with T. N. Srinivasan in *India*, for the NBER (New York: Columbia University Press, 1975); and in my own *Anatomy and Consequences of Exchange Control Regimes*, which synthesizes the results of the NBER project. On the whole, I would say that the planning-oriented IS strategy was followed by the Indian subcontinent, Ghana, and Egypt, whereas the bulk of Latin America followed the anarchic Hirschmanesque approach as a result of consistently and dramatically over-valued exchange rates there. For this reason, the IS strategy has given way rather rapidly in Latin America, as reluctance in adjusting exchange rates has largely disappeared,

called the market-reliant strategy of IS industrialization—had been followed, the results would have been dramatically better.[11]

The different forms of IS strategy are almost never differentiated in the
literature that downgrades the IS and romanticizes the export-promotion
strategies. I note these important distinctions simply because I believe,
reading Prebisch directly today and in derivative writings earlier, that
Prebisch was closer to an optimal IS program than the way IS strategy
turned out to be mostly implemented. A clarification from Prebisch on this
important issue would be most helpful to historians of thought. To restate,
while he did urge protectionism, what precisely was the manner in which
this protectionism was to be implemented? Only by getting a firm answer
from Presbisch to this question can we determine whether his prescription
of an IS strategy was wise or not.

Indeed, to determine this fully, we also need to evaluate elasticity
pessimism itself. Here history would seem to have come out on the side of
those who did not share this pessimism. We need not be too upset by this,
since even the nonpessimists did not foresee the dramatic rise in world
trade that followed the postwar liberalization of trade and payments. The
pessimists lost, but the optimists were rewarded by fortuitous circumstances and the kind of good luck that comes when the gods smile on one.
The fact remains, however, that the pessimists were wrong. And it also
remains true that the countries, such as those now called the Gang of Four,
which saw and seized the opportunity implied by the phenomenal growth
of world trade, also participated in it and shared in the affluence it
brought. In consequence, the engine of growth did operate for them, but it
passed by most of the elasticity-pessimistic periphery in a self-fulfilling
prophecy! Prebisch today suggests that he changed his views as this engine
in the center chugged away noisily. But it seems as if his increasing
skepticism toward continued IS strategy in Latin America was prompted
more by what he, in a typically Latin American fashion, calls the exhaustion of the easy first phase of IS in consumer goods industries and the need
to have larger markets for the costly second phase IS in heavy industry,[12]

whereas in India the IS, inward-looking thrust still continues because of its planning-
oriented, intellectual basis.

11. The across-the-board protection, which would be uniform on balance, has many
advantages which can be argued both on strictly economic and on political grounds.
Unlike Prebisch, Nurkse, and others who were elasticity pessimists and therefore were
essentially arguing for IS strategy on optimal-tariff grounds, Haberler appears to have
been arguing for IS strategy on grounds we would today call "noneconomic" (and
taking them as specified by others rather than himself).

12. I call this a particularly Latin American viewpoint since, in India, we have always
thought this sequencing notion to be an invalid inference from empirical observation of
how countries have invested to a planning prescription of how a country ought to
invest. The so-called second phase of heavy industrialization in fact occurred in India
simultaneously with the first phase because India had excellent iron ore, an abundance
of skills, entrepreneurship, and a program for increasing investments that required an

rather than by any significant awareness that the IS strategy should yield definitely, in the light of newly demonstrated possibilities of expanding world trade, to a far greater outward-looking industrialization than before.

[2]

Let me turn to the second issue I noted earlier: the evolution of Prebisch's thoughts on developmental problems.

Prebisch glides very hastily over his fourth stage, with UNCTAD. I would urge him to enlarge that simply because the creation of UNCTAD was one of his crowning achievements, despite the deplorable tendency on the part of several developed-country economists to treat it as if it was UNWASHED and UNKEMPT. Indeed, the North-South dialogue is currently stalled, though the post-Cancun situation seems a trifle more promising, as argued by me elsewhere.[13] But in the long sweep, UNCTAD will indeed be seen as an important contribution of Prebisch.

What does intrigue me, however, is Prebisch's fifth, and final, stage where he frontally brings political economy onto the center of the stage. I have always felt that this cannot be avoided if we are to take policymaking seriously; and if development is to be explained, we indeed have to take politics seriously. Thus, if we discuss multinationals, it is misleading to consider them as if they merely augment the opportunities open to the host country, and it is also misleading for economists simply to describe the policies that an ominiscient and benign government should implement to utilize to advantage the augmented capital and technical inflows implied by the multinationals' entry. The policymaker must rather take into account the fact that the entry of multinationals may itself constrain the policy choices that can be made; for example, the entry of politically powerful multinationals may carry with it the threat of destabilization if "radical" policies are sought to be imposed by the host country in the national interest, as indeed was the case in Chile.

But while I applaud Prebisch's entry into this wider realm of political economy, I must confess that I have serious misgivings about the thesis that he develops. I have problems with the precise elements of his scenario of the oncoming, inevitable crisis of capitalism in the periphery, but I shall resist the temptation to restate arguments I developed at some length

---

increasing domestic availability of capital goods—which, given the elasticity pessimism, the planners assumed they could not import in required quantities except at high social cost.

13. "The Significance of Cancun," *Third World Quarterly* (July 1982). My latest thoughts on these issues are in chapters 1 and 2 in Jagdish N. Bhagwati and John G. Ruggie, eds., *Power, Passions, and Purpose: Prospects for North-South Negotiations* (Cambridge, Mass.: MIT Press, forthcoming).

elsewhere.[14] I shall rather express reservations of a very different order that reflect the difficulties attending any attempt to treat political economy seriously. As soon as we endogenize politics and therefore policymaking, we have to worry that there may be no degree of freedom left to say what ought to be done from the policy viewpoint. For policy, having been endogenized, cannot be arbitrarily set at any level. Thus, consider the standard analysis of the effects of import competition on domestic income. In the orthodox $2 \times 2 \times 2$ model with two factors, two traded goods, and two countries, we know that free trade is the best policy for a small country without domestic distortions. Therefore, the "optimal" response to import competition—that is, terms of trade improvement—is to retain free trade and to profit from the improved terms of trade. But this standard economic policy prescription ceases to be relevant if we endogenize policy. Thus, if we were to model a two-party political system, so that the standard model is now a $2 \times 2 \times 2 \times 2$ model and there are cost functions for the political process of lobbying for and against a tariff, the model can be solved for an endogenous tariff.[15] But as soon as we do this, the result of import competition is yet another endogenous tariff. To ask, in this model of endogenous policymaking, what free trade implies is to ask an unrealistic question, for who shall bring this free trade policy about?

I am afraid that Prebisch is caught in this dilemma and does not fully realize it. He transits from his second and third stages, where his analysis of what the periphery should do (implement the IS strategy) is very much in the old tradition of asking what an omniscient and benign periphery government ought to do, to his fifth stage, where the analysis shifts gear to how the capitalist system in the periphery is "deterministically" locked into a developing and unavoidable crisis. Then he still hopes that somehow market socialism will solve this crisis. But, even if it can, who will bring it into being? Perhaps the smart thing to do is to prognosticate, not advocate, and let history judge who is right.

14. "Comment on Raúl Prebisch, 'The Latin American Periphery in the Global System of Capitalism,'" in *Proceedings of the Congress of the International Economic Association, Mexico City, 1980*, vol. 1, Shigeto Tsuru, ed. (London: Macmillan, forthcoming).

15. See the tariff-making models of Robert Feenstra and Jagdish N. Bhagwati, "Tariff Seeking and the Efficient Tariff," and of Ronald Findlay and Stanislaw Wellisz, "Endogenous Tariffs, the Political Economy of Trade Restrictions, and Welfare," both in Jagdish N. Bhagwati, ed., *Import Competition and Response* (Chicago: University of Chicago Press, 1982).

Paul N. Rosenstein-Rodan

PAUL N. ROSENSTEIN-RODAN was born in Crakow, Poland, in 1902, and spent his early life in Vienna. He received his doctorate from the University of Vienna in 1925. In 1930 he became a British citizen and taught at University College of the University of London for the next seventeen years. In 1947 he went to the World Bank where he became the Assistant Director of the Economics Department and Head of the Economic Advisory Staff. He was Professor of Economics at the Massachusetts Institute of Technology, 1953–68, and at the University of Texas, 1968–72. His present position is Professor of Economics and Director of the Center for Latin American Development Studies at Boston University, where he has been since 1972.

Rosenstein-Rodan began his professional work in economics in 1925 with studies on the frontiers of the Austrian theory of consumer demand. His early studies were in pure economic theory—the concepts of complementarity in consumption and production, the time sequence of economic adjustments, and economies of scale. All of these later carried over to his applied work in development economics.

At MIT he pursued research on problems of economic development, especially as director of projects in Italy, India, and Chile. From 1962 to 1966 he served on the Committee of IX of the Alliance for Progress and became increasingly engaged in Latin American development research.

He has been honored with decorations from Italy (1958), Venezuela (1967), and Chile (1970), and became a Fellow of the American Academy of Arts and Sciences (1961), Fellow of the Institute of Social Studies, The Hague (1962), and Fellow of the Academia Pontifica Tiberina, Rome (1967).

His principal publications include "Grenznutzen" (Marginal Utility) (1927), translated in *International Economic Papers*, no. 10 (New York: Macmillan, 1960); "Das Zeitmoment in der Mathematischen Theorie des Wirtschaftlichen Gleichgewichtes," *Zeitschrift für Nationalökonomie*, vol. 1 (1929); "La Complementarietà: Prima delle Tre Etappe del Progresso della Teoria Economica Pura," *La Riforma Social*, vol. 44 (1933); "The Role of Time in Economic Theory," *Economica*, New Series (1934);

"Problems of Industrialization of Eastern and South-Eastern Europe," *Economic Journal* (June-September 1943); "The International Development of Economically Backward Areas," *International Affairs* (April 1944); "Disguised Unemployment and Underemployment in Agriculture" (Cambridge, Mass.: MIT Center for International Studies, 1956); "International Aid for Underdeveloped Countries," *Review of Economics and Statistics* (May 1961); "Notes on the Theory of the 'Big Push,'" (Cambridge, Mass.: MIT Center for International Studies, 1957), reprinted in *Economic Development for Latin America*, Proceedings of a conference held by the International Economic Association, Howard S. Ellis, ed. (London: Macmillan, 1961); as editor, *Capital Formation and Economic Development* (Cambridge, Mass.: MIT Press, 1964); "The Consortia Technique," *International Organization*, vol. 22, which also appeared in Richard Newton Gardner and Max F. Millikan, eds., *The Global Partnership* (New York: Praeger, 1968); "A Study on Independent International Evaluation of National Development Effort," TD/&/Suppl. 15 (New Delhi: UNCTAD, December 11, 1967); "Criteria for Evaluation of National Development Effort," *Journal of Development Planning*, no. 1 (1969); "The Have's and Have-Not's Around the Year 2000," in Jagdish N. Bhagwati, ed., *Economics and World Order: From the 1970's to the 1990's* (New York: Macmillan, 1972); and *The New International Economic Order* (Boston, Mass.: Boston University, 1981).

Natura Facit Saltum:
Analysis of
the Disequilibrium Growth Process

DURING THE SECOND WORLD WAR, I proposed in London the formation of a group to study the problems of economically underdeveloped countries instead of the more usual work on current economic problems related to the war. If we were to emerge alive, we should want not to return to the previous status quo but to form a better world. A study group was organized at the Royal Institute for International Affairs (Chatham House) and worked from 1942 till 1945 on problems of "underdeveloped countries." This term appeared then for the first time. My 1943 article in the *Economic Journal* served as a basic document for the group and is now in many anthologies of economic studies of the Third World.[1]

Eastern and Southeastern Europe were selected as a model not because of any special interest in those countries, but because their governments in exile were in London and because Eastern and Southeastern Europe (like Latin America) constitute a group of similar but not identical models. If one compares India, Spain, and Ecuador everything is different. What is cause and what is effect is anybody's guess. When one takes a group of similar countries, they differ from each other in one or two but not in all respects; it is then easier to examine what is cause and what is effect.

Natura Facit Saltum

If I were to give one characterization to my early thoughts about development, it would be "natura facit saltum"—nature does make a jump, the opposite of the motto "Natura non facit saltum" that Alfred Marshall thought appropriate for economics. Not traditional static equilibrium theory but an analysis of the disequilibrium growth process is what is essential for understanding economic development problems.

1. Paul N. Rosenstein-Rodan, "Problems of Industrialization of Eastern and South-Eastern Europe," *Economic Journal*, vol. 53 (June–September 1943), pp. 202–11. This was a chapter from the report of the Economic Group of the Committee on Reconstruction, the Royal Institute of International Affairs. Important predecessors of the theory of development are Harrod-Domar, Joan Robinson, Keynes, and Colin Clark.

The *Economic Journal* article of 1943 attempted to study the dynamic path toward equilibrium, not merely the conditions which must be satisfied at the point of equilibrium. What matters is "the pursuit curve."[2] The pursuit curve shows the dynamic path toward equilibrium—not only the conditions at the point of equilibrium. Equilibrium points are like a compass showing the direction toward the North Pole or South Pole without implying that one is on the North Pole or South Pole. We are therefore concerned not only with the question of the existence of equilibrium, but the possibilities of nonexistence of equilibrium.

The 1943 article introduced four innovations which subsequently became so generally accepted that it is difficult to understand why they originally aroused so much opposition. The first innovation was a concern with "excess agrarian population" (disguised unemployment), which, although a weakness, may represent a source of development and strength. The second was the concept of "pecuniary" external economies, which yielded economies of scale—that is, increasing returns which were fully treated in Alfred Marshall's footnotes but considered to be a "second order of smalls." To take advantage of them, however, planned industrialization comprising simultaneous planning of several complementary industries is needed. The third new idea was that before building consumer goods factories, a major indivisible block of social overhead capital or infrastructure must be built and sponsored because private market initiatives will not create it in time. Low wages should have been a sufficient incentive to create a textile industry in India in the post-Napoleonic era and not in Lancashire, England. Indian wages were 50 or 60 percent lower than the low wages in England. There was no danger of currency manipulation or trade obstacles under British control; the prospect of building a textile mill in Bombay instead of Manchester or Coventry seemed most attractive. Further analysis revealed, however, that in order to build a factory one would have to build a bridge or finish a road or a railway line or later an electric power station. Each of these elements in the so-called social overhead capital requires a minimum high quantum of investment which could serve, say, fifty factories but would cost far too much for one. One cannot build a bridge small enough to allow only a hundred crossings a day. The efficient minimum would be profitable for fifty factories but not for one. The necessary minimum capital outlay outside of the textile mill

---

2. A dog pursues a hare, without anticipation, along the shortest distance at which he sees him (a straight line). Meanwhile the hare runs from point 1 to point 2. When the dog sees him again in this new position he again runs along the shortest distance (a straight line) in which he sees him. Meanwhile the hare runs to point 3, and so on. The line along which the dog runs is what we want to explain. It is determined by a straight-line distance wherever the dog sees the hare. The overwhelming majority of the points of the pursuit curve are disequilibrium points. It may be called "state of equilibrium" if the dog ultimately catches the hare.

(Pareto had mentioned it but never worked it out.)

would more than compensate for the advantage of cheaper labor. Lower wages are not a sufficient incentive for investment.

Industrialization meant (and still means today) urbanization. What are towns compared with rural zones? They are areas of relatively higher wages. Industrialization proceeded by concentrating in areas of high wages (towns), not in the rural areas. The rich countries were the urban zones and the poorer countries the rural zones of the world economy. That was the reason for the widening gap between developed and underdeveloped countries. The market mechanism alone will not lead to the creation of social overhead capital, which normally accounts for 30 to 35 percent of total investment. That must be sponsored, planned, or programmed (usually by public investment). To take advantage of external economies (due to indivisibilities) required an "optimum" size of enterprises to be brought about by a simultaneous planning of several complementary industries. In the process of development, pecuniary external economies play the same role as technological ones.[3]

The fourth innovation was the emphasis on "technological external economies," which are not due to indivisibilities but very largely due to "inappropriability." Under a system of slavery it paid the owner to invest in training a slave because the increase in skills would benefit the investor. When slavery was abolished, a worker trained could contract with an outside employer who did not have to bear the cost of his training. Whoever invested in the training of the worker would run the risk of not being able to appropriate the benefit of increased productivity. The training and education of workers under competitive market conditions would therefore be below optimum. This is a widespread phenomenon, not so rare as the bucolic example in a pastoral economy of not knowing whose bees alight on whose apple trees to produce honey. This example suggested a bias that technological external economies are logically interesting but practically irrelevant. In fact, the process of industrialization of underdeveloped countries was and is largely based on the advantages of training, learning on the job, and the formation of human capital (without using this terminology). In other words, technological external economies are not a second order of smalls, as already stated in 1943 and later on in the theories of human capital (Jacob Mincer and T. W. Schultz).

The market mechanism does not realize the "optimum" either in one nation or between nations because it relies on such unrealistic assumptions as linear homogeneous production functions, no increasing returns or economies of scale or of agglomeration, and no phenomenon of minimum quantum or threshold. This obscures the nature of the development process and the risks involved. Nothing in theology or technology ordains that God created the world convex downwards.

---

3. As Tibor Scitovsky correctly interpreted in his article, "Two Concepts of External Economies," *Journal of Political Economy*, vol. 62, no. 2 (April 1954).

In terms of contemporary theory, the essence of the 1943 article may seem to rest on the basic question whether perfect future markets can exist for all the commodities in the context of a future which is both open-ended and uncertain.[4] Although I recognized that future markets and future prices could provide necessary additional signaling devices, I stated that "It is a moot point whether perfect future markets for all goods can exist. [My] suspicion (without proof) is that they cannot exist for the same reasons for which perfect foresight is impossible. In reality they certainly do not exist."[5]

The seeds of my development analysis had been planted earlier when I became interested in the themes of complementarity and of the hierarchical structure of wants, together with the role of time—that is, the choice of an economic period over which an individual allocates his scarce resources.[6] The dynamics of wants and their interrelatedness were much more important to me than the neoclassical attempt at precise characterization of the properties of the utility function. Consumption complementarities, the role of time, the pursuit curve, plus external economies—all these dynamic factors were not to be considered as a second order of smalls, but even more as pervasive in a less developed country.

Big Push

My thinking during the 1940s and 1950s led to the theory of the "big push."[7] "There is a minimum level of resources that must be devoted to . . . a development program if it is to have any chance for success. Launching a country into self-sustaining growth is a little like getting an airplane off the ground. There is a critical ground speed which must be passed before the craft can become airborne."[8] Proceeding bit by bit will not add up in its effects to the sum total of the single bits. A minimum

---

4. See Sikhamoy Chakravarty, "Paul Rosenstein-Rodan: An Appreciation," *World Development*, vol. 11, no. 1 (January 1983), p. 74.

5. Rosenstein-Rodan, "Notes on the Theory of the 'Big Push'" (Cambridge, Mass.: MIT Center for International Studies, 1957), reprinted in *Economic Development for Latin America*, Proceedings of a conference held by the International Economic Association, Howard S. Ellis, ed. (London: Macmillan, 1961).

6. Rosenstein-Rodan, "Grenznutzen," in *Handwörterbuch der Staatswissenschaften*, 4th ed. (Jena, 1927), vol. 4, pp. 1190–1213; translated into English by Wolfgang F. Stolper, in *International Economic Papers*, no. 10 (New York: Macmillan 1960), pp. 71–106; "La Complementarietà: Prima delle Tre Etappe del Progresso della Teoria Economica Pura," *La Riforma Sociale*, vol. 44 (1933), pp. 157–308; "The Role of Time in Economic Theory," *Economica*, New Series (1934), pp. 77–97.

7. "Notes on the Theory of the 'Big Push.'"

8. MIT Center for International Studies, Special Committee to Study the Foreign Aid Program, *The Objectives of U.S. Economic Assistance Programs* (Washington, D.C., 1957), p. 70.

quantum of investment is a necessary—though not sufficient—condition of success.

This theory of the big push contradicts the conclusions of traditional static equilibrium theory in three respects. First, it is based on a set of more realistic assumptions of certain indivisibilities and nonappropriabilities in the production functions. These give rise to increasing returns and to technological external economies. Second, the theory is meant to deal with the path to equilibrium. At a point of static equilibrium net investment is zero. The theory of growth must be very largely a theory of investment. Third, in addition to the risk phenomena and imperfections characterizing investment, the markets in underdeveloped countries are even more imperfect than in developed countries. The price mechanism in such imperfect markets cannot therefore be relied upon to provide the signals that guide a perfectly competitive economy toward an optimum position.

Underlying the need for a big push is the pervasiveness of rural underdevelopment—excess agrarian population. Given that mass migration and resettlement are not feasible, I stated that "The movement of machinery and capital towards labor, instead of moving labor towards capital, is the process of industrialization which, together with agrarian improvement, is the most important aspect of the economic development of the depressed areas."[9]

Industrialization has to be promoted not because of terms of trade, but because external economies are greater in industry than in agriculture alone. Rejecting a strategy of self-sufficiency or an inward-looking strategy of industrialization, I argued for industrialization with the help of international investment and for a pattern of industrialization that would preserve the advantages of an international division of labor and would therefore, in the end, produce more wealth for everybody.

The crucial task of a development program was to achieve sufficient investment to mobilize the unemployed and underemployed for the purpose of industrialization. To reach an optimum size of the industrial enterprises, however, the area of industrialization must be sufficiently large. This calls for planned industrialization by the simultaneous planning of several complementary industries.

These four themes (disguised unemployment, pecuniary external economies, social overhead capital, and technological external economies) were then studied in more detail, first in Italy. Special attention was given to disguised unemployment and consequent dualism as well as the possibility of using welfare-improving policy interventions to realize a rate of growth 60 percent higher than in the previous century (that is, 5 percent a year rather than the previous 3 percent). The studies were followed up in India with special emphasis on analysis of the capital-output ratio, which was

9. "The International Development of Economically Backward Areas," *International Affairs*, vol. 20, no. 2 (April 1944), p. 161.

assumed to be too low in the India five-year plan, being in reality nearer 3 to 1 than 2 to 1. We also pointed out the importance of shadow pricing, especially the shadow price of capital exemplified by investments in electric power.

General principles of an international aid policy were first studied at the U.N. Economic Commission for Latin America (ECLA) preparatory conference for Quintandinha in the summer of 1954. These principles were used for the doctrine of aid policy in my 1961 paper[10] and later used and applied in the Alliance for Progress. The role of aid policy is ultimately a value judgment but one whose implications were spelled out best in the Alliance for Progress. The philosophy of development remains as valid as ever—it was the real operational manifesto for a New International Economic Order—although it failed by the "trahison des clercs"—that is, the sabotage of the Alliance for Progress by both the U.S. and Latin American bureaucracies.

Disguised Unemployment and Underemployment

The concept of "agrarian excess" or "surplus population" or of "disguised unemployment in agriculture" emerged in the late 1920s. But it was made one of the cornerstones of the theory of development in the 1940s and 1950s, despite the denial of its existence by such critics as Jacob Viner, Gottfried Haberler, and T. W. Schultz. Schultz had said, "I know of no evidence for any poor country anywhere that would even suggest that a transfer of some small fraction, say 5 per cent, of the existing labour force out of agriculture, with other things equal, could be made without reducing its production."[11]

In contrast to this view, I believed that disguised unemployment of more than 5 percent exists in many—though not all—underdeveloped countries. As proof of this, I offered a description and measurement of disguised underemployment in southern Italy.[12] Focusing on the direct method of measuring the static surplus—that is, an empirical sample enquiry to determine the amount of population in agriculture that can be removed from it (for forty-eight to fifty weeks a year) without any change in the method of cultivation and without any reduction in output—I

10. "International Aid for Underdeveloped Countries," *Review of Economics and Statistics*, vol. 43, no. 2 (May 1961); and "The Consortia Technique" (Cambridge, Mass.: MIT Center for International Studies, 1968).

11. T. W. Schultz, "The Role of Government in Promoting Economic Growth," in Leonard D. White, ed., *The State of the Social Sciences* (Chicago: University of Chicago Press, 1956).

12. "Disguised Unemployment and Underemployment in Agriculture" (Cambridge, Mass.: MIT Center for International Studies, 1956); and Food and Agriculture Organization, *Monthly Bulletin of Agricultural Economics and Statistics* (1956).

estimated three types of underoccupation: removal, equivalent to true disguised unemployment; irremovable frictional unemployment; and seasonal underemployment.

Disguised underemployment was important for models of dualism. It also placed emphasis on labor-intensive methods of industrialization that involve investing in consumption industries while importing heavy industry products.

Pecuniary External Economies

I had been impressed by Allyn Young's analysis that increasing returns accrue to a firm not only with the growth of its size but also with the growth of the industry and of the industrial system as a whole.[13] I believed more emphasis should be given to increasing returns through attention to the indivisibility of demand and indivisibility in the production function.

The indivisibility or the complementarity of demand means that in reality various investment decisions are not independent. Investment projects have high risks because of uncertainty whether their products will find a market. But if investment occurs on a wide front, then what is not true in the case of a single investment project will become true for the complementary system of many investment projects: the new producers will be each other's customers, and the complementarity of demand will reduce the risk of not finding a market. Risk reduction is in this sense a special case of external economies. Reducing such interdependent risks increases naturally the incentive to invest.

The low elasticities of demand in low-income countries make it much more difficult, however, to fit supplies to demands. The difficulty of fitting demand to supply on a small scale constitutes a higher risk in a small market than in a large and growing one. The complementarity of demand will reduce the marginal risk of growing and diversified investments, but it will be below a minimum "sensible" for small doses of investment. There is therefore a minimum threshold at which the complementarity of demand manifests itself. The discontinuity in the complementarity of demand may be called indivisibility of demand. To reach the threshold and take advantage of complementarity in demand, a minimum quantum of investment is required to produce the bulk of additional wage goods on which additionally employed workers will spend their additional income.[14] On the supply side, a high optimum size of firm may be required because of indivisibilities of inputs, processes, or outputs that give rise to increasing returns.

13. Allyn A. Young, "Increasing Returns and Economic Progress," *Economic Journal*, vol. 38 (December 1928), pp. 527–42.

14. Rosenstein-Rodan, "Notes on the Theory of the 'Big Push,'" section 4.

Social Overhead Capital

A most important instance of indivisibility and externalities is social overhead capital. Although subject to long gestation periods and delayed yields, the provision of social overhead capital creates investment opportunities in other industries. The provision of such "overhead costs" for the economy as a whole requires a large minimum size of investment in each infrastructure project and an irreducible minimum industry mix of different public utilities. A high initial investment in social overhead capital is necessary to pave the way for additional, more quickly yielding, directly productive investments. I considered this indivisibility one of the main obstacles to development.

Indivisibility in the supply of savings was also viewed as a major problem in low-income countries. To provide for a high minimum quantum of investment, the marginal rate of saving out of increased income must become much higher than the average rate of saving. The zero (or very low) price elasticity of the supply of savings and the high income elasticity of savings were somewhat loosely described as a "third indivisibility."

Technological External Economies

Another significant source of technological external economies was the training of labor.

The first task of industrialization is to provide for training and "skilling" of labor which is to transform [Eastern European] peasants into full-time or part-time industrial workers. The automatism of *laissez-faire* never worked properly in that field. It broke down because it is not profitable for a private entrepreneur to invest in training labor. There are no mortgages on workers—an entrepreneur who invests in training workers may lose capital if these workers contract with another firm. Although not a good investment for a private firm, it is the best investment for the State. It is also a good investment for the bulk of industries to be created when taken as a whole, although it may represent irrecoverable costs for a smaller unit. It constitutes an important instance of the Pigovian divergence between "private and social marginal net product" where the latter is greater than the former.[15]

15. "Problems of Industrialization of Eastern and South-Eastern Europe," pp. 204–05; also, "The International Development of Economically Backward Areas," p. 160.

The indivisibilities and the external economies to which they give rise plus the technological external economies of training labor were the theoretical foundations for my advocacy of an integrating, synchronizing "big push" to "jump" over the economic obstacles to development.

The Market and Programming

The recognition of the complementarity of all investment projects introduced a new set of determinants of optimum investment criteria. They rely on the *delegation* of a "plan" which must be elaborated, while the market mechanism relies on the dispersal of decisions when the program emerges as a *result* not as a previously worked out "plan" of a campaign. A program approach was considered to be logically precedent to project analysis. The dispersal of single investment decisions based on maximization of profit as the only criterion will not lead to the optimum combination. This is for the following reasons:

- The investor maximizes the private, not the social, net marginal product. External economies are not sufficiently exploited. Complementarity of industries is so great that simultaneous inducement rather than hope for autonomous coincidence of investment is called for.
- The lifetime of equipment is so long that the investor's foresight is likely to be more imperfect than that of the buyer and seller or of the producer. The individual investor's risk may be higher than that confronting an overall investment program. The costs of an erroneous investment decision are high; punishment in the form of loss of capital afflicts not only the investor but also the national economy.
- Because of the indivisibility (lumpiness) of capital, large rather than small changes are involved. Yet the price mechanism works perfectly only under the assumption of small changes.
- Capital markets are notoriously imperfect markets, governed not only by prices but also by institutional or traditional rationing quotas.[16]

For these reasons, it was stated that other criteria—especially external economies and diseconomies—had to be added to those considered by the individual investor. Program-using methods of delegation were advocated to supplement the single investor's insufficient knowledge and induce changes in his decisions or supplement them by a set of public investment projects.

16. Rosenstein-Rodan, "Programming in Theory and in Italian Practice" (Cambridge, Mass.: MIT Center for International Studies, December 1955), pp. 2–3.

Investment Programming

The programming of investment in a developing country is necessary to correct for such distortions as indivisibilities, externalities, and information failures. "Programming" is just another word for rational, deliberate, consistent, and coordinated economic policy.[17]

While a development program must be spelled out in projects, it is not a mere sum or shopping list of projects. Single-project analysis cannot simply consider each project in turn, see whether it passes the test, and accordingly decide whether to include it in the program. The various projects constituting a development program are interrelated and reinforce each other. This balance depends on whether complementary activities have been planned on the required scale. A program approach, not a project approach, is therefore necessary to determine the criteria for the productive use of capital. A change in one project may require a reshuffling and change in several other projects. Each investment project's contribution to national income depends on what other investments have been, are being, or will be realized. The complementarities introduce a new set of determinants of optimum investment, and a program approach therefore dominates project analysis.

A Shorthand Method

A bridge between the two is to establish shadow prices to correct for distorted market prices. In the late 1950s, as we focused on development programs in Italy, India, and Indonesia, our research at the Center for International Studies at MIT emphasized the shadow rate of interest, the shadow rate of foreign exchange, and the shadow rate of wages.[18] These shadow prices were to be used as a computational shorthand method for each project so that it was not necessary to solve each time the optimization problem for the investment program as a whole, of which the project is a part.

Programming is thus to be a supplement to the price mechanism and also an instrument for supplying additional information which the market mechanism cannot supply. The development program is to make use of the market mechanism, but is not to be dominated by it.

17. "Programming in Theory and in Italian Practice," p. 4.
18. See, for example, Sikhamoy Chakravarty, "The Use of Shadow Prices in Programme Evaluation," India Project C/61-18 (Cambridge, Mass.: MIT Center for International Studies, 1961).

International Aid Policy

The aim of international aid was not to achieve equality of income, but equality of opportunity. Aid should continue to a point at which a satisfactory rate of growth can be achieved on a self-sustaining basis. Ideally, aid was therefore to be allocated where it would have the maximum catalytic effect in mobilizing additional national effort. I suggested that the primary principle is to maximize additional effort, not to maximize income created per dollar of aid.[19]

Major attention was to be given to the absorptive capacity of the developing country and its capacity to repay. The first limit to be determined was the amount of aid. The second was the method of financing it. Where the capacity to repay in low-income countries is below their absorptive capacity, a proportion of aid should be given in grants, in "soft loans" (forty- to ninety-nine-year loans with a ten- to twenty-year grace period and a low rate of interest), or in loans repayable in local currency which will be re-lent for subsequent investment.[20]

The rational strategy is not to reduce a country's foreign indebtedness to zero. The rational question to ask is: How much foreign indebtedness can a country maintain in the long run? Just as any national debt or corporate debt need not be reduced if it is within sound limits, the foreign debt of debtor countries need not be amortized to zero in a sound world economy.

Retrospect and Prospect

Looking back, I now see we were overoptimistic in believing that the reservoir of disguised unemployment could be so readily absorbed. A central question that remains for development studies is why the difference between urban and rural wages has remained so high.

A basic restructuring of agriculture—involving far more than agrarian reform—is necessary to reduce the inequality between the rural and urban areas. When assessing the crisis in the Alliance for Progress, I submitted that excessive protectionism had kept the level of industrial prices so high that the domestic terms of trade between agricultural and industrial products were even worse than the world market ones. A thorough reform of tariff policy was advocated. Only when an investment actually materializes should a tariff (or subsidy) be applied. Imperfection in marketing and distribution also had to be reduced. Incentives for modernization of

19. "International Aid for Underdeveloped Countries," pp. 107–38.
20. "International Aid for Underdeveloped Countries," p. 109.

agricultural production must be provided in the form of subsidies for some inputs as well as minimum prices for two or three years at a time— "continuity is as important as the amount"—in order to reduce risks and uncertainty of selling.[21] Such policy reforms are still needed to accelerate agricultural development.

In order to reduce the inequality between the employed and the unemployed, it is necessary to establish a right to work as the minimum of equality of opportunity that modern society must provide. Full employment is an objective that cannot be replaced or compensated by anything else. Yet we are nowhere near its solution in most developing countries. A high rate of growth is necessary to provide an industrial drive sufficient to absorb the present and growing unemployment. Full employment and access to educational facilities undoubtedly remain the fundamental requirements for providing a minimum of equality of opportunity.

It may be asked: If, as we have maintained, the basic purpose of aid is to catalyze additional national effort in developing countries, who then is to judge whether this effect is forthcoming and whether it is adequate? If aid to developing countries is an income tax, the use of the tax should be decided by a consensus of all the parties. Partnership implies a consensus. The Pearson and Brandt reports foresaw both rights and duties—but the discussion stresses rights more than duties.[22]

Another problem neglected in the Pearson report is that of the multinational corporations. They present two aspects: they are very efficient in transferring capital, technology, and management; but their oligopolistic structure raises problems, not because multinationals are foreign—a national shark bites as much as a foreign one—but because they are monopolistic. All guidelines or codes of private international investment are in fact second-best attempts at an antimonopoly law. "The trouble in the past was there was not enough freedom of trade and too much freedom of international movement of capital."[23]

Today's method is unsuitable and often counterproductive; the very discussion by a credit-giving country of what the receiving country should do invariably raises objections that the latter's national sovereignty is being infringed upon. Under such circumstances, the discussion is either

21. Rosenstein-Rodan, "La Marcha de la Alianza para el Progresso," *Progresso* (Vision), 1966.

22. Lester B. Pearson and others, *Partners in Development*, Report of the Commission on International Development (New York: Praeger, 1969); *North-South: A Program for Survival*, Report of the Independent Commission on International Development Issues, Willy Brandt, chairman (Cambridge, Mass.: MIT Press, 1980).

23. Rosenstein-Rodan, "Problems of Private Foreign Investment and Multinational Corporations," in *Multinational Investment in the Economic Development and Integration of Latin America* (Washington, D.C.: International Development Bank, 1968).

incomplete and not explicitly articulated or it is bound to give rise to mutual recrimination.

The only way out of this vicious circle is to establish a committee, which is not appointed by and not responsible to either creditor or debtor governments, to make an independent evaluation of national development effort and a consequent recommendation of the amount of aid to be allocated. It is indifferent whether we call it international arbitration or mediation. It should evolve into a de facto "International Court of Economic Justice." Clearly a new form of impartial international evaluation of that sort must be adopted, which should command confidence and respect on both sides.

Today we have competence, finance, and no democracy in the international banks—and democracy and no finance in the United Nations. The 1954 ECLA report proclaimed the need for a separation of programming and financing. An independent body—not responsible to either creditors or debtors—should evaluate the programs, and resources should be allocated according to that verdict. The World Bank has a good staff (at least in the past twenty-five years), but the developing countries have no confidence in the vote of its board because creditor countries have the overwhelming majority; the developed countries, on the other hand, have no confidence in the United Nations. It is part of national sovereignty for each nation to limit its own rights. There will be no satisfactory solution to this problem without some sort of arbitration. Only an International Development Council—an International Court of Economic Justice—can solve the problem. The Committee of IX of the Alliance for Progress was an attempt to apply such an international arbitration. It failed because of sabotage on both sides, but all great ideas first fail. All progress is first proclaimed to be impossible but is then realized.

Evaluation of the Development Effort

After some four decades of concerted attention to the challenge of development, we might ask how much economics can explain. Economic theory can determine the necessary, though not the sufficient, conditions of growth. The so-called noneconomic factors account for the gap between the necessary and the sufficient. Any evaluation of development can only state that the necessary conditions for growth exist or are being created; it cannot predict with certainty that growth will actually take place. One can learn a lot from past performance, but the criteria of evaluation are ex ante concepts. They yield a probability judgment and have, therefore, to be continually checked.

Most differences of opinion among economists originate from two sources: different interpretation of data, since data are often deficient; and different interpretation of or assumptions about objectives, since the social welfare function is seldom explicitly given or even consistently felt. If both data and objectives were given, there would be a large consensus as to how to apply economic techniques, and few differences of opinion among economists would remain. Data must, however, cover not only available material and human resources, technological possibilities, and psychological preferences but also attitudes of mind and the ability to change them. A good part of the last-named factors (social attitudes) are unknown rather than given quantities, so that the data are never available. And the objectives are largely subconscious—neither quite given nor quite unknown.

A technical problem deals with multiplicity of means and *one* end: for instance, how to cross a river by boat, bridge, or some other way. We can use monetary, fiscal, foreign exchange, and commercial policy in various blends and combinations if the objective is clear. An economic problem consists of a multiplicity of means *and* multiplicity of ends. The "rationalist" assumption that we know what we want and think before making a decision is neither right nor wrong: it is an exaggeration. Our diverse *aims* ("social welfare function") are in partial conflict with each other—we can fulfill more of one and less of the other; moreover we can do it at different rates (more today, less tomorrow or vice versa) in different periods. This system of preferences is like an underdeveloped film: no contour lines are visible, but they are there. Programming (development planning) is the fluid that "develops" them: the contour lines then appear on the film.[24] The different aims—growth, employment, better income distribution—were at once emphasized; growth was only a means to achieve the other ends, since it is easier to reshuffle a growing than a stagnant income. Meeting basic needs and the assault on poverty were implicit but became more explicit in the late 1960s and 1970s.

The development momentum is now passing through a low point. The transfer of financial and technological resources to developing countries has also been disappointing. In the moral crisis of today we see in many developed countries a movement of an international Poujadism: an income tax strike. The richest country in the world, the United States, which pioneered in the field of aid, is the worst offender. When their income per head was merely 40 percent of what it now is, U.S. citizens gave 2 percent of GNP to the Marshall Plan. Today when their income is 2.5 times higher they give less than 0.25 percent for economic aid. The original philosophy of aid is still correct, and present cynics are not justified. People need and want ideals, and ideals are ultimately powerful. A great deal has been achieved in the development effort. The postwar period of development is a history of triumph—not of failure. The increase in life expectancy, the

24. Rosenstein-Rodan, "Criteria for Evaluation of National Development Effort," *Journal of Development Planning*, vol. 1, no. 1 (1970).

fall in infant mortality, the rates of growth, the achievements in any number of developing countries—nobody at the end of the Second World War would have expected so much. A billion people are still hungry, but it would now be 2 billion without the achievements that have been made.

What got lost, however, in the 1970s was international solidarity. The objective of international full employment disappeared in cynicism after Vietnam. The transition from the national welfare state to the international level must still be made. Not to do enough about inequality of opportunity and poverty when our world resources are sufficient to improve the situation is the real moral crisis of the present world, just as it was at the end of the Second World War. General cynicism is at least as unrealistic as naive idealism. We know what has to be done—we have to mobilize the will to do it.

Comment

Dragoslav Avramovic

MY COMMENTS FOCUS ON THREE POINTS. First, I want to trace the evolution of Paul Rosenstein-Rodan from a neoclassical theorist to a protagonist of a massive, organized structural change. This may be helpful in light of the resurgence of neoclassicism in development writing in recent years. Second, I shall try to identify which of Dr. Rodan's conceptual contributions have proven of use in actual development planning and policy— usually a good test of a theory. Third, I shall conclude by drawing attention to the financial crisis now affecting a large part of the developing world. It is likely to result in many changes in developing countries, and it will almost inevitably give rise to new thinking on theory and policy.

From Marginal Utility to the Big Push

Joseph A. Schumpeter, in his monumental *History of Economic Analysis*, has this to say of the early work of Professor Rodan: "A brilliant and compact survey of arguments and counterarguments [concerning the Austrian School theory of utility in equilibrium analysis] has been presented by P. N. Rosenstein-Rodan in the article 'Grentznutzen' (marginal utility) in the German encyclopedia, 4th edition, Volume IV, 1927."[1]

A long time later, in the preface to *Development and Planning: Essays in Honor of Paul Rosenstein-Rodan*, Jagdish N. Bhagwati and Richard S. Eckaus wrote: "For thirty years Paul Rosenstein-Rodan has been a leader in the efforts of the economics profession to understand the problems of the poor nations of the world and to assist in their development. He has not merely been the doyen of development theorists: he has also dedicated much of his life to policy-making by international organizations for development and to domestic policy formation within many of the less developed countries."[2]

Dragoslav Avramovic is an economic consultant with the United Nations Conference on Trade and Development (UNCTAD).

1. New York: Oxford University Press, 1954, p. 1056.
2. London: Allen and Unwin, 1972, p. 7.

When I was first asked to comment on Professor Rodan's work on growth economics, I thought that the full extent of his contribution to development theory and policy could be appreciated only if it was realized that he had come to development economics after he had mastered and contributed to neoclassical theory. How did it happen and why? Here are his answers:

> In Vienna in the 1920s I was only interested in the theory of choice, i.e., utility theory, Austrian variety, and considered any applied economics to be "impure" and of no interest. It is only later on after a year in Italy, 1929, and certainly in London that I became interested in economics as a basis for economic policy. In the Vienna days I published the main article on marginal utility in 1927 (an Italian translation in 1930 and a translation of a part of it by Stolper in English), but it is not worth referring to; these are past days.[3] The same applies to one article on complementarity in Italian, which is quoted by J. R. Hicks as having stimulated him in his theory, but is also antediluvian. More important is an early version in 1929, No. 1 of *Zeitschrift für Nationalökonomie* on "The Role of Time in Economic Theory," which had its second and considerably modified appearance in *Economica* in 1934. That one influenced somewhat my interest in development theory later on. (Letter of May 18, 1982.)

I pressed the point of the Vienna days further, suspecting that some of the essential ingredients of the development theory might already have been there. Professor Rodan's reply confirmed the suspicions: "I agree that the earlier micro-theory was relevant to development theorists very largely because the Austrian School (unlike the Lausanne School) paid major attention to the *path* towards equilibrium and not only to the conditions of stability which must be satisfied if a point is to be a point of equilibrium." (Letter of July 1, 1982.)

Specifically, as Sikhamoy Chakravarty has noted, three distinct themes can be discerned in the marginal utility article of 1927: (a) complementarity, which forms an important part of the subsequent and by now classic 1943 article, "Problems of Industrialization of Eastern and South-Eastern Europe," dealing with the basic rationale of planning, and of Rodan's later elaboration in the doctrine of the "big push"; (b) the hierarchical structure of wants, later linked to income elasticities of demand in developing countries, although its significance for planning has not yet been completely realized; and (c) the choice of an economic period over which scarce resources are allocated.[4]

3. The English translation by Wolfgang F. Stolper was published in *International Economic Papers*, no. 10 (New York: Macmillan, 1960).

4. Sikhamoy Chakravarty, "Paul Rosenstein-Rodan: An Appreciation," *World Development*, vol. 11, no. 1 (January 1983), pp. 73–75.

These arguments are summarized by Professor Rodan himself in his present paper, "Natura Facit Saltum": "The dynamics of wants and their interrelatedness were much more important to me than the neoclassical attempt at precise characterization of the properties of the utility function. Consumption complementarities, the role of time, the pursuit curve [the dynamic path toward equilibrium], plus external economies—all these dynamic factors were not to be considered as a second order of smalls, but even more as pervasive in a less developed country."

There is no doubt in my mind that the catastrophic experience of the 1930s was a major influence on the evolution of Dr. Rodan's doctrine. Implicit in the 1943 thesis was the assumption of a limited absorptive capacity of the world market. This and the example of Soviet planning must have had an effect on the Chatham House group studying the future of Eastern Europe, over which Dr. Rodan presided, although he stated clearly in the 1943 article that the Chatham House model relied on international trade, capital movements, and a mixed economy and was therefore substantially different from the Soviet model.

Programs, Projects, and Commodity Cycles

In the 1943 article the essence of national programming was laid out:

- An organized institutional framework is necessary for the successful industrialization of international depressed areas.
- A minimum of social overhead capital is necessary to induce industrialization; the supply of this minimum is beyond the capacity of individual entrepreneurs.
- The first task of industrialization is to provide training to transform peasants into industrial workers. The automatism of laissez-faire never worked properly because it is not profitable for a private entrepreneur to invest in training labor.
- Complementarity of different industries is the most important argument for large-scale planned industrialization. It would create its own additional market, thus allowing an expansion of world output with the minimum disturbance of the world markets. The planned creation of such a complementary system reduces the risk of not being able to sell, and, since risk can be considered as cost, it reduces costs.
- It is usually tacitly assumed that the divergence between the private and social marginal net product is not very considerable. This assumption may be too optimistic even in the case of a mature competitive economy. It is certainly not true in the case of a fundamental structural change in the international depressed area.
- The existing institutions of international and national investment do not take advantage of external economies of the kind described. There

is no incentive within their framework for many investments which are profitable in terms of social marginal product, but do not appear profitable in terms of private marginal product. The main driving force of investment is the profit expectation of an individual entrepreneur, which is based on past experience. Experience of the past is partly irrelevant, however, when the whole economic structure of a region is to be changed. If we create a sufficiently large investment unit by including all the new industries of the region, external economies will become internal profits out of which dividends may be paid easily.

• Government guarantees are necessary to induce the necessary movements of capital internationally.[5]

In his years at the World Bank and subsequently, Dr. Rodan made a major effort to broaden the concept of investment projects and to bring about an acceptance of country development programs as a whole as suitable bases for external financing. It has been an uphill struggle which is by no means finished. It has followed directly from the theory of internalization of external economies. Linked to the programming concept has been the use of shadow prices. Of course, Professor Rodan was not alone in advocating this approach. The widespread emergence of planning offices in developing countries, and experimentation with overall and sectoral programming and projections and with project appraisal models and techniques, can in part be attributed to the influence of development theory, to which Dr. Rodan has made such a distinguished contribution.

The late 1920s and early 1930s led to the development of the cobweb theorem: commodity prices in one period determine the quantities supplied in the subsequent period, which in turn, combined with any demand shift that may have taken place, determine later prices, and so on. The resulting fluctuations may be converging toward equilibrium, remaining neutral, or leading to a growing disequilibrium. Professor Rodan was one of several authors who seem to have contributed to the formulation of the theory at approximately the same time—according to Lionel Robbins, he was ahead of the others.[6] It is the divergent disequilibria which are particularly damaging. The damage may be especially large in commodities with a long gestation period, and may lead to overinvestment and subsequent protracted periods of depressed prices and incomes. It was from this perspective that Dr. Rodan, while at the World Bank, wrote in the late 1940s a study anticipating a massive increase in coffee prices. He warned that unless managed through an active fiscal policy, the price rise would

5. P. N. Rosenstein-Rodan, "Problems of Industrialization of Eastern and South-Eastern Europe," *Economic Journal*, vol. 53 (June–September 1943).

6. "The Role of Time in Economic Theory," *Economica*, New Series (1934), pp. 77–97. Other authors were Arthur Hanau, Henry Schultz, Jan Tinbergen, and Umberto Ricci. The term "cobweb" was apparently first suggested by Nicholas Kaldor in 1934.

lead to inflation, overproduction, and subsequent decline, but if controlled it could be used for financing diversified investments.[7] However, he did not pursue further the commodity analysis. It was Prebisch and Singer who focused on the commodity problem, including its income and investment effects, and proposed international remedies.

Crisis of the 1980s

Professor Rodan ends his present paper by drawing attention to what he calls the moral crisis of the present world, which prevents the transition of the welfare state from the national to the international level. By now, in early 1984, it is clear that what is involved is a major threat to development itself. The near collapse of capital market lending to developing countries in August 1982, the massive fall in commodity prices in 1981–82 which was only partly reversed in 1983, the enormous increase in the real international rate of interest, the cutthroat competition in the market for standard manufactures, the appreciation of the U.S. dollar—the main creditor currency—coupled with capital flight and domestic policy errors, have imposed on the major debtor countries and on most of the African continent a burden of adjustment on the order of the 1930s. Some forty to fifty developing countries are involved in debt-rescheduling negotiations or are in arrears with payments. Their internal financial situations are frequently desperate: in a number of newly industrializing countries, much of the large-scale industry is today in effect bankrupt.[8] It is caught in a squeeze of stagnating or falling domestic sales, foreign market restrictions, devaluation-induced explosions in debt service abroad, and domestic interest rates which in real terms reach 30 to 40 percent a year. The slogan of debt-led growth, proclaimed in the 1970s, has ended in a disaster. Some other slogans are on trial. Major institutional changes are under way in many developing countries; new priorities and systems of planning and management will emerge; the international scene is unlikely to remain the same; and new theories will probably be born.

7. "Increased Dollar Earnings and Coffee Inflation in Latin America," E-69a (Washington, D.C.: The World Bank, November 21, 1949).

8. Pedro-Pablo Kuczynski, "Latin American Debt: Act Two," *Foreign Affairs* (Winter 1983).

Walt Whitman Rostow

W. W. ROSTOW was born in 1916 in New York City. At the age of fifteen he won a scholarship to Yale University, then received his B.A. from Yale in 1936, his Ph.D. from Yale in 1939, and an M.A. from Oxford, where he was a Rhodes Scholar, in 1938.

His teaching career in economics and history began in 1940 at Columbia University. He returned to Oxford as the Harmsworth Professor of American History, 1946–47. In 1949 he was the Pitt Professor of American History at Cambridge University. From 1950 to 1961 he was Professor of Economic History at the Massachusetts Institute of Technology, and from 1951 to 1961 he was also a staff member of the Center for International Studies at MIT.

In 1958 he spent another year at Cambridge University, where he lectured and wrote about a subject that Keynes and his followers had neglected—that of economic development. His lectures on the "process of industrialization" led to his noted book, *The Stages of Economic Growth* (1960). In 1969 he became Professor of Economics and History at the University of Texas at Austin, where he is currently the Rex G. Baker Jr. Professor of Political Economy.

He was Assistant to the Executive Secretary of the Economic Community for Europe, 1947–49. Between 1961 and 1969 he held a succession of government posts: Deputy Special Assistant to the President for National Security Affairs, Counsellor and Chairman of the Policy Planning Council at the Department of State, U.S. Member of the Inter-American Committee on the Alliance for Progress, and Special Assistant to the President for National Security Affairs in the White House.

Rostow received the Order of the British Empire (1945), the Legion of Merit (1945), and the Presidential Medal of Freedom (1969).

His books include: *Essays on the British Economy of the Nineteenth Century* (Oxford: Clarendon Press, 1948); *The Process of Economic Growth* (New York: Norton, 1952; Oxford: Clarendon Press, 1953; 2d ed., 1960); with Richard W. Hatch, *An American Policy in Asia* (New York: Technology Press, MIT, and John Wiley, 1955); with Max F. Millikan, *A Proposal: Key to an Effective Foreign Policy* (New York: Harper,

1957); *The Stages of Economic Growth: A Non-Communist Manifesto* (Cambridge, Eng.: Cambridge University Press, 1960; 2d ed., 1971); as editor, *The Economics of Take-off into Sustained Growth* (London: Macmillan; New York: St. Martin's Press, 1963); *Politics and the Stages of Growth* (Cambridge, Eng.: Cambridge University Press, 1971); *How It All Began: Origins of the Modern Economy* (New York: McGraw-Hill, 1975); *The World Economy: History and Prospect* (Austin: University of Texas Press; London: Macmillan, 1978); and *Why the Poor Get Richer and the Rich Slow Down: Essays in the Marshallian Long Period* (Austin: University of Texas Press; London: Macmillan, 1980).

A few of his articles are "Investment and the Great Depression," *Economic History Review*, vol. 8 (May 1938); "The Terms of Trade in Theory and Practice," *Economic History Review*, vol. 3 (1950); "The Historical Analysis of the Terms of Trade," *Economic History Review*, vol. 4 (1951); "Trends in the Allocation of Resources in Secular Growth," in *Economic Progress*, L. H. Dupriez, ed. (London: Macmillan, 1955);"The Take-off into Self-Sustained Growth," *Economic Journal*, vol. 66 (March 1956); "The Stages of Economic Growth," *Economic History Review*, vol. 11 (1959); and "The Developing World in the Fifth Kondratieff Upswing," *Annals of the American Academy of Political and Social Science*, vol. 420 (1975).

His principal contributions have related to a dynamic, disaggregated theory of production and prices in which changes in population, technology, and relative prices of basic commodities are rendered endogenous, applied to both economic development via stages of economic growth and the history of the world economy.

Development:
The Political Economy
of the Marshallian Long Period

WORK ON DEVELOPMENT THEORY AND POLICY in the 1950s forced me to mobilize and bring together all I had learned in responding to the two large questions I posed in 1933–34 to frame my professional agenda: the application of economic theory to economic history, and the interplay of economic forces with the other components of the life of whole societies.

The story begins in my first two years as an undergraduate at Yale. I decided to major in history and wrote lengthy papers on facets of the English Revolution of the seventeenth century and the French Revolution which imparted some sense of the complexities of history and the inadequacy of any simple theory of causation, including economic causation.

In the autumn of my sophomore year (1933), this heady introduction to the dynamics of societies in revolutionary turmoil was crosscut by an informal weekly seminar in then modern economic theory. The teacher was Richard M. Bissell, just back from a graduate year at the London School of Economics. Bissell commanded (and commands) extraordinary powers of lucid exposition. There were four students, one of whom was Max Millikan who promptly defected from physics to economics. Bissell's impact on me was equally powerful. I did not defect from history but decided sometime in 1933–34 that I would devote my professional life to responding, as best I could, to two questions: How could economic theory be used to illuminate economic history? How did economic forces interact with social, political, and cultural forces? I had, as I noted, already set aside the notion that a simple line of causation ran from the economy to a society's other dimensions.

By the spring of 1934 I had conducted my first experiment as an economist-historian: a paper of ninety-seven pages on the British inflation during the French Revolution and the Napoleonic Wars, the subsequent deflation, and the return to the gold standard. I began believing that the theoretical structures incorporated in D. H. Robertson's *Money* (1928) and Keynes's *Treatise on Money* (1930), among other works, would

I wish to thank my colleagues Ted Carpenter, William Glade, Tomasson Jannuzi, and David Kendrick for reading and commenting helpfully on this paper in draft.

provide sufficient framework to explain what happened to prices. The beginning of my education as an independent economic theorist was the discovery that conventional monetary theory was incomplete and, on occasion, significantly misleading as a tool for explaining why prices moved as they did from 1793 to 1821. In the course of the exercise I came to understand the shrewdness of Wicksell's description of quantity theorists: "They usually make the mistake of postulating their assumptions instead of clearly proving them"[1]—a phenomenon that persists but surprises me less than it did almost a half century ago when I first encountered it.

I proceeded in my efforts to link theory and history in a doctoral thesis;[2] a substantial contribution to the Gayer study;[3] and, after a wartime interruption, my *British Economy of the Nineteenth Century*,[4] which contains essays on the pattern of business cycles and longer trend periods (Kondratieff cycles), as well as two essays on the interplay among economic, social, and political forces. By that time I had concluded that "the optimum unit for the study of economic history is not the nation, but the whole interrelated trading area; certainly that is the frame within which many of the most important national, regional, or even industrial problems [of individual countries] must be placed, if they are fully to be understood."[5] I also decided that I would have to make my own theoretical map as a matrix for teaching such a grand subject. Evidently, conventional macroeconomics, in either its monetary or Keynesian variants, would not suffice. They were incapable of dealing with the dynamics of invention and innovation, fluctuations in the supply of basic commodities, or demography. And so I began to plan the book which became *The Process of Economic Growth*.[6]

In the spring of 1950 D. H. Robertson contributed an insight which is reflected in the title of this chapter. At tea one afternoon, I told him I planned to write a book on the process of economic growth. I welcomed his advice because I had profited from his youthful work, *A Study of Industrial Fluctuations* (1915), with its rare sensitivity to the interweaving of cycles with technological and other structural changes. Robertson encouraged me to go forward with the project but said the theoretical

1. Knut Wicksell, *Lectures on Political Economy*, vol. 2, *Money*, E. Classen, trans.; Lionel Robbins, ed. (New York: Macmillan, 1934), pp. 159–60.

2. *British Trade Fluctuations, 1868–1896* (New York: Arno Press, 1981); the thesis is dated 1940.

3. A. D. Gayer, W. W. Rostow, and Anna J. Schwartz, *The Growth and Fluctuation of the British Economy, 1790–1850* (Oxford: Clarendon Press, 1953; 2d ed., Hassocks, W. Sussex: Harvester Press, 1975). This study was, in fact, completed in 1941 but not published until after the war.

4. Oxford: Clarendon Press, 1948.

5. *British Economy of the Nineteenth Century*, pp. 12–13.

6. New York: Norton, 1952; Oxford: Clarendon Press, 1953; 2d ed., 1960.

problems of growth were formidable. In particular, a theory of growth required dealing systematically with the Marshallian long period. He warned me of the pitfalls and urged me to read carefully appendix J in *Money, Credit, and Commerce* where Alfred Marshall despairs of formalizing the case of increasing returns. I read Marshall afresh and emerged with an abiding sense of how evasive, if convenient, is the convention of framing the major propositions in economic theory within the Marshallian short period. And I came to appreciate Marshall's wisdom in asserting that if one pushed beyond the propositions of static short-period equilibrium, one must deal with "real life," "the high theme of economic progress," and "society as an organism."[7]

In any case, I had for long been sure that, for a serious economic historian, there was no way to escape the challenges of dealing with economic progress and society as an organism; for in real life technologies changed unceasingly as did the conditions of supply for foodstuffs and raw materials, and the size, structure, and quality of the working force. The short period was, as Marshall said, "only an introduction to economic studies,"[8] but an economic historian or student of economic development had to face up to the more complex world beyond.

The 1950s: Development Theory

Against this somewhat eccentric background, my views on development theory and policy emerged in the 1950s from the contrapuntal interaction of three quite different activities conducted simultaneously: the crystallization of a dynamic, disaggregated theory of growth out of my study and graduate teaching of the history of the world economy; the formulation of views on the dynamics of the communist world and appropriate U.S. policies toward both the U.S.S.R. and China;[9] and the generation, with my colleagues at the Massachusetts Institute of Technology, of a collective view of the modernization process in the developing regions and of an appropriate U.S. policy toward them.

The latter two enterprises required that I come to conclusions about the nature of the U.S. interest on the world scene—a matter on which I had to form views in 1945–46 in a minor post at the State Department, as well as

---

7. Alfred Marshall, *Principles of Economics* (8th ed., London: Macmillan, 1930), p. 461.

8. Idem.

9. This part of my work was incorporated mainly in *The Dynamics of Soviet Society*, with Alfred Levin and others (New York: Norton, 1952, 2d ed., 1967); *The Prospects for Communist China*, with Richard W. Hatch, Frank A. Kierman, and Alexander Eckstein (Cambridge, Mass.: The Technology Press, MIT, and John Wiley, 1954); and *An American Policy in Asia*, with Richard W. Hatch (Cambridge, Mass.: The Technology Press, MIT, and John Wiley, 1955).

a teacher of American history in England in 1946–47 and 1949–50. My understanding was, however, enriched by my work at MIT, including a study of the interaction of American domestic life and foreign policy conducted in 1955–58.[10]

Although an author is not an authoritative judge of such matters, I would guess that there were three distinctive characteristics of my views on development theory as incorporated in *The Process of Economic Growth*. First, and most fundamental, I placed the process of economic growth explicitly in the setting of the evolution of whole societies. Economic growth was viewed as simply one manifestation of a society's total performance. In writing the book I linked the key economic variables to the noneconomic dimensions of the society through an array of propensities and insisted that, for advanced industrial as well as developing societies, the propensities mattered and had to be taken explicitly into account. As I wrote in the preface to the second edition of *The Process of Economic Growth* (p. vii):

> The propensities do not represent, then, some kind of discovery, which can be assessed one way or another. The proposition here is that no statement about the course of population or about the level of productivity or about the scale and composition of capital formation can be made, in a world of changing production functions, unless it contains implicit or explicit assumptions about the strength and the position of the propensities. The purpose of the propensities is to make those assumptions explicit and render it possible for them to be realistic; for in a world of change the state of the arts is not fixed, and profit maximization in no way covers what is involved in borrowers' or lenders' risk. Capital formation is not merely a matter of profit maximization: it is a matter of a society's effective attitude towards and response to basic science, applied science, and the risk-taking of innovation and innovational lending.[11]

Second, in *The Stages of Economic Growth*, I formulated, within this general matrix, a quite particular proposition about the crucial role of politics in the early phases of modernization:[12]

---

10. This study resulted in, among other publications, *The United States in the World Arena* (New York: Harper and Row, 1960; 2d ed., 1969).

11. Economists, Keynesian and others, appear systematically to ignore Keynes's wise *bon mot*: "If human nature felt no temptation to take a chance, no satisfaction (profit apart) in constructing a factory, a railway, a mine or a farm, there might not be much investment merely as a result of cold calculation" (*General Theory*, p. 150).

12. Cambridge, Eng.: Cambridge University Press, 1960; 2d ed., 1971, pp. 26–30. I later developed more systematically the concept of politics as a process of balancing certain abiding imperatives of government in *Politics and the Stage of Growth* (Cambridge, Eng.: Cambridge University Press, 1971).

As a matter of historical fact a reactive nationalism—reacting against intrusion from more advanced nations—has been a most important and powerful motive force in the transition from traditional to modern societies, at least as important as the profit motive. Men holding effective authority or influence have been willing to uproot traditional societies not, primarily, to make more money but because the traditional society failed—or threatened to fail—to protect them from humiliation by foreigners. . . .

. . . without the affront to human and national dignity caused by the intrusion of more advanced powers, the rate of modernization of traditional societies over the past century-and-a-half would have been much slower than, in fact, it has been. Out of mixed interests and motives, coalitions were formed in these traditional or early transitional societies which aimed to make a strong modern national government and which were prepared to deal with the enemies of this objective: that is, they were prepared to struggle against the political and social groups rooted in regionally based agriculture, joined in some cases by the colonial or quasicolonial power. . . .

Now we come to the crux of the matter. Nationalism can be turned in any one of several directions. It can be turned outward to right real or believed past humiliations suffered on the world scene or to exploit real or believed opportunities for national aggrandizement which appear for the first time as realistic possibilities, once the new modern state is established and the economy develops some momentum; nationalism can be held inward and focused on the political consolidation of the victory won by the national over the regionally based power; or nationalism can be turned to the tasks of economic, social, and political modernization which have been obstructed by the old regionally based, usually aristocratic societal structure, by the former colonial power, or by both in coalition.

Once modern nationhood is established, different elements in the coalition press to mobilize the newly triumphant nationalist political sentiment in different directions: the soldiers, say, abroad; the professional politicians, to drive home the triumph of the centre over the region; the merchants, to economic development; the intellectuals, to social, political and legal reform.

The cast of policy at home and abroad of newly created or newly modernized states hinges greatly, then, on the balance of power within the coalition which emerges and the balance in which the various alternative objectives of nationalism are pursued.

A third distinctive aspect of my formulation was more narrowly economic. It flowed from the judgment that economic growth since the late eighteenth century was distinguished from all periods of economic expansion in the longer past by the fact that, through the oblique as well as direct impact of the Scientific Revolution, invention and innovation had become a more or less regular flow.[13]

The acceptance of this proposition had two major consequences.

First, the analysis of a modern or modernizing economy could not be usefully conducted in aggregate terms: the sectors absorbing new technologies had to be examined, and the inherently decelerating path of such dynamic sectors traced out. When viewed in this fashion, the relatively stable aggregate growth rates observed in history came alive: sustained growth became a race to bring in new technologically vital sectors as the old leading sectors decelerated. This sectoral bias was strengthened by the perception that the maintenance of high and steady aggregate growth rates required adequate flows of investment to the supporting sectors such as agriculture, raw materials, infrastructure, education. The result was a particular view of what a growth theory required:

> The central theoretical effort here is to provide a systematic way of breaking through the aggregates, which we have inherited from Keynesian income analysis, in order to grip dynamic forces at work in the particular sectors on which the growth depends. The judgment is that consumption and saving, consumer goods and capital goods, are insufficient categories for the analysis of growth, cycles, or trends; and that the static cast of traditional production theory must be broken. . . . Income analysis and all its refined tools are not rejected in this way of looking at things. On the contrary. But the intellectual problem of making a theoretical framework for growth analysis is taken to be the problem of orderly disaggregation, within a dynamic model which links the broad income aggregates to the concept of sectoral equilibrium.[14]

The stages of economic growth flowed directly from this linking of the sectors to the familiar aggregates of Keynesian income analysis. The stages unfold from the interplay of sectors of increasing technological sophistication and the rise of real income per capita.[15]

A good deal of the controversy over the stages of economic growth might have been avoided—or rendered more germane—if I had driven this point home more successfully.[16] For example, the rise in the aggregate

13. This proposition, stated in *The Process of Economic Growth* and *The Stages of Economic Growth*, is elaborated at length in *How It All Began* (New York: McGraw-Hill, 1975).

14. *The Process of Economic Growth*, p. vi. As I have noted on other occasions, Simon Kuznets's *Secular Movements in Production and Prices* (Boston: Houghton Mifflin, 1930), with its focus on the dynamic paths of sectors, influenced me in this direction, as did the concurrent work of Walther Hoffmann and Arthur F. Burns.

15. The concept of stages of growth was first outlined in *The Process of Economic Growth* (see especially pp. 17, 71, 103–08).

16. *The Stages of Economic Growth*, pp. 12–16. For the playback effects of sectoral growth on the conventional Keynesian aggregates, see especially pp. 46–58. Here, for

investment rate during take-off, the rise in real income per capita, and (usually), the rise in consumption per capita were in good part caused by rapid expansion, with all its spreading effects, in the leading sectors where new technologies were being diffused; in turn, the expansion in the aggregates played back on the rate of growth in the sectors (for example, via the income elasticity of demand). I certainly tried to make this process of interaction clear, notably in a passage early in *The Stages* (p. 58), which deals with the matter head-on, entitled "A Dynamic Theory of Production." But, still, colleagues as sophisticated as Albert Fishlow could conclude that there were two theories of take-off: one sectoral, the other aggregative.[17] If I had it to do over again, I would state emphatically, right at the beginning, what I wrote in the "Introduction and Epilogue" to the volume summarizing the debate on take-off organized at Konstanz in 1960 by the International Economic Association: "the emergence of a rate of net investment sufficient to outstrip the rate of increase of population and to yield a positive net rate of growth is at least as much the result of prior [sectoral] growth as a cause of growth."[18]

In a larger sense, however, I suspect the controversy was inevitable for three reasons. First, in the Harrod-Domar world of the 1950s, it was easy and natural for economists to seize on the course of the investment rate during take-off and treat it not as a product of a complex interaction (including the role of the state in social overhead outlays) but as they were accustomed to treat it; that is, as an essentially independent variable. To this day, conventional macroeconomists have great difficulty dealing with the relation between what happens in the sectors and the behavior of the aggregates, for example, the multiple relations between the energy sector

---

example, toward the close of the exposition of take-off is one effort to make the linkage between the sectors and the aggregates (p. 58):

> What this argument does assert is that the rapid growth of one or more new manufacturing sectors is a powerful and essential engine of economic transformation. Its power derives from the multiplicity of its forms of impact, when a society is prepared to respond positively to this impact. Growth in such sectors, with new production functions of high productivity, in itself tends to raise output per head; it places incomes in the hands of men who will not merely save a high proportion of an expanding income but who will plough it into highly productive investment; it sets up a chain of effective demand for other manufactured products; it sets up a requirement for enlarged urban areas, whose capital costs may be high, but whose population and market organization help to make industrialization an on-going process; and, finally, it opens up a range of external economy effects which, in the end, help to produce new leading sectors when the initial impulse of the take-off's leading sectors begins to wane.

17. Albert Fishlow, "Empty Economic Stages," *Economic Journal*, vol. 75, no. 297 (March 1965).

18. W. W. Rostow, ed., *The Economics of Take-off into Sustained Growth* (New York: St. Martin's Press, 1963), p. 16.

and the aggregate performance of the economy. Second, the irreducible degree of sectoral disaggregation required (in my view) to deal seriously with growth—embracing infrastructure, education, agriculture, raw materials, and the major leading sector complexes—made life difficult for conventional theorists. Robert Solow's response at Konstanz was to throw the problem back on the economic historian: "if economic historians wanted help from multisector models they would have to produce much more in the way of estimates not of observable qualities but of parameters."[19] But economic growth was—and remains—too important a subject to be cut down to the size convenient for manipulation by the tools we taught our graduate students in the third quarter of the twentieth century. No great work in economics, from *The Wealth of Nations* to the *General Theory*, would have been written if the Solow criterion had been applied by the author.

Finally, and most important of all, is the inescapable role of noneconomic factors in the process of economic growth. Here Solow's observation at Konstanz and my later response are illuminating.[20] Solow properly demanded that I clarify "the rules of behavior, parameters, and initial conditions" for take-off. The heart of my response lay in these two passages:

> In one sense, the problem may not be soluble. Economic growth is the result of an interacting process involving the economic, social, and political sectors of a society, including the emergence of a corps of entrepreneurs who are psychologically motivated and technically prepared regularly to lead the way in introducing new production functions into the economy.
>
> . . . [But] one can say to Professor Solow that take-off requires by way of initial conditions the prior build-up at a certain minimum quantum of social overhead capital, to provide the technical conditions for the requisite spreading effects; and it requires a change in rules of behaviour such that new production functions available are actually brought to bear in the capital stock, within the initial leading sectors and those linked backward and laterally to them.
>
> The resulting path of change in output per head will be determined by the parameters, as well as by the scale and efficiency of the entrepreneurial corps, in the public and private sectors—efficiency being measured by the rate at which they close the gap between existing relevant technology and pre-take-off technology in the economy.

Put another way, Solow's "residual" (what is left after inputs of capital and labor are accounted for) is not the product of some antiseptic economic process transcending the physical inputs of labor and capital. It is

19. *The Economics of Take-off*, p. 472.
20. *The Economics of Take-off*, pp. 468–579 (Solow) and xxiv–xxvi (Rostow).

the result of complex societal changes which yield private and public entrepreneurs, and an educated working force, capable of and motivated to generate and/or absorb efficiently the flow or backlog of relevant technology.

Conventional theorists can, perhaps, be content with the calculation of highly aggregated residuals without peering inside the black box and can thus avoid the inelegance of a full social science analysis. An economic historian or development economist must, as I noted earlier, accept Marshall's challenge of viewing "society as an organism."

But, still, rereading the debate, I find it a bit odd; for no one can immerse himself in the living process of economic planning, whether in an advanced industrial country or in a developing nation, without transcending the Keynesian aggregates, accepting the need for a considerable degree of disaggregation, developing at least some empirical sense of the likely interplay between the sectors and the aggregates, and confronting such questions as the appropriate role of the state and education policy. I suspect that the widespread and continuing interest in *The Stages* among economists in the developing world stems from the fact that its structure can be recognizably linked to the phenomena they see about them and the problems they must try to solve from day to day in their societies. The neoclassical growth models which absorbed so much high-grade theoretical talent in the 1960s ran into the sand precisely because their method ruled out changes in most of the variables relevant to the process of economic growth.

Be that as it may, my general view of the economy—which yielded, among other things, the concept of the stages of growth—consisted in the notion of a kind of dynamic, moving Walrasian equilibrium. This system embraces as endogenous the changes in population and the working force, in technology, and in the supply of basic commodities: population and the size of the working force were determined by the dynamics of the demographic transition; major technological change was induced by economic needs; the supply of basic commodities was also induced by the dynamics of the marketplace. From this system flowed optimum sectoral levels of capacity as well as an optimum aggregate growth rate and, therefore, an optimum distribution of investment which would keep all sectors on their equilibrium paths. But the investment process was seen, in fact, as something less than omniscient. It was, in fact, subject to systematic error. Investors made their decisions in terms of current indicators of profitability without taking adequately into account the total volume of investment being induced by their common response to these indicators. This technical distortion was often accentuated by irrational waves of optimism and pessimism that swept the capital markets with respect to investment in particular sectors. The process was, of course, made possible by the lags built into the investment process, which permitted exaggerated levels of investment to proceed for some time until reality in the form of a falling rate of return over costs, induced by the boom, forced a downward reevaluation of profit expectations. Putting aside wars and other exogenous traumatic events, growth assumed, therefore, the form of cycles of varying lengths depending, notably, on the period of gestation of the type of investment undertaken and the length of its working life. And so economies made their way through history, overshooting and undershooting their optimum sectoral paths, like a drunk going home from the local pub on Saturday night.

A narrower consequence of the difference between my view and the neoclassical view was the judgment that the degree of modernization of an economy should not be measured in terms of real income per capita but in terms of the extent to which an economy had more or less efficiently absorbed the then existing pool of relevant technologies. Real GNP per capita is a convenient measuring device, and I rather doubt that I should try to persuade my respected colleagues in the World Bank to abandon it. But I believe they might agree that putting, say, low-income India and China, each with industries of very considerable sophistication, in the same cateogry, as, say, Mali and Haiti, leaves something to be desired, as does equating, say, Libya and France.

Evidently, a theoretical and historical outlook of this kind had certain implications for my approach to contemporary development problems and policy. For example:

• The brute scale of the process was dramatized in my mind by the concept of stages of growth. Historically, nations had moved into take-off in a rather stately, well-spaced-out sequence. First, Britain had graduated into take-off on its own in the 1780s; then in the second quarter of the nineteenth century, a second class graduated: the United States, Belgium, France, and Germany; in the fourth quarter, Sweden, Japan, Russia, Italy, and portions of the Austro-Hungarian Empire. In the twentieth century, Canada and Australia joined the club in the first decade and some of the Latin American countries and Turkey in the 1930s. But as the post-1945 years unfolded, virtually the whole of Asia, the Middle East, Africa, and Latin America turned with passion (if not always with success) to the goal of modernization: to get themselves into take-off or to move to the stage beyond. We have lived with the phenomenon for so long in this generation that we take it for granted as part of the international scene. But, in historical perspective, it is perhaps the most remarkable event since the coming of the first Industrial Revolution to Great Britain in the 1780s. It has altered irreversibly the balance and texture of international political, as well as economic, life.

• The transition to modernization in the developing regions was seen as inherently painful and volatile; but disruptive instability could be damped, to a degree, should the developing nations concentrate their reactive nationalist impulses on the task of modernization itself as opposed to other possible expressions of nationalist sentiment. Moreover, the dignity on the world scene which they sought was most likely to be achieved, at the earliest possible time, by demonstrating a capacity for sustained and tolerably well-balanced modernization in harmony with their respective cultures.[21] The large political objective of foreign aid was, thus, to encourage that concentration of scarce talents, resources, and political energies as well as to provide supplementary external resources.

• What we call developing nations (or, in the 1950s, underdeveloped nations) represent a very wide spectrum of societies, each in a significant sense unique and at quite different stages in their degree of absorption of the pool of modern technologies and in their current capacity to absorb them efficiently. Useful development (and foreign aid) policies thus had to be designed in the light of where each country stood along this spectrum, its absorptive capacity, its particular resource endowments, and other unique features.

• The concept of optimum sectoral levels of capacity underlined the critical need for adequate levels of investment in agriculture, infrastructure, education, and in other supporting sectors as well as in industry.

• The concept of take-off suggested the possibility that developing nations would eventually move to self-sustained growth when soft loans would no longer be required.

• Successful movement into reasonably well-balanced self-sustained growth, rooted in national aspirations, was judged to represent a way of minimizing the likelihood of successful external intrusion, communist or otherwise. In the case of China, it was judged that the relative success or failure of economic and social progress in non-communist Asia would have significant playback effects on China's domestic and foreign policy.[22]

Thus, the analysis of economic growth, as I envisaged it, became an exercise in the dynamic analysis of whole societies. In general, the integration of the social sciences—long accepted in our profession as a goal—is not likely to be achieved by an integration of the various social science disciplines themselves. It is best approximated by focusing on a problem and bringing to bear around that problem all that the various social

21. One of the most heartening manifestations of nationalism in rapidly modernizing societies is the systematic effort to reach back to and dramatize the historical roots of their cultures, an effort reflected in new museums, archeological finds, and monuments throughout the developing world.

22. Here, for example, is a passage from the 1955 *An American Policy in Asia* (pp. 36–37): "if Free Asia succeeds in meeting successfully the challenge of that region's aspirations, we shall see a new phase in the Chinese revolution. As a matter of Asian history, the Sino-Soviet alliance in its present form is the wrong way to meet China's authentic desire for independence and dignity on the world scene; the Chinese Communist New General Line is the wrong way to meet China's authentic desire to modernize and to develop its economy. A strong and creative Free Asia can both frustrate Peking and demonstrate to the Chinese that a more attractive alternative exists. At some future time the profoundly pragmatic Chinese people will choose their own version of that alternative."

science disciplines can provide by way of illumination. That, for example, was the method of Gunnar Myrdal in his remarkable study of race relations in the United States, *An American Dilemma*. For me and many others, the problem of development served that integrating purpose in the 1950s.

As individuals, most of us felt, I suspect, some kind of moral or religious impulse to help those striving to come forward through development. In that sense we were in the line that reached back a century and more to the missionaries from Western societies who went out to distant and often obscure places, not merely to promulgate the faith but also to teach and to heal. But we were reticent about these impulses and properly so. A missionary approach was no longer appropriate to proud, aspiring, highly nationalistic developing nations. Equally important, the aid policies of the advanced industrial countries, while strengthened by such abiding moral and religious impulses among their citizens, could not be sustained for the long pull unless they were underpinned by more conventional concepts of national interest.

CENIS and Foreign Aid

Although my research in the 1950s led to particular views about an appropriate U.S. policy toward development, and I spoke and wrote a good deal on this matter as an individual, my most useful contribution to policy was, no doubt, as part of the collective effort mobilized in the 1950s at the Center for International Studies (CENIS) at MIT.

CENIS was set up in 1951 under the leadership of Max Millikan, with my active support and participation. The Korean War convinced some of us that the struggle to deter and contain the thrust for expanded communist power would be long and that new concepts would be required to underpin U.S. foreign policy in the generation ahead, quite aside from the task of dealing directly with the communist world. We believed that a portion of academic talent should be devoted to generating these concepts, and, as individuals, we were prepared to make that allocation. We hoped that we could do more by remaining in academic life than by returning to Washington as public servants, as I was asked to do and seriously considered doing. We also believed that, if high standards of academic professionalism and integrity were sustained, work on contemporary and foreseeable problems of the active world could add to the body of scientific knowledge. We were conscious that most of the great works in economics—from Adam Smith's *The Wealth of Nations* to Keynes's *General Theory*—were also, to a degree, tracts for their times. This view was supported by the senior administrators of the university, notably the provost, Julius Stratton. In a discussion with Millikan and me, he noted that many advances in the physical sciences—including advances in theory—had derived from the effort to solve practical problems. He said we could go forward with our enterprise on the understanding that we would maintain rigorous intellectual standards and, of course, complete intellectual independence of the government. He also noted that we would have to raise our own funds.

We decided to concentrate our initial efforts in two areas: the study of communist societies and the study of problems of development—economic, social, and political. The former work came to be financed by the federal government;[23] the latter was wholly financed by private funds, notably from the Ford and Rockefeller Foundations.

CENIS's work on development began formally in 1952 and included intensive studies of India, Indonesia, and Italy. Aside from Millikan and me, the members of the senior staff engaged in economic development problems were Everett Hagen, Benjamin Higgins, Wilfred Malenbaum, and P. N. Rosenstein-Rodan. Rodan had, of course, been at work on development problems longer than any of us—since his research on Eastern Europe in London during the Second World War. We were also closely in touch with our colleague Charles Kindleberger, whose wide portfolio of interests included the field of economic growth in both a historical and a contemporary context. James E. Cross, Dan Lerner, Ithiel Pool, and Lucian Pye contributed insights from political science and sociology. Younger economists, including George Baldwin, Francis Bator, Richard Eckaus, and George Rosen, also got into the act, as did a then junior political scientist, Donald Blackmer, and a remarkable former schoolmaster and novelist, Richard Hatch, who served as critic, editor, and conscience of CENIS.

The senior scholars working on development problems at CENIS came at them from quite different perspectives. We were a strong-minded as well as variegated lot held together by a common commitment to the problems of development, by ties of mutual respect and affection that often grow out of such common commitments to large purposes, and, above all, by the graceful and sensitive leadership of Max Millikan.

The most complete synthesis of our argument was incorporated in a short book entitled *A Proposal: Key to an Effective Foreign Policy*, completed in August 1956.[24] It represented the fruition of a draft written by Millikan and me in the wake of a meeting at Princeton in May 1954. The draft passed through a series of stages over the subsequent two years,

---

23. The Central Intelligence Agency (CIA), in its function as agent for the National Security Council, financed the studies of communist societies. If Congress had not been so penurious (and suspicious) they would have been more naturally financed by the Department of State. However, the CIA at no time tried to influence our analysis or conclusions, which were published in the normal manner of scholarly works. It did not even blink when our study suggested that communist China might well be admitted to the United Nations—a rather contentious issue in the mid-1950s.

24. New York: Harper, 1957.

responding to specific occasions when the issue was debated in the Executive Branch and the Congress. Its collective character is suggested by the fact that fourteen names are explicitly noted as contributing.

I cannot recount here the full range of our crusading. Aside from publishing our views in various forms, we worked closely with sympathetic members of the Congress in both parties and with like-minded officials in the Executive Branch. We maintained ties to officials in Western Europe, the developing regions, and international organizations, notably the World Bank. Above all, we were stubborn and patient, weathering a sequence of frustrations and setbacks, arguing the case for enlarged development aid year after year from 1953 until President Kennedy's wholehearted adoption of it in 1961.

We were, of course, by no means alone. For example, among the academic groups at work on development, Edward Mason organized and led a first-rate team at Harvard that worked closely with the government of Pakistan. A good many of the land grant colleges established, through Point Four, fruitful lines of collaboration with developing countries in agriculture. The major foundations helped generously as development moved close to the top of their agenda. As the 1950s wore on, the stage became increasingly crowded with development crusaders of considerable distinction. Among them were Chester Bowles and Adlai Stevenson, Nelson Rockefeller and Milton Eisenhower, C. D. Jackson, five doughty Senators—John Sherman Cooper, William Fulbright, Hubert Humphrey, John Kennedy, and Mike Monroney—and, highly effective in quite different domains, Barbara Ward and Eugene Black. In the foreign offices and even the treasuries of the Atlantic world there were a good many anonymous, but equally committed, public servants arguing the case and trying to move things forward from day to day, often against determined bureaucratic opposition. What CENIS supplied was a coherent program based on insights generated from a wide spectrum of approaches to the process of modernization, including the professional work conducted by CENIS in developing countries, plus a rationale for the U.S., Western European, and Japanese interest in development, thought through and articulated with considerable care. It is for others to judge, but I would guess *A Proposal* in all its versions was a quite influential piece of work, which in no way guaranteed its validity.

With some oversimplification of a reasonably sophisticated exposition, the argument of *A Proposal* can be paraphrased as follows:

The bulk of the world's population, for the first time in history, is caught up in a revolutionary transition which is

> rapidly exposing previously apathetic peoples to the possibility of change. . . . The danger is that increasing numbers of people will become convinced that their new aspirations can be realized only through violent change and the renunciation of democratic institutions . . . the dangers of instability inherent in the awakening of formerly static

peoples would be present even in the absence of the Communist apparatus. . . . But the danger is, of course, greatly intensified by the focus which both Communist thought and Communist organization give.

U.S. assistance should not aim "to insure friendship and gratitude," or "to enable the recipient countries to carry a much larger burden of military buildup against Communist armed forces," or "to stop Communism by eliminating hunger." U.S. assistance should contribute to "the evolution of societies that are stable in the sense that they are capable of rapid change without violence."

This judgment flows directly from a definition of the U.S. national interest which is taken to be "to preserve a world environment within which our form of democratic society can persist and develop." Two priority tasks follow from that definition:

> The first of these is to meet effectively the threat to our security posed by the danger of overt military aggression. . . .
>
> The second . . . is to promote the evolution of a world in which threats to our security and, more broadly, to our way of life are less likely to arise. Success in this task would mean the freeing of a large volume of resources from military to more constructive uses. More important, it would mean protecting our society from the pressures inevitably associated with a garrison state, pressures which threaten our most cherished values. It is this task with which this book is mainly concerned.

External economic assistance can be effective only if it is meshed with and designed in ways which contribute to the society's own efforts to move toward "political maturity." This implies that six conditions be met in the process of economic and social modernization.

> A. There must be posed for the leadership and the people of each country challenging and constructive internal tasks which will look to the future of their societies. . . .
>
> B. [These tasks] must relate to the emerging aspirations of all classes and regions in the society. . . .
>
> C. The new countries must find ways of developing young and vigorous leadership. . . .
>
> D. Related to the recruitment of new leadership is the need for greatly increased social, economic, and political opportunity. . . .
>
> E. Related to this fact is the requirement . . . of finding ways to bridge the existing gulf between the urban classes, often Western educated, and the countryside. . . .
>
> F. Perhaps the most critical requirement for the growth of political maturity is that the people of the new nations develop confidence, both as a nation and as individuals in small communities, so that they can make progress with their problems through their own efforts.

Technically, aid programs must be geared to the particular circumstances of each developing country. In general, developing countries were viewed as constituting a wide spectrum at different stages of economic growth. Where they stood in the spectrum determined the amount of capital and technical assistance they could efficiently absorb.[25] Broadly speaking, three stages were distinguished: the preconditions for take-off, take-off, and self-sustained growth,

> the long period of regular if fluctuating progress . . . [when] the structure of the economy changes continuously—sometimes painfully—as technique improves. The character as well as the scale of appropriate external assistance will vary with these stages, rising and becoming more diversified in take-off, falling gradually away with the attainment of self-sustained growth when, in time, developing countries could come to rely on normal commercial sources of international finance.[26]

Against this background the proposal consisted of an international plan to generate sufficient resources to meet all requirements for external assistance which could be justified by absorptive capacity, plus enlarged technical assistance to accelerate the increase in absorptive capacity. The

---

25. Four reasonably objective criteria were defined in *A Proposal* to test whether the overriding standards of absorptive capacity and creditworthiness were being met.

A. It must be within the technical and administrative capabilities of the receiving country to carry out its proposed project with reasonable efficiency, over the time period of the loan or grant.

B. Steps must have been taken to insure that the rest of the economy of the receiving country is being developed sufficiently to make the proposed project fully productive in the time period envisaged by the loan.

C. The receiving country must have an over-all national development program designed to make the most effective possible use of its resources; this should include not only a series of interrelated capital projects but also necessary educational and training programs.

D. The receiving country's national development program must be consistent with the requirements of expanding world commerce and the international division of labor.

26. The introduction of the concept of stages of growth into the argument had two substantial political and psychological consequences. In the developing regions it provided an operational focus for efforts to accelerate economic growth that was manageable, as it were, within the lifetime of a human being. If one stared in the 1950s at the gap between a real income per capita of, say, $100 and $3,000, one could conclude the task of modernization was hopeless or irrelevant to one generation's efforts. If the task was defined as achieving self-sustained growth, rather than the U.S. level of real income per capita, it was easier to roll up one's sleeves and go to work.

Within hard-pressed parliamentary bodies, commitment to sustained development assistance was easier to achieve if it was believed such aid would level off and ultimately decline as take-offs occurred in one country after another and the bulk of the developing world made its way to the stages beyond, relying increasingly on conventional sources of capital.

price tag was estimated at an additional \$2.5 billion to \$3.5 billion a year (about \$7.5 billion to \$10.5 billion in 1981 U.S. dollars), of which about two-thirds was judged to be then an equitable U.S. share.

Administratively it was proposed that the program be conducted mainly by existing institutions, but that the World Bank create a special instrument "to co-ordinate information, set the ground rules, and secure acceptance of the criteria for the investment program."

As for the linkage between economic development and the emergence of stable political democracies, we may, in retrospect, have been a bit too hopeful; but we were by no means naive. One CENIS publication of the 1950s posed and answered bluntly the question of linkage: "Is there any guarantee that the free Asian nations will emerge from rapid economic growth politically democratic? No such guarantee can be made. The relation between economic growth and political democracy is not simple and automatic."[27] We were, however, firmly convinced that a concentration of scarce resources, talents, and political energies on the task of development, undertaken with reasonable balance, was likely to maximize the chance that societies would move through the modernization process with minimum violence and human cost and yield governments whose policies roughly approximated the will of the governed.

Alternative Views of Development Policy in the 1950s

The struggle for enlarged development aid in the 1950s took place in the United States, at least, as an argument against the adequacy of existing aid policy and against certain alternative conceptual formulations. With regard to policy, the Korean War led to large programs of military aid and military support for countries around the periphery of the U.S.S.R. and China. The programs were designed to build and sustain sufficient military and economic strength to deter another such direct military adventure. They left most other developing nations beyond the scope of U.S. aid policy.

In addition, we had to contend with quite particular alternative views of the appropriate relation between advanced industrial countries and developing countries. One such formulation was, in its own way, positive. It suffused, for example, the 1954 Randall Commission Report on foreign economic policy. It took the view that the task of U.S. policy was to lead the world economy, as rapidly as possible, back to an approximation of the world before 1914: liberal if not free trade, unrestricted movement of private long-term capital, and convertible currencies. The pre-1914 world

---

27. *An American Policy in Asia*, p. 50. The palpable lack of automatic linkage between real income per capita and the capacity to sustain democracy was one factor which led me to write *Politics and the Stages of Growth* (1971).

economy did not, in fact, operate in such an engagingly uninhibited way, but the somewhat romanticized memory of that era exercised a powerful hold over many minds. And the influence of that memory had some positive consequences; for example, it encouraged those who accepted the concept to struggle against protectionist impulses in the United States and helped set in motion the succession of global negotiations to reduce trade barriers. But, implicitly at least, this vision of the task did not recognize that distinctive and difficult problems existed in the developing regions for which free trade, free private capital flows, and convertible currencies were not sufficient answers. By and large, holders of this view, while opposing development aid, were willing to support technical assistance, narrowly defined.

Among those who recognized the distinctive problems of the developing regions, P. T. Bauer was, without doubt, the most sophisticated intellectual analyst who took a reserved stance toward development aid and set explicit, highly restrictive economic and political criteria for expanding such aid. Since Lord Bauer speaks for himself in this book, I will simply summarize my perception of the difference between his views and those of CENIS.

Bauer believed the objective of foreign aid should be to promote democracy by promoting private enterprise; CENIS held that the objective of foreign aid was to encourage the development of societies capable of undergoing rapid change with minimum violence, and that such societies were most likely to evolve in democratic directions, although the early achievement of Western-style democracy was not guaranteed.

Bauer believed foreign aid should be used as a lever actively to promote development programs which maximized promptly the role of the private sector and the market mechanism; whereas CENIS believed that this was a second-order criterion, that its strict application would be politically counterproductive, and that the ultimate role of the private sector would be determined by the dynamic evolution of the economy and its political system as a whole.

With respect to the important case of India, Bauer and CENIS agreed that a high-productivity agriculture was essential for sound development and that the Indian second five-year plan was somewhat out of balance. CENIS, however, held that the vitality of the Indian private sector (and its consequently increasing foreign exchange requirements) was one of the causes of the strain on India's foreign exchange resources and that enlarged foreign aid would permit the private sector to go forward with increased élan.

Bauer and CENIS shared, of course, a human, intellectual, and policy concern with the fate of the developing regions in general, which was by no means universal. The differing views summarized here were part of an insiders' debate among those who felt that the destiny of the developing world mattered to the West. A great many political figures (and, indeed, economists), implicitly or explicitly, simply ignored the issues involved; but when politicians of negative bent were forced by events to take a position, they often reached out for the kind of rationale Bauer formulated.

Things Learned since the 1950s—Some Painful

Looking back over the quarter century since the debate about development policy was at its height, I find that some of CENIS's views (and my own) were fairly well vindicated.

• Supported by external aid, the aggregate average performance of the developing regions in the 1960s and 1970s approximated or exceeded our earlier hopes, falling in the range of 4.5 to 5.5 percent a year, yielding an average increase in GNP per capita of 1.6 percent for low-income countries and 3.8 percent for those in the World Bank's middle-income range (generally, my drive to technological maturity). The former figure approximated the nineteenth-century performance of the presently advanced industrial countries during take-off (1.7 percent); the latter substantially exceeded the earlier performance during the drive to technological maturity (2.1 percent).[28] These aggregate growth rates were strongly reflected in such basic social indicators as length of life and level of education: by World Bank calculations life expectancy increased from 42 to 57 in low-income countries between 1960 and 1979, from 53 to 61 in middle-income countries; population per physician more than halved in both categories; adult literacy rose from 27 to 43 percent in low-income countries between 1960 and 1976, from 53 to 72 percent in middle-income countries; and the numbers enrolled in secondary schools and higher education about doubled in both categories. As we all know, there is a long way to go; but sustained economic growth in the third quarter of the twentieth century was not a statistical artifact nor a process insulated from the life of the average citizen.

• The four major differences between the development process in the historical past and that of the contemporary world identified in *The Stages of Economic Growth* (pp. 140–42), both positive and negative in their implications, were correctly identified and have left their mark: a larger backlog of unapplied technologies, the availability of foreign aid, higher rates of population increase, and a corrosive setting of Cold War. The effort to move forward in modernization in the context of population growth rates two to three times higher than those of the nineteenth century has been, in many ways, the most distinctive of those differences, with widely ranging pathological consequences.

28. *Why the Poor Get Richer and the Rich Slow Down: Essays in the Marshallian Long Period* (Austin: University of Texas Press, 1980), pp. 266–67.

• The strong emphasis in *The Stages* (pp. 21–24) on the multiple roles of a dynamic agriculture in permitting successful industrialization has been validated, as has the stabilizing political and social consequences of a successful modernization of rural life.

• Vital private sectors have, in a good many countries, proved compatible with a framework of national economic planning and some government ownership and operation of industry.

• Nations which concentrated their political energies on reasonably well-balanced economic and social modernization have, by and large, reconciled political stability with rapid change better than those which looked primarily abroad for a gratification of their nationalist ardors or indulged in passionate ideological domestic political struggles.

• Our hopes for the emergence of a pragmatic China, more open to the world, influenced by the economic and social success of non-communist Asia, has been, for the time, realized.

• The contours of what I have defined as the stages of take-off and the drive to technological maturity can, in an unforced way, be clearly perceived among the developing countries which have moved beyond the preconditions for take-off. It would be inappropriate to use this occasion to argue afresh and in detail the concept of stages of economic growth. I responded to the lively debate of the 1960s in appendix B of the 1971 edition of *The Stages*. My further review and use of the concept in *The World Economy: History and Prospect*[29] strengthened my confidence in its validity. But a few retrospective observations on the debate may be helpful.

Take, for example, a much argued question of the 1960s: Do net investment rates rise markedly during take-off? The key problem was empirical: reasonably reliable pre-take-off and take-off investment rates were available for few countries. Subsequent research and the unfolding of growth in the developing regions over the past generation has greatly improved our knowledge of this matter.[30] Of the twenty countries ana-

---

29. Austin: University of Texas Press, 1978.

30. The most intensively argued case was that of Great Britain. In difficult, pioneering estimates, Phyllis Deane and W. A. Cole (*British Economic Growth, 1688–1959* [Cambridge, Eng.: Cambridge University Press, 1969], p. 263) calculated that the rise of the investment rate during the period I define as take-off (1783–1802) was unlikely to have amounted to more than an additional 1.5 percent. Later calculations suggest strongly that the rise in the British investment rate was more substantial. See, notably, François Crouzet, ed., *Capital Formation in the Industrial Revolution* (London: Methuen, 1972), especially the editor's introduction and chaps. 3–6; and Charles Feinstein, "Capital Formation in Great Britain," in Peter Mathias and M. M. Postan, eds., *The Cambridge Economic History* (Cambridge, Eng.: Cambridge University Press, 1978), vol. 7, pt. 1, pp. 28–96, with key estimates on p. 91. In general, the evidence now available on the British economy in the late eighteenth and early nineteenth centuries has led to a fairly solid consensus on the acceleration of growth in the period 1783–1802, which leaves the matter a question of choice among alternative vocabularies for describing the acceleration.

lyzed in part five of *The World Economy: History and Prospect* (containing, as of 1976, about two-thirds of the world's population and 80 percent of global real product) investment rates for the relevant period are available for all but five (Japan, U.S.S.R., Turkey, Brazil, and Iran). In the fifteen other cases, a substantial surge in investment rates can be observed during take-off; although it is, as one would expect from the analysis of this point in *The Stages*, by no means uniform.

More generally, the believed conflict between Kuznets's concept of "entrance into modern growth" and the take-off turned out to be empirically trivial or nonexistent. As I point out in a lengthy note in *The World Economy* (pp. 778–79), our criteria differ, to a degree, but our dating of the critical transition for the eight important countries examined by Kuznets is similar—indeed, in seven cases almost identical.

As for the stages beyond take-off, the sectoral data now available permit quite firm dating for the movement to more sophisticated and diversified industries, which defines the drive to technological maturity, and for the (usually) subsequent movement to the automobile and durable consumers goods, which characterizes high mass consumption.

In general, then, I would hold that the views we developed in the 1950s hold up reasonably well in retrospect. But a good many realities have been forced on us by events that we did not fully anticipate in the 1950s, of which I shall cite only five.

First, defense support—economic aid to compensate for abnormal domestic military outlays—proved an effective instrument of development assistance in a number of cases, such as the Republic of Korea, Taiwan, and Turkey. It was rooted in direct U.S. national security interests of a fairly stable kind and bought time for these and a few other economies to weather some difficult days, find their feet, and move into self-sustained growth. In retrospect, it deserves higher marks than it was granted by development purists like myself in the 1950s. The other side of that coin, however, is that the development crusaders of the 1950s were less successful than we would have liked in persuading Western governments that steady, large-scale support for the development process was in their interests, quite apart from the occasions when the communist threat was palpable.

Second, disruptive external expressions of nationalism proved harder to avoid than we would have hoped, notably in South Asia and Africa. (There was not much basis for hope in the Middle East even in the 1950s.) The failure of India and Pakistan to find the terms in the 1960s on which they could live peacefully together and cooperate economically was notably costly to all parties in the region and to the cause of foreign aid itself. And so was the failure of the Organization for African Unity in the 1970s to fulfill its earlier vision of excluding external powers from African affairs and settling regional conflicts on an intra-African basis.

Third, despite the relatively satisfactory average aggregate performance of the developing regions and a number of quite remarkable success stories, we confront some hard and recalcitrant cases for which there are no easy answers. Why, for example, set on the same island, should Haiti have one-fourth the real income per capita of the Dominican Republic and one-eleventh of its growth rate over the past two decades? Is there any satisfactory solution for some of the smaller African countries south of the Sahara short of becoming part of larger subregional economic groupings?

Fourth, the normal tendency for income distribution to become more skew in the early stages of growth was exacerbated in a good many countries by excessive rates of population increase, inadequate priority for the modernization of rural life, and relatively poor performance in tax collection, which reduced the resources available for social services, notably in rural areas. Where these conditions were substantially mitigated (as in Taiwan, Korea, and Sri Lanka), patterns of income distribution were achieved approximating those in advanced industrial societies and indexes of social well-being were substantially higher than the averages for developing countries.

Fifth, while Bauer's fear of a large government role in development proved, I believe, excessive and did not set many developing countries on the road to serfdom, government bureaucracies in a good many countries proved relatively inefficient and self-perpetuating beyond the time when they may have been needed to do jobs the private sector could not do. A powerful "state bourgeoisie" has been created in some developing countries whose interests may not converge with those of the nation as a whole.[31] Put another way, the balance between the public and private sectors deserves reexamination in developing countries as the capacities of the private sector have increased and government bureaucracies have conformed to the dynamics of Parkinson's Law.

Yet another major issue which some have viewed as a special problem of development in the period since, say, 1950 is the question of "dependencia." For example, Paul Streeten, in summarizing criticisms of the stages of growth, wrote:

> Logically, it should have been clear that the coexistence of more- and less-advanced countries is bound to make a difference (for better or worse) to the development efforts and prospects of the less advanced, compared with a situation where no other country was ahead or the distance was not very large. The larger the gap and the more interdependent the components of the international system, the less relevant are the lessons to be learned from the early starters.[32]

31. For a perceptive discussion of this phenomenon in Latin America, see William P. Glade, "Economic Policy-Making and the Structures of Corporatism in Latin America," Offprint Series no. 208, Institute of Latin America Studies, the University of Texas at Austin, 1981. It should, perhaps, be immediately noted that advanced industrial societies have not been immune from the generation of self-interested state bourgeoisie.

32. Paul Streeten, "Development Ideas in Historical Perspective," in *Toward a New Strategy for Development* (New York: Pergamon Press, 1979), pp. 26–27.

In fact, I discussed explicitly in *The Stages* (pp. 139–44) the question of similarities and differences among early comers and latecomers in a passage subtitled "Take-offs, Past and Present." But the vogue of dependencia justifies a few further observations.

I once presented a paper wholly devoted to the theme.[33] It begins by evoking the British sense of its neocolonial relation to the Dutch Republic in the seventeenth century. The French felt the same way, helping goad Colbert into his modernization policies. Alexander Hamilton in 1791 urged a policy of industrialization on the United States in the face of the nation's continued heavy dependence on British manufactured imports, in terms which, like the theme of a symphony, run through the literature of the latecomer down to the present day: "Not only the wealth but the independence and security of a country appear to be materially connected with the prosperity of manufactures."[34] As for gaps in real income per capita, as nearly as we can calculate, Japan in the mid-1880s, as take-off began, stood at $158 (U.S. 1967 dollars), Great Britain, at $750; Italy in the mid-1890s, at $300, Great Britain, at $842.[35] The Russian gap at its time of take-off in the 1890s was almost certainly greater.

In short, the problem embraced in the notion of dependencia is at least three centuries old; it persisted throughout the nineteenth century; it did not prevent the nineteenth-century latecomers from mounting higher average per capita rates of growth than the early comers and substantially catching up with them; and the process of narrowing the gap has continued through the twentieth century for many latecomers which have managed to move into self-sustained growth.[36] The normally S-shaped long-term path of growth is a healing force in the human community.

Nevertheless, even though the problems of dependencia are historically familiar and palpably surmountable, they are, to a degree, real. For example, just as Latin America is achieving reasonable virtuosity in the last round of new technologies (for automobiles, durable consumers goods, and chemicals), the industrial North is generating a new round of technologies (in industries based on genetics, minicomputers, lasers) on which Latin America will once again have to draw. There are difficulties with patents and other problems the developing nations wish to mitigate or remove in effecting the transfer of technology. Related to them, but going beyond, are problems as well as opportunities posed by the existence

33. "From Dependence to Interdependence: An Historian's Perspective," Conference on Economic Relations between Mexico and the United States, Institute of Latin American Studies, University of Texas at Austin, April 1973.

34. Alexander Hamilton, "Report on Manufactures, December 5, 1971," in Samuel McKee, Jr., ed., *Papers on Public Credit, Commerce and Finance* (New York: Columbia University Press, 1934), p. 227.

35. For data and discussion, see my *Why the Poor Get Richer and the Rich Slow Down*, chap. 6.

36. See *Why the Poor Get Richer*, especially pp. 259–69, for statistical evidence on this point.

of multinationals. This is a large, much canvassed subject, and I shall therefore confine myself to a few conclusions.

A good deal has been done within the international community to mitigate the problems arising from large differences in stage of growth and technical virtuosity; for example, trade preferences for developing countries and codes of behavior for multinationals. The latter problem is not as acute, in fact or in international debate, as it was even a decade ago.

The intensity of the problem relates, in part, to the size of the country and its domestic market. In take-off, for example, the larger domestic markets of, say, Mexico and India provided a more spacious framework for the expansion of import-substitution consumer goods industries than, say, those of Peru, Uruguay, or the nations of Central America. In the drive to technological maturity, Brazil finds it easier to develop efficient steel, metalworking, and chemical plants than Chile or even Argentina. Canada, despite its full attainment of high mass consumption and its rich natural resource base, still struggles, as it has for more than a century, to keep its dependence on the United States—which is ten times larger—within politically and psychologically (as well as economically) manageable bounds.

But we should exercise some care in evoking the question of size. First, the size of a population does not necessarily represent the size of its effective market: a substantial part of Latin America, let alone India, has only a tenuous link to the market system. The effective market is much smaller than the population, and income per capita can vary greatly, even at similar stages of growth, depending on the ratio of population to arable land, natural resource endowments, and so on. Second, a purposeful, energetic people, with a good educational base, a framework of political stability, and an ample supply of innovating entrepreneurs and public administrators, can build a highly sophisticated industrial society on a small population base by exploiting with vigor the possibilities for exports. This is what Sweden and the other Scandinavian nations have done. In Asia, it has happened in Korea and Taiwan and, even more remarkably, in Hong Kong and Singapore.

These cases are worth underlining because the felt costs of dependence are clearly an inverse function of the vigor with which economic development and export markets are pursued as well as of relative stages of growth and size.

In the end, I am inclined to believe that the costs of dependencia are outweighed by the advantage for developing countries of a large backlog of unapplied technologies, and that the burden of dependence, notably technological dependence, is partly psychological. In urging an expanded hemispheric effort to increase Latin American scientific and technological capacity, the Herrera report responded to this sentiment.[37] I suspect that

37. Organization of American States (OAS), "Hemispheric Cooperation and Integral Development," OEA/Ser. T/II, OTC 15-80 (Washington, D.C., August 6, 1980).

this component of the problem will be eased only when the developing regions begin substantially to contribute to, as well as draw upon, the global pool of technology. In time, this will surely happen. But there are real problems as well with technical dependence, notably the fact that international research and development (R&D) may not focus sharply enough on the particular problems of a developing country or region. Indeed, this is a problem not only for developing countries but also, as suggested earlier, for Canada and even for certain American states and regions. For example, the special energy, water, and transport problems of Texas helped increase the sense of urgency for a radical expansion of R&D within the state in the report of the Texas 2000 Commission.[38]

The list of both anticipated and unanticipated facets of experience over the past quarter century could, of course, be extended. But the greatest challenge the editors of this volume laid before us was in their final questions: How do you view development economics today? How could it be improved?

Development Economics in the Fifth Kondratieff Upswing

My view of contemporary development economics and policy is, to put it simply, the product of a linkage of growth analysis to the concept of trend periods (or Kondratieff cycles) as I have interpreted them. In my concept of a dynamic general model of the economy, the stages of growth emerge from the efficient absorption in particular sectors of a sequence of progressively more sophisticated technologies generated currently in the world economy or available to a latecomer as a backlog. My view of trend periods (or Kondratieff cycles) also flows from the interplay of sectors and aggregates: the severely lagged process of adjusting supplies of foodstuffs and raw materials (including energy) to the requirements set up by the growth of the world economy.

In mid-1972 I turned to writing a long-planned history of the world economy over the past two centuries.[39] At the close of 1972 the world economy experienced a convulsive rise in the relative price of grain, followed shortly by a convulsive rise in the price of energy. Set against the background of what had been happening to international grain and oil markets in the 1960s, these events, and their repercussions, suggested, as I worked away on my history, that the world economy had entered a protracted period of relatively high basic commodity prices for the fifth

38. *Texas 2000 Commission Report and Recommendations* (Austin: Office of the Governor, March 1982), especially pp. 6, 9, and 29–31.

39. This effort is incorporated in the following books: *How It All Began* (New York: McGraw-Hill, 1975); *The World Economy: History and Prospect; Getting from Here to There* (New York: McGraw-Hill, 1978); and *Why the Poor Get Richer and the Rich Slow Down*.

time since 1790. The succession of irregular, but clearly marked, phases of relatively expensive and relatively cheap basic commodity prices had interested me from my earliest work as an economic historian.[40] I concluded that this was the phenomenon at the core of the long cycles Kondratieff had identified (but never explained) and which Joseph Schumpeter had, in my view, incorrectly associated with the rhythm of major technological innovations.

Historically, the upswings were generally periods of inflationary tendency, with high interest rates, pressure on urban real wages, and a shift of income in favor of producers of basic commodities. Capital and migrants flowed to the countries and regions producing such commodities; and, in time, the expansion of output in the basic commodity sectors overshot equilibrium levels to yield a protracted reversal of trends in the international economy. From this perspective, the great boom period 1951–72 was the fourth Kondratieff downswing, and we have spent the past, uncomfortable decade in the fifth Kondratieff upswing.

The falling or relatively low basic commodity prices of the 1950s and 1960s yielded an approximately 25 percent favorable shift in the terms of trade for the advanced industrial countries, cut foreign exchange earnings of traditional export products from the developing regions, and helped generate, notably in Latin America, a new development doctrine and strategy centered on the believed long-term trend in the terms of trade. The price trends of the 1950s also—though it is rarely noted—provided cheap energy and food to those developing countries which were rapidly industrializing and urbanizing. The advanced industrial countries and a good many of the World Bank's middle-income countries were thus assisted by the contours of the fourth Kondratieff downswing, the former, of course, more than the latter.

As we all know, things have been quite different since the close of 1972. The forces which have come to rest on the developing nations in the past decade include:

- The deceleration of growth rates in the advanced industrial countries, as they failed to face the imperatives and exploit the possibilities of the fifth Kondratieff upswing, and the consequent weakening of markets of exports from the developing countries
- A radical shift in the terms of trade and income distribution in favor of energy-exporting countries and regions and against oil importers
- Balance of payments pressures on the oil-importing, developing nations including, in some cases, a precarious expansion of high-interest loans contracted to maintain even reduced economic and social momentum

40. My undergraduate studies, aside from the initial examination of the period 1793–1821, were, in effect, of the second Kondratieff downswing (1873–1896), which was also the subject of my doctoral thesis, and the third Kondratieff upswing (1896–1914).

- A progressively increased reliance of the developing nations, taken as a whole, on imported food
- Underinvestment in raw materials, in part because of nationalist inhibitions on private foreign investment
- Gross environmental deterioration in a number of regions because of deforestation and the loss of arable acreage.

My perception of where the world economy has stood since the close of 1972, in the long erratic rhythm of trend periods (or Kondratieff cycles), led to a particular judgment about the appropriate agenda for North-South economic cooperation. The central common task is to work in partnership to assure that the sectors supporting the continuity of industrial civilization are expanded and sustained: energy, agriculture, raw materials, water, and other environmental sectors. The task of this generation is to do consciously what its predecessors did, mainly (but not wholly) in response to market incentives—for example, in opening up the American West in the second Kondratieff upswing; Canada, Australia, Argentina, and the Ukraine in the third; Middle East oil in the fourth. The task in the last quarter of the twentieth century embraces a wider range of sectors than it did previously.

In the 1950s, when basic commodity prices were declining, we could focus on the need for enlarged lending on easy terms for general development purposes, with each country designing a plan responsive to its unique circumstances and its stage of growth, including its absorptive capacity. That need has not disappeared from the agenda nor has the endless struggle to contain protectionist pressures in the industrial North. But I, at least, have no doubt that the heart of North-South economic cooperation in the 1980s—as it should have been in the 1970s—lies in the kind of sectoral functional cooperation I have outlined here.[41]

I believe, therefore, that the ideological framework and agenda of the New International Economic Order that emerged in 1974, in the wake of the quadrupling of the international oil price, however psychologically explicable, was basically misconceived and anachronistic.

Although my judgment about the appropriate North-South agenda arose from a quite special idiosyncratic intellectual setting, others, out of their own experiences and frames of thought, have come quite independently to similar conclusions. In this matter I was heartened by the consensus that emerged among seven of us on the Herrera Committee;[42] the increasingly sharp focus of the World Bank on key resource sectors; the passages in the Brandt Commission report on resources, notably

---

41. For an elaboration of this argument, see *The World Economy: History and Prospect*, pt. 6; *Getting from Here to There*, chaps. 4, 5, 6, and 13; *Why the Poor Get Richer and the Rich Slow Down*, chap. 7; "Latin America Beyond Take-off," *Americas*, vol. 31, no. 2 (February 19, 1979); and "Working Agenda for a Disheveled World Economy," *Challenge* (March/April 1981).

42. OAS, "Hemispheric Cooperation and Integral Development."

chapters 5, 6, and 10.[43] The Cancún meeting of October 1981 also spent considerable time on agriculture and energy, but the efficacy of the action taken in its wake is still to be assessed.[44] In that regard I have argued for some time that much of the work on this functional agenda should be conducted regionally, centered on the regional development banks and their related political institutions (such as the Organization of American States and the Organization of African Unity), with an active role in all the regions for the World Bank, the Food and Agriculture Organization, and other relevant global agencies.

If a sense of communal interest and communal purpose can be reestablished by enterprises in these critical sectors, I am confident that progress can be made in the other areas of mutual North-South interest. Perhaps, above all, the participants and negotiators should be officials who bear direct responsibility for policy toward these sectors in their national governments rather than foreign office officials, expert in the rhetoric (and counterrhetoric) of the New International Economic Order and the rather sterile resolutions a decade of negotiations has yielded.

A Few Reflections

The first question to ask in a reflective exercise of this kind is, of course: Has development lending been a good thing? Are the lives of men, women, and children in the developing regions better than they would have been if, say, the doctrine of the Randall Commission had prevailed and the advanced industrial countries had confined themselves to technical assistance or no aid whatsoever in their relations with the developing regions?

No such counterfactual question in history can be firmly answered. One simply cannot trace out all the substantial consequences of removing one significant variable from the equation. Any attempt to answer the question is, therefore, inherently arbitrary, impressionistic, and personal.

It is possible to argue that development is, in the end, primarily a matter of self-help, and aid, while not trivial, clearly not decisive. Overall total investment in the developing regions has been generated overwhelmingly from domestic resources—say, 90 percent; and net official development

43. *North-South: A Program for Survival*, Report of the Independent Commission on International Development Issues, Willy Brandt, chairman (Cambridge, Mass.: MIT Press, 1980).

44. President Reagan offered, in this respect, an opening which has not thus far been picked up and exploited by any of the leaders in the developing countries. Among the five principles he set out for "a positive program of action for development" was: "Guiding our assistance towards the development of self-sustaining productive activities, particularly in food and energy." *Public Papers of the Presidents of the United States: Ronald Reagan, 1981* (Washington, D.C.: U.S. Government Printing Office, 1982), p. 982.

assistance may now account for only about 6 percent of total gross investment. But in certain cases the availability of development aid clearly bought time for nations to find their feet and go forward on their own; and the flows of development assistance from abroad encouraged private investment and stimulated domestic investment, public and private, in certain important sectors. In other cases, however, it may have postponed, at some cost, confrontation with reality. I am inclined to think, for example, that at least some of the PL 480 loans and grants in the 1950s and 1960s were counterproductive. They carried with them the illusion that U.S. grain surpluses, beyond the capacity of commercial markets to absorb, were a permanent feature of the world economy. They may well have slowed the adoption of effective agricultural policies in certain developing countries.[45] And any knowledgeable observer of the scene can cite both individual loans and country loan programs that yielded, to put it mildly, disappointing results. Like the private sector, the world of official development assistance has had its Edsels.

It has also been argued that without development aid, with its encouragement of planning, the economies of the developing countries would have been less centralized and more reliant on the price system and the bracing winds of competitive private enterprise. This I disbelieve. The odds are that the strains of their balance of payments would have pushed developing countries toward more authoritarian solutions, and they would now be more dominated than they are by compulsive central planning mechanisms and less open to the disciplines of domestic and international price competition.

But I am skeptical that any kind of satisfactory approximation of an answer can be established by argument, one way or another, in these more or less economic terms. I would judge the decisive considerations to be three:

First, the existence of institutionalized development aid elevated the stature of the men and women in the governments of developing countries who were seriously committed to economic and social development and capable of formulating the case for assistance in terms of internationally recognized standards. After all, external resources are, in the short run,

---

45. I would not attribute to the existence of food imports under PL 480 the primary reason for the systematic neglect of agricultural and rural life which was—and remains—one of the most troubling features of policy in developing countries. That neglect flowed mainly from a convergence of political realities and understandable, but misguided, intellectual biases within developing countries. In the short run, the cities were more volatile and, in a sense, politically dangerous. There was a powerful temptation, therefore, to provide the cities cheap food even at the cost of wise, longer-run agricultural policies. PL 480 loans were evidently attractive to many political leaders in developing countries, and to their finance ministers as well, because they provided a prompt increase in current governmental revenues. Meanwhile, intellectuals argued that agriculture was a quasi-colonial activity, value added was higher in industry than in agriculture, industry was needed urgently to underpin military strength, and so on.

extremely important to hard-pressed governments in developing regions; and those capable of negotiating successfully for such resources become important national assets. From close observation of many developing countries, I have no doubt that the domestic priority of development was thus heightened.[46]

Second, in an inherently divisive world, with ample capacity to generate international violence, institutionalized development aid has been perhaps the strongest tempering force, quietly at work, giving some operational meaning to the notion of a human community with serious elements of common interest.

Third, as noted earlier, the existence of institutionalized development aid helped damp, to a significant degree, the domestic conflicts inherent in the modernization process in those countries which pursued reasonably balanced, purposeful, and sustained development programs. This reduction of conflict, rather than the prompt adoption of the institutions of Western democracy, was a critical part of the case for foreign aid.

Be that as it may, at least one development crusader of the 1950s has no regrets for his enlistment in a cause he has supported for more than three decades. But looking back at the intellectual struggle for development aid of the 1950s and at the political figures who joined early in the campaign, I would underline a chastening fact. The path-breaking victories won in the form of the International Development Association, the Inter-American Bank, the India and Pakistan consortia, the Alliance for Progress, and the Decade of Development did not come about because, at last, we persuaded the opposition that we were right. They came about because a series of crises in the developing regions forced on responsible politicians an acute awareness of the political and strategic danger of not assisting the process of development in Latin America, Africa, the Middle East, and Asia. It was Vice President Nixon's difficulties in Lima and Caracas in May 1958 (promptly and skillfully exploited by President Kubitschek) that shifted the balance of power within the Eisenhower administration toward support for the Inter-American Bank and other positive responses to Latin America's development needs, long urged upon it. Castro's emergence in 1959 as a working ally of Moscow was not irrelevant to easy congressional acceptance of the Alliance for Progress. Similarly, the somewhat romantic image of economic and social progress in China, during Mao's Great Leap Forward, assisted John F. Kennedy, John Sherman Cooper, and Eugene R. Black, via the Banker's Mission to India and Pakistan of

---

46. The historians of the World Bank, Edward S. Mason and Robert E. Asher, share my view of the importance of this point, but more wistfully: "The Bank can ally itself with the development-minded elements in the country and reinforce their efforts. But the Bank's biggest handicap is its inability to guarantee that development-minded officials will come into power or remain in power" (*The World Bank since Bretton Woods* [Washington, D.C.: Brookings Institution, 1973], p. 648). My point is, of course, that many more development-minded officials rose to power and stayed in power than would have been the case if development aid had not been institutionalized.

early 1960, in setting in motion the World Bank consortia for those countries. Again, the Lebanon-Jordan crisis of August 1958 led President Eisenhower to propose a generous plan for regional development in the Middle East which, unfortunately, was not taken up. In fact, the whole critical period when the long-run foundations for development assistance were laid was framed by the protracted anxieties, in the United States and elsewhere, that followed the Soviet launching of the first satellite in October 1957. The story of the transition to large-scale sustained development aid, is, in fact, a vivid illustration of Jean Monnet's dictum: "people only accept change when they are faced with necessity, and only recognize necessity when a crisis is upon them."[47]

Nevertheless, the work of the development crusaders was not irrelevant. When governments in the advanced industrial world were forced by events to turn to the tasks of development, there existed a body of thought and doctrine, based on research, debate, and some practical experience, which permitted sensible courses of action to be fashioned quickly. Perhaps most important of all, development thought and doctrine had been thrashed out between economists of the North and South. This lively process proceeded not only in universities, but also on the occasion of research and aid missions to developing countries and within the secretariats of the World Bank, the United Nations, and the regional economic commissions. It was, clearly, a two-way process of mutual education. The existence of this common frame of reference, often underpinned by close human ties, rendered North-South collaboration much easier than it would otherwise have been when the institutional framework for development assistance was built and put to work in the late 1950s and early 1960s. One of our major current tasks is to build, in the quite different environment of the 1980s, a new North-South intellectual consensus to underpin a sustained partnership effort. The concepts underlying the New International Economic Order did not fulfill that function and the exceedingly serious and well-meant effort of the Brandt Commission to do the job did not quite succeed.

However philosophical we may be about the role of Cold War–related crises as the catalyst which altered the political balance in the struggle of the 1950s for enlarged development assistance, the Cold War had its costs. The flow of aid has, to a degree, remained responsive, in both its direction and scale, to the intensity of the Cold War dimension in policy toward the developing regions. But it is also true, to a degree, that development aid was institutionalized, notably through the enterprise of the World Bank in the regimes of Eugene Black, George Woods, and Robert McNamara, and through the regional development banks. It is no small thing that, by World Bank calculations, official development assistance was $25.5 billion in 1981 from the members of the Organisation for Economic Co-operation and Development, and perhaps $7 billion from the Organiza-

47. Jean Monnet, *Memoirs* (Garden City, N.Y.: Doubleday, 1978), p. 109.

tion of Petroleum Exporting Countries.[48] Aid from communist governments to non-communist developing countries approximated $2.6 billion in 1979. There are those who believe these sums are too low, too high, and/or misdirected or misused in one manner or another. Foreign aid has never been a subject that lent itself to easy consensus or complacency. Nevertheless, it is a unique historical phenomenon that the advanced industrial countries have recognized an interest in the economic fate of the developing countries worth the regular allocation of something like 0.35 percent of GNP.[49] Still, the seriousness of the larger northern governments about development assistance has tended to fluctuate with the scale and locus of conflicts in the South. This has reduced one of the advantages we believed would flow from the kind of steady long-term approach some of us advocated in the 1950s—that is, it reduced the possibility of heading off crises that might otherwise occur. Moreover, aid granted in the midst of crisis is generally less efficient, dollar for dollar, than aid granted steadily in support of ongoing development programs.

My final reflection concerns a still larger issue: Is regular growth still a legitimate objective for the developing regions? Do global resource limitations decree that the old devil, diminishing returns, will soon generate a global crisis unless the developing regions and the advanced industrial countries level off promptly, adopt new, less materialistic criteria for the good life, and even things out within the human family by drastic redistribution of income and wealth within national societies and among nations? This was, of course, the theme of *The Limits to Growth*.[50] That study was subjected to the careful criticism its radical conclusion deserved, and the flaws revealed in the analysis diminished the inevitability of its apocalyptic judgment, as the authors came to acknowledge.

But quite aside from the potentialities for continuing to fend off diminishing returns through man's ingenuity—as we have done for two centuries—there is no evidence that *The Limits to Growth* prescription is politically, socially, and psychologically viable. On the contrary, the thrust for higher real incomes by less advantaged groups and nations is one of the most powerful forces operating on the world scene, and so is the deter-

---

48. World Bank, *World Development Report 1982* (New York: Oxford University Press, 1982), pp. 140–41.

49. In terms of development theory and policy as my colleagues and I conceived of it in the 1950s—and as I conceive of it now—the criterion of the proportion of GNP allocated by the advanced industrial countries to developing countries is irrelevant and misleading. Measuring official development assistance in this way implies that the objective is the transfer of resources from rich to poor. The "correct" criterion is to assure that absorptive capacity is matched by the availability of capital for development programs which are in appropriate sectoral balance. This would not, of course, exclude emergency aid, on a human welfare basis, to countries experiencing one kind or another of economic emergency.

50. Donella H. Meadows, Dennis L. Meadows, Jørgen Randers, and William W. Behrens III (New York: Universe Books, 1972).

mination of advantaged nations and social groups to sustain and even improve their material status. Thus far the tensions generated by these ambitions have been softened because the pie to be divided has been expanding. It is one thing to quarrel about fair shares when all are gaining in real income; the struggle for fair shares is a more dour matter in the face of a static or low growth rate in real income per capita.

But trees do not grow to the sky. It is wholly possible, even certain, that, with the passage of time, man's perceptions of affluence will change—or change will be forced upon him. More than two decades ago, in writing *The Stages of Economic Growth*, I raised the question of what would happen in the richer societies when "diminishing relative marginal utility sets in, on a mass basis, for real income itself" (p. 91). The problem was much discussed in the 1960s. A margin of the more affluent young went into revolt against the values of material progress and the consequences of those values as they perceived them. They sought nonmaterial objectives. And a no-growth strand exists in the politics of most advanced industrial countries. But it is not a majority view. The fact is that, among both the early comers and latecomers to industrialization, we must count on a protracted period of effort to continue to grow. Right or wrong, the odds are that the effort will be made, and serious policymaking should be based on that probability. As a black colleague of mine once said, the disadvantaged of this world are about to buy tickets for the show; they are quite unmoved by the affluent emerging from the theater and pronouncing the show bad; they are determined to find out for themselves.

That determination underlines the urgency of the kind of North-South cooperation I outlined earlier. The problems of energy, food, raw materials, and the environment that we confront in the world economy may not decree an end to industrial growth after, say, a run of 250 years from the late eighteenth century. But those problems are real and still degenerative; that is, they will worsen with the passage of time unless present national and international policies change.

In the end, those policies should reflect the universal stake, shared equally between the North and South—and, I would add, East and West— in a continuity of industrial civilization which would permit us to level off in population and, later, in real income per capita when we are so minded, not when faced by bitter Malthusian or other resource-related crises. The most primitive self-interest should, then, bring nations and peoples closer to accepting the injunction of the poet after whom I happen to be named, to which I have often returned:

> One thought ever at the fore—
> That in the Divine Ship, the World,
>   breasting Time and Space,
> All peoples of the globe together sail,
>   sail the same voyage,
> Are bound to the same destination.

Comment

Gerald Helleiner

PROFESSOR ROSTOW offers in his paper a characteristic blend of history, theory, insight, and provocation. Whatever one may think of his approaches or his conclusions, it can never be said that his work makes dull reading! When I was asked to discuss the Rostow paper—knowing the span of his interests and experience—I expressed doubt as to whether my own background was appropriate for this task; and that was *before* I had seen the paper. I am terribly conscious of the weak credentials I bring to this task and of the fact that when the MIT group set about writing their "tract for the times"—a couple of decades *after* Professor Rostow had embarked upon his earliest enquiries into economic history—I had not myself even finished secondary school. But let me turn to my task.

Professor Rostow's paper is an amalgam of two quite different kinds of stories. The first concerns his interpretation of the interrelationship between economic theory and economic history at a quite general level; in this we see Rostow the much respected scholar of long-term change and development. The second is a story of U.S. foreign policy and the evolution of U.S. attitudes toward the developing countries since the early 1950s; in this we see instead Rostow the advocate, the political participant, and servant of the U.S. public interest. The two stories are intertwined, but I should like to address them separately.

We are familiar with the Rostovian emphases on noneconomic dimensions in societal performance, "the crucial role of politics" in modernization, and the importance of science and technology in modern economic growth; and many of us were brought up on his "characterization of stages in development." In this paper, however, I have been particularly struck by a number of other propositions, especially three with which I fundamentally agree:

- "The optimum unit for the study of economic history is not the nation, but the whole interrelated trading area," a conclusion Professor Rostow had already recorded in 1948, from which he was thence-

Gerald Helleiner is Professor of Economics at the University of Toronto.

forth led, he says, to address history in terms of "the evolution of the world economy as a whole."

- "The analysis of a modern or modernizing economy could not be usefully conducted in aggregate terms."
- The post-1945 turning of "virtually the whole of Asia, the Middle East, Africa, and Latin America . . . with passion . . . to the goal of modernization . . . in historical perspective . . . is perhaps the most remarkable event since the coming of the first Industrial Revolution to Great Britain in the 1780s. It has altered irreversibly the balance and texture of international political, as well as economic, life."

The facts of national-level decisionmaking and national-level historical statistics tend to drive most of us, as they have driven Professor Rostow, back to the questions of *national* experiences, interests, and policies. But the implications of these three propositions for the future study of *world* economics and politics are profound, and two of them are worth spelling out. First, sectoral or industry-level investigations and analysis may be among the most appropriate means for approaching an understanding of global political and economic developments. (Global macroeconomics is also necessary but not yet very much in fashion.) An "orderly disaggrega-tion" of the global economy might best proceed in terms of sectors or industries rather than nations. International trade would then be absorbed into studies of global industries, in which industrial organization and location theories might provide a more appropriate intellectual framework than conventional trade theory. Market structures at the global level, within particular sectors and industries, would then probably receive more attention than they now do, as would their effects (if any) upon global intersectoral terms of trade. If one pursues these Rostovian lines, one can—and to some extent Rostow does, at least for "protracted periods"—end up, in fact, with Raúl Prebisch and Hans Singer! Whether or not Professor Rostow enjoys this company, I am sure he would agree on the need to vastly improve our modeling and understanding of sectoral developments and interrelationships at the global level.

Second, in view of the remarkable post–Second World War events of which he writes, the admirable concern with "the aspirations of all classes and regions, greatly increased social, economic, and political opportun-ity," and the like,[1] *all at the national level*, should be logically and appro-priately applied at the world level. So should the expressed concern regarding the appropriate balance between the public and private sectors, although the direction of suggested change might well be reversed.[2] I speak

---

1. Expressed in *A Proposal: Key to an Effective Foreign Policy* (New York: Harper, 1957) and in Professor Rostow's reflections on this work here.

2. See, for instance, former MIT colleague Charles Kindleberger, who notes that while "there may be too much government at the national level . . . there may also be too

of analysis and of logic, not of political rhetoric. The Rostovian propositions I have noted imply the logical need for global data and global analysis in the fields of income distribution, market imperfections, and failures, and the potential for governmental activities of the conventional kind to deal with them.

About Professor Rostow's main thesis concerning the "Marshallian long period," however, I must express some doubts. If I have understood him correctly, nations and now the world possess optimal sectoral capacities which are related to rates of growth of the labor force, technical change, and the supply of basic inputs. From this "system" flows an optimal aggregate growth rate and an optimal distribution of investment. The world lurches its way through history, overshooting and undershooting its optimal sectoral paths.

It is by no means clear how these sectoral "optima" are to be ascertained or indeed what is typically the maximand in their determination. It is therefore not clear how one is to know when one is on target and when one is not. Nor is it clear whether the engine of growth is powered best by remaining firmly upon the prescribed sectoral paths or by persistent disequilibria; Albert Hirschman would certainly say the latter.

In any case, these phenomena can be related, Rostow argues, to Kondratieff long swings, in which the prices of basic commodities figure prominently. In the early 1970s sharp increases in the relative prices of grain and energy, according to his view, ushered in "a protracted period of relatively high basic commodity prices for the fifth time since 1790." On the historical evidence following a period of inflation, high interest rates, and falling real wages, this can be expected eventually to lead to expanded output in the basic commodity sectors, which will overshoot equilibrium and thus generate a "protracted reversal of trends in the international economy."

From this analysis, Professor Rostow is led to his view that it is now most important for the world economy "to assure that the sectors supporting the continuity of industrial civilization are expanded and sustained: energy, agriculture, raw materials, water, and other environmental sectors." And, it seems, these needs cannot now be left to the "magic of the marketplace." Hence he sees functional cooperation in these critical sectors as "the heart of North-South economic cooperation in the 1980s." He also continues to argue for regional approaches to such cooperation.

When it comes to assessing the longer-run significance of current events, I have always noticed that historians are prone to greater, rather than less, caution than the average professional of my acquaintance. Professor Rostow is clearly the exception required for my rule. Can his provocative

---

little government internationally." Charles P. Kindleberger, *Government and International Trade*, Princeton University Essays in International Finance no. 129 (Princeton, N.J., 1978), p. 17.

proposition about the post-1972 "protracted period" of high basic commodity prices *really* be taken seriously?

Can all his "basic commodities" be so cavalierly lumped together? In what way were the events in grain and oil markets in the early 1970s logically linked, and to what degree were either of them the product of long-run influences of the sort which interested Alfred Marshall? What is the underlying explanation of this purported new trend in relative prices? And how long is a "protracted period" anyway? Most of the exporters of "basic commodities" of my acquaintance will be very surprised to hear that they are in the middle of a protracted upswing.

For the record, oil apart, there is no statistically discernible trend in the relative prices of Professor Rostow's basic commodities from the early 1970s to the early 1980s. Following the burst in 1973–74, food prices have risen at lower rates than overall wholesale price indices; they are now roughly at the same relative price level as they were in 1972. Agricultural raw material prices never did soar disproportionately in the early 1970s, and have since declined in relative terms. The experience with metals is quite variable, but the IMF metals (dollar) price index since 1975 and the prices for some, such as copper, are now much lower in real terms than in 1972. (If current relative prices are said to be "temporary," the product of global recession, I can only reply that "theories" must be capable of disproof—and suggest that an alternative testing methodology be provided.)

Who really needs the Rostovian crystal ball anyway? If the message is that we should now think hard about investing more in energy, food, and certain strategic raw materials (for that seems to be what is meant by "basic" commodities), Professor Rostow has plenty of company. But few have dressed their views up as long-term development theorizing. Moreover, most of those with a Southern concern view energy and food questions from a decidedly *non*-Rostovian perspective that does not encompass "the continuity of industrial civilization." They see energy issues as primarily a matter of ensuring adequate firewood or biomass alternatives for masses of rural poor, and food issues much less in terms of production than in terms of poverty, entitlements, security, and distribution.

To see the future of North-South relations in terms of Professor Rostow's interpretation of long-run economic history is therefore, in my opinion, to see it rather murkily. This leads me to Rostow's second story, the evolution of U.S. policy toward the developing countries. This story is told from the perspective of what some of my social science colleagues would call a "participant observer." The tale is a fascinating one, if ultimately also a sad and sobering one. The sadness derives above all from the contrast between the vision, foresight, and basic wisdom of the "mutual interest" case for foreign aid presented by Millikan and Rostow in the 1950s and the blinkered and dogmatic character of current U.S. approaches. But sadness and sobriety also must accompany one's reflections upon how such visionary initiatives as the Alliance for Progress worked out in practice. Professor Rostow himself calls attention to the fact that the key decisions in the sphere of development aid were were typically made in response to crises and not because of the force of the mutual interest case. That long-run case has still not been accepted by politicians who must face electorates in the short run.

In one major respect the second Rostow tale is curiously dated—indeed, even out of touch with the North-South debates of the mid-1970s, let alone the 1980s. That is in its primary focus upon foreign aid. This is curious in view of Professor Rostow's stated respect for the "mutual education" and "sustained partnership" attainable through North-South intellectual debate. Development assistance has not been of primary importance in this debate for some time. At the same time that he himself concentrates on an older debate, he dismisses the more recent North-South agenda as "psychologically explicable . . . [but] basically misconceived and anachronistic." Each to his own taste in these matters. But it certainly cannot realistically be suggested that Professor Rostow's views of the appropriate future North-South agenda, rather than those he dismisses, have been shared by the Brandt Commissioners or the participants in the Cancún Summit.

The mutuality of Northern and Southern interests have been argued most vigorously in these and other places with respect to general international trade and monetary regimes, and not simply in sector-specific terms. With or without the South, the problems of coordinating macroeconomic management, achieving structural adjustment, and controlling a resurgent protectionism are now before the industrialized world. What happens to the North in as long a run as I am prepared to contemplate (I am not sure whether it is a Marshallian one, but it is a good deal shorter than the famous Keynesian long run) depends far more on events in these spheres than on the sector-specific issues of Professor Rostow's prime interest. The expanded role of the developing countries in Northern trade and finance should and will make them more significant actors in the resolution of these issues than previously. The principal challenge to current Northern policy is to bring the developing countries into these matters in an orderly and mutually acceptable manner.

It must also be said that in some areas Northern and Southern interests do not coincide, and it is misleading to pretend otherwise. Areas of conflict—actual or potential—are no less important for North-South consideration and for analytical attention than those of apparent mutual interest. Even in the "basic commodity" areas in which Rostow wants us to invest our time and money, he surely underestimates the degree to which Southerners will have views of their own as to the priorities and mechanisms (as I have already suggested above). In terms of the current North-South debate, Professor Rostow's perspective is, understandably, thoroughly Northern. It is not helpful to pretend, again, that this particular perspective flows from a generalized economic development theory. An orderly process of change, of which Professor Rostow seems to approve, is bound to have many dimensions. Whatever one's own global development theory—and most of us do not possess a very coherent one—the main foreign policy story is simply that the developing countries are going to have to be listened to much more than they used to be.

Comment

Azizali F. Mohammed

PROFESSOR ROSTOW has summarized three decades of his work on economic history, the development process, and the political economy of international assistance in his paper. The most fascinating part of the paper describes the evolution of Rostow's thinking. I shall leave this aside, except to remark that it is not surprising that a mind so well endowed would have found itself at the center of a professional controversy that kept historians and economists busy for a decade, if not longer.

His vision of a society proceeding through a succession of discrete and identifiable stages is arresting in itself, but of even greater interest is the world view within which it is embedded. Rostow places the 1950s and the 1960s in the downswing phase of the fourth Kondratieff cycle when energy was cheap and the terms of trade favored the industrial countries. These countries grew vigorously in a relatively inflation-free environment and were able to pull the rest of the world along, while at the same time dispensing substantial amounts of foreign aid. The world entered the upswing phase of the fifth cycle in the early 1970s. Food and energy prices rose and aid turned scarce. Industrial countries were faced with a combination of deteriorating terms of trade and domestic inflation when they tried to ignore the real income transfer that was implicit in the new structure of relative prices. The upswing brought harder times for developing countries that were not energy exporters and that went heavily into debt as interest rates first turned positive and then touched "real" levels of 5 percent and more for the first time.

Yet the Rostovian prognosis remains essentially optimistic. The upswing phase of the cycle has its compensations as rising input costs, especially of energy, trigger a new burst of resource-saving innovations. While the countries that benefit from this stimulus resume their momentum, life can be made easier for everyone, according to Rostow, if the North and the South can work harmoniously together to expand supplies of energy, food, and raw materials. What is not clear is whether the

Azizali F. Mohammed is Director of the External Relations Department at the International Monetary Fund.

developing world is necessarily rendered better-off by these developments. How would the terms of trade evolve? Would they tilt back in favor of the industrial countries? Would the losses of the energy exporters and of the suppliers of labor to them be offset by equivalent gains of the oil-importing countries? Would aid flows be maintained in real terms? If disenchantment with aid proves to be irrevocable, how would the weakest countries manage in the next phase of the cycle if they did so poorly in the last? One looks in vain for some intimations of an answer.

Moving to a lower level of abstraction, the take-off stage holds our attention. A quarter century from the time the concept was propounded, it is pertinent to inquire how it has fared in the interval. A great deal of Rostow's work has gone into the construction and refining of the mechanism that catapults an economy into take-off. The propulsion is supplied by one or more leading sectors, but all sectors remain in a state of flux as production functions change, new technologies become available, and new linkages reach out into the economy. Rostow has been careful to emphasize that the propulsive mechanism is delicate and unpredictable. Although a good part of the action is focused on the leading sectors, the energies accumulating there are derived from several sources: new inventions or the absorption of available technology; the emergence of a corps of entrepreneurs who invest in and exploit the market possibilities; and an external challenge that serves to focus national political energies. To these conditions Rostow would add a productive agriculture and a modicum of aid. But these elements must fall into precise alignment, and whether they do or not remains largely fortuitous.

In his recent work Rostow has continued his investigations into the dynamics of leading sectors. One would have hoped in this paper for a progress report. How well have the stages stood up against the facts about the newly developing countries? In viewing the development experience over the past three decades one might be forgiven for not being able to see the scaffolds of Rostow's schema. And we remain without guidance on the identification of potential leading sectors, the fostering and nurture of "growth points" through suitable incentives, the strengthening of linkages with policy measures, the revival of sectors that have begun to flag, and the criteria for determining which sectors have to be abandoned.

This leads to a more general point. Twenty years ago at the close of a conference on the stages of growth, Robert Solow wondered about the analytical quality of Rostow's system. Were economic historians simply retailing descriptions of idealized economic stages? Was stage theory simply a literary device? He went on to add that if economic historians were ever to collaborate fruitfully with the garden-variety economists, the rules of the game had to be clearer. For the stage theory to be usable, it had to be more precise about behavioral relationships, parameters, and initial conditions. Reading this paper, one is assailed with the same doubts. Economic evolution as we experience it in these difficult times is a random walk on a muddy track. Developing nations must pull themselves out of the slime and pick their way with whatever guidance economic theory and empirical experience can offer them. The good advice of international institutions can help avert the most egregious of mistakes, but governments are leery of taking outside advice unless no alternative remains. We could certainly all use a historical perspective. That is why the promise of Rostow's work has been so heartening.

We shall, however, need more guidance from him before his ideas can provide us with a handle on policies and measures that affect the process of development. For example, Rostow sees modernization partly as a process by which countries absorb existing technology. To some extent he finds the ability of latecomers to acquire already developed technologies as the key to their rapid rise up the ladder of economic development. His latest work hints at a closing of the gap between the rich and the poor countries in large part because of this process. But there is little to relate this hypothesis to the dwindling of aid flows and the evident inability of many poor countries to adequately prepare their rapidly growing populations for the technological age that has already dawned for the industrialized countries of the world. What role does he see for the aid institutions and, in the absence of official finance for disbursement by these institutions, does he foresee them turning into agencies for technical assistance in the main?

My next point goes in a somewhat different direction. Perhaps Rostow, in casting his disciplinary net so widely, cannot possibly be attentive to the analytical needs of low-brow practitioners of the dismal science and to the international civil servants who follow in their wake. From the start, he has been willing to knock on the doors of all the social sciences to find answers to the problems of development. In some respects his stage theory is as ambitious and catholic as that of Marx. But there are important differences in the choice of ingredients and in the distribution of emphasis. The tension between classes is central to Marxian thought, and a rich story is written around the energies that are released by the clash of class interests. One searches Rostow's writings in vain for a sense of the complexity of social frictions, the abrasion of one class or group interest by others, the often destructive political conflicts. All of these are surely integral to the evolution of developing societies. Rostow does refer to the emerging state bourgeoisie and the lack of convergence between its interests and those of the masses, but gives no indication of wanting to incorporate this widespread phenomenon into his theory. Perhaps it is too much to ask that his theory take account of the many sides and angles of society, identify the stresses within, or even track the complex changes in institutions, modes of thinking, and cultural practices that are taking place inside.

My last comment concerns the role of foreign aid. A good portion of the paper is devoted to the concerns underlying aid policies in the 1950s. His own views are a trifle veiled because he speaks on behalf of that elite body of scholars who populated CENIS during that decade. Nevertheless, one senses his deep humanitarian concerns and his powerful convictions on the efficacy of aid. He admits that some kinds of assistance, such as the PL 480 program, might in hindsight appear to have been counterproductive. But on balance, foreign assistance must have done more good than harm. It promoted economic welfare, assisted governments seriously committed to modernization to proceed with change with the minimum of violence, and gave scope to men of vision, enterprise, and intellect.

I have no difficulty with these claims but doubt that they give us a complete picture. Because the assistance provided by the industrialized nations in the 1950s and the 1960s was harnessed to strategic goals, it may have—even if unintentionally—bolstered regimes whose policies went against the grain of popular demands and aspirations, generating tensions that have surfaced in many parts of the world. The aggregate indicators, to which Rostow refers, undoubtedly point toward a rate of growth which by historical standards is quite impressive. But as he would be the first to recognize, such indicators can be deceptive. In many countries, economic polarization may have proceeded hand in hand with GNP growth. Some of the statistics on the spread of poverty and deprivation in developing societies have been well documented by the World Bank, but these are not cited.

Rostow believes that aid brought about a certain concentration of talents. I happen to agree that the efforts of aid-giving agencies, bilateral or multilateral, did promote better economic management in a number of countries and helped raise the caliber of policymakers in the economic ministries. I am also convinced that aid accelerated the coalescence of an entrepreneurial class in some countries. But there is a negative side to the ledger that we would do well to recognize. The economic, political, and bureaucratic milieu that was nurtured by foreign aid created its own problems. As noted earlier, Rostow himself refers to the problem of the state bourgeoisie. This is one facet of a larger problem, which is the emergence of bureaucratic and entrepreneurial elites of considerable talent, who are identified with aid-givers and, by virtue of that fact alone, disassociated from their own people and seen by them as aliens.

But enough of these quibbles. Professor Rostow has favored us with an eminently satisfying repast. No theory in the social sciences is so flawless that a diligent search will not reveal one deficiency or another. Rostow has tried to transcend the limitations of our discipline more vigorously than most. Over the years we have all benefited from his efforts. This paper shows that his vigor remains undiminished and that we can rely upon it as a continuing source of insight for many years to come.

H. W. Singer

HANS SINGER was born in 1910 in the Rhineland. He first studied economics and social problems at the University of Bonn where he was much influenced by his teachers Joseph Schumpeter and Arthur Spiethoff.

Singer was able to leave Germany in 1933 and was admitted to King's College, Cambridge, where he actively shared in the Keynesian analysis and Keynesian values. He received his Ph.D. from Cambridge in 1936. He was then engaged in the Pilgrim Trust Unemployment Enquiry and helped to produce *Men without Work* (Cambridge, Eng.: Cambridge University Press, 1938). His interest in unemployment statistics led to a series of articles in the *Review of Economic Studies* and to the Frances Wood Memorial Prize of the Royal Statistical Society. His study of the depressed areas of Wales, Durham, Merseyside, and Lancashire was also to have a relation to his later studies of the regional poverty areas in Northeast Brazil, northern Thailand, and Kenya.

His first academic post was at Manchester University (1938–43). In 1944 he joined the Ministry of Town and Country Planning and in 1946 joined Glasgow University. In 1947 he entered the United Nations during its early days and immediately helped to build up its Economics Department which then had a section of only two persons concerned with underdeveloped countries. He was to remain with the United Nations for the next twenty-two years.

His early development work found expression in *Formulation and Economic Appraisal of Development Projects: Lectures on Special Problems Delivered at the Asian Centre on Agricultural and Allied Projects*, 2 vols. (New York: U.N. Technical Assistance Administration, 1951). Numerous visiting missions, official reports, and consultancies to various governments and international organizations followed, including direction of the establishment of the African Development Bank, the World Food Program, and the U.N. Special Fund.

Since 1969 he has been a Professorial Fellow at the Institute of Development Studies and Professor of Economics at the University of Sussex, now Emeritus.

Among his books are *Unemployment and the Unemployed* (London:

King, 1940); *Economic Development of Under-Developed Countries* (in Portuguese; Rio de Janeiro: Vargas Foundation, 1950); *Economic Development of the Brazilian North-East* (New York: U.N. Technical Assistance Report, 1955); with others, *The Role of the Economist as Official Adviser* (London: Allen and Unwin, 1955); *International Development, Growth and Change* (New York: McGraw-Hill, 1964); with others, *Perspectives in Economic Development* (Boston: Houghton Mifflin, 1970); *The Strategy of International Development* (London: Macmillan, 1975); *Technologies for Basic Needs* (Geneva: ILO, 1977); *Rich and Poor Countries* (London: Allen and Unwin, 1979); and, with others, *The International Economy and Industrial Development* (London: Wheatsheaf Books, 1982).

Some selected articles are: "The Process of Unemployment and the Depressed Areas, 1935–38," *Review of Economic Studies*, 1938; "Economic Progress in Under-developed Countries," *Social Research*, 1949; "Distribution of Gains between Investing and Borrowing Countries," *American Economic Review*, Papers and Proceedings, May 1950; "International Approaches to Modernization Programmes," *Milbank Memorial Fund Quarterly*, April 1950; "Capital Requirements for the Economic Development of the Middle East," *Middle Eastern Affairs*, February 1952; "Mechanics of Economic Development," *Indian Economic Review*, August 1952 and February 1953; "Obstacles to Economic Development," *Social Research*, Spring 1953; "Terms of Trade—Barter vs. Factoral—and Gains from Trade," *Contribuicoes a Analise do Dosenvolvimento Economico*, Rio de Janeiro, 1957; "Comment on C. P. Kindleberger's 'The Terms of Trade and Economic Development,' " *Review of Economics and Statistics*, February 1958; "Trends in Economic Thought on Under-Development," *Social Research*, 1961; "External Aid: For Plans or Projects?" *Economic Journal*, September 1965; "The Notion of Human Investment," *Review of Social Economy*, March 1966; and "Dualism Revisited," *Journal of Development Studies*, October 1970.

Singer's most recent work relates to the New International Economic Order, food aid, appropriate technology, and the problems of newly industrializing countries.

The Terms of Trade Controversy and the Evolution of Soft Financing: Early Years in the U.N.

THE FIRST PART of this paper is mainly autobiographical, as seems justified by the occasion: How did I come to be in the United Nations during those early years, and why did I do what I did? The second part deals with my 1949–50 paper on the "Distribution of Gains between Investing and Borrowing Countries," with the benefits of an extra thirty-two years of hindsight.[1] It is argued that the views then expressed have been well vindicated, and that a reformulation in more contemporary terms would now command increasing support. The third part deals with the story of the Special United Nations Fund for Economic Development (SUNFED) and the International Development Association (IDA), the World Bank affiliate, as it appeared to one involved in the discussions of soft financing of development in the 1950s and from the viewpoint of someone on the U.N. side. According to my dictionary, a pioneer is "somebody who prepares the road for the main body"; it is exactly my contention that the "wild men" in the U.N. with their SUNFED prepared the road for the main body, the World Bank.

Autobiographical

In trying to think about the years 1947–51 and how I first came to concentrate on terms of trade and then afterwards on the need for soft development financing, I must start by being autobiographical.[2]

I had been invited to join the United Nations in 1946. In April 1947 I arrived at the U.N. I have described elsewhere the curious linguistic misunderstanding—a difference between the American and English usage

---

1. The paper was presented at the annual meeting of the American Economic Association, 1949, and published in *American Economic Review*, Papers and Proceedings, vol. 40 (May 1950), pp. 473–85.

2. This will involve some name-dropping. As Geoffrey Keynes (the younger brother of J. M.) has said in his autobiography, it "sounds too much like performing an exercise in name-dropping, the most unattractive of all occupations, which no-one enjoys" (*The Gates of Memory* [Oxford: Clarendon Press, 1982], p. 1).

of the term "country planning"—which assigned me to the development work within the Division of Economic and Social Affairs.[3] On reflection, I can think of several strands of connection between the new problems that I now had an opportunity to study and my earlier interests.

I had always been greatly interested in the problems of the "depressed areas"—those parts of the United Kingdom such as Wales, Scotland, Merseyside, and the Northeast that had been particularly hard-hit by unemployment and that had distinctly fallen behind the rest of the country in terms of incomes and standards of living. Before the war, I had published, with David Owen and Walter Oakeshott, the Pilgrim Trust unemployment enquiry, *Men without Work* (Cambridge University Press, 1938). I had lived in the depressed areas among unemployed people and thus been able to make proposals for policy based on more than purely academic study of unemployment problems. As a follow-up to the joint book with David Owen and Walter Oakeshott, I produced by myself *Unemployment and the Unemployed* (Allen and Unwin, 1939) and a number of separate papers and articles (many of the latter published in the *Review of Economic Studies*). I had continued this interest in Glasgow University, where I was engaged in a study of differentials in development indicators between Scotland and England, subsequently published (jointly with C. E. V. Leser) as *Industrial Productivity in England and Scotland* (University of Glasgow, Department of Social and Economic Research, 1950). The results were also presented as a paper to the Royal Statistical Society (*Journal of the Royal Statistical Society*, 1950). Clearly this work on depressed areas and unemployment was a forerunner to the work on developing countries. I had already been forced to think about "vicious circles" and "poverty traps." During the Kenya ILO Employment Mission,[4] in particular 1971–72, I often thought back to my work in the 1930s.

As part of my concern with unemployment problems, I felt involved in the development of a social welfare state immediately after the war. I was an admirer of Sir William Beveridge and an ardent propagandist for the Beveridge report. In 1943 I had written one of the Fabian Society research pamphlets, *Can We Afford Beveridge?* My answer, perhaps predictably, was that not only could we afford it, but we could not afford not to afford it. The same point was made in an article on "Beveridge Plan Economics" published as a special issue of the *Westminster Newsletter* in 1943. Obviously, a partisan of the social welfare state would be attracted by the thought and possibilities of a global welfare state represented by the United Nations in those hopeful first days of naive utopianism.

3. H. W. Singer, "Early Years, 1910–1938," in Sir Alec Cairncross and Mohinder Puri, eds., *Employment, Income Distribution and Development Strategy* (London: Macmillan, 1976).

4. *Employment, Incomes and Equality in Kenya* (Geneva: International Labour Office, 1972).

There was also a more intellectual link. As my fellow "pioneer" Albert Hirschman has pointed out,[5] in some sense Keynes was the real creator of development economics insofar as he broke with "mono-economics"—the view that economics consists of a body of universal truth applicable in all countries and in all conditions. Keynes showed that, on the contrary, the rules of the game applicable to a condition of unemployment are not the same as those of classical full employment economics. It was a natural step—as Albert Hirschman has shown—to apply this view of different rules of the game to countries at different stages of development. As a student of Keynes during the formative years of the *General Theory* (1934–36) in Cambridge, I was certainly intellectually preconditioned to think in terms of different rules of the game applying to developing countries, and the idea of nonorthodox policies in relation to them. Only a few years later, in 1954, Arthur Lewis published his path-breaking article on "Economic Development with Unlimited Supplies of Labour," which carried the analogy between the existence of unemployment in an industrial country and the existence of surplus labor in a developing country a decisive step further.[6]

My other teacher before Keynes was Joseph Schumpeter, under whom I had studied in Bonn before he left for Harvard. Thus I had been brought up on economic development from my first student days. Through Schumpeter I had acquired a lasting interest in problems of technical progress and technical innovation as well as in long-run economics. This interest in long-run trends and technical progress was fostered in Cambridge by my supervisor (and another "fellow pioneer"), Colin Clark, to whom I owe a great debt. Even in Keynes's work, I had always been particularly interested in some of the long-run aspects, such as his essay on "Economic Possibilities for our Grandchildren," and was never quite happy with the dictum that "in the long run we are all dead." I would say that this interest in the long run, in technical progress, was another ingredient and guide toward work on long-term trends in terms of trade.

Keynes and Beveridge were both proponents of active state intervention. This preconditioned me to take a direct interest in the problems of development planning, much in vogue in the immediate postwar era with a special focus on India.[7] P. C. Mahalanobis became the prophet (or guru) of the development economists in this respect, and Calcutta became their Mecca.

5. "The Rise and Decline of Development Economics," in *Essays in Trespassing* (New York: Cambridge University Press, 1981).

6. *Manchester School of Economic and Social Studies* (May 1954). Even earlier, Arthur Lewis had become a key member of the U.N. Committee on Measures for Economic Development.

7. My lectures in Lahore were published under the title *Economic Development Projects as Part of National Development Programmes* (New York: United Nations, 1951).

One of my first operational assignments was to participate in the training courses for Indian and Pakistani officials in connection with the World Bank–financed Indus River Basin scheme. My attention was also directed toward the Indian subcontinent by an early friendship with my fellow student, V. K. R. V. Rao, who during the early years of the United Nations, as chairman of the U.N. Sub-Commission for Economic Development, formulated the first ideas for global soft financing (see below).

The other area of early involvement was Brazil. Here again, personal factors were at work: apart from family links, there was an early friendship with Roberto Campos, then a young Brazilian delegate in U.N. economic committees, and later on through him with a number of other Brazilian economists, including Eugenio Gudin, at that time the minister of finance.

One result of the assignment in Brazil was a series of lectures at the Getulio Vargas Foundation in Rio de Janeiro, subsequently published in Portuguese. But more important were my early visits and studies of the Brazilian Northeast. Here certainly the experiences of earlier work on depressed areas in the United Kingdom came vividly to my mind. One of the first things to establish was that the problem of the Northeast was a development problem and not simply a problem of natural disaster (the "secca" or drought). The latter was the prevailing view, although a group of young Brazilian economists[8] were already hammering at the national conscience that more could be done than simply building roads to get the people out and building some reservoirs to keep them and some of their cattle alive while they were waiting for evacuation. I heartily joined the fray at their side.[9]

The work in the Brazilian Northeast was also linked with the work on terms of trade or distribution of gains which will form the next part of this paper. The Northeast was a major source of all Brazilian primary exports other than coffee—and of course at that time Brazilian exports were almost entirely primary products. The prices obtained by exporters of these Northeastern products were depressed by chronic overvaluation of the cruzeiro, while the prices they paid for domestic manufactures from São Paulo were inflated by heavy protection and resulting inefficiency and high profit margins. Thus the work on this particular case of a depressed area formed a direct link with the concern regarding terms of trade. My work in Northeast Brazil was also directly connected with the establish-

8. These included Roberto Campos, Octavia Bulhoes, Celso Furtado, and Romulo Almeida, all destined to play major roles in Brazilian development.

9. My reports on the Northeast were published in English as a U.N. Technical Assistance Report (1953) and subsequently as a book in Portuguese (*Estudo sobre o Desenvolvimento Economico do Nordesta* [Economic development of the Brazilian Northeast] (Recife: Commissão de Desenvolvimento Economico de Pernambuco, 1962). An English version of some of these reports was also included in *International Development, Growth and Change* (New York: McGraw-Hill, 1964), as pt. 6.

ment of a regional development bank, Banco do Nordeste. This provided a link with work on development financing, and even more specifically with involvement some dozen years later (while stationed with the U.N. Economic Commission for Africa in Addis Ababa) with the establishment of the African Development Bank in Abidjan.

My appointment—simultaneously with the U.N. post—as a member of the Graduate Faculty of the New School for Social Research in New York resulted in regular evening teaching and forced me to place my thinking about development into a more systematic framework. The underlying theory of development for my course in the Graduate Faculty was based partly on the importance of infrastructure—which drew on the earlier work of Rosenstein-Rodan and Thomas Balogh—partly on the idea of the need for balanced growth, where I was most influenced by Ragnar Nurkse, and partly on the ideas of Gunnar Myrdal, with his emphasis on cumulative causation and vicious circles. But the main components of my lectures at the New School were international trade problems on which I had concentrated at the United Nations and to which I now turn.

Terms of Trade—Distribution of Gains from Trade and Investment

In retrospect, I can see a number of reasons why I selected the problems of distribution of gains from trade and investment as a principal area of study. When I arrived at the United Nations in 1947, the negotiations for the creation of an International Trade Organization (ITO) were proceeding in Havana. Keynes at Bretton Woods had considered the creation of such an organization to increase and stabilize primary commodity prices; it would have been the third pillar, in addition to the World Bank and the International Monetary Fund (IMF), of the international system he envisaged.[10] As early as 1938, in a paper on "The Policy of Government Storage of Foodstuffs and Raw Materials" delivered in Cambridge to the British Association, Keynes had advocated buffer stocks for primary commodities, and he came back to the idea when he started thinking in 1941 about postwar reconstruction. He shared the idea that primary commodity prices would have a long-run downward trend, and that industrial countries like Britain therefore had nothing to worry about in reducing instability and fluctuations around the trend. James Meade played a big part in helping Keynes develop ideas which "contributed notably to the Charter of the ITO." Keynes's proposals for a Clearing Union (subsequently, the IMF) included the functions of what later became the UNCTAD

10. For Keynes's "newly-found enthusiasm at Bretton Woods for the Commercial Policy side of the international plans," and specifically for the ITO proposals, see R. F. Harrod, *The Life of John Maynard Keynes* (New York: Harcourt, Brace, 1951), p. 620.

Common Fund, that is, financing buffer stocks and "ever-normal granaries."[11] But this British initiative was shelved in 1942, in view of U.S. resistance, to be revived only in the Havana charter for an ITO.

A strong influence among the early colleagues in the United Nations was that of Folke Hilgerdt, the Swedish economist who had already shaped the League of Nations publications on the Network of World Trade. Working with him was Carl Major Wright, a Danish economist who was particularly interested in the relationship of primary commodity prices to trade cycles and economic growth in the industrial countries. Two other staff members in the trade section were Walter Chudson (United States) and Percy Judd (Australia), the latter being very expert in the economics and details of commodity agreements.[12] Discussions with these four must have drawn my attention quickly to problems of terms of trade. It was natural for me to link development work (a new area in the United Nations) with the well-established and much more highly advanced work proceeding in the field of trade analysis. Through Hilgerdt's work and then through Gunnar Myrdal—who had been influenced by his countryman Hilgerdt— I also became familiar with the possibility of backwash effects of conditions in industrial countries, certainly cyclical (Hilgerdt and Wright) but possibly also structural (Myrdal), on the trade of the primary exporting countries, with prices and terms of trade acting as a mechanism of transmission. Even though Raúl Prebisch's terminology of "center" and "periphery" and the phraseology of the "dependency" school were not specifically known to me at that time, the essence of such concepts certainly was in my mind, albeit less articulately.

While mainstream economics concentrated on the problem of allocative efficiency (where comparative advantages ruled supreme), my interest was from the beginning more in the direction of distributive justice, or rather distributive efficiency as I saw it as a follower of Alfred Marshall, R. H. Tawney, and William Beveridge.[13] This reflected a past concern with unemployment and the welfare state, and foreshadowed a future interest in basic needs and problems of children. It seemed to me that to think of

11. Ibid., pp. 531–32, 533, 550. UNCTAD is the acronym for the U.N. Conference on Trade and Development.

12. He was also for many years the secretary of ICCCP, the "Interim" Coordinating Committee on Commodity Problems: Rien ne dure que l'interim!

13. The distinction between allocative efficiency and distributive justice has been clearly made on lines coinciding with my own thinking by Detlef Lorenz, most recently in his "Notes on Unequal Exchange between Developing and Industrialized Countries," *Intereconomics* (January-February 1982), and more fully in "Non-Equivalent Exchange and International Income Distribution," *German Economic Review*, vol. 8, no. 4 (1970), pp. 280–83. Recently I have learned much on "unequal exchange" from my colleague at the Institute of Development Studies, David Evans. Note, however, that my formulation in the "Distribution of Gains" paper "did not question the likelihood of gains all-round from international trade, only the likely distribution of such gains: a compromise between laisser-faire and exploitation."

the distribution of gains in terms of only the amount of labor saved by specialization was to neglect an essential element. The assumption of equal exchange in impartial "fair" markets seemed in conflict with the facts of unequal market and technological power.[14] The dice were loaded against one of the trade partners. As in other such situations, acts of positive discrimination were called for, hence the attempt to create an ITO.

It should also be remembered that the general assumption around 1946–48 was that the Second World War would be followed by a period of recession and unemployment, just as after the First World War, with expected repercussions on primary commodity prices. Here was a basic assumption predisposing one to some degree of pessimism about primary commodity prices in spite of the rise which had taken place during the war and immediately after.

Anticipating some of the subsequent argument, those who were skeptical about the future underlying trend of primary commodity prices from the 1948–49 levels onward can perhaps claim that their projection was a fortiori justified, since it held even though the industrial countries entered into an unprecedented period of twenty-five years of full employment and steady growth. The stagnation and depression of the later 1970s corresponded more to the broad assumption of 1946–48 as to what would happen, at least periodically, in industrial countries; and this certainly had a depressing effect on the terms of trade on non-oil-producing primary product exporters among the developing countries. It should be emphasized, however, that neither in my 1949 U.N. publication on *Relative Prices of Exports and Imports of Underdeveloped Countries* based on U.K. data,[15] nor in my 1949–50 paper in the *American Economic Review*, did I make any specific analysis or assumption on conditions or cycles in the industrial countries. My interest, different from Folke Hilgerdt's and Carl Major Wright's, was in structural differences between the industrial countries exporting manufactures and exporters of primary commodities. The paper suggested that such structural differences between countries and markets would set up a tendency for primary commodity prices to decline relative to those of manufactured goods, and for asymmetrical changes in demand and volume. The effect would be for the benefits from trade and investment to be increasingly unequally distributed between the two groups of countries, more or less regardless of the state of activity in the industrial countries or the coming and going of trade cycles, short-term or Kondratieffs.

The collapse of the attempt to create an ITO and establish anything like a postwar regime of stabilized and controlled commodity prices, let alone a new international currency system based on commodities, was of course

14. The concept of a "dominant country" was developed by François Perroux within a few years of the delivery of the 1949–50 paper, "Distribution of Gains."
15. New York: United Nations, Department of Economic Affairs, no. 1949, II, B.3.

another element predisposing one to pessimism. Perhaps the 1949–50 paper can take some credit for being influenced not unduly by the rise of the preceding ten years[16] and more by the declining trend of the preceding sixty years,[17] and also for treating the 1870–1939 decline as a structural rather than a cyclical (even long-term cyclical) affair.

Arthur Lewis, in his Nobel lecture, with his long-term perspective on growth and fluctuations since 1870, draws attention to two relevant features: that the coefficient linking primary commodity trade with industrial production in the developed countries has consistently been less than unity (he puts it at 0.87); and that the expected favorable cyclical effect on terms of trade of primary exporters from high levels of activities in the developed countries "did not happen this time."[18] Both these statements clearly are in line with my thinking.

My paper did not contain an explicit projection—projections were not as popular or as easily quantified then as now. It was based on the historical analysis on which I had worked in the United Nations during 1947–48 and which was published by the U.N. in 1949[19] *before* the paper for the American Economic Association meeting (December 1949) was written. However, the paper clearly argued that the historical downward trend in terms of trade for primary products from the 1870s to 1939, or even to 1949, was due to general forces and the nature of relations both within and between industrial and developing countries, which could be expected to continue in the absence of major changes (a New International Economic Order as we would now say). Thus the paper was an implicit projection and was generally considered as such. Treated as a projection, one can certainly claim that it has passed the test better than most other economic projections. From 1948 or 1949, when the projection was made, up to 1973, there was a tendency toward further deterioration of the terms of trade of primary products exported by developing countries relative to their manufactured imports. After 1973, of course, a judgment on this projection depends on the treatment of the Organization of Petroleum

16. The paper has a specific subheading, "The False Impression of Recent Changes in Terms of Trade."

17. The subsequent critics of the Prebisch-Singer thesis have to some extent cast doubt on the statistical evidence of the period 1870–1939 or 1870–1949 by attributing the changes in terms of trade to the differential development of international transport costs and international prices FOB. However, this criticism, pronounced particularly by P. T. Ellsworth ("The Terms of Trade between Primary Producing and Industrial Countries," *Inter-American Economics Affairs*, vol. 10, [1956], pp. 47–65), as well as the criticism that quality changes would reverse or obliterate the existing trend have been shown by Spraos to be largely irrelevant. See J. Spraos, "The Statistical Debate on the Net Barter Terms of Trade between Primary Commodities and Manufactures," *Economic Journal*, vol. 90 (March 1980).

18. W. A. Lewis, "The Slowing Down of the Engine of Growth," *American Economic Review* (September 1980), p. 556.

19. *Relative Prices of Exports and Imports of Underdeveloped Countries.*

Exporting Countries (OPEC) and oil. If oil is excluded as a special case,[20] then the projection would hold true up to 1982.[21]

If oil is *not* excluded as a special case, then of course the projection fails to be true. It can rightly be said that the 1949–50 paper failed to anticipate the rise and power of OPEC after 1973. Even on that basis, however, a projection which turns out to be valid for a quarter century still has some claim to be judged as vindicated.

There is another point in defense of the 1949–50 paper. This was meant less as a projection than as a *policy guide*. The developing countries were advised to diversify out of primary exports wherever possible, by development of domestic markets and by industrialization, either import-substituting (ISI) or export-substituting or a combination of both. (Export-substituting industrialization, in 1949, seemed a long way off for the less developed countries (LDCs), so the emphasis was more on ISI.) To the extent that they succeeded, they would escape the consequences of deteriorating terms of trade and lower productivity growth directly for themselves, and perhaps also enable other LDCs to do so. In fact, there was considerable industrialization of LDCs after 1949, especially after 1960. To that extent, even if—or to the extent that—the empirical data do not support the implicit projection (especially as to terms of trade of *countries* as distinct from *commodities*) this does not necessarily invalidate the paper. It can be argued that the actual data incorporate the result of the remedial or compensatory action taken, in line with the 1949–50 paper. We do not know what the data would have been without such action—the deterioration in terms of trade would presumably have been even sharper than it was.

A Restatement

In 1971 I had a chance to "revisit" the 1949–50 paper, putting more emphasis on relations between types of *countries* rather than types of *commodities* (following Charles P. Kindleberger) and on the nature and

20. As is also done by Spraos, "Statistical Debate." Obviously, when oil and OPEC are excluded as a special case, it would also be necessary to exclude the higher oil prices from the import price index of oil-importing primary exporting developing countries, but the above formulation avoids this problem by relating primary product export prices only to manufactured imports, which excludes oil at least directly. Oil prices are included as a cost element in manufactured import prices, and a more refined analysis would have to try to eliminate that element of the rising import prices which is due to rising oil prices (since the latter benefits developing rather than industrial countries). However, a look at the figures will lead to the clear judgment that, even if the effect of higher oil prices is eliminated from increased prices of manufactures imported by developing countries, it would still be true that their terms of trade continued to deteriorate between 1973 and 1982.

21. See the next section below on the empirical trend in the terms of trade.

distribution of technological power.[22] The present occasion seems to call for a restatement in more contemporary terms of the essential points of the paper. I hope that such a restatement will also help to remove some misunderstandings and to answer some of the criticism.

The 1949–50 paper concentrated on the issue of distributive justice or fairness or desirability in sharing out the gains from trade. It did not deny the existence of such gains nor did it claim that deteriorating barter terms of trade are direct evidence of a welfare loss by developing countries. That could have been done only by studying factoral terms of trade, for which the data were not available. The paper did, however, look into productivity trends, and by implication argued that if productivity in manufacturing increases faster than productivity in primary production—surely a justifiable assumption then and now—it must be assumed that the distribution of welfare gains based on double factoral terms of trade (allowing for change in productivity in the production of exports and imports) would a fortiori become even more unequal (unfair, undesirable). Even that, of course, would not mean that no trade would be better than trade, especially if exports of primary products are "vent for surplus" or provide additional employment. Naturally, deteriorating terms of trade mean a welfare loss for the developing countries as compared with a situation in which their terms of trade do not deteriorate while everything else, specifically including export volume and factoral terms of trade, is exactly the same—but that is clearly a hypothetical comparison.

There has been a great deal of discussion about "engines of growth." The Brandt report,[23] with its story of mutual interests and interdependence, is based on the picture that during the 1950s and 1960s the industrial countries were the engine of growth for the LDCs; but it envisaged a future in which these roles might be reversed and the LDCs could serve as an engine of growth for the rest of the world. The 1949–50 paper throws some doubt on the first part of this story. Its implication is that the LDCs, even during the 1950s and 1960s, by providing the industrial countries with steady supplies of primary commodities (and also, I would now add, of simple manufactures and labor), on terms increasingly favorable to the industrial countries, were an engine of growth for the industrial countries throughout the twenty-five "golden years" after the end of the war.[24]

22. "The Distribution of Gains Revisited," paper presented to a Conference at the Institute of Development Studies in Sussex, May 1971, and reprinted as chap. 4 of *The Strategy of International Development*, Sir Alex Cairncross and Mohinder Puri, eds. (London: Macmillan, 1975).

23. Report of the Independent Commission on International Development Issues (Brandt Commission), *North-South: A Programme for Survival* (Cambridge, Mass.: MIT Press, 1980).

24. Not least by enabling them to concentrate on high-technology lines of activity and to consolidate their technological leadership.

The 1949–50 paper is based on a view of commodity markets in which less emphasis is placed on the traditional neoclassical competitive market paradigm and more on bargaining power, financial power, and control of marketing, processing, and distribution. More recently this position of the 1949–50 paper has been shared by Gerald Helleiner in his summary of the result of the Refsnes Seminar. He identifies the competitive market paradigm with "Northern analysis" and the paradigm of the 1949–50 paper with the South, and he continues:

> There is emerging a relevant literature within the Western tradition which, in effect, is at least partially legitimising the Southern approach by applying the tools of empirical analysis to particular commodity markets. These theoretical "bits and pieces" have not yet percolated through either to introductory Western textbooks or to Western economic policy-makers; but their volume may already be great enough to permit the thought that the dominant paradigm may yet shift to that of the South.[25]

In this sense, as well as in that of empirical verification, the original paper may perhaps be claimed to have been vindicated. At any rate, Helleiner states that the Prebisch-Singer analysis represents "another rich area for theoretical exploration." Although he thinks it has not proved "persuasive or rigorous enough to have been incorporated into the central core of trade theory," he does credit it with "an enormous intuitive appeal."[26]

Helleiner also refers to another aspect of my paper. The paper tried to incorporate foreign investment activity—or, in Helleiner's more contemporary language, "transnational corporate activity"—into the model (as was indicated by the very title of my paper). It thus implies a concept of the terms of trade based upon the national retained value from exports rather than conventionally measured prices for export products.

A contemporary version of this may be seen in the statement by A. Maizels:

> With transfer pricing being used as one of a package of instruments designed to maximize the global profits of a TNC, the neo-classical approach to the process of price formation is invalidated. Moreover, the concept of "export value" (usually measured f.o.b.) of commodities shipped from a developing country itself needs to be modified to take account of remittances abroad, e.g., as royalties or management fees to a parent (TNC) which are, in effect, leakages from domestic incomes.

He then adds the following footnote to this quotation: "The alternative

25. "The Refsnes Seminar: Economic Theory and North-South Negotiations," *World Development*, vol. 9, no. 6 (1981), p. 545.
26. Ibid., p. 550.

concept of 'retained value' would thus seem to be more relevant than the usual f.o.b. export value, *especially for analysis of the division of benefit*" (my emphasis).[27] Maizels, like Helleiner, feels that:

> Analysis which focuses solely on shifts in supply and demand, and thus on changes in market prices, will not reveal the underlying relationships between the TNCs and producers in developing countries. For that, it is necessary to place the supply/demand analysis in the context of the structures of control and decision-making which govern the production and trade of a given commodity, and to show how these structures influence the price outcome.[28]

That is precisely what my 1949–50 paper tried to do, although not as explicitly and articulately as Helleiner and Maizels. The original paper mixed together, without clear distinction, elements in the supply/demand analysis (such as Engel's law and low-income elasticity) pointing to deteriorating terms of trade, and elements relating to market structure and technological-financial power. This may have led to misunderstandings and contributed to criticism. With the benefit of hindsight, I should have avoided the use of "terms of trade," with its narrower professional meaning of net barter terms of trade relating to prices only, and used instead "framework of trade" (or perhaps "Terms of trade" with a capital T) or some similar concept. That in fact was the intention in omitting "terms of trade" from the title of the paper and referring instead to "investing and borrowing countries."

To me, the empirical evidence seems convincing, and the intellectual trends indicated by Helleiner and Maizels inevitable. The thesis of deteriorating terms of trade obviously touches raw nerves and rouses strong resistance; hence all the emphasis on the changing quality of manufactures, new commodities, falling transport costs, factoral terms of trade, and so on. To my mind, the study by Spraos, discussed below, has shown convincingly that these difficulties of measurement do not go to the heart of the matter, even empirically.

In the last resort I am quite ready to accept Paul Streeten's conclusion:

> While many of the criticisms of the doctrine that the terms of trade of primary producers steadily deteriorate appear to be damaging, the core of the doctrine may well survive the onslaughts. This core is that in the world economy there are forces at work that make for an uneven distribution of the gains from trade and economic progress generally, so that the lion's share goes to the lions, while the poor lambs are themselves swallowed up in the process.[29]

27. A. Maizels, "A Conceptual Framework for Analysis of Primary Commodity Markets," October 1981, p. 4; processed.

28. Ibid., pp. 24–25.

29. Paul Streeten, *Development Perspectives* (London: Macmillan, 1981), p. 217.

The title of "Distribution of Gains" also indicates that I did not question the basic doctrine of comparative advantages that trade is a positive-sum game resulting in gains to the trading partners. But it did seem to be legitimate to ask further questions as to *who* gains. This then led me in the paper to consider the possibility that in a certain institutional and power set-up the longer-term and dynamic impact on one of the trading partners could be negative, and that at least temporary delinking might be preferable until a better basis for trade with more evenly distributed gains could be developed. That, after all, was no more than an extension of the old infant industry argument into an infant economy argument.

If I may analyze the 1949–50 paper in terms that I did not then use, I would take a dual position:

1. That international trade between primary exporting developing countries and industrial countries is as much a question of power relationships as of classical markets and comparative advantages, and that domestic power relationships within industrial and developing countries are as relevant as power relationships between industrial and developing countries.

2. That the impact of trade of the type prevalent in 1949–50 on developing countries includes not only the "engine of growth" effects emphasized by the classical economists and the theory of comparative advantage, but also potential backwash effects related to a more dynamic concept of comparative advantage; and that such effects on developing countries may under certain conditions offset, or more than offset, any engine of growth effects.

Such backwash effects would be strengthened by a further factor which was not directly discussed in the 1949–50 paper but to which I turned immediately after writing the 1949 U.N. study on *Relative Prices of Exports and Imports* and the 1949–50 paper. This was the chronic instability of primary commodity prices and export proceeds. It was thus natural to follow with the study on *Instability of Export Proceeds of Underdeveloped Countries.*[30]

If trade was not the engine of growth, nor was the foreign investment that went with the development of primary product exports, then what *was* the engine of growth? To that, the two answers to which I was pushed were (1) a shift from primary products to manufactured goods and (2) the development of a system of international aid. A shift to manufactured products was mainly by way of import substitution—the development of manufactured exports (export substitution) by developing countries was difficult to visualize in 1949–50 to the extent in which it actually later happened in the newly industrializing countries. The chief argument for giving priority to industrialization seemed to be the dynamic advantages.

30. New York: United Nations, 1952.

With the benefit of hindsight, however, I would agree that the limits of the ISI strategy were not fully realized. Yet today, when LDCs have become large net food importers, import substitution in the name of rural development and promotion of domestic food production has become very popular and part of the established wisdom—an indication that the objections were perhaps more to industrialization than to import substitution.

Still later in the 1960s, I related these problems more to the power relationships created by technical progress. In the original 1949–50 paper, I emphasized the power relationships *within* the developing countries (which prevented their producers of primary products from appropriating productivity gains)[31] and the different power relationships *within* industrial countries (which enabled producers of manufactured goods to appropriate their productivity gains in the form of higher incomes). The power relationship *between* industrial and developing countries I brought in only through investment (transfer pricing and so on). I was not at that time aware of anything like product cycle trade theories, nor had I then studied the unequal distribution of expenditures on research and development (R&D) as a basis for divergent growth of industrial and developing countries. In my 1971 "revisit" I tried to fill this gap and explain tendencies toward deteriorating terms of trade for primary exporters by linking them to technological leadership. This, in a way, brought me back to the teachings of Schumpeter. At Bonn I had been brought up on his theory of economic development and the idea that quasi-monopolistic profits were made by those producing new and sophisticated goods requiring high technological power. It did not then seem such a big step to translate this idea from internal to international relations and from simple divergencies in GNP growth rates to unequal exchange and changes in terms of trade.

One corollary of this shift in thinking was that the argument for tendencies of terms of trade to decline was widened to include the high-technology manufactured goods exported by industrial countries relative to the simpler manufactured goods exported by developing countries, as well as the primary commodities exported by the two categories of countries. This last view is certainly underlined by the statistics which show that in fact the terms of trade of Third World countries have declined in relation to those of industrial countries, even if the analysis is restricted to trade in manufactured goods only or to primary commodities only.

Empirical Recent Trend of Terms of Trade

The most satisfactory and up-to-date series for our purposes is the index of thirty primary commodities exported by developing countries (excluding gold and petroleum) deflated by the U.N. index of manufactures

31. Soon to be so impressively developed by Arthur Lewis in "Economic Development with Unlimited Supplies of Labour," *Manchester School of Economic and Social Studies* (May 1954).

exported by developed countries, calculated by the IMF Research Department. The latest information goes back to 1957 and brings the story up to February 1982 (see table next page).

Between 1957 and February 1982, the terms of trade of LDC primary exports in relation to developed-country manufactured exports had deteriorated by 32 percent. This deterioration applied to all four major groups of primary commodities: food by 27 percent, beverages by 28 percent, agricultural raw materials by 45 percent, metals by 28 percent. If we take the four-year average 1957–60 as our base figure, the overall deterioration is reduced from 32 percent to 26 percent and the other subindices accordingly. If we compare 1957–60 with 1978–81, the deterioration is still 14 percent. It is difficult to see how in the face of such data there can be any quibbling over what the tendency of terms of trade has been, provided the exclusion of oil is accepted. And do not these remarkably uniform figures for the four groups suggest some common factor at work? This general impression does not exclude the recognition of cyclical factors that complicate the selection of dates for measuring trade: in 1973 and 1974 the terms of trade improved temporarily beyond 1957, and 1977 again came close to doing so. The temporary improvement was quite spectacular for food in 1974 and for beverages in 1977. But the most recent figures for February 1982 are the lowest on record for all commodities together, as well as for food, agricultural materials, and metals (but not beverages) separately—is not this what a trend means? Looking at the full set of 120 annual data for 1957–81, we find that only 20 show an improvement over 1957, 2 show no change, but 98 show a deterioration.

Whether subsequent events have borne out the implicit projection in the 1949–50 paper of a declining trend in terms of trade, either for primary commodity exports of developing countries or for developing countries generally, is a question that has been specifically raised and answered by Professor J. Spraos.[32] Spraos gives the net barter terms of trade between primary products and manufactures since 1950. According to his data based on U.N. statistics, this index of terms of trade deteriorated between 1950 and 1970 from 114 in 1950 to 85 in 1970, a deterioration of 25 percent. It can of course be objected that 1950 was a year in which primary commodity prices were particularly good. To this it could be replied that (1) the Korean war peak of primary commodity prices and terms of trade was in 1951 rather than 1950; (2) the data are based on 1913 = 100, so that the 1970 figure shows a 15 percent deterioration compared with 1913, reversing the improvement which had taken place between 1913 and 1950;[33] and (3) after all, 1950 is the year following the delivery of my paper to the American Economic Association; and (4) in any case, the

32. "Statistical Debate"; see specifically pp. 121–26.
33. The UNCTAD series, although slightly different, tells essentially the same story as the U.N. figures.

Price Indices of Primary Commodities
(1975 = 100)

Year	All commodities[a]		Major groups, deflated[b]			
	Nominal[c]	Deflated[b]	Food	Beverages	Agricultural raw materials	Metals
1957	57	127	90	171	163	131
1958	53	118	84	171	137	123
1959	52	117	85	146	154	121
1960	52	115	83	133	158	121
1961	50	109	79	124	145	119
1962	49	106	80	120	138	115
1963	52	113	96	118	142	114
1964	55	118	90	133	139	139
1965	54	112	82	118	132	149
1966	56	114	81	121	133	157
1967	52	106	81	119	119	132
1968	52	105	79	120	116	137
1969	56	110	82	121	119	145
1970	58	107	82	129	103	145
1971	55	96	78	112	96	118
1972	62	100	83	113	116	109
1973	95	132	110	120	178	137
1974	122	138	144	117	141	140
1975	100	100	100	100	100	100
1976	113	112	81	189	123	105
1977	137	125	72	302	117	104
1978	130	103	71	190	109	95
1979	152	106	71	177	117	109
1980	166	104	86	140	110	108
1981	142	94	79	115	105	99
1982						
Jan.	133	86	66	119	90	95
Feb.	134	86	66	125	90	94

a. Overall index of thirty primary commodities exported by developing countries (excluding gold and crude petroleum).

b. Deflated by the U.N. index of manufactures exported by developed countries.

c. In terms of U.S. dollars.

Source: IMF Survey (April 5, 1982), p. 110.

above statements all remain true, albeit to a reduced extent, if 1948 or 1952–53 are taken as starting points.

Between 1970 and 1977, if petroleum is excluded, there was a further deterioration of 9 percent in the net barter terms of trade between primary products and manufactures.[34] Superimposed on a 26 percent deterioration from 1950 to 1970, this would leave a total deterioration between 1950 and 1977 of 33 percent. If petroleum is included, obviously the picture changes dramatically.

Another series given by Spraos is based on World Bank indicators of market prices of primary products divided by a unit value index of total manufactures exported from developed market economics to developing countries. This indicator shows an even greater deterioration of terms of trade between 1950 and 1970 than the U.N. index based on a comparison of unit values: by 36 percent if petroleum is included, and by 33 percent if petroleum is excluded. However, this particular index based on market prices shows no further deterioration between 1970 and 1977, but rather an improvement by 4 percent (even with oil excluded), so that over the total period 1950–77 the two indicators agree very closely.

Looking at the whole period 1900–70, Spraos finds generally negative trends for the different series but finds them "statistically insignificant." Spraos agrees, however, that "a counter-case [for significant deterioration] could be made" and that anyone finding evidence of persistent deterioration "is entitled to this conclusion."[35] One may add that, even if the individual trends he calculates are statistically insignificant when taken one by one, the fact that they all point in the same direction surely adds significance. At any rate, there is no hint of any sign that terms of trade have improved (always excluding petroleum). Be that as it may, in this paper we are concerned only with the implicit postwar projection from the 1949–50 paper onward, not with the entire 1900–70 period.

On second thought—and with hindsight of the actual fairly rapid shift in the exports of developing countries in the direction of an increasing share of manufactures—the paper should have given warning of the gradual weakening of the export concentration of developing countries on primary commodities. If there was a continuous tendency for the industrial countries to absorb technical progress in the form of higher producer incomes, and specifically wages (while there was no such tendency in the developing countries, and the pressure of surplus labor would prevent a rise in wages), then the natural consequence would be that developing countries could gain comparative advantages in the export of manufactures, especially where technology was simple and/or labor-intensive. In spite of protectionist tendencies in industrial countries, this is of course what has happened. The 1949–50 paper failed to foresee or emphasize

34. Spraos, "Statistical Debate," p. 123, column 5.
35. Ibid., pp. 124 and 125.

this; nor did it foresee that the developing countries would become major net importers of food. Hence the prices of primary commodities relative to those of manufactured goods became less and less suitable as an indicator of the terms of trade of developing countries.

The argument should also have logically led me to project that the terms of trade of the poorer low-income developing countries would deteriorate more than the terms of trade of the higher-income developing countries, which shifted more to the export of manufactured goods. For the low-income developing countries, the arguments for deterioration of terms of trade based on the characteristics of primary commodities would have been added to the arguments based on the characteristics of different countries; while for higher-income developing countries they would go in offsetting directions. This seems to be fully borne out by the data.

This is illustrated by data obtained from UNCTAD.[36] The series runs from 1960 to 1978 and shows that the terms of trade of developing countries with per capita income of under $400 in 1976 have changed distinctly less favorably than those with per capita income of $400–$800, and these in turn less favorably than those with per capita income over $800. Unfortunately, the data are affected by the fact that the better-off groups include the OPEC countries, but we can eliminate this factor by looking at the series from 1960 to 1973 only. We then find that the poorest developing countries (under $400) show a deterioration in terms of trade between 1960 and 1973 of 11 percent; the middle group ($400–$800) shows an improvement of 6 percent, and the better-off group (over $800) shows an improvement of 3 percent. With the benefit of hindsight, the 1949–50 paper should have pinpointed the least developed countries not breaking into manufactures instead of referring to developing countries generally.

The point first made by Charles Kindleberger, that the tendency toward deterioration is more a matter of the characteristics of different countries than of different commodities, is borne out by a comparison of the unit values of primary commodities exported by developing and developed countries respectively. This series based on 1953 = 100 shows that, between 1953 and 1975, with petroleum excluded, the unit values of primary exports of LDCs fell by 27 percent in relation to the unit values of primary commodities exported by developed countries.[37] Similarly, it can be shown that the unit values of manufactures exported by LDCs also deteriorated in relation to those of exports of manufactures from developed countries.

Thus the deterioration of terms of trade of developing countries can be attributed to the combined effects of three factors: the relative deterioration of unit values for primary commodities exported by developing

---

36. UNCTAD *Handbook of International Trade Statistics* (New York, 1978), p. 62.

37. The data for LDCs are drawn from the UNCTAD *Handbook of International Trade Statistics* (1976), p 60; these include, in the Standard International Trade Classification (SITC), 0 + 1 + 2 (except 27) + 4 + 68. The data for developed countries come from the U.N. *Yearbook of International Trade and Statistics*, various issues.

countries in relation to primary export unit values of developed countries; the relative deterioration of manufactured export unit values of developing countries relative to manufactures exported by developed countries; and the lower proportion of manufactures in total exports of LDCs (for which unit values have increased more), and a higher proportion of primary commodities in their exports (for which unit values have increased less). The Kindleberger effect and the Prebisch-Singer effect are both parts of the explanation.

Some Policy Matters

Paul Streeten considers that "the debate over the course of the terms of trade has been shunted onto the wrong track, by disputing the question as to whether they had deteriorated historically. The relevant question is not what are the terms of trade compared with what they were, but what are they compared with what they should and could be." Moreover, Streeten suggests that *direct* action to improve terms of trade by producers' associations is very difficult and that such associations "are notorious for their instability, for the more successful the agreement is in raising the price, the stronger the incentive for individual members to defect."[38]

If such direct action is difficult, we are driven back to other possible alternatives:

Changing the underlying bargaining relations, if not by commodity power, then by countervailing power in other directions, for example, pressure on the multinationals and advances in technological dissemination to obtain lower import prices by more balanced bargaining, more effective procurement, or diversification of sources of imports.

*Emphasizing collective self-reliance by more intra-*LDC *trade and intra-*LDC *investment*. In intra-LDC trade, terms of trade obviously cease to matter for the collective position of LDCs, since one LDC's loss must be another LDC's gain. For agricultural primary commodities (but not metals or manufactures), there has been some progress in reducing the impact of unfavorable relative prices by increased intra-trade, but even in this category the bulk of trade remains between developing and developed countries. The day when intra-trade offers LDCs the same protection against relative price changes as the developed countries now enjoy seems as far distant as ever.

National delinking (autarky/import substitution). This again is not happening. At least up to 1976, exports were still rising faster than GNP even for the low-income LDCs (those with GNP per capita under $300 in 1975); exports were 13.8 percent of their GNP in 1960 and 15.7 percent in 1976. Hence the importance of unfavorable terms of trade for primary

---

38. "Approaches to a New International Economic Order," *World Development*, vol. 10, no. 1 (January 1982), p. 8.

exports has increased rather than diminished.[39] In terms of imports and total trade, the evidence against any national delinking is even stronger.

Export substitution. In this sense a good deal of movement has occurred, both in shifting exports of primary commodities to more highly processed stages, and also in shifting altogether to exports of manufactured goods not based on domestic primary production (or at least not replacing primary exports). Manufactured exports from the LDCs in 1979 offset over 25 percent of their manufactured imports, as compared with only 11 percent in 1963. This certainly is a major change that reduces the incidence of unfavorable relative prices of primary exports. It is, however, subject to four major qualifications.

First, the shift was only partial, greatly affecting the medium-income countries and the newly industrializing countries, but much less the low-income countries. Even in the least developed countries, however, the share of manufactured exports to total exports has risen, although less than in other developing countries. The share of processed and manufactured goods in their total exports increased from 12 percent in 1964 to 18 percent in 1977. In exports of food and beverages, the processed share remained at 10 percent from 1964 to 1977, but for industrial materials it increased from 7 percent in 1964 to 14 percent in 1977.[40] However, all these percentages are too small to modify significantly the impact of falling relative prices of primary commodities.

Second, even with the shift to processed and manufactured exports the terms of trade problem did not disappear, although it shifted from factors relating to commodities to factors relating to countries (the Kindleberger case).

Third, further shifts to manufactured exports are threatened by recession and protectionism in developed countries.

The fourth major qualification is that it is a fallacy of composition to assume that what is possible for one or some of the LDCs or newly industrializing countries can work if all, or the great majority, of developing countries seek to pursue export substitution (export-led growth) at the same time. A recent analysis has concluded, on the basis of a simulation exercise, that "generalisation of the East Asian model of export-led development would result in untenable market penetration into industrial countries . . . from approximately one sixth to approximately three fifths of their manufactured imports." The analysis concludes that protectionist response would be inevitable, and hence "it is seriously misleading to hold up the East-Asian G-4 [Gang of Four] as a model for development because that model almost certainly cannot be generalised without provoking protectionist response ruling out its implementation."[41]

39. Ibid., p. 1, notes 8 and 4.

40. United Nations Industrial Development Organization (UNIDO), *A Statistical Review of the World Industrial Situation* (Vienna, 1981), p. 12.

41. William R. Cline: "Can the East Asian Model of Development Be Generalised?" *World Development*, vol. 10, no. 2 (February 1982), pp. 88 and 89.

Volume increase. A fifth possible policy response to deteriorating barter terms of trade is to increase the *volume* of trade in primary commodities so as to obtain better income terms of trade (export revenue divided by import prices) and maintain import capacity. This is also a form of export substitution, except that it is not accompanied by diversification into processed products of other manufactures. The fallacy of composition applies here, too. An individual country can protect itself against declining terms of trade in primary products by increasing its world market share in the primary product concerned, but if all exporters of the product tried to do this simultaneously they would only succeed in driving the price even lower.

In any case, the quantum of primary exports from LDCs has in fact increased *less* than the quantum of exports—or even of primary exports—of developed countries. Between 1959 and 1970 the quantum of primary LDC exports (excluding oil) increased by 74 percent, but that of developed countries by 152 percent—more than twice as fast. Thus the *relative* deterioration of income terms of trade has been even more rapid than that of the net barter terms of trade. (The absolute income terms of trade, on the usual definition equating them with import capacity, have improved, of course.) International trade has been a better engine of growth for the developed countries than for the LDCs.[42]

Even in overall terms, and in spite of the group of fast-growing LDC exporters of manufactures, the volume lag of LDCs is clear. Between 1948 and 1970, world trade volume (excluding socialist countries and largely indicative of developed-country trade) increased by 7.3 percent a year, but the export volume of LDCs by only 5.3 percent. In the decade 1970–80 the figures are 5.8 percent and 3.1 percent respectively. For the least developed countries, typically primary exporters, the respective growth rates were only 4.4 percent and a dismal −0.4 percent for 1960–70.[43] At least in this relative sense, volume changes have increased any gap created by the worsening terms of trade, and in that sense trade pessimism has not been proved wrong.

The rapid decline in the prices of primary commodities exported by developing countries relative to the manufactured goods imported by them during the early 1980s has been dramatic. The main factor has been the depression or slow growth of the industrial countries; the elasticity of commodity prices in response to changes in world industry production seems to have sharply increased during the past decade.[44]

42. There is, however, the well-known qualification that, insofar as the growth of developed-country trade is largely due to trade with other developed countries—much of it within the same product with only minor differences—the benefit to the developed countries is less than the quantum figures would suggest.

43. The figures are based on the UNCTAD *Trade and Development Report, 1982*, pp. 26 and 38.

44. See "Commodity Prices in the 1970s," *Bank of England Quarterly Bulletin*, vol. 21, no. 1 (March 1981), p. 47. According to the calculations based on the Bank of

Aid Not Trade?

I have listed five possible policy reactions to worsening terms of trade. This leaves the sixth alternative, that is, to compensate for declining terms of trade (and lagging import capacity) by financial transfers. These can be in the form of investments by multinational corporations, bank lending, or official development assistance (ODA).[45] To rely on multinational investments runs the risk of introducing cumulative elements into trade imbalances, if transfer pricing, export restrictions, lack of local training and local capacity for R&D (research and development of products), and repatriation of profits (including profits on locally raised funds) are not controlled by codes of conduct, countervailing power, or enlightened policies. The cumulative factor arises when trade imbalance makes the resources of multinationals attractive, but multinational activities may then contribute to new trade imbalances (most clearly in the case of transfer pricing that directly affects terms of trade). Bank lending leads to indebtedness; the recent rise in indebtedness of LDCs means that some 20–25 percent of export earnings is not available for imports. This is equivalent to declining terms of trade.[46] Hence bank lending, like direct foreign investment, when considered as a remedy for poor terms of trade can be self-defeating; both postpone the problem at the expense of intensifying it.

This leaves ODA, or aid, which was in fact the natural avenue to which the interest of the United Nations, and my own with it, turned in those years as a result of trade pessimism. Hence the idea of the need for soft financing for development was born and developed at the same time as the work on terms of trade, and with a clear intellectual link between the two. It is difficult to realize today how revolutionary, indeed subversive, this idea was considered at the time.[47] The near-commercial operations of the

---

England's model, the short-run elasticity of commodity prices in response to changes in world industrial production has increased from 0.39 in 1957–69 to 3.08 in 1970–79. The long-run elasticity has increased from 2.18 in 1957–69 to 4.34 in 1970–79. This increased elasticity also applies to the three categories of primary commodities taken separately: metals, agriculture, and raw materials and foodstuffs.

45. ODA would include direct compensation for insufficient export proceeds, such as the IMF compensatory facility, the newly added food financing facility, and the export earnings stabilization scheme (STABEX system) under the Lomé convention between the European Economic Community (EEC) and ACP countries (Africa, Caribbean, and Pacific).

46. Future calculations of income terms of trade might well be based on export earnings *minus* debt payments.

47. The word "subversive" in this context has a very direct meaning—those were the days of the Hiss trial and the McCarthy committee. Those advocating soft aid for developing countries, specially when suggesting this be done under U.N. auspices, were

World Bank (minus IDA then, of course) were the most that could be permitted, and that only because they came from a respectable, firmly Western-controlled banking institution. By contrast, the United Nations appeared as a hotbed of irresponsible wild men, radical utopians who could at most be entrusted with minor extensions and offshoots from the technical assistance work announced in January 1949 as Point Four in President Truman's inaugural speech. The official policy was "Trade Not Aid" (although in practice the opponents of aid were often opposed to trade liberalization and the proponents of trade liberalization were in favor of aid).[48]

The attempt to create a major soft aid mechanism within the United Nations—unsuccessful in the main—centered around the proposal for SUNFED, the Special United Nations Fund for Economic Development. The story begins in 1949—the same year as the paper on "Distribution of Gains" was presented to the American Economic Association—and seemed to have ended in the late 1950s with the almost simultaneous establishment of IDA and the U.N. Special Fund (the main component[49] of what is now the United Nations Development Programme [UNDP]). Quite recently, however, the proposal has been prominently revived by the Brandt Commission and placed once again on the international agenda.

The story which ended with IDA and UNDP can be described as a battle of acronyms.[50] In 1949, it started with UNEDA (United Nations Economic Development Administration). This was the proposal by V. K. R. V. Rao in his capacity as chairman of the U.N. Sub-Commission for Economic Development, the body which I served as a member of the Development Section of the secretariat (which even by that time had hardly more than a half dozen professionals). The proposal was made during the third session of the subcommission (1949), although I seem to remember a tossing-about of similar ideas during the earlier sessions. Since no quick unanimous support in the subcommission seemed attainable, Rao submitted this as his personal proposal, appended to the report of the subcommission; it was also reproduced in a simultaneous secretariat report on *Methods of Financing Economic Development in Under-developed*

---

often treated as outcasts and out to weaken the Free World. Because of its association with aid and its suggestion of unequal exchange, trade pessimism alone was often enough to put you in the "subversive" category.

48. Senator Taft, when asked what he thought of the policy of "Trade Not Aid," is said to have replied: "I agree with the second part of it." Si no e vero e ben trovato!

49. The other was the Expanded Technical Assistance Programme (ETAP).

50. In presenting the story, I have the advantage of leaning on the account given by John G. Hadwen and Johan Kaufmann, *How United Nations Decisions Are Made* (Leyden: A. W. Sythoff, 1960), especially chap. 5, "The Story of SUNFED and the Special Fund." Another good account, although more from a Bank perspective, is in Edward S. Mason and Robert E. Asher, *The World Bank since Bretton Woods* (Washington, D.C.: Brookings Institution, 1973).

Countries[51] for the U.N. Economic and Social Council (ECOSOC). The UNEDA proposal combined the technical assistance element leading to ETAP, SUNFED, and UNDP with proposals for soft financing for "schemes of development which cannot be financed from the country's own resources and for which loans cannot be asked on strict business principles." Special emphasis was laid on financing regional projects which seemed particularly suitable for multilateral financing under U.N. auspices. The Indus River Basin problem arising from the separation of India and Pakistan was then much in our minds as a prototype of such regional projects.

The ETAP part of UNEDA was already on the cards in 1949. But the financing part predictably made heavy weather with ECOSOC and less so with the General Assembly. In the time-honored U.N. fashion—by no means limited to the United Nations—the divisions were temporarily resolved by asking for more secretariat studies. In this way, the Rao initiative was kept alive. Thus it was that my own work, subsequent to the studies on terms of trade, turned toward the problems of soft financing for development—an issue which remained a lively center of debate and (often vicious) controversy for the next decade. The leading protagonists of a new soft aid U.N. agency were then India, Rao's home country, Chile, and Yugoslavia.[52] (The outlines of the nonaligned movement were beginning to emerge.) I would say that if anybody deserves the title of grandfathers of IDA, it would be V. K. R. V. Rao and Hernan Santa Cruz—but that may not be orthodox World Bank history!

The United States and United Kingdom from the beginning of the debate in 1949 combined hostility to soft financing with hostility to the idea of a rival to the World Bank. In the latter respect they were presumably strongly backed by the management of the World Bank, and at least ostensibly also in the opposition to the general principle of soft loan finance. To what extent the Bank's opposition to a new soft financing agency (voiced consistently in succeeding years by Eugene Black in his appearances before ECOSOC and elsewhere) was one of conviction or of political tactics is difficult for me to say. It was certainly good political tactics: the cause of soft financing at that point must have seemed hopeless, even dangerous. In the early 1950s the Korean commodity boom and the rising foreign exchange reserves of the LDCs made the cause even more implausible—the 1949–50 paper and the 1948 U.N. study did not look exactly convincing at that moment. In any case, the World Bank could be confident that if the prospects should change, the new agency would come to the World Bank, not the United Nations—certainly some of us in the United Nations never had any illusions on this. So it fell to us in the U.N.

51. Document E/1333/Rev. 1, no. 1949.II (New York: United Nations, 1949).

52. Through their economic representatives, Hernan Santa Cruz for Chile and Leo Mates and Janos Stanovnik for Yugoslavia, the latter now executive director of the U.N. Economic Commission for Europe (ECE).

secretariat to play the role of the "radical," "politically naive," "amateur-ish," "inexperienced" "utopians," but in the event we kept the cause alive until it became acceptable, when it was time for the "responsible," "pragmatic," "experienced," "professional," "well-tried" institution to move in and take over. Mason and Asher not only repeatedly and gener-ously credit the SUNFED movement with preparing the ground for IDA,[53] but they go further in attributing to the wild men in the United Nations the function of frightening the conservative donors sufficiently to look to IDA as a welcome escape from less welcome schemes. Mason and Asher also specifically credit this situation with the earlier establishment of the Inter-national Finance Corporation (IFC).[54] Escott Reid, in fact, suggests that "some of the more sophisticated leaders of poorer countries" deliberately put on the pressure for SUNFED in order to induce the rich countries "to counter this pressure by supporting the creation of a soft-loan affiliate of the World Bank and by providing it with ever-increasing financial resources."[55]

I was and am quite satisfied with this distribution of roles as "fall guys" for Eugene Black and IDA and happy with the respectability acquired by the idea of soft multilateral financing—all the more so since the United Nations got a valuable consolation prize in the form of the Special Fund, a prize made even more valuable because it brought Paul Hoffman in as managing director. I was in charge of the preparatory work for the Special Fund until his arrival. That was the beginning of an unclouded rela-tionship, with unlimited admiration and support on my part.[56] I was always conscious of the link with the Marshall Plan (however precarious) that working with Paul Hoffman provided. The fact that Arthur Lewis came as his deputy and David Owen became his associate administrator when the UNDP was formed was almost too much of a good thing; I felt thoroughly enthusiastic about this addition to the U.N. family.

But I am running ahead of my story. In 1949 the U.S. and U.K. argument that the World Bank was an "experienced," "well-established" develop-ment agency whereas a new U.N. agency would be new and untried was

53. *The World Bank since Bretton Woods*, pp. 347–49; p. 380 on the "persistent peaceful pressure" in the United Nations; p. 386 on how IDA "offset the urge for SUNFED"; on p. 592 they state: "The General Assembly and ECOSOC were severely critical of the Bank during the first post-war decade, but in the process helped to create a climate suitable for the establishment of the IFC and IDA as affiliates of the Bank."

54. Ibid., p. 347: UNEDA and SUNFED "were so repugnant to conservative Secretaries of the U.S. Treasury that, by comparison, the notion of an IFC came in time to seem positively attractive."

55. Escott Reid, *Strengthening the World Bank* (Chicago: Adlai Stevenson Institute, 1973), p. 134.

56. I should make it clear that I did not join the staff of the Special Fund but remained in the Department of Economic Affairs. I did, however, undertake a number of assignments for the Special Fund/UNDP, especially the establishment of the first country program, for Kenya.

not in fact particularly convincing. The World Bank then had little experience in development matters, as distinct from reconstruction. Ten years later when the United States and United Kingdom abandoned their opposition to the principle of soft financing, the case for relying on the experience of the Bank had, of course, become much stronger. So the objection to a new U.N. agency was sustained, and Eugene Black could make his "180 degree shift" in favor of soft loan financing.[57] When the objection to soft financing was dropped, the argument for it was first strongly linked with the concept of infrastructure or "non-self-liquidating" projects, necessary to make agricultural and industrial investment productive though not themselves directly productive. For some time, the hope was that a special financing agency for infrastructural investment would be accepted, but this idea never took off.

In 1951 there came weighty support for the UNEDA idea from the expert group submitting a U.N. report on *Measures for the Economic Development of Under-Developed Countries*.[58] This group was a forerunner of the Pearson and Brandt commissions in the wide scope of its terms of reference. In fact, at this point UNEDA became IDA (International Development Authority, not "Association" as in the later World Bank IDA). This U.N. version of IDA was to distribute "grants-in-aid for specific purposes" and to verify their proper utilization. The 1951 group also proposed a target of $1 billion annually for intensified lending by the World Bank, this target to be reached within five years. Thus the 1951 report, while proposing a new U.N. agency, was anxious to avoid any impression of competition or substitution between the World Bank and the new Authority. But this was not enough to overcome the objections of the main donors at the 1951 ECOSOC and General Assembly, although a majority vote of the General Assembly asked for studies on the detailed plan which would govern the detailed rules and operations of a new "special fund." This then became the origin of the Special Fund, although the latter had quite different functions. As often in the United Nations, the label survived even if the substance did not. UNEDA had become IDA and then became the Special Fund, soon to become SUNFED. My own work for the next few years centered on preparing reports on the Special Fund and working with the various rapporteurs, committees, groups, and bodies concerned with the Special Fund.

SUNFED made its appearance in 1953 in the title of the report of the "Committee of nine distinguished persons."[59] Since the word SUNFED became a highly emotionally charged battle cry and since the "initials had

---

57. Mason and Asher, *The World Bank since Bretton Woods*, p. 383.
58. Document E/1986, no. 1951.II.B.2 (New York: United Nations, 1951).
59. *Report on a Special United Nations Fund for Economic Development*, document E/2381, no. 1953.II.B.1 (New York: United Nations, 1953).

some appeal" and "played a significant part in the debates which followed,"[60] perhaps a minor footnote to the history of the initials may be permitted. The subject of the report was originally called the "United Nations Fund for Economic Development." It was only shortly before translation and printing was due that it was realized (I believe by me) that the initials of this new animal would read UNFED. That was too close to the truth and would no doubt be used by critics (including the World Bank) to discredit and ridicule the whole idea. So at the last minute it was decided to come back to the "special fund" (in the lower case) on which the general resolution of 1951 had requested studies. Thus "Special" was rapidly prefixed, and UNFED became SUNFED. SUNFED seemed to have a nice science-fiction flavor (or perhaps we would today call it an environmental flavor). The opponents of the proposal used this science-fiction association to criticize the proposal for its starry-eyed absence of anything down-to-earth. Perhaps it would have been better to stick to UNFED, thus proclaiming ourselves as realists!

Subsequently in 1953–55 the negotiations, at the specific request of the General Assembly, became largely the responsibility of M. Raymond Scheyven of Belgium, at that time the president of ECOSOC. I continued to work under his direction and that of various ad hoc bodies looking into specific aspects. One aspect was the financing of SUNFED by savings from disarmament—a proposal renewed twenty-five years later by the Brandt Commission. During this period, the Nordic countries and the Netherlands emerged as supporters of SUNFED, establishing a special position friendly to that of the LDCs which they have maintained ever since. It was also in casting around for possible financing for SUNFED that I became very interested in 1954 in the establishment, under Public Law 480, of the U.S. food aid program and in the possibility of an international food aid program which had begun to emerge in Rome.[61] This interest led to my involvement in laying the ground for the U.N./FAO World Food Programme,[62] and it has remained an active interest.

After several years of delaying action and play-acting—too tedious to report in detail but essential to keep the idea alive—a stage was finally reached in 1956 when a statute for SUNFED was to be drafted by a

60. Hadwen and Kaufmann, *How United Nations Decisions Are Made*, p. 90.

61. Probably first in the minds of S. R. Sen, then director-general of the FAO, and Mordecai Ezekiel, his economic adviser. I believe Thomas Balogh (Lord Balogh) was also involved. There was also a direct link with the local counterpart funds arising from P.L. 480 and the financing of IDA. See Mason and Asher, *The World Bank since Bretton Woods*, pp. 381–87.

62. As chairman of the committee which prepared the report "Development through Food." V. K. R. V. Rao, the originator of the UNEDA proposal, was a member of this committee, thus further emphasizing the link between food aid and the soft financing movement.

governmental committee under the chairmanship of U Thant (then Burmese delegate to the United Nations, soon to become secretary general[63]—a treasured relationship for me. Once matters had reached this stage, some kind of action became inevitable, and the little groups of SUNFED activists for the first time felt that all our efforts, and all the abuse, over eight years or so had not been totally in vain. The return for the United Nations itself began to emerge clearly at that time when, as a compromise solution, the financing of project studies and analysis, natural resource surveys, and pilot projects was proposed and accepted. The decisive break was the proposal by Paul Hoffman in 1957 (in an article in the *New York Times Magazine*) proposing a U.N. experimental fund of $100 million for surveys of natural resources and pilot projects. This represented an emphasis on the borderland between technical assistance and investment, and on this basis I helped develop the concept of pre-investment activities (in a paper entitled: "An Example of the New Pragmatism: Toward a Theory of Pre-investment").[64] There were some analogies to the infrastructure concept: just as the development of infrastructure is a precondition for agricultural and industrial activities, so pre-investment activities are necessary for any form of investment, including investment in infrastructure. This proposal by Paul Hoffman was readily acceptable to both the proponents and opponents of SUNFED, and both camps could hail it as a victory. In fact, it was more a victory for the opponents. Mason and Asher, with some justification, described the blowing-up of the pre-investment function as "a mystique well beyond its intrinsic importance in the investment process."[65] However, I would argue that from the point of view of the United Nations rather than the World Bank it was a politically necessary and useful "mystique." That the United Nations should emerge with the minor prize was inevitable, given the distribution of political support. The proponents obtained the terminological satisfaction of preserving the blessed name of Special Fund for the new mechanism, and they could save face by maintaining that the Special Fund was a step toward SUNFED.[66] Shortly they would obtain the more substantive satisfaction of seeing the principle of multilateral soft loan financing accepted, although not under the umbrella of the United Nations. The day came when this was no longer "unpractical" but became "responsible." Apparently, what had been

63. *Final Report of the Ad Hoc Committee on the Question of the Establishment of a Special United Nations Fund for Economic Development*, General Assembly document A/3579 and Add.1 (New York: United Nations, 1957). Johan Kaufmann was the rapporteur of this committee.

64. Reprinted as chap. 2 in H. W. Singer, *International Development: Growth and Change* (New York: McGraw-Hill, 1964). Not surprisingly, Paul Hoffman picked this chapter out in his introduction to the book.

65. *The World Bank since Bretton Woods*, p. 592.

66. In fact, on paper this was the case since a U.N. Capital Development Fund was set up.

"unpractical" had never been the principle, but the machinery proposed—though this was not how the matter was put in earlier years. All's well that ends well? Let us hope that both IDA and the UNDP will survive and grow to give a positive answer to that question.

It would be nice to end on such a happy note, but if I am honest, as an autobiographer should be, I cannot suppress one slightly sour postscript. I have already noted the full—and in my mind correct—emphasis given to the SUNFED pressure in the history of IDA (and IFC) by Mason and Asher in their *World Bank since Bretton Woods*. But when Dag Hammarskjöld, presumably with the U.N. role in creating IDA in mind, asked Eugene Black for a "special institutional link" between the IDA and the United Nations, "President Black politely but firmly rejected this suggestion."[67] A pity. That could have been the perfect happy ending. Although Eugene Black acknowledged in his reply that "clearly the creation of the IDA will intensify the need for close cooperation at the working level," the liaison committee established as a result, in the laconic words of Mason and Asher, "is now inactive." Need I add that since these words were printed (in 1973) this committee has remained inactive? So SUNFED/IDA did not really bring the United Nations and the World Bank together. And now an old pioneer's memory nerves twitch when he sees the Brandt Commission (Mr. McNamara's own brainchild) propose a World Development Fund—over the objections of the World Bank. Perhaps the threat of the World Development Fund will once again serve to rescue the ailing IDA? Or will there be other "180 degree shifts"? No projections are ventured.

67. All quotations in this paragraph are from Mason and Asher, *The World Bank since Bretton Woods*, p. 569.

Comment

Bela Balassa

DR. SINGER'S BEST-KNOWN PAPER is "The Distribution of Gains between Investing and Borrowing Countries," presented at the December 1949 meeting of the American Economic Association and published in the *American Economic Review* of May 1950. The paper has been reprinted in practically all readings volumes on economic development and has been read by an untold number of students. It has also led to the pairing of Singer's name with that of Raúl Prebisch, in referring to the Prebisch-Singer thesis on the alleged tendency for the secular decline of the terms of trade of the developing countries. The terms of trade issue was central to Singer's 1950 article as it is to his present paper.

Singer suggests that "treated as a projection, one can certainly claim that [the historical downward trend in terms of trade for primary products exported by developing countries] has passed the test better than most other economic projections." He further submits that "the terms of trade of Third World countries have declined in relation to those of industrial countries, even if the analysis is restricted to trade in manufactured goods only or to primary commodities only." These differences are said to be reinforced by "the lower proportion of manufactures in total exports of LDCS (for which unit values have increased more), and a higher proportion of primary commodities in their exports (for which unit values have increased less)," with the extent of the deterioration of the terms of trade being greater at lower levels of development. I will submit these propositions to scrutiny.

The first question relates to the choice of the time period. Singer states that "in this paper we are concerned only with the implicit postwar projection from the 1949–50 paper onward, not with the entire 1900–70 period." At the same time, results for a relatively short period are affected to a considerable extent by the choice of the initial and the terminal years. In the present case, the choice of the initial year introduces a bias as, in conforming to the old adage "what goes up, will come down," primary

Bela Balassa is Professor of Political Economy at Johns Hopkins University and consultant to the World Bank.

product prices could not have remained at the lofty levels reached during the early 1950s, the period of the Korean war. At any rate, just as Prebisch has done, in his original article Singer considered long-term tendencies; hence, in judging the validity of the proposition, data for a longer period would be needed.

The only terms of trade estimates pertaining to a longer period that Singer cites are those reported by Spraos for 1900–70. According to Singer, "even if the individual trends [Spraos] calculates are statistically insignificant when taken one by one, the fact that they all point in the same direction surely adds significance." However, the individual results do *not* point in the same direction. The trend coefficient derived by the use of the U.N. index is positive, representing a terms of trade improvement for the developing countries; a negative result is obtained only if the U.N. index is spliced to the World Bank's index for the postwar period. We thus have a positive and a negative result, neither of them statistically significant, which hardly establishes a trend.[1]

The U.N. statistics utilized by Spraos uniformly employ unit value indices.[2] Yet, as a succession of writers have pointed out, changes in *unit values* do not appropriately represent changes in *prices*, and lead in particular to an overestimation of increases in the prices of manufactured exports. This is hardly surprising if we consider that, for example, the unit value of machinery is measured as the ratio of value to weight, so that a shift toward lighter materials ipso facto raises unit values.

Singer dismisses these objections, claiming that Spraos "has shown convincingly that these difficulties of measurement do not go to the heart of the matter, even empirically." In so doing, Singer—as well as Spraos— have overlooked the monumental work of Kravis and Lipsey, who painstakingly collected price observations for the exports of metal products by the United States, the United Kingdom, the Federal Republic of Germany, and Japan. The export price indices derived from the data show a 13 percent average increase in the prices of machinery and transport equipment between 1953 and 1964, compared with a 24 percent rise in the U.N. unit value index for the same product categories.[3]

Kravis and Lipsey have subsequently extended the country, commodity,

1. J. Spraos, "The Statistical Debate on the Net Barter Terms of Trade between Primary Commodities and Manufactures," *Economic Journal*, vol. 90 (March 1980), table 2. Spraos notes that combining the U.N. index with the one constructed by Yates for the 1913–53 period would give rise to an upward adjustment in the prices of manufactured goods, but this index has a low level of reliability and using the calculations made by Maizels would involve a downward adjustment of the same order of magnitude (ibid., pp. 124–25).

2. The World Bank utilized a unit value index for manufactured goods and a price index for primary products.

3. Irving B. Kravis and Robert E. Lipsey, *Price Competitiveness in World Trade* (New York: National Bureau of Economic Research, 1971), table 8.8.

and time coverage of their investigation and have estimated a price index for manufactured goods exported by the developed countries to the developing countries. The index shows a 127 percent increase between 1953 and 1977, the time period covered by the estimates, compared with a rise of 162 percent in the U.N. unit value index for these exports. Deflating by the U.N. price index for the world exports of primary products other than petroleum, the authors find that the terms of trade of manufactured goods exported by the developed to the developing countries, relative to the prices of nonfuel primary products, declined by 6 percent during the period. This compares with an increase of 13 percent estimated from the U.N. unit value indices for manufactured goods and for food and raw materials.[4]

I have adjusted the Kravis-Lipsey estimates by replacing the U.N. price index for the world exports of primary commodities other than petroleum by the price index estimated by the World Bank for thirty-three nonfuel primary commodities, weighted by the exports of the developing countries. The index shows an average price increase of 154 percent for these primary products between 1953 and 1977 compared with an increase of 145 percent in the U.N. index.

Utilizing the World Bank's index, then, we observe a decline of 10 percent in the terms of trade of the developed countries in their exchange of manufactured goods for primary products other than fuels with the developing countries during the 1953–77 period. An even larger decline is shown if adjustment is made for quality change. In the case of the United States, where Kravis and Lipsey made such estimates, a 105 percent rise in the unadjusted price index for machinery and transport equipment in 1953–76 gives place to a 77 percent increase in the adjusted index—a downward adjustment of 14 percent.[5]

The comparison of the U.N. and the World Bank indices points to the conclusion that the prices of nonfuel primary products exported by the developing countries rose more rapidly than average world primary product prices during the period under consideration. This conclusion is confirmed by Michaely's estimates that show unit value indices for primary products exported by low-income countries to have risen by 27 percent between 1952 and 1970, compared with an increase of 10 percent for primary products exported by high-income countries. Michaely's results further show a 27 percent improvement in the terms of trade for primary

4. Irving B. Kravis and Robert E. Lipsey, *Prices and Terms of Trade for Developed-Country Exports of Manufactured Goods*, National Bureau of Economic Research Working Paper no. 774 (Cambridge, Mass., September 1981), tables 1, 5, and 6.

5. Bela Balassa, *Adjustment to External Shocks in Developing Economies*, World Bank Staff Working Paper no. 472 (Washington, D.C., July 1981), table 3.

products in the case of low-income countries, compared with a 23 percent deterioration for high-income countries, during the period.[6]

The unit values of manufactured goods exported by low-income countries also increased more rapidly (45 percent) than those exported by high-income countries (19 percent) between 1952 and 1970. In the same period, the terms of trade for manufactured goods improved by 14 percent in low-income countries and deteriorated by 12 percent in high-income countries.

For all merchandise trade taken together, Michaely has observed an improvement of 19 percent in the terms of trade for the low-income countries, and a deterioration of 15 percent for the high-income countries, during the 1952–70 period. He has further established that terms of trade changes are negatively correlated with income levels in a fivefold classification scheme: the changes between 1952 and 1970 were -26, -11, -8, $+11$, and $+47$ percent as one moves from the top to the bottom quintile.[7]

Michaely's results thus reinforce the findings of Kravis and Lipsey and indicate that the developing countries have improved their terms of trade relative to the developed countries in the post-Korean war period. It is further observed that primary and manufactured commodities exported by the developing countries increased more in price than goods in the same categories exported by the developed countries and that improvements in the terms of trade were inversely correlated with the level of economic development.

These results pertain to the post-Korean war period, for which Kravis and Lipsey have collected price observations. Although the period is relatively short, it begins with high primary product prices, as noted above. Kravis and Lipsey have further calculated changes in the terms of trade between "Industrial Europe" and the developing countries, by replacing the world export unit value indices of the United Nations with unit value indices for the manufactured exports of Industrial Europe to the developing countries and for the primary imports of Industrial Europe from these countries in the 1872–1953 period.

The results show no change in the terms of trade of Industrial Europe relative to the developing countries between 1872 and 1953.[8] In view of

---

6. More exactly, the calculations pertain to price changes for goods classified by income level, when the income level of exports (imports) is derived as an income-weighted average of exports by individual countries. The cited results refer to data for the lower half and the upper half of the distribution. The relevant formulas are provided in Michael Michaely, "The Terms of Trade between Poor and Rich Nations," in *Trade, Income Levels, and Dependence* (Amsterdam: North-Holland, forthcoming).

7. Ibid., table 2.

8. Kravis and Lipsey, *Prices and Terms of Trade for Developed-Country Exports of Manufactured Goods*, table 7.

the upward bias of the unit value indices for manufactured goods, it follows that the use of price indices would show a deterioration in the terms of trade of Industrial Europe, and an improvement in the terms of trade of the developing countries, during this period.

The cited estimates effectively refute the Prebisch-Singer thesis on the alleged tendency for the secular deterioration of the terms of trade of the developing countries. This is not to say that particular countries may not experience a deterioration in their terms of trade. Thus, the oil-importing developing countries have suffered as a result of the tenfold rise of petroleum prices since 1973.

But how about the choice of appropriate policies for the developing countries? Singer suggests "in defense of the 1949–50 paper [that] this was meant much less as a projection than as a *policy guide*. The developing countries were advised to diversify out of primary exports wherever possible, by development of domestic markets and by industrialization, either import-substituting (ISI) or export-substituting or a combination of both." One finds no prescription for export expansion in the 1949–50 article or in any of the contributions to the Prebisch-Singer thesis, however. Rather, the prescription—widely cited in the literature—called for introducing an anti-export bias in the system of incentives, with a view to improving the terms of trade of the developing countries and accelerating their economic growth.

This policy prescription failed to consider that, apart from petroleum, there are few commodities whose prices the developing countries could increase and thereby reduce the volume of their exports. Even in the case of tropical beverages, for which such action may be effective, repeated attempts made by the producing countries have not led to an agreement by reason of their different economic interests.

In regard to the large majority of primary commodities, the anti-export policies applied have led to a decline in the world market shares of the developing countries. Singer takes note of this decline, claiming that "volume changes have increased any gap created by the worsening terms of trade, and in that sense trade pessimism has not been proved wrong," without recognizing that it was the policies many developing countries followed in application of the Prebisch-Singer prescription that led to such a result. He also resurrects the old shibboleth about the possible adverse effects of trade on economic growth in the developing countries. Theoretical considerations as well as the evidence of the last quarter of the century indicate, however, that it is anti-export policies that have adverse effects on economic growth.

Johnson has shown that, in countries that are price-takers in world markets, the protection of the capital-intensive industrial sector under incomplete specialization may lead to immiserization in the event that the rate of capital accumulation exceeds the rate of growth of the labor force.[9] This possibility becomes a certainty if foreign capital is invested in the protected industry and it receives the full (untaxed) value of its marginal product at protection-distorted prices.[10]

It has further been observed that export expansion and economic growth in the developing countries are positively correlated. This was the case in the pre-1973 period, characterized by the rapid expansion of world trade, as well as in the post-1973 period, characterized by external shocks in the form of the quadrupling of petroleum prices and the world recession.[11] Apart from the gains from international specialization according to comparative advantage, the results reflect the fact that export expansion permits utilizing large-scale production methods and attaining higher levels of capacity utilization, with the "stick and carrot" of foreign competition providing further inducements for technological improvements.

Nor has export expansion been limited to the Gang of Four (the Republic of Korea, Taiwan, Hong Kong, and Singapore) as Singer alleges. In the mid-1960s several major Latin American countries, including Brazil, reduced the anti-export bias of their incentive system, with favorable effects for exports and economic growth. In the mid-1970s Chile and Uruguay, and in the early 1980s Turkey, made the shift from inward to outward orientation.

And although no one would suggest that all developing countries should aim at the high export shares of the four East Asian economies, of which two are city-states, I have shown that an annual rate of growth of 12.5 percent in the manufactured exports of the developing to the developed countries between 1978 and 1990 would not lead to an absolute decline in the production of any of the industries of the latter.[12] At the same time, it should be remembered that developing countries do not tend to accumulate reserves, so that increases in their export earnings are spent on imports, mostly from developed countries. Thus, even though a rate of export expansion in excess of 12.5 percent may lead to temporary disloca-

9. H. G. Johnson, "The Possibility of Income Losses from Increased Efficiency or Factor Accumulation in the Presence of Tariffs," *Economic Journal* (March 1967).

10. R. A. Brecher and C. F. Diaz Alejandro, "Tariffs, Foreign Capital, and Immiserizing Growth," *Journal of International Economics* (November 1977).

11. Gershon Feder, "On Exports and Economic Growth," *Journal of Development Economics* (February–April 1983); and Balassa, *Adjustment to External Shocks in Developing Economies.*

12. "Prospects for Trade in Manufactured Goods between Industrial and Developing Countries, 1978–1990," *Journal of Policy Modelling* (September 1980); republished as Essay 9 in *The Newly Industrialized Countries in the World Economy* (New York: Pergamon, 1981).

tion in the developed countries, both groups would benefit from increased trade through the exploitation of their comparative advantage.

Comparative advantage is changing over time, with the export structure being upgraded in the course of economic development. In addition to Japan, which has progressed from the exportation of unskilled labor-intensive commodities to high-technology products, the relevance of the "stages approach" to comparative advantage is apparent in developing countries at different levels of industrialization as well as in a cross-section relationship.[13]

The application of the stages approach to comparative advantage also indicates the possibilities for trade among the developing countries. These possibilities are far from being realized today, largely because high protection in many of these countries tends to discriminate most heavily against countries at similar, or at lower, levels of development. The adoption of an outward-oriented development strategy, involving a reduction in the bias against exports and in favor of import substitution, would thus contribute to increased trade among the developing countries themselves.

The adoption of an outward-oriented strategy would also involve reducing the bias of the incentive system against primary activities. Such a change in incentives would promote exports as well as import substitution in primary products, in particular food and fuels. But efficient import substitution may also occur in manufactured goods, such as machinery, that often suffer discrimination in developing countries.

These considerations may explain why, in the 1973–78 period, outward-oriented developing countries not only were more successful in increasing their exports but also did better in import substitution than inward-oriented economies. As a result, their economic growth accelerated while GDP growth rates declined under inward orientation.[14]

It follows that, if appropriate domestic policies are applied, export expansion and efficient import substitution will go hand in hand. At the same time, in industries that need to be promoted as "infant industries," the measures of promotion should extend to exports, lest high-cost import substitution occur in the confines of small domestic markets. But the infant industry argument does not imply that unrestricted trade would lead to losses to one of the partners or that delinking would be an appropriate strategy as Singer suggests.

I now come to the second half of the title and of the paper, the evolution of soft financing. According to Singer, "ODA, or aid . . . was in fact the natural avenue to which the interest of the United Nations, and my own

13. Bela Balassa, "A 'Stages Approach' to Comparative Advantage," in *Economic Growth and Resources*, Vol. 4, *National and International Issues*, Irma Adelman, ed. (London: Macmillan, 1979); republished as Essay 6 in Bela Balassa, *The Newly Industrialized Countries in the World Economy*.
14. Balassa, *Adjustment to External Shocks in Developing Economies*.

with it, turned . . . as a result of trade pessimism." Although one cannot consider foreign aid as a compensatory measure for a decline that did not in fact occur in the terms of trade of the developing countries, it may usefully complement trade in particular in countries at lower levels of development.

One should, however, put into perspective the relative importance of trade and aid. In 1979 official development assistance amounted to $28 billion while the nonfuel exports of the developing countries to the developed countries were $116 billion and nonconcessional flows, largely private capital, $53 billion. Although some authors have pointed to the possibly adverse effects of foreign aid on production and on savings, these adverse effects can be avoided if appropriate domestic policies are followed.

More generally, as the example of the sub-Saharan African countries discussed in the so-called Berg report indicates,[15] the effective use of foreign aid also presupposes the application of appropriate domestic policies by the developing countries. IDA—and the World Bank in general—can continue to play an important role in this regard, not only because of its professionalism and apolitical character, but also because of the emphasis on improving the domestic policies of the recipients, including the increased outward orientation of their economies.

15. World Bank, *Accelerated Development in Sub-Saharan Africa: An Agenda for Action* (Washington, D.C., 1981).

Jan Tinbergen

NOBEL LAUREATE JAN TINBERGEN was born in 1903 in The Hague, the Netherlands. He received his doctorate in physics from the University of Leiden in 1929, and since then has been honored with twenty other degrees in economics and the social sciences. He received the Erasmus Prize of the European Cultural Foundation in 1967, and he shared the first Nobel Memorial Prize in Economic Science in 1969.

He was Professor of Development Planning, Erasmus University, Rotterdam (previously Netherlands School of Economics), part time in 1933–55, and full time in 1955–73; Director of the Central Planning Bureau, The Hague, 1945–55; and Professor of International Economic Cooperation, University of Leiden, 1973–75.

Utilizing his early contributions to econometrics, he laid the foundations for modern short-term economic policies and emphasized empirical macroeconomics while Director of the Central Planning Bureau. Since the mid-1950s, Tinbergen has concentrated on the methods and practice of planning for long-term development. His early work on development was published as *The Design of Development* (Baltimore, Md.: Johns Hopkins University Press, 1958).

Some of his other books, originally published or translated into English, include *An Econometric Approach to Business Cycle Problems* (Paris: Hermann, 1937); *Statistical Testing of Business Cycle Theories*, 2 vols. (Geneva: League of Nations, 1939); *International Economic Cooperation* (Amsterdam: Elsevier Economische Bibliotheek, 1945); *Business Cycles in the United Kingdom, 1870–1914* (Amsterdam: North-Holland, 1951); *On the Theory of Economic Policy* (Amsterdam: North-Holland, 1952); *Centralization and Decentralization in Economic Policy* (Amsterdam: North-Holland, 1954); *Economic Policy: Principles and Design* (Amsterdam: North-Holland, 1956); *Selected Papers*, L. H. Klaassen, ed. (Amsterdam: North-Holland, 1959); as coauthor, *Programming Techniques for Economic Development* (Bangkok: U.N. Economic Commission for Asia and the Far East, 1960); with H. C. Bos, *Mathematical Models of Economic Growth* (New York: McGraw-Hill, 1962); with others, *Shaping the World Economy* (New York: Twentieth Century Fund, 1962); *Essays in Regional and World Planning* (New Delhi: National Council of Applied Economic Research, 1964); *Central Planning* (New Haven, Conn.: Yale University Press, 1964); with others, *The Case for an International Commodity Reserve Currency* (Geneva: UNCTAD, 1964); *Development Planning* (New York: McGraw-Hill, 1967); *Income Distribution: Analysis and Policies* (Amsterdam: North-Holland, 1975); and, with others, *Reshaping the International Order* (New York: Dutton, 1976).

Some of his articles on economic development and economic planning are: "Capital Formation and the Five-Year Plan," *Indian Economic Journal*, January 1953; "Problems Concerning India's Second Five-Year Plan," *Public Finance*, February 1956; "The Optimum Choice of Technology," *Pakistan Economic Journal*, February 1957; "The Use of a Short-Term Econometric Model for Indian Economic Policy," *Sankhya: The Indian Journal of Statistics*, April 1957; "International Coordination of Stabilization and Development Policies," *Kyklos*, March 1959; "Problems of Planning Economic Policy," *UNESCO International Social Science Journal*, March 1959; "The Appraisal of Investment Projects: The Semi-Input-Output Method," *Industrial India*, 1961; "Planning in Stages," *Statsoknomisk Tidskrift*, January 1962; and "Wanted: A World Development Plan," *International Organization*, January 1968.

Development Cooperation
as a Learning Process

My understanding is that this book deals with a twofold learning process: the one through which, in the last half-century, all who participate in the process of cooperation have gone and the one that goes on inside each of us. The former could not have existed without the latter: in order to change one's mind one has to be honestly convinced of the necessity for accepting the change.

Like a number of others in the field of economics I deserted the subject of my education, physics, under the influence of the phenomena of poverty—to begin with, in my own country. I made this switch in 1929, the very year the Great Depression started. The latter created still more poverty, even in the industrialized world. Intellectually, it was the cyclical component in economic movements that first caught our minds. I had the privilege to work, first, at the Netherlands Central Bureau of Statistics on business cycle research, and from 1936 to 1938 at the League of Nations secretariat at Geneva (so my first experience abroad was not exactly in a poor country).

Soon after my family's return to the Netherlands, the country was invaded by the German army and cut off from the remainder of the world. This gave me plenty of time to think over a number of problems left open by the work so far on economic movements. Two of the resultant issues of concentration seem to fit the present essay. One is that in addition to understanding cyclical movements we need understanding of the trends around which these cycles are supposed to fluctuate. The other is the desperate need for international cooperation instead of cruel conflicts. Both issues found their expression in written form. *International Economic Cooperation* was the title of an amateurish book I published after the war.[1] The first subject was dealt with in a theory of trend movements, published in German in 1942 and translated into English in 1959.[2] This

---

1. Amsterdam: Elsevier, 1945.

2. First published as "Zur Theorie der langfristigen Wirtschaftsentwicklung," *Weltwirtschaftliches Archiv*, vol. 55 (1942), pp. 511–49. As a check on the non-Nazi attitude of the journal editors, I had quoted a considerable number of Jewish authors.

trend theory in fact was a theory of development in an embryonic state, though narrowly economic and not inspired by personal experience in the Third World. At most, therefore, it can be seen as a prelude.

Its (shaky) empirical basis was a collection of heterogeneous data on France, Germany, the United Kingdom, and the United States, 1870–1914. The theoretical frame was at the level one could expect for the early 1940s. A first distinction was made between periods in which production is determined by the supply side and those in which it is determined by demand. For long-term movements the supply side was considered more relevant. Production, and hence real income, was assumed to depend on the supply of labor and of capital. The relationship determining production was assumed to be a Cobb-Douglas function with disembodied exponential technological development; the exponents of labor and capital were three-fourths and one-fourth respectively. The supply elasticity of capital with regard to its price (interest) was assumed to be zero; labor supply was given values ranging from -1 to infinity. The supply of labor was also assumed to depend proportionally on population, itself growing exponentially. Capital formation was taken to be a fixed proportion of real income. Other assumptions with regard to the supply elasticity of capital and the development of population over time were considered. For the central case described in the preceding sentences two main results were offered: (1) the time shape of production and (2) the growth rates, for the middle of the period considered, of capital, labor, and product for four different values of labor supply elasticity.

The whole exercise was meant as a supplement to business cycle theory and was typically inspired by the situation in developed countries and by the absence of massive unemployment in the phase of prosperity. Hence my qualification that it was a prelude, and a theoretical one at that, to the sort of development theories we need for developing countries.

First Confrontation with Developing Countries

During the first postwar decade I was mainly assigned the task of heading the Central Planning Bureau of my own country, the Netherlands, but I did visit a Third World country, India. In 1951 I was a guest at the International Statistical Institute, at the initiative of its prominent member, P. C. Mahalanobis. As the institute's secretary, I went to New Delhi as well as to Calcutta. Although in Holland we had been hungry during 1944–45, the last winter of the occupation by Hitler's army, the poverty

---

The editors accepted my text without changing it. The paper was translated as "On the Theory of Trend Movements," in L. H. Klaassen, L. M. Koyck, and H. J. Witteveen, eds., *Jan Tinbergen: Selected Papers* (Amsterdam: North-Holland, 1959), pp. 182–221.

prevailing in India—as a normal situation—was such a contrast that it redirected my thinking and main activities.

In 1955 I left the Dutch planning office and accepted a full-time professorship, with research possibilities, at the Netherlands School of Economics (now the Economics Faculty of Erasmus University), Rotterdam, combined with a similar task in the Netherlands Economic Institute, which operated on a contract basis and to a large extent paid its own way. This brought me to at least a dozen other countries in the three underdeveloped continents. Most intensively I was involved in Turkey and Egypt. In order to contribute to what seemed to me to be the highest priority from a humanitarian standpoint, it was necessary to use my "comparative advantages," which I assumed to reside in my (self-made) economic thinking. One of the clearest characteristics of underdevelopment is, of course, capital scarcity. This shows up in the most diverse observations even a superficial visitor can make: not only the quality of dwellings, but also the overcrowded trains, trams, and buses and, typically, the small size of the average shop, not to speak of the number of trades practiced in the open air.

Simultaneously, the contrasts between poor and rich, which are definitely much greater than in Western Europe, reflect at least two features: differences in and scarcity of *human* capital and other differences in power. I use the word "other," since differences in human capital constitute differences in economic power, but the word "power" is less used by economists than by sociologists.[3] Upon closer observation, errors in economic decisionmaking are seen as another possible cause of underdevelopment. This at least was my conclusion when in 1957 I was shown a highly automated textile factory in Egypt, with a capital intensity far out of gear with the country's endowment of capital and labor.

Some of My Teachers

The twofold learning process referred to in the introductory section cannot be discussed without mentioning some personalities who have strongly influenced my thinking. If important contributors to development

---

3. Often this difference in terminology creates the misunderstanding that economists altogether disregard the phenomenon of power. They deal with at least two types of power whose reduction requires different instruments: the power of scarcity, just mentioned, and the power of monopoly. Scarcity can be reduced by production; that is, scarcity of human capital can be reduced by increased education, which is production of skill. Monopoly can be reduced by competition. The economist does suggest some means to reduce undesirable power. But the sociologist is able to add more possibilities—for instance, the reduction of discrimination because of caste or sex, which in many developing countries is very striking.

theory are lacking in my list, it may be because of my bad luck in not meeting them or the mistake I made in not reading them.

In my learning process Paul Rosenstein-Rodan was the pioneer, partly because of his very early research on how to develop Southeastern Europe, but especially his famous MIT study.[4] Probably this is the most careful basis for the "1 percent target," which has been the most characteristic uniting thought of all who have participated in the campaign for development cooperation—from Hans Singer via the Pearson Commission and the United Nations Development Planning Committee to the Independent Commission on International Development issues (Brandt Commission).[5] Singer was the main author and proponent of a program for "the" U.N. Development Decade, 1961–70. In Latin America's Comisión Económica para America Latina (CEPAL) and later at the world level (UNCTAD), it was Raúl Prebisch whose persistence I have always admired. My first steps in technical assistance missions were guided by Manuel Perez Guerero in Cairo, where he was resident representative of the United Nations Development Programme. Later, in his own country, Venezuela, his courage would show me some of the nonintellectual ingredients needed for a development policy worth the name. Several of my younger colleagues, among them Leida van Oven and Jan Breman, made similar contributions. An impressive guide in the slums of Dakar was my French colleague, Jacques Burnicourt. The practical American approach was symbolized by Edward S. Mason, with his pupils in every region of the world.

The Need for a General Framework

By a happy coincidence, one of my first tasks in the field of development policy was set by an invitation from the World Bank to compose a general guide to civil servants in both developing and developed countries confronted with responsibilities in the field of development policy. In their heavy day-to-day decisionmaking they have to consider so many concrete details that they cannot "see the woods for the trees." This invitation, which I gladly accepted, forced me to adapt my experience with the Dutch approach to planning, and what I had learned in discussions with Western

4. "International Aid for Underdeveloped Countries," *Review of Economics and Statistics*, vol. 43 (1961), pp. 107–38.

5. See Lester Pearson and others, *Partners in Development* (New York and London: Praeger, 1969). For the work of the U.N. Development Planning Committee, see *Towards Accelerated Development*, no. E.70.II.A.2 (New York: United Nations, 1970); *Renewing the Development Priority*, no. E.73.II.A.7 (New York: United Nations, 1973); *Continuity and Change: Development at Mid-Decade*, New York, no. E.75.II.A.6 (New York: United Nations, 1975); and *Launching a Third Decade of Development*, no. E.79.II.A.7 (New York: United Nations, 1979). The report of the so-called Brandt Commission is *North-South: A Program for Survival* (London and Sydney: Pan Books; Cambridge, Mass.: MIT Press, 1980).

and Eastern European politicians about many variants of it, to the situation in developing countries as far as I knew it. The book that resulted was *The Design of Development*.[6]

Among the difficulties the underdeveloped countries had to face, some were well known: the tendency toward too ambitious goals and projects, the failure to avoid inflationary tendencies, the waste of resources in various sorts of bottlenecks or by inexperienced national politicians, together with the widespread disease of corruption—often simply as consequences of poverty and underdevelopment, but also in part a response to colonial relationships or local culture.

One necessary ingredient for a more efficient and somewhat less inequitable development was a better understanding of the main economic interrelations and of the orders of magnitude of the phenomena at stake—and hence of the limits to what a nation with modest endowments could attain. Also essential were minimum standards of law and order, a minimum of financial and monetary policies, and social stability. Previously, these had been provided, up to a point, by colonial rulers, although then they had been biased by colonial interests rather than by those of the colonized country. Another basic need, that of a minimum of schooling, was recognized but not dealt with.

The general orientation needed could, to a considerable extent, be provided by statistics. Only ten years or so earlier, in the 1940s, developed countries had integrated into their national accounts a bookkeeping system for the nation as a whole. Even if only rudimentary, an idea of the orders of magnitude involved could help stimulate a sense of proportion—something many politicians lacked, even in developed economies, during the Great Depression. These sets of figures, and attempts to set future goals for them, serve as a basis not only for government decisions and negotiations, but also for market analyses of private firms.

In *The Design of Development* I discussed some of the techniques available and used for setting realistic targets and deriving appropriate policy instruments, including estimates of future production, consumption, and investment; evaluation of public investment projects; the choice of appropriate industries; and the means to stimulate private initiatives. The text also deals with some technical instruments to support evaluation, including what we now call shadow prices. Some central problems will be dealt with below in more detail.

The Early Approach: Physical Capital and Project Appraisal

With physical capital so visibly in short supply in underdeveloped countries, it is understandable that early theories gave a central place to

6. Baltimore, Md.: Johns Hopkins University Press, 1958.

the need to expand these countries' stock of capital goods, whether infrastructure or superstructure. Two main problems immediately arise: how much capital would be needed and on what should it be spent?

Rosenstein-Rodan had made his path-breaking contribution to the question of the total amount and its distribution over countries. Its hard core was the Harrod-Domar model and its central concept the capital-output ratio, meaning that the portion of national product to be available for investment should be several times the annual rate of growth of national product desired.[7] Self-sustained growth of a country would be attained when its savings equal the necessary investment. Development cooperation was seen as providing the temporary supplement to what could reasonably be expected to be saved by the better-off in countries where the average income meant a very low level of well-being.

Choosing concrete figures for each of the concepts implied a lot of arbitrariness, and striving for an "optimal" policy needed a number of heroic guesses. A logical start was, of course, to observe the recent past and then opt for a somewhat higher figure. In practice, the narrowest of all the bottlenecks often determined its actual dimension. In many of the least developed countries this was the absorptive capacity (that is, the number of sufficiently concrete blueprints for projects); for many of the more developed countries the bottleneck was the donor's willingness to supply capital. But all sorts of other bottlenecks turn up during the execution of a given project: material supplies, certain types of skilled workers (from manual to managerial), and various bureaucratic shortcomings.

The second main question—on what objects should the capital be spent?—has given rise to a new industry: project appraisal. Essentially the answer is that the project promising the highest present value of all future yield should be preferred. Estimating the yields to be expected in each consecutive year requires a detailed knowledge of the project's construction time and costs, as well as the income for the nation concerned (if not for the world at large!). Engineers will usually know the volume figures involved much better than economists,[8] who can make their contribution when it comes to the pricing component. The idea of shadow prices, or, in earlier terminology, opportunity prices, comes in for markets not in equilibrium; in particular, factor markets often show structural disequilibria. The most difficult question, of course, is the time discount: intuitive answers or political compromises usually have to come in here.

7. Otherwise well-trained development economists often ignore the time dimension that the capital-output ratio has; this may be about three years. A correct definition of the capital-output ratio is "the time period for which output equals capital invested." The word "ratio" is somewhat misleading.

8. For a related experience, see T. C. Koopmans, "The Transition from Exhaustible, Renewable or Inexhaustible Resources: Economic Growth and Resources," Cowles Foundation Paper no. 533 (New Haven, Conn., Yale University, 1981), p. 6.

On one important point there is less room for compromise—a proper choice among all competing projects has to be taken into account. This point helped me when President Sukarno of Indonesia was trying to get the approval for a nonsense project into which he had been talked by the representative of an European firm specializing in rotating restaurants on top of towers. The minister of finance, the president of the Central Bank, and I were able to postpone the decision on the strength of our statement that, after all, a decision could be made only after all other projects had been appraised. The tower was not built.

A Philosophical Interlude: The Role of Environment in Its Widest Sense[9]

On the occasion of a publication to honor the well-known Swedish economist Johan Åkerman in 1961, seven authors were asked to present their views on the "theory of growth."[10] Characteristically for that time, problems of the Third World were scarcely of concern to Western economists. Except Albert Hirschman,[11] they all concentrated on the development of industrialized countries, taking up the well-known approaches by Gustav Cassel and Joseph Schumpeter. Having been asked to give my view, I attempted to list some parameters which are needed if we are to understand the differences between developed and underdeveloped economies and the very existence of the latter. (This was a typical rich-country economist's way of posing the problem. But historians and sociologists had been aware—long before their views were known to me—that "developed" countries have been the exceptions in human history.)

In my contribution I attempted to sum up some extra-economic phenomena that presumably help determine the level of development. My list was very incomplete and consisted of climate, social institutions, state of technology, and race. Two possible theories were mentioned, elements of which might be found relevant to a general theory of differences in level of development. One was Toynbee's theory of "too strong challenges," from which an explanation of underdevelopment may be derived (as in the case of the Eskimo society). Race may play a role, since we know there are racial differences. Objective scientific treatment of this subject is obstructed, however, by the emotions aroused by two extremist views: one

9. I am calling this section a philosophical interlude because I do not think that research on these questions has a high priority.

10. H. Hegeland, ed., *Money, Growth and Methodology: Essays in Honor of Johan Åkerman* (Lund, Sweden: Gleerup, 1961).

11. A. O. Hirschman, *The Strategy of Economic Development* (New Haven: Yale University Press, 1958).

assumes a priori that the subject is taboo; the other, that whites—and even more particularly, German-defined "Aryan" peoples—are superior in all respects. The underestimation of Japanese capabilities is one very clear error made by a number of whites.

Other elements of a theory of underdevelopment must be looked for in the differences between the individuals of a homogeneous racial group. Thus, the Europeans who populated the United States of America are not a representative sample. Presumably they are a selection of more active and enterprising individuals. In many countries we find similar groups selected from the Chinese and the Indians. In all three cases—Europe, China, and India—those who stayed home may have been less active and enterprising than those who moved. This suggests that the poorest nations may be found in the areas of oldest settlement.

The International Division of Labor and Technology

Given the goal of increasing the prosperity of the Third World, the natural means is to raise productivity. This immediately leads to the next question: which activities—or productive sectors—should be chosen? In view of the rapid growth of population, which is expected to continue for some time, increased productivity in agriculture should be one target. More generally, we may follow Eli Heckscher and Bertil Ohlin and the theory of international trade which point out that the activities developed should be those that require inputs of the factors of production in abundant supply. For many developing countries this means some types of natural resources and, as a rule, unskilled labor. Capital, on the other hand, is scarce—both physical and human capital. According to the Heckscher-Ohlin principle, developing countries will maximize their national product if they concentrate on natural-resource-intensive and labor-intensive activities. In other words, processing of their own natural resources is the sort of activity to recommend, especially if labor-intensive processes are known.

In this respect, some underdeveloped countries have better prospects than others. Since textile and garment industries are labor-intensive, countries producing natural fibers—cotton or jute—are in a favorable position. The same applies to leather and leather products and timber products. Countries with iron ore deposits are in a less favorable situation since steelmaking is capital-intensive. Often the dilemma is that the processing starts with capital-intensive phases and only the later phases, such as toolmaking and production of machines, are more labor-intensive. Similarly, processing of bauxite requires much capital and energy to begin with, whereas the final phases—production of aluminum utensils—are more labor-intensive. One may even argue that these technological consid-

erations make the process of import substitution an attractive industrialization strategy because it implies a start at the final phases of the
production of finished goods. Both strategies—processing of natural resources and import substitution—require that trade impediments be
avoided. To attain maximum efficiency, the first strategy requires the
absence of import barriers in developed countries; the second strategy, the
absence of protection by the developing country itself.

Another aspect of the recommendations formulated is the range of
choices between different technologies for a given industry. For some
industries this range is wide, whereas others hardly have any choice. In
textile industries, for example, the range is fairly wide; one example is that
the number of spindles or looms supervised by one worker may be varied.
Empirical studies show that, obviously, the balance should be chosen so as
to occupy as fully as possible the more expensive of the two factors: where
labor is cheap the machines should be kept busy, and where it is expensive
the workers should be used as fully as possible.

Economists agree that the technology chosen should be "appropriate"
or "adapted" to the conditions under which it is used. G. K. Boon even
uses the term "geotechnology" to remind the reader of this adaptation.[12]
Among transnational enterprises few have given systematic thought to the
optimal choice of technology. One is Philips Lamps, the well-known
Dutch multinational. Other characteristics of the production process determine the prices of products, and hence competitiveness on the world
market. With the help of many concrete examples Boon has also shown
the importance of lot size, that is, the quantity of one brand manufactured
in one run. Clearly this depends on the size of the market served: the world
market permits long runs.

Empirical work by Chenery and collaborators has shown that in cross-
section as well as historical comparisons there is a clear link between level
of development and capital intensity of industrial production.[13] Japan, the
country which showed the quickest development, displays the phenomenon quite clearly. In the 1930s it frightened the Western world by its
export offensive in cheap textiles; later it became the world's shipbuilder,
motor car producer, and optical instruments supplier; now it is leading in
electronics, automation, and robots.

A well-known objection against the main recommendation—to start
with labor-intensive activities—is that these are low-income industries and

12. See G. K. Boon, *Technology and Sector Choice in Economic Development*
(Alphen aan den Rijn, The Netherlands, and Rockville, Md.: Sijthoff and Noordhoff,
1978) and, from the same publisher, his *Technology and Employment in Postwar
Manufacturing* (1980) and *Technology Transfer in Fibres, Textile and Apparel* (1981).

13. Hollis B. Chenery and others, *Structural Change and Development Policy* (New
York: Oxford University Press, 1979).

hence not attractive. This objection overlooks the difference between income per producer and income per potential producer (or employable worker). If high-income (capital-intensive) industries are chosen, the number of employables who actually become employed producers will fall far short of the total employable population. It can be shown that total national product is maximized if employment is maximized, which happens if relatively labor-intensive industries and technologies are selected.[14] Out of a maximum national product, more can be used for investment and hence for growth; so the future national product will then be maximized too.

Another aspect of the international division of labor should not be lost sight of either: the well-known existence of nontradables. In this category, although the number of material products is limited—mainly buildings and some building materials—the number of services and their total value are considerable. For an average-size economy about half of the national product consists of nontradables. This fact has far-reaching consequences, especially for countries where the balance of payments is in deficit. To eliminate such a deficit the usual advice is to reduce national expenditures (consumption and investment outlay) so as not to surpass national income. What has not always been understood is that this advice implies a considerable reduction in the national product itself—something difficult for developing countries to accept. Hence this is, in its unqualified form, not the best advice. Reduction of spending in order to equilibrate the balance of payments is relevant only for tradables. Reduction of the production of services such as education, for instance, or health care, not only fails to make sense; it does harm to the country's development.[15]

The existence of nontradables also affects the application of the well-known input-output method of planning. If one aim is a given increase in the final demand of some tradable product, this does not necessarily require increases in the output of other tradables which are inputs into its production. It may be better to import such inputs. Only the increased inputs of nontradables have to be produced in the country itself. The traditional input-output method may be adapted to these arguments; at the Centre for Development Planning in Rotterdam the amended method has been baptized "semi-input-output method" and has been set out in detail by A. Kuyvenhoven with an elaborate application to Nigeria.[16] This study had been preceded by the work of L. B. M. Mennes and others, who

14. Jan Tinbergen, "Maximizing National Product by the Choice of Industries," Discussion Paper no. 60, Centre for Development Planning, Erasmus University, Rotterdam, 1981.

15. Jan Tinbergen, "Spardefizit und Handelsdefizit," *Weltwirtschaftliches Archiv*, vol. 96 (1965), pp. 89–101.

16. *Planning with the Semi-Input-Output Method* (Leiden and Boston: Martinus Nijhoff, 1978).

dealt with the distinction between geographical areas of different size, combined in a hierarchical system.[17] The basis for this spatial dimension of planning had been laid by H. C. Bos, who studied the optimal dispersion of economic activities in centers of various size and composition.[18]

The Necessity of a Public Sector

An interesting evolution of views has taken place on the question of where to draw the frontier between the private and the public sector. In the United States many politicians and some economists have a strong preference for the private sector. The World Bank has been influenced by its American surroundings more than has the United Nations:[19] in its work the frontier was drawn between the infrastructure and the superstructure. For quite some time it was assumed that the latter, which consisted of all material production (primary and secondary sectors), would automatically come into existence once the transportation system and public utilities had been created by public authorities. So in the beginning World Bank loans were primarily for infrastructural projects. Only much later was the need felt for a specialized agency dealing with industrialization, mainly under the pressure of developing countries, and the United Nations Industrial Development Organization (UNIDO) was created.

It would be tempting to deal with the problem in a theoretical way, especially with the aid of welfare economics and management science, and against the background of a discussion of socialist views. I shall resist that temptation and choose an empirical approach—one too rare in the discussion of alternative social systems—taking the history of two countries which at the time to be considered were not under socialist rule.

Around 1900 in the Netherlands the Dutch State Mines were created. The government had to take this initiative because neither private capital of sufficient volume nor private initiative was available to exploit the national coal deposits to the extent needed for the country's development. A few decades later state farms were established on land newly recovered from the sea. This state ownership was only temporary, in order to prevent

17. *The Elements of Space in Development Planning* (Amsterdam and London: North-Holland, 1969).

18. *Spatial Dispersion of Economic Activity* (Rotterdam: Rotterdam University Press, 1964).

19. *The Design of Development*, published in 1958, had actually been written for the World Bank in 1955. At their request, I dealt with an additional example of state financing, in the Dutch steel industry. The report was accepted but not published then; I am afraid the president of the Bank at that time did not agree with the opinion I expressed. Three years later it was published: the director of the Economic Development Institute, created by the Bank for teaching purposes, considered it a useful text.

the first generation of settlers from becoming bankrupt. On previous occasions—the reclamation of the Haarlemmermeer—unexpected difficulties in the early years had ruined the first generation of settlers, notwithstanding their qualities as farmers. In both cases, public and private enterprises existed and their relative performance could be compared: in neither were cost differences large—state mines were slightly more efficient than private mines, whereas state farms were slightly less efficient than comparable private farms.

The other case is Turkey, where in 1923 the great modernizer Atatürk established "state economic enterprises" in various modern industries, again because private initiative was unable to raise the necessary capital.

As an outcome of many discussions and on the basis of experience with various alternative management structures, many European economists and politicians have concluded that the type of ownership of the means of production is much less important for an enterprise's efficiency than the quality of its management. Among other features, the tendency toward bureaucracy should be minimized. So efficiency considerations need not be a stumbling block if public enterprise is chosen as a means for furthering a country's development. Rather, the nonavailability of sufficiently large private capital is the decisive point.

Education—The Longest Production Process

The study of economic cycles, started in the 1920s, has drawn attention to the significance of the time needed for a number of productive processes. In the German Institute for Business Cycle Research (Institut für Konjunkturforschung, headed by Ernst Wagemann), Arthur Hanau was the first to analyze the so-called hog cycle, in which a considerable role was played by the length of the production process, including the time the farmer needed to react to hog prices.[20] Periods about twice as long are shown by the adaptation process of the market for pork. In the Anglo-Saxon literature, this became known as the cobweb theorem, since the graphical presentation of the successive steps in the adaptation process looks like a cobweb. Similar, but somewhat more complicated, mechanisms can help explain the intensive swings in coffee and rubber prices, where again the duration of the production process is the main explanatory factor (for example, the time needed before a coffee tree first bears beans). It is also well known that investments in mining or oil exploration require time periods of the order of magnitude of a decade, not to speak of the time needed to recover investment.

---

20. Arthur Hanau, "Die Prognose der schweinepreise," *Vierteljahrshefte zur Konjunkturforschung*, Sonderheft 18 (1930).

Perhaps the longest production process of considerable relevance to the development process is the investment in human capital, as we now like to say (Jacob Mincer was perhaps the first to use that expression[21]). Schooling is the best-known element in training, preceded by informal training in the family between birth and the age of about six and followed by another informal process of training on the job. Schematically, the schooling process can be seen as three consecutive six-year periods (at least in my own country), known as primary, secondary, and third-level schooling. The subdivision is different in different countries and subject to change, but for a considerable portion of the labor force it takes two decades to produce an experienced worker. Recently Russell W. Rumberger made the most elaborate estimates of schooling required for the main occupational groups of the American labor force.[22] They range from 7.5 years for the laborers to 15.6 years for the professional and kindred workers. Gradually the importance of human skills for the development process was discovered, and this contributed to a change of emphasis from physical to human capital.

Because of the length of the education process, it is very probable that at the time a person completes his schooling the situation in the labor market differs considerably from that prevailing when he made his final decision about the process. Of course this last decision need not coincide with the initial choice. At the moment of graduating from high school, it is still possible to choose a college or university education different from that originally intended.[23] So in fact a duration of only four to six years is typically at stake. Longer periods are involved for teachers in particular, since a change in the labor market will affect the demand for various kinds of teacher indirectly, through the number of students. And what about the teachers of the teachers?

A number of studies have been made dealing with how best to redirect the schooling system if, for instance, an acceleration of development is desired.[24] Transitional structures have to be designed, based on the length of the processes mentioned. If need be, temporary or second-best solutions are available, of course. Thus, jobs may be entrusted to persons not fully schooled for them. Also, quick courses may be organized to produce the most urgent skills needed.

An educational policy that is at first sight surprising arises if a newly independent nation wants to get rid of expatriate teachers as soon as

21. "Investment in Human Capital and Personal Distribution of Income," *Journal of Political Economy*, vol. 66 (1958), pp. 281–302.

22. *Overeducation in the U.S. Labor Market* (New York: Praeger, 1981).

23. This is not always true, since some types of secondary schools do not give access to all university studies.

24. Hector Correa and Jan Tinbergen, "Quantitative Adaptation of Education to Accelerated Growth," *Kyklos*, vol. 15 (1962), pp. 776–86.

possible. It turns out that the quickest way to achieve that goal is to attract more expatriates temporarily in order to raise the number of nationals among the teachers. (This does not apply to subjects such as the national language or history taught in that language.)

Not All Cultural Features are Sacrosanct

From the very beginning, those in favor of development cooperation have been warned not to impose their own cultures on those assisted. These warnings spring from a view often held by cultural anthropologists that all cultures should be respected in every detail. The answer of "development assistants" usually could be that they were concerned about something that no culture whatsoever disagreed with: the prevention of starvation. Unfortunately, for quite some time to come the question of cultural imposition is hardly relevant, as starvation will be with us longer than we once hoped.

The issue is not completely irrelevant, however. Long before development cooperation became a branch of political activity, Christian missionaries worked in developing countries that were most frequently still colonies. Simultaneously Muslims succeeded in spreading their religion; so did communists.

Looking at the present situation I am inclined to defend two theses. First, Western culture is not something to be very proud of in all aspects. It now shows several features of degeneration, it has been outspokenly materialist in the sense of being greedy, and it has suffered from serious inconsistencies. There is a wide gap between Christian preaching and acts by so-called Christian nations or politicians: the few who have really lived up to Christian principles, among them many missionaries, are exceptions.

My second thesis is that most cultures are not static, and that cultural exchange is something to aim for. Most cultures show some attractive qualities alongside unattractive, even repulsive, features. In many cultures, the way women are treated leaves much to be desired. Also the way animals are treated is sometimes repulsive and cruel. It seems better to have an open mind with regard to other cultures, to be tolerant about many issues, even willing to learn, but also prepared to defend alternatives. In the light of today's energy and food problems much is to be learned from authors such as Tévoédjrè or Elgin, to mention only two out of a long list.[25]

25. Albert Tévoédjrè, *La Pauvreté: Richesse des peuples* (Paris: Les editions ouvrières, 1978); and Duane Elgin, *Voluntary Simplicity* (New York: William Morrow, 1981).

The DD II Circus and the RIO Circle—Gratifying Experiences

Around 1965 it became clear that the first Development Decade had not inspired the large and middle-size industrial countries to change their policies in the direction suggested by the U.N. designation of the decade as one in which special efforts should be made. This contributed to the creation of the U.N. Committee for Development Planning in Resolution 1079 (xxxix), July 23, 1965, by the Economic and Social Council. Until 1972 I had the privilege of being the chairman of this committee. The product of our deliberations is a booklet of forty-six pages entitled "Towards Accelerated Development—Proposals for the Second United Nations Development Decade," brought out early in 1970.

The committee had eighteen members. This modest size was outnumbered considerably by the number of observers who attended the meetings and took an intensive part in the discussions. All members of the United Nations family of institutions—from the International Monetary Fund and the World Bank to the Universal Postal Union—and a number of nonmember international agencies such as the Organisation for Economic Co-operation and Development and its counterpart the Council for Mutual Economic Assistance (Comecon), as well as the European Economic Community, were represented. I think the word "Circus"—with due respect, of course—reflects the nature of the deliberations rather faithfully.[26] Certainly for the chairman there was never a dull moment, and it gave me great satisfaction to have been entrusted with this post for some time. I don't venture an estimate of the yield of our efforts.

It was a rather different experience, but also a very stimulating one, to act as the coordinator of what I shall call the RIO Circle. The group whose meetings I had to "coordinate" (in fact, to chair) had been composed in consultation with Dr. Aurelio Peccei, president of the Club of Rome, in 1974, to report on the New International Economic Order, as defined and adopted as an aim by the United Nations General Assembly. It is no exaggeration to say that this was a circle of friends, and that the more informal and profound discussions held there were of a totally different

26. The observers surely provided the committee with useful information and suggestions, but their behavior was hardly distinguishable from that of the members. I remember that on one occasion I requested the observers to refrain from asking the floor until the committee's members had made their interventions. Immediately one of the observers asked the floor for a matter of order: he voiced a protest against my request. Even so, the atmosphere of the meetings was pleasant throughout. And thanks are due to those who, in succession, acted as rapporteur, often Josef Pajestka, and to the U.N. secretariat staff who assisted our work. Scientifically, a major step forward was Jacob Mosaks's world model from which some of the key figures in our report were derived.

character. Many attempts were made to go beyond accepted scientific views and produce a number of innovations—reflecting the Club of Rome's feelings of urgency toward mankind's problematical future. Thus, the optimal level of decisionmaking for problems with different areas of impact throughout the world was one of our innovations. Another was sovereignty as a functional concept instead of a concept of property. A third concept of a novel character was package deals, composed so as to contain elements attractive to all negotiating parties.

It is regrettable that, partly as a consequence of today's stagflation, and partly as a consequence of a general shortsightedness, the Foundation RIO had to stop its activities in 1982—let us hope temporarily.

Shifts in Priorities

As illustrated by the preceding sections, during its short history the development strategy for underdeveloped countries has been subject to an intensive learning process. This may be characterized as an attempt to shift to other activities so as to avoid repeating previous mistakes and to fight negative forces blocking the road toward higher prosperity, in this case the well-being of the poor masses in the Third World.

Some of the clearly negative forces we are facing are ignorance in many forms, shortsightedness (one type is narrow nationalism), polarization (which often implies waste of energy), and cynicism (which discourages action).

In the preceding sections I discussed a number of the shifts from less to more satisfactory approaches: for example, from the creation and transfer of physical capital to that of human capital; from foreign, capital-intensive technologies to appropriate, or adapted, less capital-intensive technologies, which in many cases implies a shift from large to smaller projects; and from employment creation in cities to its creation in villages or small towns. I also discussed a shift from external (intergovernmental) to internal policies and, somewhat related, from paternalism to self-reliance.

Polarization in ideas, which implies reinforcement of extremist political forces, both within and between nations, is useful sometimes in order to demonstrate the existence of a problem, but it is an incomplete process which must be supplemented by a synthesis. This thesis (the well-known dialectic philosophy dealing with the consecutive phases of thesis-antithesis-synthesis) may be illustrated by an almost simplistic example. Some politicians hold that markets are self-regulatory and can solve many problems without intervention by public authorities. Others are in favor of regulation of markets with the aid of buffer stocks, minimum and maximum prices, and quotas. So far this is a polarized situation. The synthesis can be created from the moment we understand that there are essentially two types of markets, stable and unstable. Stable markets can indeed be left to themselves, but unstable markets need regulation, as noted above where I mentioned a few unstable markets: those of pork, coffee, and rubber.

One more lesson should be learned from the past. The corresponding shift might be said to be from idealism to long-term common interest. Around the 1950s, development cooperation was seen as an act of idealism required by the few among the developed world's citizens who propagated it. Those who formulated the Brandt report point out that development cooperation is a policy in the long-term self-interest of developed countries. The tragedy is that even that down-to-earth view is not shared by the shortsighted politicians whom we have elected. The world is in desperate need of statesmen as Churchill defined them—politicians who think of the next generation and not only of the next election—people of the stature of, for instance, the founding fathers of the European Community and their American counterparts who launched the New Deal and, later, the Marshall Plan.

Comment

Michael Bruno

IN THE FOLLOWING COMMENTS I shall not discuss Tinbergen's seminal contributions to general economic science.[1] Tinbergen was a cofounder of econometrics (and the Econometric Society) and his contributions to the statistical study of business cycles and other dynamic processes (such as the cobweb process) would in themselves have earned him a major place in the modern revolution of economics as a quantitative science. I shall also resist the temptation of commenting in detail on the various development issues brought up in Tinbergen's paper for this volume. Tinbergen has thought and worked on many aspects that development economists have been and still are occupied with, such as the choice of "proper" technology, the role of international competitiveness in investment allocation, the design of educational planning, and the interplay of economic and social factors in development. His thoughts and contributions in all of these were always of considerable relevance and importance, but they were not unique. His unique contribution, to my mind, lies in the adaptation of his own pioneering thoughts on the *Theory of Economic Policy*, developed at the Dutch planning office in the postwar years, to the subsequent *Design of Development*. I shall confine my comments to that phase of his work, perhaps in part because many of my own generation of development economists often started their thinking and analysis under the deep imprint of Tinbergen's planning methodology.

The most important lesson that Tinbergen and the postwar Dutch planning school taught us is that economic planning and economic policy could be expressed in a form that combines sound economic theory with applied empirical content. The main body of a plan should be based on a theoretical construct or "model," be it a simple Harrod-Domar model with a rudimentary consumption function or a more complex input-output framework. It should involve quantitative targets and quantitative

Michael Bruno is Professor of Economics at the Hebrew University.

1. For an excellent survey and overall evaluation of Tinbergen's work, see Bent Hansen, "Jan Tinbergen: An Appraisal of His Contribution to Economics," *Swedish Journal of Economics*, vol. 71 (1969), pp. 325–36.

policy instruments, and it should be based on a set of equations or constraints of a technical, behavioral, or institutional nature which link the important variables into a systematic conceptual framework.

Tinbergen did not lose sight of the fact that there may be an inconsistency between a "top-down" macro approach and a "bottom-up" micro project approach to planning. He realized early on that there is need to fill a macro plan with detailed project planning, making use of accounting prices and allowing for both public investment planning and private investment promotion. A macro plan should later be revised in the light of project information. Subsequent writers (Henri Theil probably being the first) pointed out the limitations of Tinbergen's formal fixed-target approach (with sensitivity analysis on the chosen parameters) and the advantage of combining modern welfare economics (that is, social optimization) with the underlying Tinbergen structure. Much was said and written on the difference between "consistency" planning and planning for "optimality."

The evolution of formal development planning in the late 1950s and 1960s dealt with economy-wide application of linear, nonlinear, and dynamic programming techniques. These more sophisticated techniques were greatly helped by the rapid advance of electronic computers, which did not exist in the early planning days. Such models have certainly helped in the process of thinking about trade and development policy issues, about the link between macro planning and the actual derivation of shadow prices for micro-investment decisions. But in one basic sense the more advanced techniques have not helped us progress much beyond the stage already developed by Tinbergen. Data limitations and uncertainty about the response of public and private agents still make the relatively simple consistency frameworks, such as the semi-input-output method developed by Tinbergen, the most useful ones when it comes to the actual design of a formal development plan in a developing country.

We all know that the formal planning techniques designed by Tinbergen and his followers have serious limitations. The best-designed set of simultaneous equations is no substitute for a good development strategy, which very often has important qualitative, and unquantifiable, dimensions. Issues of centralization and decentralization in development planning, the problem of assessing the area of effective government control, as well as social and political questions often escape the structured planning model format. I am sure Tinbergen himself would want to disown some of the naiveté with which formal programming techniques have often been implemented. Even as early as twenty-five years ago, he stated an eclectic view: "It must first be made clear that programming is not an alternative to common sense; it cannot replace common sense and it should not. It does supplement it, particularly with regard to the orders of magnitude of the phenomena involved. In the design of development all information and all methods available should be put to use. This seems the more desirable

since information of the traditional type, the usual statistics, is often
insufficient and inconsistent."[2]

Finally, one must stress the fact that Tinbergen has set a very important
example by his own personal involvement in actual development policy,
first in his own country and later on the international scene. Everywhere he
has always been led by very deep humanitarian convictions. These clearly
transpire again in Tinbergen's present paper. It is for this reason that his
great impact on development economics and practitioners transcends the
important legacy of introducing formal programming techniques.

2. *The Design of Development* (Baltimore, Md.: Johns Hopkins University Press,
1958), pp. 9–10.

Postscript

Development Dichotomies

Paul P. Streeten

Economists consist of two groups: those who don't know, and those
who don't know that they don't know.

—WIDELY ACCEPTED SAYING

THE WORLD IS DIVIDED into two groups of people: those who divide the
world into two groups of people, and those who don't. As I evidently
belong to the former, I believe that the nature of various divisions can
throw light on what has come to be known as the rise and decline of
development economics.

Albert Hirschman, in his stimulating contribution to the international
symposium on Latin America at Bar Ilan University in 1980,[1] used two
criteria for classifying development theories: whether they asserted or
rejected the claim of mutual benefits in North-South relations; and
whether they asserted or rejected the claim of monoeconomics that there is
a single economic discipline, applicable to all countries and at all times.
Using this classification, he derived four types of theories. Orthodox
(neoclassical) economics asserts both claims. Neo-Marxist and dependence theories reject both claims. Development economists tend to reject
the monoeconomics claim—the reason for their existence calls for a
distinct subject—but to assert the mutual benefit claim, whereas paleo-
Marxists assert the monoeconomics claim (except insofar as class deter-
mines consciousness) but reject the mutual benefit thesis.

One may want to quibble with Hirschman's classification. Development
economists constitute a large group, many of whom would reject the
mutual benefit claim without regarding themselves as neo-Marxists or
dependence theorists. Others would assert the unity of economics, while
considering it legitimate to carve out special areas for development economics, to which particular branches or modifications of the single disci-

Paul P. Streeten is Professor of Economics and Director of the World Development
Institute at Boston University.

1. "The Rise and Decline of Development Economics," in *Essays in Trespassing:
Economics to Politics and Beyond* (New York: Cambridge University Press, 1981).

| | Monoeconomics | |
	Asserted	Rejected
Mutual benefit — Asserted	Orthodox economics	Development economics
Mutual benefit — Rejected	Marx?	Neo-Marxist theories

pline apply. In other words, there are development economists who analyze interest conflicts, and development economists who are neoclassical. Jon Elster has pointed out that Marx in his *Theories of Surplus Value* makes the point that capitalist countries exploit "backward" countries even though both parties gain from exchange.[2] And Joan Robinson wrote: "The misery of being exploited by capitalists is nothing compared to the misery of not being exploited at all."[3] Mutual benefit is therefore not denied.

Hirschman attributes the decline of development economics (as reflected, for example, in the difficulty of filling chairs in development economics)[4] to a combined (though not concerted) onslaught from both neoclassical economics (with the charge of misallocation resulting from deviation from neoclassical principles) and neo-Marxist economics (with the charge of justifying dependence and exploitation). He also attributes its fall to the political disasters that struck many countries of the Third World.

Unity in Diversity

In 1963 Dudley Seers argued that the economics of the North does not apply to the different societies of the South.[5] Twenty years before that, Paul Rosenstein-Rodan suggested that indivisibilities, complementarities, externalities, and economies of scale were concepts much more relevant to

2. Jon Elster, "Trespassers," *London Review of Books*, vol. 4, no. 17 (September 16–October 6, 1982).

3. *Economic Philosophy* (Harmondsworth, Middlesex, Eng.: Penguin, 1966), p. 46.

4. Though not as reflected in the attendance at an 8:00 A.M. meeting of the American Economic Association at which the economics of development and the development of economics were discussed.

5. "The Limitations of the Special Case," *Bulletin of the Oxford University Institute of Statistics*, vol. 25, no. 2 (May 1963), pp. 77–98. Robert Solow reminded me of Stephen Potter's well-known ploy to acquire a reputation for profundity and sophistication. The reply to any generalization is, "Not in the South."

developing economies than to those of the already industrialized countries.[6]

The "economics of the special case," applicable to advanced industrial societies, had to be broadened to encompass different relationships. Stimulated by the generalization of the "special case" of fully employed economies to conditions of industrial unemployment in advanced countries, Rosenstein-Rodan, Arthur Lewis, and others broadened our vision to encompass underemployment and low labor utilization in underdeveloped countries. Although it was later discovered that labor utilization in poor countries introduces quite different issues from those raised by Keynes for advanced countries, and although some of the writings criticized the application of Keynesian concepts to underdeveloped countries, there can be no doubt that Keynes's attack on orthodox economics provided a stimulus for the exploration of labor use in developing countries. Joan Robinson's analysis of disguised unemployment in industrial countries provided the inspiration for the analysis of underemployment in underdeveloped countries.[7]

Albert Hirschman, among others, has noted that the exploration of Southern societies, with different tools of analysis, has often led to new illuminations and discoveries in our own Northern societies, thereby reestablishing the unity of the analysis. Hirschman cites the case of underemployed rural labor, "development with unlimited supplies of labor," the role of labor surpluses in European economies, and theories of dual labor markets on the one hand, and the analysis of underemployed resources in developing countries[8] that have to be activated and theories of satisficing and X-efficiency, on the other. My own work on the production function, in collaboration with Gunnar Myrdal in *Asian Drama*,[9] similarly showed that many of the criticisms originally developed for South Asia also apply to Western Europe and the United States. Dudley Seers's odyssey from the economics of the special case to the discovery of dependency and dominance within Europe and even within a single European country is another illustration. Structuralist theories of inflation, originally constructed for the underdeveloped countries, also found new application in the advanced countries of the North. Clearly, much of the work on the

6. "Problems of Industrialization of Eastern and South-Eastern Europe," *Economic Journal*, vol. 53 (June-September 1943).

7. "Disguised Unemployment," in *Essays in the Theory of Employment* (Oxford: Blackwell, 1947), pp. 60–74.

8. Hans Singer has pointed out to me that the influx of foreign workers into European economies was the result of the pressure of excess demand for labor, whereas in developing countries there was excess supply. Today, when we suffer from a labor surplus, the story is quite different. It is also true that the theories of dual labor markets in industrial countries have developed without influence from the developing-country models.

9. New York: Pantheon, 1968.

advanced countries had been done independently and in ignorance of development work. But the parallels and coincidences are remarkable.

Dudley Seers, in his recent provocative essay entitled "The Birth, Life and Death of Development Economics" in the volume of essays in honor of Kurt Martin, writes:

> Virtually all countries are suffering now from structural rather than global problems. For very few would an acceleration of growth *per se* be a solution to social problems such as unemployment. All countries face powerful external forces, especially the policies of the transnational corporations, and experience the strains of absorbing modern technology. So insights from the development field could usefully be imported into the social sciences in the so-called developed countries too, which include several where neo-classical analysis and prescription did not once seem obviously implausible. I refer to appropriate technology and concepts familiar in Latin American writings, such as self-reliance, marginalization and cultural dependence.[10]

The examples could be multiplied in which an analysis originally designed for underdeveloped economies finds application in the most developed. They range from small-scale technology in the face of energy shortage and the alienating effects of large-scale organizations, to lessons from the study of caste with relevance for trade union rivalries (craft versus industrial unions) in industrial countries, to the analysis of the "Dutch disease," first explored by Arthur Lewis for Jamaican bauxite and Dudley Seers for Trinidad oil, long before it gained respectability through Dutch natural gas. But, as Albert Hirschman says, "whereas such a finding makes for reunification of our science, what we have here is not a return of the prodigal son to an unchanging, ever-right and -righteous father. Rather, our understanding of the economic structure of the West will have been modified and enriched by the foray into other economies.[11]

The move toward awareness of the universal nature of some problems originally explored in the development context was accompanied by growing differentiation of countries in the Third World to the point where it could be questioned whether a special branch of economics—development economics—applied to them all. To some extent this was the result of the analysis of the coexistence of different countries at different stages of development, and their interaction. The relations between richer and poorer countries were reflected both within the industrial and among the developing countries, and the analysis of these relationships followed along a spectrum or a hierarchy with both greater differentiation and unification.

The history of development economics can be regarded as a progress

10. *Development and Change*, vol. 10 (1979), p. 714.
11. *Essays in Trespassing*, p. 9.

from large generalizations and high abstractions to greater specificity and concreteness. This applies to countries within the Third World, which was found more heterogeneous than originally thought, as well as to concepts such as national income or employment. Many early errors in development theory resulted from the transfer of assumptions and relations from one country or region to others, where they did not apply. No longer was it thought that each country must be studied in its unique specificity, or that useful generalizations can be made for all countries in the Third World; but there was a move toward a country typology, regarded as useful for the application of policies. The principal criteria in this typology were country size (measured by population), which is relevant to the importance of foreign trade and the scope for using labor-intensive techniques for exports, degrees of dualism and labor surplus, relevant to the application of different models of development; endowment with natural resources and particularly an indigenous energy base which distinguishes oil exporters from oil importers; relative size of the agricultural and the industrial sectors; and government strategies.

In combination, the two discoveries—that many problems of the countries of the South are shared by the North, and that few problems are common to all countries of the South—contributed to the decline of the early certainties, or at least the large generalizations, of development economics.

Mutual Benefits versus Conflict

The mutual benefit thesis is not as straightforward as may appear at first sight. Even when there are benefits for all, the division of them may give rise to conflict. A pure concession or sacrifice by one partner, however, may contribute to an order that is regarded as fair and acceptable, and is therefore accepted. Acceptance of this order may contribute to peace and help avoid confrontations and conflicts, and therefore turn out to be in the long-term interest of the partner making the concession.

A related point is the question of the meaning of welfare. It is not just a matter of command over economic resources, but command in relation to wants. Gains from, say, international trade have then to be assessed in relation not only to additional income but also to additional wants, expectations, and aspirations that are generated by the extra income. It is then quite possible, indeed likely, that gains in income are accompanied by losses in welfare, because wants grow faster than command over resources—the appetite grows faster than what it feeds on. This is not largely because of advertising and sales promotion, but it is often the result of the unequal division of the gains from trade; even with equal division between countries, there can be greater inequalities within countries. The inequalities contribute to the reference groups whose income levels shape the wants of the lower groups. On this definition of welfare, it is then possible that the countries with large gains from trade fail to benefit because their internal inequalities are great, and the developing countries do not benefit because international inequalities are great. It is, of course, possible to define welfare in a different way, such as a widened range of choice, though this definition has been disputed by psychologists.

The mutual benefit thesis might be seen as the old harmony doctrine served in a new sauce, and it is doubtful whether anybody seriously believed in it, except in a very extenuated form or for purposes of political propaganda. This is not to deny that there are areas of action from which all participants benefit, particularly international trade and capital movements. And attention should be given to full exploration of these areas, particularly where there are obstacles to the achievement of these interests. But it would be a strange fluke of coincidence if these were the same actions that would have to be taken to pursue developmental goals—whether of growth, or growth with equity, or basic needs. The extenuated version is the one that would place international solidarity and morality under the heading "benefits."

It is also doubtful whether development economics asserted universally the mutual benefit thesis. Surely many writers saw the existence and possibility of conflicts of interest between nation states. Very few moral philosophers would attempt to construct a political theory on purely egoistic lines. Why then try to construct an international economic theory for national egoisms? Since we all accept the readiness of individuals to sacrifice their interests to the national community, the challenge of normative development economics is to construct the moral and institutional basis for applying sentiments and principles of solidarity beyond the national frontiers to the fledgling world community. Another obvious objection to the current fashion of the mutual interest thesis is that, where mutuality exists, people usually act accordingly (with some exceptions such as prisoner's dilemma situations in which rational, self-interested action leads to mutual impoverishment), and no great economic, political, or philosophical analysis is needed to propagate such action. The challenging task is not to show areas of common or mutual interests or benefits, but to show how conflicts, when they arise, can be resolved.

The current preoccupation with mutual and common interests (the two are not the same, though often confused) is surprising in view of the fact that national policies are not normally justified on grounds of mutual and common individual, household, or local interests, social contract theories notwithstanding. Most of us accept the principle that the rich have an obligation toward the poor in the national community. Once this is accepted, the question arises whether humanity is a community in the same sense. It is, of course, possible to reject this on social contract grounds: why should I do anything for the world since it has done nothing for me? But there are embryonic global institutions that do render services to their members, and a social contract is not the only ground on which obligations by the rich to the poor can be justified.

Even if such global obligations were accepted, the objection may be raised that the existence of nation states and national governments interferes with the discharge of the obligations of individual rich members to individual poor members. No doubt there is something in this objection. Those advocating development aid, and North-South cooperation generally, on the moral ground of the obligation to help the poor have not devoted enough time and effort to showing that such efforts actually achieve their aim, or, if not, how these efforts should be designed so that they do achieve the aims, without infringing too much on national sovereignty. As a result, attacks on aid by an alliance of left and right have, with a few notable exceptions, not been seriously answered by the proponents of aid. The principal reason moral obligations must be accepted by governments (as well as by individuals) is that certain objectives can be achieved only through collective action, as in developing indivisible projects, or stepping up growth rates by adding foreign savings in the form of aid, or intervening on behalf of children of poor households, a particularly vulnerable and particularly neglected group. In such situations, in order to express the moral motives of each individual, it is necessary to force others, and oneself, to contribute (through taxation) if the aim is to be achieved.

Formal versus Informal Intellectual Sectors

Another distinction is suggested in a sentence by Dudley Seers.[12] It has its analogy in the distinction between the two sectors in developing countries: one sophisticated, organized, modern, large-scale, and "formal"; the other simple, nonorganized, small-scale, and "informal." The formal sector is cultivated by the economics departments of the established universities where students are trained in sophisticated techniques and where the standards of excellence are derived from the discipline. The informal sector is made up of what the profession often dismisses as cranks, dissidents, "poets," journalists, and novelists.[13]

The insights of members of the informal sector have three advantages over those of the formal sector. First, these people often know better how to communicate with a wide audience. They do not use jargon and do write simply and vividly. Second, they use their eyes and ears and tell what they observe. Third, not having been drilled in the professional paradigms

12. "The Birth, Life and Death," p. 717.
13. E. F. Schumacher once wrote (in an unpublished paper): "Some people call me a crank. I don't mind at all. A crank is a low-cost, low-capital tool. It can be used on a moderately small scale. It is non-violent. And it makes revolutions."

and being free of the blinkers that these impose, they often treat important issues ignored by the professionals. But since they do not have a rigorous formal framework, their insights, in spite of widespread impact, are often ephemeral and fade out fairly soon.

The formal sector has the virtues of its defects. It attracts brilliant students and generates a body of knowledge that can be admired, taught, and elaborated. But its elegance diverts attention from its irrelevance. In isolating the quantifiable and technically tractable and neglecting the rest, workers in the formal sector occasionally pour out the baby instead of the bath water.

Areas in which the informal sector has pioneered advances are corruption, the culture of poverty, and global concerns. The profession, understandably, has focused on the nation state. Concerns at a much lower level and at a transnational level (not the same as international concerns) have been relatively neglected.

David Henderson, in a review of a book by Albert Hirschman, suggests that one way of classifying economists

> is to distinguish "constructivists" from sceptics. The former group, while recognizing that orthodox economic analysis is far from all-embracing, chooses nonetheless to emphasise its usefulness in relation to issues of policy, and the dangers of ignoring or going against it. By contrast, the sceptics acknowledge that the orthodox approach is both elegant and helpful within its limits, but prefer to stress the narrowness of these limits, and the inadequacy of the theory both as a guide to social reality and as a basis for deciding policy.[14]

This is a useful distinction. It raises interesting questions about the relations between these two groups. Clearly, the skeptics would have nothing to work on were it not for the constructions of the constructivists. But, the constructivists would lapse into dogmatism were it not for the skeptics. Almost every economist contains elements of each of the two groups. On the one hand, the skeptics, when they go their classrooms or give practical advice, cannot do without the kit of the constructivists. On the other hand, some of the most distinguished members of the profession, when they give presidential addresses, sound the tone of the skeptics, though they return to constructivist activities in their daily work. Among these doyens of the profession are Henry Phelps Brown, David Worswick, Wassily Leontief, Ragnar Frisch, Frank Hahn, Kenneth Arrow, and Lloyd Reynolds.[15] Could it be that this reflects a tension in their subversions between accepting and rejecting the orthodox paradigm?

14. *The Banker*, vol. 132, no. 677 (July 1982), pp. 128–29.
15. G. D. N. Worswick, "Is Progress in Economic Science Possible?" E. H. Phelps Brown, "The Underdevelopment of Economics," and N. Kaldor, "The Irrelevance of Equilibrium Economics," all in the *Economic Journal* (1972); W. Leontief, "Theoreti-

It is possible to hold the view that the most important function of a construction, be it a model, a paradigm, or a theory, is to show up the limitations of other constructions and thereby add to the flexibility of our intellectual muscles, rather than to shed light on reality. Their function is therapeutic, not didactic. The introduction of institutional considerations in the analysis of rural land/debt/wage relationships by neo-Marxists shows up the limits of neoclassical analysis, but equally neoclassical analysis shows that the crust of institutions can be broken, as well as hardened, by market forces. An analysis of intrafamily relationships in terms of time allocation and maximizing behavior can throw light on an alternative analysis conducted in terms of power relations and force, and vice versa. For reasons such as these, it is of the utmost importance to keep the dialogue between different ideological schools in development studies going, and not to permit a breaking up into noncommunicating groups.

Flat Earthers versus Round Earthers

Ian Little divides development economists according to a different criterion. He says (in private correspondence with me) that he does not regard stages of growth and W. W. Rostow (the division suggested by me) as being very important or dominant. "At least until fairly recently I see the story as one of a battle between structuralists who see the world as bounded and flat, and consisting of stick-in-the-muds, who have to be drilled—and neoclassicists who see it as round and full of enterprising people who will organize themselves in a fairly effective manner!"[16]

Little's distinction is an important one and underlies much of the dispute between neoclassicists and structuralists. If one believes that resources, in response to the right incentives, flow easily and quickly, at minimal costs, from one line of activity into another, so that the economy is rather like toothpaste or syrup, the implications for policymaking and for mutual benefits are quite different from what they are if one believes that the economy consists of hard, specific pieces of capital goods and individuals trained in specific skills and located in specific areas, who can be remolded only at great cost, or after a long time, or not at all.

The neoclassicists stress the importance of getting prices right. Peter

---

cal Assumptions and Non-Observed Facts," *American Economic Review* (1971); Kenneth Arrow, "Limited Knowledge and Economic Analysis," *American Economic Review* (1974). See also, J. K. Galbraith, "Power and the Useful Economist," *American Economic Review* (1973); Sir Donald MacDougall, "In Praise of Economics," *Economic Journal* (1974); O. Morgenstern, "Thirteen Critical Points in Contemporary Economic Theory," *Journal of Economic Literature* (December 1972).

16. The distinction has been elaborated in I. M. D. Little, *Economic Development: Theory, Policy, and International Relations* (New York: Basic Books, 1982).

Timmer's remark remains valid: "Getting prices right is not the end of economic development, but getting prices wrong frequently is."[17] Everybody would agree that other things are necessary for efficient and equitable management of an economy, but there is disagreement about the relation between the correct prices and these other measures. According to one interpretation, getting prices right without the other measures is better than nothing. According to the other, the combined set of measures is necessary and the "right" prices by themselves may leave things unchanged or make them worse. Overvaluing a single element in a complex system such as that of prices (in this view) is worse than overvaluing the currency.

If a country suffers from one type of evil (such as very unequal land distribution) the addition of another evil (such as the "distortion" of low food prices) may improve things. An early formulation of the theory of the second best by Pigou during the Great Depression is apt: "A man ordered to walk a tight rope carrying a bag in one hand would be better off if he were allowed to carry a second bag in the other hand, though of course if he started bagless to add a bag would handicap him."[18]

A difficulty with the distinction between neoclassicists and structuralists is that, though their arguments are inspired by different visions of the world, the debate is often about instruments.[19] In this debate, instruments that form part of a complex kit are then singled out and identified with the ultimate purpose they serve. Thus the success stories of the Republic of Korea and Taiwan are used by orthodox economists to proclaim export promotion as the key to equitable and rapid growth. And export promotion in turn is often identified with the absence of government intervention and the free play of market forces. But the reasons for the success of Korea and Taiwan are much more complex. The countries promoted labor-intensive import substitution as well as exports; early import substitution led to later exports; the labor force employed in exports is a small proportion of the total labor force; and government intervention as well as the public sector played a very important part. In my view, the singling out of export promotion through liberal trade policies is a false account of the success stories.[20]

---

17. Peter Timmer, "Choice of Techniques in Rice Milling on Java," *Bulletin of Indonesian Economic Studies*, vol. 9, no. 2 (July 1973), p. 76.

18. Quoted in T. W. Hutchison, *On Revolutions and Progress in Economic Knowledge* (New York: Cambridge University Press, 1978), p. 184.

19. Sukhamoy Chakravarty has pointed out that both grossly oversimplify the problems posed by the costs of information in implementing economic policies.

20. See Paul Streeten, "A Cool Look at Outward-Looking Strategies for Development," *World Economy*, vol. 5, no. 2 (September 1982), and "Trade as the Engine, Handmaiden, Brake or Offspring of Growth," *World Economy*, vol. 5, no. 4 (December 1982). For a critique of this view, see the replies by P. D. Henderson and Bela Balassa in the same journal (November 1982 and June 1983).

The structuralists tend to be equally guilty of oversimplification. Having correctly observed and analyzed numerous occasions when the market malfunctioned, they immediately jump to the conclusion that central state action must replace it, in spite of evidence that some state interventions have produced results worse than the market. Instead of concluding that the state should incorporate the market as a powerful instrument of planning, and prices as useful instruments of policy, they dismiss them.

There is a deeper issue underlying Little's distinction. It is whether measures introduced to cushion the victims of the competitive struggle, or measures to ensure fairness in the allocation of resources, may be not merely ineffective, but counterproductive. There has been a large literature on the detrimental effects of social security on incentives, the misallocation caused by equitable controls that encourage "rent-seeking" activities, and the way monopolies are reinforced by what Raj Krishna has called "first-round socialism." There is a smaller body of literature on the detrimental effects of international aid, although a good deal has been written on food aid. The advocates of the compassionate society and world solidarity have to think harder about how to achieve their objectives in these areas without cutting away the ground on which they stand.

This is the place to remember two pioneers of development economics, now dead, who were both opposed to state intervention, central planning, and protectionism, but whose vision of the world was quite different. We owe them many now widely accepted ideas.

Ragnar Nurkse wrote at a time when the accumulation of physical capital was considered to be of strategic importance in the development process: "The problem of development is largely . . . a problem of capital accumulation." He analyzed carefully not only the limits then generally recognized to be set by the supply of savings, but especially those set by demand: "The inducement to invest is limited by the extent of the market."[21] Allyn Young's reinterpretation of Adam Smith's famous dictum that the division of labor was limited by the extent of the market was the starting point of Nurkse's analysis of balanced growth. Together with its obverse—that the extent (size) of the market is limited by the division of labor; that is, by the application of capital—the two propositions provide the basis of economic progress.

Nurkse was interested in the links between international trade and development. He was pessimistic about international trade as an engine of growth and therefore stressed the balanced expansion of domestic markets in accordance with income elasticities of demand. But he did not draw protectionist conclusions from his trade pessimism, nor did he believe that balanced growth necessarily called for central planning. He thought that

21. Ragnar Nurkse, *Some Aspects of Capital Accumulation in Underdeveloped Countries* (Cairo: National Bank of Egypt, 1952), pp. 1 and 2.

prices could be allowed to do their work in guiding the allocation of factors of production.

Some of Nurkse's doctrines have not survived the test of time. Although his emphasis on capital accumulation and industrialization has been confirmed by experience, until the 1970s trade turned out to be much more buoyant than he had expected. The international demonstration effect, which he took over from James S. Duesenberry and applied to international trade, was not as powerful a course of balance of payments deficits as he had thought. Disguised unemployment, implying zero marginal productivity of agricultural labor, was found flawed both logically and empirically. But Erik Lundberg was insightful when he wrote in his introduction to Nurkse's Wicksell Lectures (1959) about "the delicate manner in which he uses—but does not overuse—available statistics, as well as his sense for finding balanced proportions between theory and historical fact in interpreting the trends of economic development."[22] As other pioneers have shown, in economics it is not important to be right.

The second pioneer is Jacob Viner. Though he had his odd quirks—working with a model based on perfect competition and full employment and insisting on the prevalence of increasing unit costs, dismissing all forms of state planning and intervention, and passionately advocating free trade—he was prescient in his emphasis on agricultural improvement as a precondition for development. He was also a lone, early voice stressing the need to pay attention to reductions in absolute poverty as a test of development. In fact, he is a very early advocate of basic needs.

> Were I to insist, however, that the reduction of mass poverty be made a crucial test of the realization of economic development, I would be separating myself from the whole body of literature in this field. In all the literature on economic development I have seen, I have not found a single instance where statistical data in terms of aggregates and of averages have not been treated as providing adequate tests of the degree of achievement of economic development. I know, moreover, of no country which regards itself as underdeveloped which provides itself with the statistical data necessary for the discovery of whether or not growth in aggregate national wealth and in *per capita* income are associated with decrease in the absolute or even relative extent to which crushing poverty prevails.

In discussing obstacles to development Viner writes: "The first requirements for high labour productivity . . . are that the masses of the population shall be literate, healthy, and sufficiently well fed to be strong and energetic."[23] He is thus a pioneer of the basic needs approach, both in its

---

22. *Patterns of Trade and Development* (London: Oxford University Press, 1959), p. 7.

23. Jacob Viner, *International Trade and Economic Development* (Oxford, 1953), pp. 100 and 103.

humanitarian and in its human productivity aspects. He also clearly saw the problems caused by population growth and argued that the rate of growth will decline only after higher income levels have been reached.

Viner remained an inveterate nineteenth-century free trader and resisted the claims of the central planners, the protectionists, and to a large extent even the Keynesian revolutionaries. He was an opponent of official development assistance. Viner is critical of the moral basis of development aid. International charity he saw as an inferior instrument of international cooperation: "Unlike private charity, intergovernmental gifts on a recurrent basis are bound to accumulate protocol, conditions, limitations, humiliating to the recipient to comply with and ungracious of the donor to exact."

"As an economist, I revert to the ungracious role of my predecessors of the nineteenth century, and insist that whatever may be the case in the field of domestic charity, or even of regional charity within national boundaries, it is bad economics, bad politics and, perhaps, even questionable ethics, to make one-sided gifts a substantial and permanent element in our relations with the outside world, no matter how superior our resources may be to theirs." Viner did, however, draw a distinction between charity and payments resulting from obligations, injustice, morality, or solidarity and acknowledged that these had their place at least in domestic relations.

He gave perhaps the best reply to Keynes's famous dictum about the long run:

> A brilliant English economist discovered a few years ago that in the long run we are all dead, and ever since economists have been somewhat apologetic and shamefaced about their ancient habit of taking the long view. It has been suggested, however, that the "we" in this epigram is somewhat ambiguous, and that in its ambiguity resides all its force. It is the special function of the social scientist to attract attention to the policies necessary if assurance is to be had that there shall still be life, if not for us, then for our descendants, after the short run is over.[24]

Hedgehogs versus Foxes

"The fox knows many things, but the hedgehog knows one big thing," wrote the Greek poet Archilochus in the seventh century B.C. Development economics also has its hedgehogs and its foxes.

Knowing many things or knowing one big thing may refer to causes and obstacles or it may refer to aims and objectives. We have had a large number of theories explaining the absence of development, or too slow or distorted development, in terms of a single cause, or rather a single barrier, the removal of which would release the natural forces of progress. Neo-

24. *International Economics* (Glencoe, Ill.: Free Press, 1951), pp. 372, 371, 110.

Marxists and dependency theorists see in neocolonialism and imperialistic exploitation the chief barrier. Early non-Marxist writers stressed a shortage of savings. Low savings in turn have been ascribed (for example, by Ragnar Nurkse) to low incomes or to the international demonstration effect.[25] Others, including Nurkse, see the main obstacle in the lack of incentive to invest. Still others see it in the difficulty of constructing overhead capital which requires large, indivisible investments. A more recent group of writers has shifted attention from inadequate physical capital to lack of human capital. Others have identified deteriorating terms of trade and the rules of the international game as the villain.

It would not be difficult to show that none of these theories holds water, though many point to obstacles that have stood in the way in some regions at some periods. Countries have failed to develop well in which these obstacles were not present, and others have successfully developed in spite of their presence.

It would be normal for an economist not to emphasize a single barrier but to analyze the social system in terms of a set of interacting conditions. Few economists would nowadays maintain that it is only land or only labor or only capital that produces output (though the history of thought shows that such views were held). Could one not apply an extension of the production function to the "product" development, and show that it depends on the cooperation and interaction of several variables, some economic, others noneconomic, which are complementary to some degree but also to some extent substitutable for one another? By training, if not by instinct, economists are foxes rather than hedgehogs.

A similar division applies to the definition of objectives. Some define them in terms of national product and its growth, or only material product excluding services; others in terms of life expectancy or other human indicators; still others in terms of participation, quality of life, or liberation. The pluralists see a blend of many objectives and tolerate different visions of the good society.

Linear versus Nonlinear Paradigms

I have suggested another dividing line. Allegiance to one of two schools of thought is most easily tested by a response to the Lewis test:[26] if the advanced countries were to sink under the sea in the year 2000, would the developing countries (after a period of adjustment) be better or worse off? As in a litmus test, those who say "worse" are the Blues, those who say "better" are the Reds.

25. Ragnar Nurkse, *Problems of Capital Formation in Underdeveloped Countries* (Oxford, Eng.: Blackwell, 1953).

26. W. Arthur Lewis, *The Development Process*, United Nations Executive Briefing Paper no. 2 (New York, 1970), p. 12.

The distinction is, of course, related to the mutual interest thesis. According to the doctrine of the Blues, development is a linear path along which all countries travel. The advanced countries have, at various times, passed the stage of take-off and the developing countries are now following them. The prime concern of governments is to organize the march along the development path.

Applied to the area of international relations, this view led to the call on rich countries to provide the missing components to developing countries and thereby to help them break bottlenecks and overcome obstacles. These missing components may be capital, foreign exchange, skills, or management. The doctrine provided a rationale for international financial aid, technical assistance, trade, and private foreign investment.[27] By breaking bottlenecks, rich countries could contribute to development efforts a multiple of what it cost them and thus speed up the development process in less developed countries at minimal cost to themselves. The two-gap models were a rationalization of foreign assistance. Moreover, the ultimate purpose of aid was to be rid of aid when, beyond the point of take-off, indigenous efforts are sufficient for further advance.

The linear view ruled out options of different styles of development. Inexorably, all countries were bound to pass through the five Rostovian stages. Historically, the view can be criticized as excessively determinist. Even Germany and Russia followed different paths from the English Industrial Revolution, and the differences were greater for the recently industrializing countries. Economically, the doctrine is deficient because it ignores the fact that the propagation of impulses from the rich to the poor countries (and among the poor countries) alters the nature of the development process; the latecomers face problems essentially different from the early starters, and the late latecomers find themselves in a world of demonstration effects and other impulses, both from the advanced countries and from other latecomers, which present opportunities and obstacles, incentives and inhibitions, quite different from those that England or even Germany, France, and Russia faced in their preindustrialization phase.

The Red response to the Lewis litmus test has gained adherents with the spreading disenchantment about development and about the international contribution to it. According to this view, the international system of rich-poor relationships produces and maintains the underdevelopment of the poor countries (the rich "underdevelop" the poor, in André Gunder Frank's phrase). In various ways, malignly exploitative or benignly neglectful or simply as a result of the unintended impact of events and policies in rich countries, the coexistence of rich and poor societies renders

27. See Hollis Chenery and Alan Strout, "Foreign Economic Assistance and Economic Development," AID Discussion Paper no. 7 (Washington, D.C.: U.S. Agency for International Aid, 1965), and *American Economic Review*, vol. 56 (1966).

more difficult or impossible the efforts of the poor societies to choose their style of development. The dominant groups in the developing countries—politicians, entrepreneurs, salaried officials, employees—enjoy high incomes, wealth, and status and, since they are subservient to the international system of inequality, conformity, and underdevelopment, they perpetuate it. International integration leads to national disintegration. Not only Marxists but also a growing number of non-Marxists have come to attribute a part of underdevelopment and of the obstacles encountered in the process of development to the existence and the policies of the industrial countries of the North, including Japan and the U.S.S.R.

According to one line of this second view, aid is not a transitional phenomenon to be ended after take-off, but a permanent feature claimed as a matter of right, and paid like an international income tax. According to a more radical line, aid is itself part of the international system of exploitation essential to maintain reactionary regimes, and self-reliant, independent development has to rid itself of it.

The conclusion drawn from this perception is that the developing countries should put up barriers between themselves and the destructive intrusions of trade, technology, transnational corporations, and educational and ideological influences, and should aim at "delinking" or "decoupling," at pulling down a poverty curtain, at insulating and isolating themselves from the international system. It is paradoxical that the socialist or radical advocates of delinking propose something that was triggered off by capitalist hostility to the U.S.S.R., China, and Cuba.

Proponents of the Blue perception point to Singapore, Hong Kong, Taiwan, Korea, and West Africa as outstanding examples of areas that benefited from commercial integration into the international system of trade, aid, investment, and money; and they cite the introduction of export crops into the colonies—rubber into Malaya, cocoa into the Gold Coast and Nigeria, tea into India—as powerful stimuli to their progress. Central Asia, large parts of Africa, and the interior of South America, however, lacked contact with the West and are among the least developed areas.

Proponents of the Red perception point to Indonesia, India, China, and Japan. The country with the greatest degree of contact with the West is Indonesia, where the Dutch were present for more than 300 years. Next comes India, where the British gradually expanded their foothold; then China, where trade along the coast created enclaves from which trade with the interior was forced on the country; last, Japan where the Tokugawa enforced a policy of no contact with the West except through a small Dutch trading group. Yet, they point out, Japan started to grow first and made rapid progress; China is well on the way; India comes next, and Indonesia last. The order of economic advance is the reverse of the degree of contact with the West.[28] Albert Hirschman observes that in Latin

28. See E. E. Hagen, *On the Theory of Social Change* (London: Tavistock, 1962).

America "industrial progress was particularly vigorous during the World Wars and the Great Depression, when contacts with the industrial countries were at a low ebb."[29]

Inevitably, a brief summary of the two views is bound to oversimplify. Rostow for the first kind of perception, and Frank for the second, are the popular rather than the academic models. Jacob Viner, Gottfried Haberler, Ragnar Nurkse, Harry Johnson, G. M. Meier, Hla Myint, I. M. D. Little, Maurice Scott, Jagdish Bhagwati, Anne Krueger, Bala Balassa, and others espoused the view that countries have much to gain from linking themselves up with the international system, and particularly from pursuing trade policies that avoid discrimination between exports and import substitution. Raúl Prebisch, Hans Singer, Gunnar Myrdal, Albert Hirschman, and François Perroux, not to say anything of Marx and List, had long ago developed approaches to development that separated "spread" or "trickle down" effects from "polarization," "backwash," "domination," or "immiserization" effects. And many raised doubts from the beginning as to whether everything would be fine if all countries would only pursue free trade policies and establish competitive markets. But probably because of their more careful formulations, the impact of their thinking, important though it was, was peripheral, not mainstream. More recent proponents of the second perception include Samir Amin, E. A. Brett, F. E. Cardoso, Franz Fanon, Celso Furtado, Johan Galtung, Colin Leys, Ann Seidman, Osvaldo Sunkel, and Tamas Szentes.

A reconciliation between the two perceptions (that development can be speeded up by integration into the international system and that underdevelopment is caused and perpetuated by it) is possible along the following lines. The advanced industrial countries emit a large number of impulses of two kinds: those that present opportunities for faster and better development than would otherwise have been possible, and those that present obstacles to development and stunt growth. I submit that the Lewis test is not a helpful way of presenting the problem, however useful it is as a litmus test for sorting out ideologies. The developed countries propagate a large number of impulses to the developing countries. Reasonable men may differ about the net balance of these impulses; for example, whether any defects of admitting transnational companies are offset by the availability of a stock of scientific, technological, and organizational knowledge, or whether the harm done by the brain drain is greater or less than the benefits from foreign technical assistance, or whether the inflow of grants and loans at concessionary interest rates is counterbalanced by aid-tying, faulty project selection, hard terms and conditions, and flight of capital.

The interesting question then is not, Do the developing countries benefit or lose from their coexistence with developed countries? but How can they

29. "The Rise and Decline of Development Economics," p. 17.

pursue selective policies that permit them to derive the benefits of the positive forces, without simultaneously exposing themselves to the harm of the detrimental forces? Countries should scrutinize the details of the whole balance sheet, the entries on the credit and debit side, and not only the net balance. Looked at in this way, the question becomes one of designing *selective* policies for aid, trade, foreign investment, transnational companies, technology, foreign education, movements of people, and so on. Neither complete insulation nor wide-open integration but a policy of enlightened discrimination may present the correct answer.[30]

This approach does tend to take a somewhat Olympian or Platonic view of policymaking. If policies are regarded as a function of political interests and pressure groups, the picture changes. The Reds would say such policies are impossible and the Blues that they are unnecessary. My reply would be that although I regard policies as partly dependent variables, determined by all the other variables in the social system, a process of experience and learning, as well as of constituency building for reforms, is capable of bending policies in the right direction.

According to this view, not all transnational corporations would be welcomed on favorable terms, but only those deemed to make a positive contribution to development, and on terms that insist on fair sharing of the benefits. The contracts between host governments and foreign companies would be carefully drawn up so as to derive the benefits of direct investment without its drawbacks, while leaving sufficient incentives to the company to operate efficiently on the desired scale. The existence of oligopoly rents ensures that such bargaining is possible and fruitful. Trade would be neither completely free nor autarkic, but, combined with a system of excise taxes and domestic controls, would discriminate according to social priorities. Exports would be taxed where demand elasticities are favorable. Not all forms of foreign technology and foreign products would be adopted without modification, but only those suited to the needs of the country. Others would be adapted and, where adaptation is impossible or too costly, indigenous innovation would be encouraged. Simi-

---

30. Ian Little has criticized this position on the following grounds: "Of course, such a position always puts the critic at some disadvantage, because he seldom wants to advocate *laissez-faire*, and the policies described will usually contain some elements that he would himself advocate—for example, export taxes or hard case-by-case bargaining in the case of mineral exploitation. Nevertheless, the picture of 'enlightened discrimination' drawn by Streeten seems to me to come too close to Indian policy over the past twenty years, and too close to maximum surveillance and control for it to be likely to do anything but retard growth without any offsetting benefit. There is a mass of evidence, in works already cited and elsewhere, that discrimination is seldom very enlightened." I. M. D. Little, "The Developing Countries and the International Order," in R. C. Amacher, G. Haberler, and T. D. Willett, eds., *Challenges to a Liberal International Economic Order* (Washington, D.C.: American Enterprise Institute, 1979), p. 278.

lar principles of discrimination would be applied to subsidizing education abroad and inviting technical assistance at home. Multilateral clearing and payments arrangements with like-minded countries would be established, so that constraints on hard currency earnings would not prevent the expansion of mutually beneficial trade. International reserves would be held in the form of a diversified portfolio of currencies to minimize the risk of losses. All of this would require scarce administrative skills, but pooling can economize on these, international cooperation can help, and learning will improve performance.

There are alternative styles of development, and one type of society may prefer to develop by adopting or adapting technologies and products from abroad, while another will find its identity by raising a curtain (it may be of bamboo or cactus) around its own frontiers or the frontiers of a group of like-minded countries with similar income levels and needs. A judicious selection of features of outward- and inward-looking strategies is likely to give the best results—such as drawing on foreign research and developing indigenous research or drawing on and adapting foreign technology and products. The lessons of industrializing Germany, France, Japan, and Russia, which used and adapted foreign ways, blending new institutions with old traditions, are not directly applicable because international income gaps were narrower then and the dimensions of the demographic problem, which determine the scale of the need for jobs, were quite different. In their early stages of development, however, these countries looked not at the established markets of England but at new opportunities and the growing markets of other newcomers. The main point is that there is a choice among styles of development which admit different blends of indigenous and foreign impulses. If the developed countries are enlightened, they will not feel threatened by the discriminatory features in such approaches but will cooperate with the developing countries in evolving their individual styles.

Big versus Small

There are those who believe that bigger is better, and those who think that small is beautiful. (We dismiss those who confuse big with great.) The spokesman of the former is the late P. C. Mahalanobis; of the latter, the late E. F. Schumacher. Both views have been influential.

The most influential advocate of "large planning" was Prasanta Chandra Mahalanobis (1893–1972). Although not an economist by training, he modified the simple Harrod-Domar model of growth in such a way as to justify investment in heavy industry in India. Multisector models with different capital-output ratios in each sector can easily be derived by modification of the Harrod-Domar model. Mahalanobis's two- and four-sector models have been among the most influential.[31] These models have been criticized both on empirical grounds—that the sectors do not correspond to "fillable boxes"—and on logical grounds. Mahalanobis assumes that investment is distributed between two sectors, consumer goods (for example, looms) and capital goods (for example, machine tools). We thus have two capital-output ratios: investment/extra consumer goods and investment/extra capital goods. The former is assumed to be lower than the latter, but the rate of growth of investment depends now on the rate of growth of output in the capital goods sector and thus on the allocation of investment between the two sectors. There is an implicit assumption that foreign exchange resources for importing capital goods are strictly limited, so that foreign trade "productivity" is zero. Thus the proportion of total investment allocated to the capital goods sector (together with its capital-output ratio) becomes the crucial variable determining the long-term rate of growth of consumption goods. In his four-sector model the consumption sector is subdivided into modern industry, small-scale industry including agriculture, and services. This model was used by Mahalanobis to explore the employment implications of different investment patterns.[32]

The two-sector model has been criticized from various points of view.[33] It has been argued that no empirical meaning can be given to the distribution of investment between the two sectors, since most industries supply products to both. The model has also been criticized for implicit and unwarranted assumptions about exports; for neglecting supply limitations other than capital goods; for ignoring depreciation, raw materials, and all intermediate goods; for confusing a technological capital coefficient with an economic choice as to how much of the product of the capital goods sector should be used for investment; for treating the productivity of investment and the capital-labor ratio as independent; for inadequately considering the relation of demand to supply; for assuming capital-labor ratios to be constant; for neglecting the benefits to development that arise from expanding some types of consumption; and for not distinguishing

31. P. C. Mahalanobis, "Some Observations on the Process of Growth of National Income," *Sankhya*, vol. 12, pt. 4 (September 1953), and "The Approach of Operational Research to Planning in India," *Sankhya*, vol. 16, pts. 1 and 2 (December 1955).

32. Since the statistics of planning require the planning of statistics, Mahalanobis's contribution to both sample surveys and the statistical techniques also make him a pioneer in development planning.

33. See, for example, Shigeto Tsuru, "The Applicability and Limitations of Economic Development Theory," *Indian Economic Journal* (April 1962); K. N. Raj, "Growth Models and Indian Planning, *Indian Economic Review* (February 1961); K. N. Raj and A. K. Sen, "Alternative Patterns of Growth under Conditions of Stagnant Export Earnings," *Oxford Economic Papers*, vol. 13, no. 1 (February 1961); the contributions in *Oxford Economic Papers*, vol. 14, no. 1 (February 1962), and the reply by Raj and Sen, *Oxford Economic Papers* (June 1962). See also Evsey D. Domar, "A Soviet Model of Growth," in *Essays in the Theory of Economic Growth* (New York: Oxford University Press, 1957), which discusses the very similar model of the Soviet economist G. A. Fel'dman.

between capital goods in general, machine-making goods, and heavy and basic industries. When all criticisms are taken into account, certain valid conclusions still remain. In the absence of all other limitations on production if there is a machine that can either reproduce itself or produce other kinds of products, the production of other kinds of products can be raised at some later date by a greater allocation of capital now to the reproduction of the machine. (In addition to this versatility assumption a second assumption is necessary; that is, that the capital stock cannot be shifted between the two sectors.[34]) Alternatively, if other limitations on production are postulated, the tautological proposition is left that if the growth of an economy is limited by a bottleneck in the production of capital goods (however defined), removal of this bottleneck will accelerate growth. In India's first development plan, emphasis was placed on the marginal propensity to save. It has been healthy to distribute the emphasis among other constraints, such as the availability of capital goods, and to show that these may prevent the savings potential from materializing. To raise the investment-income ratio is obviously not enough. Decisions will also have to be taken as to how the investment is to be distributed among different activities. Not only the aggregate of savings but also its distribution is important. Any bottleneck—skilled labor, administrative ability, foreign exchange—could be selected as a constraint, and the proportion of expenditure (or effort) devoted to reducing this constraint could be made the determinant of development.

The Mahalanobis model also adds a constraint set by savings, though it is an odd and rather special constraint. If it is assumed that savings can be raised only by introducing capital-intensive methods of production, then emphasis on heavy industry and capital goods becomes a means of enforcing savings. In terms of the Harrod-Domar model, in which the growth rate (g) equals the savings-income ratio (s) divided by the capital-output ratio (k), s becomes a function of k, and k is a function of the distribution of investment; by changing the direction of investment we can increase the average k, thereby raising s more than proportionately and thus raising the growth rate g. The main reason seems to be that people cannot eat machines. But before choosing this method of increasing g we should be certain that there are no ways of reducing k that would reduce s less than proportionately.

In spite of the numerous criticisms advanced against the Mahalanobis model, his conclusions and recommendations were broadly right for India at the time, the major exception being his neglect of foreign trade opportunities.[35] The principal reason he gave for encouraging the

34. See Sukhamoy Chakravarty, "Some Aspects of Optimal Investment Policy in an Underdeveloped Economy," in *Towards Balanced International Growth*, H. C. Bos, ed. (Amsterdam: North-Holland, 1969).

35. See T. N. Srinivasan, "P. C. Mahalanobis," in *International Encyclopedia of the Social Sciences*, vol. 18. There can be little doubt that the neglect of manufactured

machine-making sector is to reduce, in time, the unit cost of making capital goods through learning effects, economies of scale, and specialization. For a country the size of India, this was the most important ground for building up the capital goods sector. In his *A Theory of Economic History*, Sir John Hicks attributes the mainspring of the Industrial Revolution not, as is commonly thought, to the textiles sector, but to the capital goods sector, in which ever cheaper ways were found to make machines to make machines.[36]

Ernst Friedrich Schumacher (1911–77) stands at the opposite pole from that of P. C. Mahalanobis. It is ironical that the Indian disciple of Tagore from Bengal enthusiastically advocated large-scale facilities to produce cement, electricity and steel, while the product of the high-technology education of Germany, Great Britain, and the United States emphasized, above all, the need to protect the process of organic growth and foresaw spiritual disaster in any attempt to speed up development through a program of large-scale industrialization.[37]

To the economic content of Schumacher's message the neoclassical economist might reply that, with proper pricing policies that reflect the relative scarcities of the factors of production, the right combinations between capital and labor would emerge. But the scale of the problem is such that tinkering with prices would not help. Incomes per capita in the poor countries are perhaps one-tenth of what they are in rich countries; savings rates are about one-half; and the rate of growth of the labor force is three times as high, say, 3 percent instead of 1 percent. This means that investable resources per worker are only one-sixtieth what they are typi-

---

exports was a fault of Indian planning. But the creation of a capital goods sector need not have been at this expense.

36. New York: Oxford University Press, 1969, pp. 147–48.

37. In the 1960s, when capital accumulation was the rage on both the left and the right, and when the "stages of economic growth" dominated official thinking, Schumacher argued that countries with large labor surpluses and capital shortages should adopt "intermediate technology," at a cost of between $100 and $1,000 per workplace; neither $10,000, nor $10. Village tools were too primitive, Western machines too complex. "Modern man has built a system of production that ravishes nature and a type of society that mutilates man," he wrote, in an essay on "Economics as if People Mattered" (*Small is Beautiful* [New York: Harper and Row, 1973]). He wanted technology to have a human face. What initially was developed for the poor countries found application in the advanced industrial countries of the West and he had a wide following among the young, especially in America.

The notion of an intermediate or appropriate technology was applied not only to manufacturing industry and agriculture (simple power tools, not tractors and combine harvesters), but also to the social sectors (health, sanitation, water supply) and to the scale of institutions: small, decentralized, participatory. In his later writings he emphasized the unity of man as consumer and producer. His thought had been developed when he was economic adviser to Burma and India, where Buddhist and Gandhian philosophy had impressed him. But the policy of previous Indian governments to replace large firms by small establishments in the production of textiles and footwear was misguided.

cally in an advanced, industrial country ($1/10 \times 1/2 \times 1/3$). Assuming, unrealistically, completely fixed coefficients between capital and labor, the transfer of rich-country technology would create jobs for only between 1 and 2 percent of the extra labor force streaming into the market every year, without making an impact on the large pool of already existing unemployed. Even with a considerable degree of flexibility, it is impossible to remove unemployment. And the appropriate technology for these countries just does not exist. Only 3 percent of research and development (R&D) expenditure is spent in the developing countries containing three-quarters of humanity (and by no means all of this expenditure is on problems specific to them); 97 percent is spent in the rich countries with only one quarter of mankind. This amounts to a ratio of 100:1 of R&D expenditure per capita between rich and poor countries. No wonder appropriate technology for low-income societies does not exist.

Utopians versus Pedants

Finally, there is my favorite division between utopians and pedants. There is, on the one hand, an admirable species of man and woman: professional, dedicated, conscientious, with fine minds and great attention to details. They are, without derogatory connotations, the pedants. But they have come to know so much about how things are and how they work that they have acquired a vested interest in preserving the status quo. When faced with proposals for reform, they are like inverted Micawbers— waiting for something to turn down. They can always think of ten very good reasons why it cannot be done. If we think that there must be a solution to every problem, they have at least two problems to every solution.

On the other hand, there is another group of people with fewer but more vocal members. They present us with visions of different possibilities of the future. Just as the first group is passionately devoted to preserving things as they are, so this group passionately dislikes precision, both in analyzing what exists today and in drawing up the blueprints of their ideas for a better society in the future. They are the utopians. They are careless about details but they are the visionaries, the keepers of our faith.

The division of humanity into pedants and utopians is, as the sociologist Peter Berger has said, deplorable.[38] What we need is to marry the two: pedantic utopians or utopian pedants—who cultivate, with informed fantasy, imaginative but carefully worked-out visions of alternative social possibilities.

The pedants tend to advocate models that have, by their standards,

38. *Pyramids of Sacrifice: Political Ethics and Social Change* (New York: Basic Books, 1974).

worked: export orientation, reliance on market forces, reduced interventions by the central government. The utopians want to experiment with a wide range of institutional arrangements: socialist communities with complete common ownership; cooperatives with some private property and shared services; completely private ownership of the means of production; even institutions where nobody owns assets and groups of trustees administer the productive activities. The pedants think in linear terms, the utopians wish to adopt many options. The blend between the two is necessary because the objectives and the technology often prescribe the social institutions, and some options are ruled out. But there is not complete rigidity between technology and institutions, and the marriage of the utopians and the pedants would explore the available range.

Conclusions

Some of the foregoing discussion can be criticized for being too compromising. Eclecticism and compromise are not attractive to scholars. And it is true that two different scientific paradigms cannot coexist for long. But the declension is: I (and Hegel) synthesize, you compromise, he/she is anemic. The intention was not compromise but to show either that the alternatives were wrongly posed or that only a double-pronged attack will achieve the objective.

What lessons can be learned for the future course of development economics should it turn out that the news of its death has been exaggerated?

1. The transition of development economics from the economics of a special case to a new global economics of shared problems, but with greater differentiation of approaches and analyses, both unifies and differentiates the subject. It calls for a much finer typology of countries and regions, according to the questions posed.

2. The call for an appropriate intellectual technology that is rigorous within the bounds permitted by the subject calls for a unification of the formal and informal intellectual sectors.

3. The need for multidisciplinary work at the deepest level, where nonconventional but relevant variables are incorporated in the models, is generally accepted. The precise way of doing it is much more difficult to specify.

4. A selective policy of discrimination or alternating phases is capable of producing a synthesis between those who advocate total linking to the international market system and those who advocate delinking. The purpose would be to make use of the beneficial impulses propagated by the world system, without admitting the detrimental impulses, and to build a base on which external influences could be used.

5. Three dimensions now somewhat neglected need strengthening. One

is the historical dimension, so that we understand how things came to be what they are, so that we may know the limits of and opportunities for desirable changes. The second is the global dimension, so that we view international relations in a manner that transcends the boundaries of the nation state. The interaction of national policies and the international system, alliances of interests across national boundaries, appropriate institutional responses to global problems are all issues that should have a higher place on our research agenda than they have now. The third is the dimension of what Harvey Leibenstein has called Micro-Micro Theory. It covers not only what goes on inside the firm, but also inside the farm, the household, and possibly inside any one individual with conflicting desires. The basic needs work has shown that institutional arrangements are very important in meeting basic needs, and of the three institutions—market, public sector, and household—the household has, until recently, been neglected by economists. In addition, the origins and diffusion of technological innovation deserve more attention.

6. Large-scale and small-scale activities should not be regarded as alternatives, but should be made mutually supporting or at least not mutually destructive—Mao's strategy of walking on two legs. Large-scale, modern activity should not destroy the small-scale, informal sector. The difficulty is to design policies which enable the small-scale sector to grow, without depriving the large-scale sector of resources that would have a higher productivity there: these may be capital, managerial talent, wage goods, or foreign exchange.

7. Finally, we need a combination of careful attention to detail with visions for alternative ways of arranging and managing our affairs. This implies exploring institutional options and their dependence on certain technological processes and economic objectives.

Index

Absolute poverty, 161, 348
Africa, 6, 33, 52, 249
African Development Bank, 279
Aggregate indicators, 234, 235–37, 263, 271, 348
Agricultural commodities, 30, 37, 178, 225–26, 268; export of, 72, 177, 122–25, 138, 139–40, 142
Agricultural labor force, 65, 70, 134–35, 170, 211; productivity of, 32–33, 65–66, 82, 124, 139–40, 348. *See also* Rural unemployment
Agricultural policy, 122, 128, 218, 257*n*
Agricultural productivity, 65–66, 76–77, 121, 128, 133, 142, 160, 322
Agriculture, 102*n*, 201, 242, 248, 269; capital formation in, 29–30, 31, 35, 48–49, 75; modernization of, 217–18
Alliance for Progress, 136, 195, 212, 217, 219, 258, 266
Allocation of resources. *See* Resource allocation
American Dilemma, An, 151, 153, 168, 240
Antagonistic growth, 106–09, 115–16
Appropriate technology, 170, 209, 323, 330, 332, 340, 358*n*, 359, 360
Arab countries, 152
Argentina, 104–06, 124, 175
Arrow, Kenneth, 54–55
Asher, Robert E., 258*n*, 299, 302, 303
Asia, 37, 153–55, 239*n*, 245, 248, 249; agriculture in, 29, 31
Asian Drama, 153–55, 158, 168, 170, 339
Australia, 72
Austrian School, 3, 61, 222–23
Autarky, 54, 80, 293–94

Authoritarian government, 161, 191, 196, 257

Backward linkages, 94, 96, 236
Balance of payments, 103–04, 136, 137, 202, 324, 348; pressures on, 133, 160, 172, 179, 254, 257
Balanced growth, 127, 141, 199, 200*n*, 347. *See also* Unbalanced growth
Balogh, Thomas, 279, 301*n*
Banfield, Edward C., 99
Bangladesh, 49–50
Bank of England model, 295*n*
Basic needs, 210, 220, 223, 319, 348
Bauer, P. T., 246–47, 250
Becker, Gary, 131
Berg report, 311
Beveridge, Sir William, 276, 277, 280
Beveridge report, 15, 276
Bhagwati, Jagdish N., 53, 222
Big push doctrine, 30, 105, 136, 210–12, 222–24
Birth control, 156, 160
Bissell, Richard M., 229
Black, Eugene, 130, 298, 299, 300, 303
Bolivia, 9
Boon, G. K., 323
Bos, H. C., 325
Boserup, Ester, 102*n*
Brandt Commission, 255–56, 259, 266, 284, 300, 301, 318; on foreign aid, 163–64, 172, 218, 297, 303, 331
Brazil, 9, 102–03, 124, 278
Breman, Jan, 318
Bretton Woods conference, 9–10, 11, 136, 279
British West Africa, 15; trade organization in, 28, 29–30, 31, 35–36, 39, 45

British West Indies, 121–22

Brogan, Sir Dennis, 74

Buck, J. L., 65

Business cycles, 193, 280, 315–16, 332. *See also* Keynesian analysis (of business cycles); Trade cycles

Business interests, 158*n*, 187

Cairncross, Alec, 16–17, 63

Campos, Roberto, 278

Canada, 73

Cancún meeting, 256, 266

Capital, 130–31, 163, 200*n*, 203, 236, 319–21, 330. *See also* Human capital

Capital accumulation, 15–16, 59, 179, 182, 189, 191, 193, 347, 348, 358*n*; versus consumption, 185, 186, 187, 188, 195. *See also* Agriculture (capital formation in)

Capital formation, 5, 13, 35, 131–32, 134–35, 145, 316

Capital goods, 356–58

Capital investments, 16, 74–75, 237. *See also* Infrastructure (investment in)

Capital market, 215, 226

Capital-output ratio, 50, 75, 211–12, 320, 355–56

Capital supply, 27, 34–35, 316

Cassel, Gustav, 321

Caste. *See* Social structure

Center for International Studies (CENIS), 240–45, 246–47

Center-periphery system, 114, 124, 176–81, 184, 190, 194, 197, 198, 280. *See also* Peripheral capitalism

Central Intelligence Agency (CIA), 241*n*

Central planning, 17–18, 42, 55, 257, 347, 348, 349

CEPAL (Comisión Económica para América Latina). *See* United Nations Economic Commission for Latin America

Challenge of World Poverty, The, 159

Chenery, Hollis B., 79, 127, 137, 200*n*, 323

Chicago School, 112, 113

Chile, 203, 298

China, 80, 158*n*, 239, 248; agriculture in, 65

Choice-theoretic models, 112

Chudson, Walter, 280

Circular and cumulative causation, 152, 168

Clark, Colin, 277

Clark-Fisher hypothesis, 36

Classical economics, 3, 45–46, 75. *See also* Neoclassical economics

Club of Rome, 329, 330

Cobb-Douglas function, 74, 316

Cobweb theorem, 225, 326, 332

Cocoa industry, 28, 31

Colombia, 9, 14*n*, 90–91, 93, 95, 102, 114

Colonial economics, 6, 7–8

Colonialism, 5, 8, 155, 197, 319

Comisión Económica para América Latina (CEPAL). *See* United Nations Economic Commission for Latin America

Commercial policy. *See* Trade policies

Commodities, 41, 181, 194, 210, 225–26. *See also* Agricultural commodities; Consumption goods; Manufactured goods; Primary commodities

Common Fund, 279–80

Communist countries, 231, 240–41, 243; foreign aid from, 260

Comparative advantage, 94, 138, 169, 170, 192, 280, 287, 309–10; of manufactured goods exports, 138, 291; of primary commodities exports, 129, 138, 193

Competition, 101, 179, 189, 192, 211, 226, 317*n*, 348

Complementarity activities, 126, 210, 213, 216, 223, 224

Conditions of Economic Progress, The, 59–60, 61, 64, 65, 68, 70, 78, 80, 81

Conspicuous consumption, 182, 185, 195

Consumption, 4, 5, 35, 82, 103, 130, 137, 154, 159, 210. *See also* Capital accumulation (versus consumption); Domestic consumption

Consumption goods, 22, 67, 163, 171, 252, 356

Cooperative society, 38*n*

Corruption in government, 154, 155, 157, 159

Credit market, 160, 188

Cuba, 9, 258

Cultural differences, 328; in labor productivity, 29, 32–33, 46–48, 52–53

Currie, Lauchlin, 14*n*

Customs unions, 127, 141

Debt-led growth, 226

Decisionmaking, 102, 117, 191, 213, 263, 317. *See also* Investment decisions

Delinking, 104, 190, 193, 293–94, 360

Demand, 184, 286; elasticities of, 176, 178, 193, 198–200, 213, 295; income elasticities of, 20, 73, 179, 223. *See also* Supply

Democratic government, 108–09, 157–58, 189, 191, 196, 242, 245, 246

Dependency theory, 96, 123–25, 129, 140–41, 190, 195, 250–53, 280, 337–40, 350

Depressions, 159, 166, 172. *See also* Great Depression

Design of Development, The, 319, 325n, 332

Development aid, 151, 166, 257–60, 343

Development cooperation, 320, 328, 331

Development Decades, 329–30

Development Planning, 131

Developmental economics, 4, 6–7, 8, 34, 121, 337–41

Developmental Projects Observed, 101

Direct investment, 29, 31, 45, 194

Disequilibrium in development, 105, 169, 194, 207–08, 225

"Distribution of Gains between Investing and Borrowing Countries," 275, 287, 304–05

Distributive justice, 280–81, 284

Division of labor, 347; international, 179, 211, 322–25

Dobb, Maurice, 16–17

Domestic consumption, 142, 178

Domestic investment, 19, 103, 256

Duesenberry, James S., 348

Dutch disease, 125–26, 340

Dutch planning school, 318–19, 332–33

East Asia, 171, 202, 294, 309–10

ECE. *See* United Nations Economic Commission for Europe

Eckaus, Richard S., 222

ECLA. *See* United Nations Economic Commission for Latin America

Econometrics, 332, 333–34

Economic history, 229–30, 236, 237, 238, 253–55, 262–63, 269–70, 282, 316, 358

Economic liberalism, 188, 191

Economic stability, 6, 13, 172

Economic surplus, 185–86, 195. *See also* Surplus labor

Economic Survey, 123

Economic Theory and Underdeveloped Regions, 152, 168

Economics of 1960, The, 72–73

Economics of Subsistence Agriculture, The, 76

Economies of scale, 208, 209, 213

Education, 101, 159–60, 218, 247, 317n, 319, 324, 332, 355; investment in, 131, 326–28

Efficiency, 99–101, 196, 238, 280. *See also* X-efficiency theory

Eisenhower, Dwight, 258, 259

Elites, 162, 166, 195, 271

Elkan, Walter, 38

Ellsworth, P. T., 282n

Elster, John, 338

Employment, 73, 187, 330; full, 5, 11, 12, 15, 218, 221, 277, 348. *See also* Unemployment

Employment policies, 14–15

End of Laissez-Faire, The, 76

Engel's law, 79–80, 82, 286

"Engines of growth," 284, 287

Entrepreneurs, 31, 45, 96, 129, 199, 214, 225

Equilibrium in development, 105, 136, 199, 211, 223, 237, 320. *See also* Disequilibrium in development

Europe, 124, 152, 207, 224, 307–08, 318, 339; industrialization in, 4–5, 214

Evans, David, 280n

Exchange, 3, 193, 280n, 281

Exit mechanism, 100–01

Export industries, 158, 177–79, 341, 346

Export substitution, 181, 194, 283, 287, 294, 295

Externalities, 126, 143, 208, 209, 211, 213–15, 216, 224, 225

Factors of production, 169–70, 211, 316, 321–24, 358–59; prices of, 152, 168

Failure complex, 93

Far East. *See* Asia

Finance, 130–37, 180, 222, 225, 296, 299. *See also* Capital

Fiscal policies, 35, 102, 169, 225–26

Fishlow, Albert, 235

F.o.b. export value, 285–86

Foreign aid, 8, 18–19, 42, 53–54, 247, 265–66, 268–69, 347; political objectives of, 136–37, 158n, 239–40, 241–45. *See also* Brandt Commission (on foreign aid); Development aid; Poverty (foreign aid to alleviate)

Foreign aid policies, 159, 161–64, 212,

Foreign aid policies (*cont.*)
  217, 220, 239–40, 270–71. *See also*
  Official development assistance
Foreign debt, 164, 217, 218–19, 296
Foreign exchange, 14, 103, 122, 128,
  141, 194; rates, 11, 54, 147, 169, 178,
  201, 216
Foreign investment, 4, 13, 48–49, 141,
  194, 211, 287, 309
Foreign investment policies, 130, 166,
  169
Foreign policies, 241–46, 267, 269, 328
Formal sector, 343–45
France, 71, 89
Frank, André Gunder, 351, 353
Friedman, Milton, 40, 101
Full employment, 5, 11, 12, 15, 218, 221,
  277, 348

Galbraith, John Kenneth, 66
Galenson, Walter, 130
Gandhi, Mohandas, 63
Gang of Four, 171, 202, 294, 309–10
Gayer study, 230
General Agreement on Tariffs and Trade
  (GATT), 10, 189
*General Theory of Employment, Interest
  and Money, The*, 34n, 60
Ghana, 28, 122, 133–34, 201n
Gilbert, Milton, 46n, 67, 68, 80
Government, 131–32, 137, 146, 166,
  239n; intervention by, 5, 39–40, 55,
  178, 193, 195, 277, 346, 347; policies,
  17–18, 180, 211; regulation by, 76,
  188; role of, 6, 14–15, 27, 31, 250,
  263–64. *See also* Authoritarian gov-
  ernment; Corruption in government;
  Democratic government; Nationalism;
  Soft state
Government enterprises, 325–26
Great Britain, 9, 155–56, 208, 276; employment in, 15, 60–61, 70, 276; investment by, 298, 299–300; investment
  in, 248n; national product, 59, 68, 69
Great Depression, 11, 14, 60–61, 123,
  175, 178, 198, 319, 346
Gross national product. *See* National product
Gudin, Eugenio, 278

Haberler, Gottfried, 21, 200, 202n
Hagen, Everett, 75–76, 81
Hammarskjöld, Dag, 303
Hanau, Arthur, 326

Hancock, Sir Keith, 29
Harrod, Roy, 67
Harrod-Domar model, 16, 48, 74, 320,
  332–33, 355, 357
Haswell, M. R., 76
Havana charter, 10, 280
Hayami, Yujiro, 66, 77
Hayek, Friedrich A., 61
Heckscher, Eli, 322
Heckscher-Ohlin theory, 168–69, 322
Helleiner, Gerald, 285
Henderson, David, 344
Herrera Committee, 252–53, 255
Hicks, Sir John R., 22, 223, 358
Hidden rationalities, 91–94, 99, 112, 114
Hilgerdt, Folke, 168, 280, 281
Hirschman, Albert, 127, 201, 264, 277,
  321, 337, 339, 340, 352–53
Hirschman hypothesis, 98–99
History of Economic Analysis, 222
Hoffman, Paul, 299, 302
Human capital, 32, 52, 209, 317, 327,
  330

IBRD (International Bank for Reconstruc-
  tion and Development). *See* World
  Bank
IDA. *See* International Development Asso-
  ciation; International Development
  Authority
ILO. *See* International Labour Office
IMF. *See* International Monetary Fund
Immigration policies, 53
Import restrictions, 10, 158n
Imports, 76–77, 163
Import substitution (IS) industrialization,
  12, 96, 198, 199, 202, 252, 283, 287–
  88
Import substitution, 14, 125–29, 141–
  42, 179–81, 193–96, 293, 310, 323,
  346
Import substitution strategies, 10, 21,
  170–71, 201–02, 204
Income, 106n, 109, 184, 195, 204, 260,
  268, 316; disparities, 170–71, 181–82,
  184, 192, 193, 195, 341–42; loss, 177,
  179, 185; per capita, 142, 167–68,
  171, 348; producer, 40, 140, 324; real,
  66, 78, 80–81, 261, 316; statistics, 35,
  46, 159. *See also* Wages
Income distribution, 134, 189, 194, 250,
  254, 268
Income redistribution, 5, 154, 170, 191,
  194

India, 80, 155–58, 208, 298; agriculture in, 33, 49, 134, 135, 246; census of, 64; economic plans of, 17, 130, 170, 201–02n, 211–12, 246, 354n, 355–58; education in, 156, 157; land reform in, 135, 156, 157; national product of, 62–63, 167; population growth in, 156; poverty in, 316–17

Indonesia, 321

Inducement goods, 29, 35

Inducement mechanism, 95

Indus River Basin scheme, 278, 298

Industrial investments, 97, 103, 193

Industrial planning, 97

Industrial sector, 130, 160, 308–09

Industrialization, 73–74, 99, 121–29, 138–39, 177–79, 184–85, 209, 248, 310, 325, 348; labor needs, 160, 211, 213, 214, 224; qualitative model of, 4–5

Industrialization of Backward Areas, 4–5

Industrialization policies, 12, 17, 169, 177, 180, 193, 208, 287–88

Inequalities, 152–54, 156, 159, 166, 168, 195, 196, 217–18, 221

Inflation, 134–36, 145–47, 182, 184, 186–88, 195, 229, 254

Informal sector, 38, 343–45

Infrastructure, 30, 45, 224, 279, 302, 320; investment in, 75, 105, 169, 180, 208–09, 214, 300, 325

Innis, Harold, 97

Input-output method of planning, 324

Institutional approach, 153–54, 158–59, 258, 345

Institutional reforms, 166, 170, 195

Interest rates, 160, 216, 226

International Bank for Reconstruction and Development. *See* World Bank

International commodity agreements, 9–10, 48

International Development Association (IDA), 53, 275, 297, 300, 303, 311

International Development Authority (IDA), 300

International economic cooperation, 163, 182–83, 315–16. *See also* North-South cooperation

International economic relations, 176–77, 265, 337, 361

International Labour Office (ILO), 66–67, 97, 276

International Monetary Fund (IMF), 9, 102, 131, 164, 182, 279–80

International organizations, 219, 256, 258, 329–30

International trade, 4, 6, 11, 22, 27, 136, 166, 202, 279, 341, 347–49

International Trade Organization (ITO), 10, 279, 281

International trade theory, 126–27, 141, 152, 180, 263, 322

Investment, 22, 27, 35, 193–94, 201, 211, 224–25, 236, 237–38. *See also types of investment*

Investment decisions, 76, 213

Investment planning, 94, 180, 200, 202n

Invisible hand, 113, 116

IS industrialization. *See* Import substituting industrialization

Italy, 66–67, 90, 211, 212–13

Jamaica, 125–26, 340

Japan, 158n; economic development of, 71, 73, 75, 310, 323; employment in, 53, 65, 77

Johnson, H. G., 308–09

Judd, Percy, 280

Kenya, 71, 276

Keynes, John Maynard, 9, 60–61, 68, 232n, 279

Keynesian analysis, 6, 11, 19, 34n, 172, 230, 237, 349; of business cycles, 3, 132; of income, 234; of inflation, 229; of investments, 76; of money, 230; of unemployment, 14–16, 277

Kindleberger, Charles, 263n, 283, 292–93, 294

King, Gregory, 79

Kondratieff cycle, 72, 230, 253–55, 264, 268, 281

Korea, Republic of, 158n, 346

Korean War, 240, 245, 289, 305

Kravis, Irving B., 46n, 67, 68, 70–71, 80, 305–06, 307

Krishna, Raj, 347

Kuznets, Simon, 7, 81, 167, 249

Kuyvenhoven, A., 324

Labor, 130–31, 322; training of, 129, 143, 209, 214–15, 224. *See also* Division of labor; Employment

Labor force, 134, 160, 177, 186, 187, 188. *See also* Agricultural labor force

Labor migration, 29, 31–32, 53, 70, 126, 134, 141, 145, 211

Labor productivity, 4, 67–68, 71, 98–101, 281, 343. *See also* Cultural differences (in labor productivity)

Labor supply, 37–38, 132–33, 144, 145, 170

Laissez-faire, 76, 224, 280*n*, 354*n*

Land reform, 128, 130, 158*n*, 159, 170

Land tenure, 32, 181

Latin America, 9–10, 93, 201*n*, 251–53, 258; balance of payments in, 136, 193, 194, 195; common market in, 178, 194; employment in, 97; industrialization in, 177, 192, 194, 198, 202, 352–53; inflation in, 12, 102–03, 127, 135–36, 188; trade policies in, 14, 180, 254, 309

Leibenstein, Harvey, 95, 130, 361

Lewis, W. Arthur, 3–4, 82, 197, 277, 282, 288*n*, 299, 339, 340, 350

Lewis test, 350–55

Limits to Growth, The, 260–61

Lindblom, C. E., 92

Linkages, 96–98, 117, 177, 201*n*, 234–36, 245, 253, 288, 323, 347. *See also* Backward linkages; Delinking

Lipsey, Robert E., 305–06, 307

Little, Ian, 22*n*, 345, 347, 354*n*

Loans, 130, 296, 325. *See also* Foreign debt; Soft loans

Lorenz, Detlef, 280*n*

Lundberg, Erik, 348

McClelland, David, 99

McNamara, Robert, 161, 303

Macroeconomics, 7, 230, 235–36, 263

Mahalanobis, Prasanta Chandra, 130, 199–200, 277, 316, 355–58

Mahalanobis model, 17, 355–56

Maizels, A., 285–86

Malaysia, 28, 41, 44, 45

Malthusianism, 68, 81, 82, 261

Mandelbaum, Kurt, 4–5

Manoilescu, Mihail, 125

Manufactured goods, 287; export of, 22, 128–29, 138, 142–43, 170, 176, 180–81, 194, 288–95, 306; terms of trade for, 176, 217

Manufacturing sector, 121, 129, 130, 143

Marginal net product, 214, 215, 224, 225

Marginal utility, 3, 132, 222–24, 261

Market mechanism, 209–10, 215

Market theory, 46, 54–55

Markets, 189–90, 192, 252, 263, 360

Marshall, Alfred, 207–08, 231, 237, 264, 265, 280

Marshall Plan, 14, 88–90, 91, 111, 171–72, 220, 299

Martin, Alison, 131

Marx, Karl, 133, 144, 338

Marxism, 69, 352. *See also* Neo-Marxism

Mason, Edward S., 242, 258*n*, 299, 302, 303

Mates, Leo, 298*n*

Meade, James, 279

Measurements for the Economic Development of Under-Developed Countries, 12–13, 300

Measurements for International Economic Stability, 13

Mennes, L. B. M., 324

Mexico, 160

Michaely, Michael, 306–07

Micro-Micro Theory, 361

Military aid, 245, 249, 271

Mill, John Stuart, 4

Millikan, Max, 229, 240–41, 265

Mincer, Jacob, 327

Modernization, 51–52, 130, 231, 238–39, 242, 247, 262–63, 270

Modernization policies, 232–34, 251

Monetarism, 102, 229–31

Monetary policies, 102, 147, 169, 187–88, 189

Money, Credit, and Commerce, 231

Money supply, 135, 145, 187

Monoeconomics, 337

Monopoly, 317*n*

Mosaks, Jacob, 329*n*

Multinational corporations, 143, 190, 192, 203, 218, 285–86, 293, 340, 350; and technological progress, 129, 179, 203, 252, 323

Mutual benefit thesis, 256, 284, 338, 341–43, 345, 351

Myint, Hla, 6–7, 22, 122

Myrdal, Gunnar, 7, 10–20, 130, 240, 279, 280, 339

Nakayama, Ichiro, 77

Naoroji, Dadabhai, 62–63

National and International Measures for Full Employment, 12

National Income and Outlay, 59, 80

National product, 13, 69, 80–81, 137, 151, 161, 167, 320, 322, 324. *See also* Per capita product

Nationalism, 5–6, 232–33, 238–40, 249, 263, 330

Nehru, Jawaharlal, 156–57

Neoclassical economics, 20, 130, 191, 210, 237, 285, 337, 338, 358; criticism of, 54, 104, 132, 169, 238, 345–56; support for, 169–70, 175, 178

Neo-Marxism, 337, 338, 345, 349–50

Netherlands, 126, 161, 325–26

New International Economic Order, 10, 164–65, 212, 255, 256, 259, 282, 329

New Zealand, 72; national product of, 69–70

Nigeria, 28, 41, 160, 324

Noneconomic factors, 202n, 232, 236–37, 262

North-South cooperation, 255, 256, 261, 264, 343

North-South dialogue, 182–83, 193, 203, 259, 265–66, 285, 337, 338–41

Nurkse, Ragnar, 16, 20, 134, 145–46, 199, 200, 202n, 279, 347–48, 350

ODA. See Official development assistance

OECD. See Organisation for Economic Co-operation and Development

Official development assistance (ODA), 53–54, 161–63, 171–72, 195, 296–97, 310–11, 349

Ohlin, Bertil, 322

Oil, 340; prices, 160, 255, 283n, 290–91, 309

OPEC. See Organization of Petroleum Exporting Countries

Opportunity prices. See Shadow prices

Organisation for Economic Co-operation and Development (OECD), 123, 127, 201, 259

Organization of Petroleum Exporting Countries (OPEC), 259–60, 282–83

Overpopulation, 128, 133

Owen, David, 276, 299

Pacing devices. See Pressure mechanisms

Pajestka, Josef, 329n

Pakistan, 73, 278, 298

Pearson Commission, 218, 300, 318

Peccei, Aurelio, 329

Per capita product, 7, 247, 293

Per capita real income, 6, 159, 238, 358

Perez Guerero, Manuel, 318

Peripheral capitalism, 183–85, 189–91, 192–95, 203–04

Petroleum. See Oil

Petty, William, 70, 79, 81

Physiocrats, 69

Pigou, Arthur C., 346

Planning, 15, 199–201, 223, 324–25, 333. See also Central planning; Dutch planning school; Industrial planning; Investment planning

Poland, 75

Polanyi, 68

Political economy, 42, 83, 106–08, 114, 203–04, 248, 262

Political power, 42–43, 186, 188

Population growth, 7, 34, 75–76, 136, 156, 160, 167–68, 220–21, 247, 349; and agricultural productivity, 78, 81–82; and savings, 13, 50. See also Overpopulation

Population pressure, 4, 34, 102n, 168

Population size, 252, 341

Poverty, 4–5, 16, 27, 30, 48, 152, 160–61, 315, 316–17; attempts to alleviate, 15, 221, 315; foreign aid to alleviate, 137, 161–62, 166. See also Absolute poverty

Power relationships, 124, 153, 286, 288, 293, 317

Prebisch, Raúl, 11, 263, 280, 318

Prebisch-Singer thesis, 21, 226, 282n, 285, 293, 304, 308

Pressure mechanisms, 94–95, 101, 103

Price mechanism, 211, 215

Prices, 20–21, 66–67, 141, 184, 216, 230, 345–46; statistics on, 41, 290, 305–08. See also Primary commodities (prices); Shadow prices

Primary commodities, 94, 184, 283; export of, 20, 176, 177–79, 181, 193, 198, 288; price stabilization policies, 9–10, 38–41; prices, 123–25, 140, 225–26, 253–54, 255, 264–65, 268, 278, 279, 304–11; terms of trade for, 21, 72, 123, 139, 176, 198, 217. See also Cocoa industry; Oil; Rubber industry; Sugar industry

Primary production, 94, 187, 193–94, 284, 325

Principle of oscillation, 104

"Problems of Industrialization of Eastern and South-Eastern Europe," 4, 5, 199, 207–08, 210, 214, 223, 224

Process of Economic Growth, The, 230, 232

Production, 4, 29–30, 94, 187, 194, 282, 322–25. See also Factors of production

Production functions, 74, 209, 211, 236, 316, 339, 350

Productivity, 16, 184–85, 186, 189, 193, 284, 322. *See also* Agricultural productivity; Labor productivity

Profits, 132, 238

Programming, 215–16, 219, 220, 224–25, 333–34

Proposal: Key to an Effective Foreign Policy, A, 241–44

Protectionism, 10, 22, 129, 147, 178, 291, 294, 347; advantages of, 169, 179–80, 198–99, 200, 202*n*; opposition to, 137, 217, 246, 255, 294, 308–09

Purchasing power, 46, 67, 68, 70

Pursuit curve, 208

Quantitative models, 4–5, 7

Racial differences, 321–22. *See also* Cultural differences

Randall Commission, 245, 256

Rao, V. K. R. V., 62, 278, 297–98, 301*n*

Rate of return, 131, 231, 238

Reagan, Ronald, 256*n*

Recessions, 281, 294. *See also* Depressions

Redistributive power, 186, 188–89

Regional development, 104, 105, 152, 278–79, 298

Regional Employment Program for Latin America and the Caribbean, 97

Reid, Escott, 299

Relief aid, 166, 171

Resource allocation, 3, 122, 139, 179, 194, 210, 223

Resources, 153, 255, 256, 260, 261, 323, 341

Rio Conference on Inflation and Growth in Latin America, 135–36

Robertson, Sir Dennis H., 199, 229, 230

Robbins, Lionel, 61, 225

Robinson, Austin, 62

Robinson, Joan, 62, 338

Rosenberg, Nathan, 95

Rosenstein-Rodan, Paul N., 4–5, 15, 127, 136, 199–201, 241, 279, 318, 320, 338–39

Rostow, W. W., 345, 351, 353

Rubber industry, 28, 29, 31–32, 38–39, 41

Rumberger, Russell W., 327

Rural unemployment, disguised, 5, 133, 144, 208, 212–13, 217, 348

Russia. *See* U.S.S.R.

Ruttan, Vernon W., 66

Samuelson, Paul, 168, 198, 200*n*

Santa Cruz, Hernan, 298

Satisficing theory, 95, 339

Savings, 5, 13, 132, 133, 134, 136, 137, 147; and investment, 19, 49, 50, 103, 214, 320, 350

Scheyven, Raymond, 301

Schultz, Theodore W., 52

Schumacher, Ernst Friedrich, 355, 358–59

Schumpeter, Joseph A., 222, 254, 277, 288, 321

Second-best, theory of, 194, 196, 346

Sectors: balance between, 67–71, 78, 79–80, 190, 234, 235–36, 237, 263–64, 355–56; growth of, 81, 105, 106, 235*n*, 239

Seers, Dudley, 126, 127, 338, 339, 340, 343

Self-sufficiency, 128, 138, 142–43, 211, 340

Sen, S. R., 301*n*

Sequential growth, 94–95, 102, 106

Service industries, 67–69, 70–71

Shadow prices, 126, 130, 212, 216, 225, 320

Shifting Involvements: Private Interest and Public Action, 116

Singapore, 158

Singer, Hans, 15, 263, 318, 339*n*

Smith, Adam, 3, 45, 69, 116, 121, 122, 347

Social change, 6, 7, 108–09, 237

Social indicators, 167, 220–21, 247, 250

Social overhead capital. *See* Infrastructure

Social structure, 156, 157, 177, 181, 184, 185–86, 340

Social wage, 131

Socialism, 191, 196, 347

Soft financing, 275, 278, 296, 298–300, 310

Soft loans, 171, 217, 239, 300

Soft state, 154, 159

Solow, Robert, 74, 200*n*, 236, 269

Southeast Asia, 28, 29, 31–32, 171

Soviet Union. *See* U.S.S.R.

Special United Nations Fund for Economic Development (SUNFED), 275, 297, 298–99, 300–03

Spraos, J., 282n, 283n, 286, 289, 291, 305

Sri Lanka, 171

Stages of economic growth, 234–35, 237, 244n, 253, 269–70, 310, 345, 351

Stages of Economic Growth, The, 232–35, 237, 247–48, 249, 251, 261

Stagnation, 3, 27, 49, 124

Stamp, Dudley, 82

Standard of living, 7, 10, 13, 81, 122

Stanovnik, Janos, 298n

Statistics, 68, 166, 168, 247, 288–92, 319, 348. *See also* Income (statistics); Prices (statistics on)

Stone, Sir Richard, 63

Strategy of Economic Development, The, 88, 94, 96, 98, 100, 102, 103–04, 105–06, 110

Stratton, Julius, 240

Streeten, Paul, 250, 286, 293, 354n

Structural inflation, 12, 102, 127, 141, 339

Structuralism, 20, 195, 199–200, 280, 281–82, 339–40, 345, 346–47

Subsidies, 181, 194, 218

Substitution, 37–38, 66. *See also* Export substitution; Import substitution

Sugar industry, 141

SUNFED. *See* Special United Nations Fund for Economic Development

Supply, 40, 140, 213, 286, 316. *See also* Demand

Surplus labor, 13, 17, 134–35, 145–46, 277, 291, 339, 341

Sweden, 151, 154, 161, 162, 164

Taiwan, 158n, 170, 346

Tariff, 10, 200, 202n, 204, 217

Taxation, 132, 134, 137, 194, 220, 343

Technical assistance, 244, 246, 256, 297, 298, 355

Technical dependence, 251–53

Technological external economics, 209, 214–15

Technological innovation, 189–90, 277

Technological power, 284, 286

Technological progress, 140, 176, 177, 184, 192, 254, 288, 291. *See also* Multinational corporations (and technological progress)

Technology, 5, 185–86, 238, 247, 262,

270, 322–25, 354–55. *See also* Appropriate technology

Terms of trade, 14, 106n, 124, 179, 192–93, 204, 254, 278, 279, 304–11; for manufactured goods, 176, 217; for primary commodities, 21, 72, 123, 139, 176, 198, 217

Textile industry, 170, 208, 322–23, 358

Thant, U, 301–02

Theil, Henri, 333

Theory of Economic Growth, 3–4

Time, role of, 126, 210, 223

Timmer, Peter, 345–46

Toynbee, 321

Trade, 37–38, 169. *See also* International trade

Trade cycles, 281–82, 288. *See also* Kondratieff cycle

Trade policies, 9, 21, 159, 170–71, 190, 204, 353

Transnational corporations. *See* Multinational corporations

Truman, Harry, 297

Turkey, 326

Two-gap model, 127, 136, 137, 141, 200n

Unbalanced growth, 92, 96, 102, 104–10, 113, 115–16

UNCTAD. *See* United Nations Conference on Trade and Development

Underdeveloped countries, term coined, 207

Underemployment, 211, 212–13, 339

UNDP. *See* United Nations Development Programme

UNEDA. *See* United Nations Economic Development Administration

Unemployment, 14–15, 125–26, 144, 211, 276, 277, 281, 359. *See also* Rural unemployment; Underemployment; Urban unemployment

UNIDO. *See* United Nations Industrial Development Organization

United Kingdom. *See* Great Britain

United Nations, 11–13, 18, 275–76, 279, 329; charter, 5, 9; foreign aid policies, 136–37, 278, 296–99, 302, 310. *See also* Special United Nations Fund for Economic Development

United Nations Conference on Trade and Development (UNCTAD), 164–65, 175, 182–83, 195, 203, 279–80, 318

United Nations Development Programme (UNDP), 297, 298, 303

United Nations Economic Commission for Europe (ECE), 151–52

United Nations Economic Commission for Latin America (ECLA), 11–12, 102, 175, 176, 181–82, 190, 194–95, 212, 219, 318

United Nations Economic Development Administration (UNEDA), 297–98, 300

United Nations Industrial Development Organization (UNIDO), 325

United States, 9, 10, 190, 240; agriculture in, 70, 82; foreign aid from, 242–43, 245, 258–59, 265–66, 297, 298–300; foreign policies, 161, 231–32, 243, 249, 262, 265; trade policies, 70, 246, 297

UN Report on the World Social Situation, 159

Urbanization, 136, 209

Urban unemployment, 133–34, 145

U.S.S.R., 68, 72, 134, 152, 259; economic plans of, 14, 51, 73, 224

van Oven, Leida, 318

Venezuela, 126

Viner, Jacob, 7, 21, 348–49

Voice mechanism, 100–01

Wages, 125–26, 131, 144, 145, 170, 208–09, 216, 291

Warfare, 15, 161, 172. See also Korean War

Wealth, 184, 211, 348. See also Income

Weber, Max, 99

Welfare economics, 125, 141, 143, 220, 271, 284, 333, 341–43

Welfare state, 14–15, 152, 221, 226, 276

Western Europe, 15, 136, 161. See also Marshall Plan

Wicksell, Knut, 152, 230

Work force. See Labor force

World Bank, 9, 172, 225, 238, 275, 297, 301, 302, 311; aid to Asia, 258–59; aid to Colombia, 90; and the Brandt Commission, 164; criticism of, 53–54, 219; policies, 102, 245, 318, 325; reputation, 74–75, 219, 298–300

World Economy: History and Prospect, The, 248–49

Wright, Carl Major, 280, 281

X-efficiency theory, 95, 339

Yamada, Saburu, 77

Young, Allyn, 213, 347

Yugoslavia, 298

Zambia, 52

The full range of World Bank publications, both free and for sale, is described in the *Catalog of Publications*; the continuing research program is outlined in *Abstracts of Current Studies*. Both booklets are updated annually; the most recent edition of each is available without charge from the Publications Sales Unit, Department B, The World Bank, 1818 H Street, N.W., Washington, D.C. 20433, U.S.A.

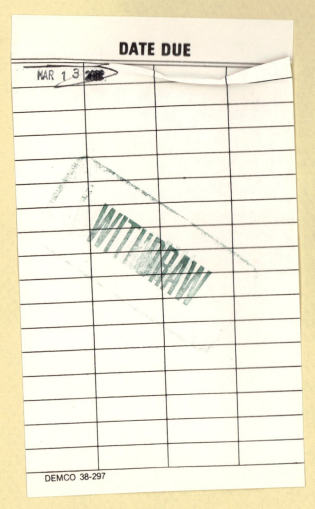